Advance Praise

"*When Disaster Strikes* is a key part of gaining the knowledge requisite to survive disasters. Read it, formulate a plan tailored to your family's particular needs, and then put your plans into action. Someday, you may be very glad that you did."

—From the foreword by JAMES WESLEY, RAWLES, editor, SurvivalBlog.com

"With his book *When Disaster Strikes*, Mat Stein has put together one of the most comprehensive emergency-preparedness manuals I've ever seen. From the smallest emergency to a total societal collapse, this book has it covered. Highly recommended!"

—JIM COBB, disaster readiness expert and cofounder, www.SurvivalWeekly.com

"*When Disaster Strikes* is an important tool for you and your family, as well as your business and community, to avoid costly mistakes during times of crisis. Stein's common-sense guide provides valuable tools and lessons learned so you can be prepared ahead of time and won't have to learn them the hard way while going through a disaster."

—JAMES LEE WITT, Chief Executive Officer of Witt Associates (www.wittassociates.com) and Director of the Federal Emergency Management Agency (FEMA), 1993–2001

"Every day, disaster strikes someone, somewhere. When it does, only a handful have the wisdom and foresight to be prepared. Mat Stein has done one hell of a job of accumulating the tremendous vault of knowledge that can set you apart as one of the few who elect to care for themselves and not wait around for someone else to do it. This book will help you prepare for just about any catastrophe that might strike—from basic first aid at the scene of an auto accident to coping with the devastating effects of an electromagnetic pulse (EMP), which would shut down society as we know it for months or years."

—JOHN MCPHERSON, survival instructor for U.S. Military Special Forces S.E.R.E. survival instructors (a "teacher of the teachers") and author, *Primitive Wilderness Living & Survival Skills*

"Mat Stein offers a sure and steady hand through turbulent times. When a storm threatens or the earth trembles, you'll be glad you have *When Disaster Strikes* close at hand."

—GEORGE NOORY, host of *Coast-to-Coast AM* and author, *Journey to the Light*

"Matthew Stein has been way ahead of the curve in recognizing the multiple fiascos we face in late-stage industrial society. This book is a concise, comprehensive, and deeply intelligent manual for getting through all that in one piece. . . . It's a darn good book—the kind of thing I actually need!"

—JAMES HOWARD KUNSTLER, author, *The Long Emergency* and the *World Made By Hand* novels

"Self-sufficiency and survival skills are essential following disasters or unforeseen events as simple as getting lost in the outdoors. For major disasters, the government has advised everyone to prepare with a minimum of supplies sufficient to survive for three days and preferably one to two weeks until aid can reach individuals in the affected communities. Matthew Stein has drawn together a unique compendium of information from various disciplines including disaster preparedness, wilderness survival, and living "off the grid." This book has specific lists, instructions, and techniques, and will satisfy people with very different interests and needs—both those who want to purchase the necessary items for the most common disasters and want to be more self-reliant for long term and those who prefer improvised and natural solutions to commercial products."

—HOWARD BACKER, MD, MPH, emergency physician and disaster planner; author, *Wilderness First Aid: Emergency Care for Remote Locations;* past President, Wilderness Medical Society

"I write survival books. Mat Stein has written a survival *encyclopedia*. Every survival topic I have ever heard of is covered in depth, breadth, and detail. This is a survival library in a single volume."

—BRUCE D. CLAYTON, PhD, author, *Life After Doomsday*

"Natural and man-made disasters can happen anywhere at any time, and Mat leaves no stone unturned—from surviving at home without heat or power, to coping with full-blown nuclear disaster and other large-scale catastrophes. *When Disaster Strikes* is a *must-have* addition to any survival library!"

—ED CORCORAN, editor, *Survivalist* magazine

"Taking his remarkable book *When Technology Fails* to the next level, Mat Stein's new book tells the reader exactly what to do, where to go or not go, what to wear, and how to take care of him/herself and loved ones in the midst of disaster. It is extraordinarily practical and empowering. When reading it, I feel confident and inspired to take the steps Stein has laid out for anyone who is willing to move beyond the denial of "it can't happen to me" and into no-nonsense preparation for the inevitable. Read it, share it with friends, give it as a gift, and keep one in the home and one at the office or in the car. It could save your life or the life of someone you care about."

— CAROLYN BAKER, PhD, author,
Navigating the Coming Chaos: A Handbook for Inner Transition

"Concise yet comprehensive, *When Disaster Strikes* gives good advice for just about every disaster situation imaginable. Medical preparedness is covered in a well-written and conversational manner that anyone can understand, with a focus on alternative remedies. Unlike some authors who just talk the talk, Mat Stein really walks the walk!"

—JOSEPH ALTON, MD, AND AMY ALTON, ARNP, CNM, hosts
of Dr. Bones and Nurse Amy's *Doom and Bloom*™ show

"Mat Stein did an amazing job on this book! *When Disaster Strikes* is an outstanding compilation of emergency-preparedness information. This is the one book I want on the bookshelves of all the people I care about, including my children."

—KATHY HARRISON, author of *Just in Case: How to Be
Self-Sufficient When the Unexpected Happens*

"If every family in the country would simply take the time to study one chapter in this book, as a family project each month—what a stronger, more prepared country we would be, and able to face the many hazards in our communities. Great job!"

—RICK TOBIN, President/CEO, TAO
Emergency Management Consulting

"If you need to know how to use emergency gear, make rope, run a generator, give first aid, or make colloidal silver, these and many more survival skills are explained in *When Disaster Strikes*, along with clear illustrations and photos throughout. This is clearly the work of an author who knows his topic and who has taken the time to research it well."

—JOHN EGAN, proprietor, prepperbooks.com and preppergroups.com

When Disaster Strikes

When Disaster Strikes

A Comprehensive Guide to Emergency Planning and Crisis Survival

Matthew Stein

Foreword by James Wesley, Rawles

CHELSEA GREEN PUBLISHING

White River Junction, Vermont

Project Managers: Patricia Stone and Bill Bokermann
Project Editors: Susan Warner and Makenna Goodman
Developmental and Copy Editor: Cannon Labrie
Proofreader: Helen Walden
Indexer: Lee Lawton
Designer: Peter Holm, Sterling Hill Productions

Printed in the United States of America
First printing October, 2011
10 9 8 7 6 5 4 3   14 15 16 17 18

Chelsea Green Publishing is committed to preserving
ancient forests and natural resources. We elected to print
this title on 30-percent postconsumer recycled paper,
processed chlorine-free. As a result, for this printing, we
have saved:

17 Trees (40' tall and 6-8" diameter)
8 Million BTUs of Total Energy
1,471 Pounds of Greenhouse Gases
7,977 Gallons of Wastewater
534 Pounds of Solid Waste

Chelsea Green Publishing made this paper choice because
we and our printer, Thomson-Shore, Inc., are members
of the Green Press Initiative, a nonprofit program dedicated to supporting authors, publishers, and suppliers
in their efforts to reduce their use of fiber obtained
from endangered forests. For more information, visit:
www.greenpressinitiative.org.

Environmental impact estimates were made using the Environmental Defense Paper Calculator.
For more information visit: www.papercalculator.org.

Our Commitment to Green Publishing

Chelsea Green sees publishing as a tool for cultural change and ecological stewardship. We strive to align our book
manufacturing practices with our editorial mission and to reduce the impact of our business enterprise in the environment. We print our books and catalogs on chlorine-free recycled paper, using vegetable-based inks whenever possible.
This book may cost slightly more because it was printed on paper that contains recycled fiber, and we hope you'll
agree that it's worth it. Chelsea Green is a member of the Green Press Initiative (www.greenpressinitiative.org), a
nonprofit coalition of publishers, manufacturers, and authors working to protect the world's endangered forests and
conserve natural resources. *When Disaster Strikes* was printed on FSC®-certified paper supplied by Thomson-Shore
that contains at least 30% postconsumer recycled fiber.

Library of Congress Cataloging-in-Publication Data
Stein, Matthew R.
When disaster strikes : a comprehensive guide for emergency planning
and crisis survival / Matthew Stein ; foreword by James Wesley, Rawles.
   p. cm.
Includes bibliographical references and index.
ISBN 978-1-60358-322-0 (pbk.)
1. Survival. 2. Emergency management. 3. Disaster relief. I. Title.

GF86.S745 2011
363.34'8068--dc23

2011029948

Chelsea Green Publishing
85 North Main Street, Suite 120
White River Junction, VT 05001
(802) 295-6300
www.chelseagreen.com

FSC
www.fsc.org
MIX
Paper from
responsible sources
FSC® C013483

This book is dedicated to my son, Joshua, daughter, Elisha, and wife, Josie. You provide me with the most awesome reason for preparing to weather whatever storms may come our way. I love you all!

CONTENTS

Foreword, ix

Acknowledgments, xi

Introduction, xiii

Part 1: General Preparations

1. Where There Is a Need, There Is a Way, 3
2. Your Preparedness Plan, 19
3. Stored Food and Other Supplies, 34
4. Home Is Where the Hearth Is, 54

Part 2: Emergency Medicine, Survival Skills, and Tools

5. First Aid, 81
6. Staying Healthy in a Crisis or Pandemic, 115
7. Emergency Survival, 140
8. Water: Requirements, Purification, and Storage, 192
9. Communication, 216
10. Self-Defense and Personal Protection, 227

Part 3: Specific Disasters and Crises: Preparations and Strategies

11. Fire!, 255
12. Earthquake!, 265
13. Hurricanes and Floods, 271
14. Tornadoes, 282
15. Winter Storms: How to Handle the Cold Without Power, 286
16. Electromagnetic Pulses and Solar Storms, 304
17. The Unthinkable: Surviving a Nuclear Disaster, 319

Afterword, 341

Appendices, 345

1. Recommended Reading, 345
2. Recommended Resources, 350

Glossary, 356

Bibliography, 359

Index, 369

About the Author, 377

Foreword

There are few books that summarize what families need to do to be *truly* ready for disasters. Certainly, there are good books in print about first aid, food storage, outdoor survival, the martial arts, and amateur radio. But there are precious few that succinctly summarize numerous topics in terms that are understandable to a layman. You are holding one in your hands now, and I hope that you appreciate its significance. It could literally mean the difference between life and death for you and your loved ones.

We live in an increasingly fragile society. As was evidenced by the earthquake, tsunami, and subsequent nuclear power disaster in Japan in March of 2011, unexpected chains of events can have a profound effect on modern, technological societies.

We are now dependent upon power grids and telecommunication networks for nearly every aspect of our lives. Chains of supply for food and fuel span thousands of miles and are dependent on power grids, telecommunications systems, and computerized "just in time" inventory-control systems. The majority of our petrochemicals come from thousands of miles away—mostly from the war-torn Middle East. It doesn't take much to disrupt any of that, and when the disruption starts, things come unraveled very rapidly. The aftermath of Hurricane Katrina in 2005 was clear evidence of that unraveling.

Hurricane Katrina was also evidence that governments are incapable of providing effective short-term relief in disasters of large proportions. In SurvivalBlog, this is what I call "YOYO" time—"You're on your own!" *When Disaster Strikes* does an admirable job of teaching you how to get through YOYO time, whether it is just twenty-four hours, or if it persists for many months.

Any number of events can disrupt the fragile web that holds modern societies together. These include earthquakes, tsunamis, wildfires, floods, tornadoes, hurricanes, naturally occurring plagues, cyber attacks, terrorist nuclear, biological, or chemical attacks, economic spasms, and solar flares. These each have unique characteristics, and highlight specific vulnerabilities in a society where hardly anything gets accomplished without Internet access.

Further exacerbating our predicament, modern societies have an increasingly stratified division of labor. In the early twentieth century, fully 30 percent of American families were employed at full-time farming, ranching, or fishing. But in the early twenty-first century, just 2 percent of the population feeds the other 98 percent. Think about the implications of that. If we were to experience a repeat of the Great Depression in today's world, how many people would go hungry, and what would the crime rate be?

For a moment, try to take on the viewpoint of an actuarial accountant—someone who estimates risks for an insurance company. Is it any wonder that insurance is so expensive these days, and that there are entire categories of risks that the insurance companies cannot or *will not* insure? Those risks are simply too great for them to insure at an affordable price.

It is for those uninsurable risks where you come in. Prepared individuals size up the potential threats and take active measures to ensure the health and safety of themselves and their family members. Steps as simple as buying a compact water filter and laying in a several-months' supply of food can make a tremendous difference between being a survivor, and being an actuarial statistic.

Matthew Stein is one of the people who have the gift of seeing "the big picture." He is also grounded in the commonsense reality of a fully experienced outdoorsman. Some of this knowledge is old-fashioned, and some of it is high-tech. Mat wisely picks and chooses between old and new, depending on the circumstances. I'd estimate that Mat has spent more time camping out and scrambling around in the granite of the High Sierras than many people have spent commuting to work in their cars. That represents a huge number of hours, and a lot of hard lessons learned. *When Disaster Strikes* encapsulates a lot of those valuable lessons, and will help you avoid some costly mistakes.

Whether it is using a home-made rocket stove or tuning a Grundig shortwave receiver, Mat really knows his stuff. More importantly, he knows how to distinguish essentials from nonessentials. After all, few of us have a millionaire's budget, so it is crucial to establish a *priority* for making preparedness purchases and getting training.

As I've written elsewhere, the modern world is full of pundits, poseurs, and mall ninjas. Preparedness is not just about accumulating a pile of "neat stuff." You need practical skills, and those come only with study, training, and practice. Any armchair survivalist with a credit card can buy a set of stylish camouflage fatigues and an "M4gery" carbine encrusted with umpteen accessories. Style points should not be mistaken for genuine skills and practicality. What is between your ears is much more important than the gear that is stacked up in your garage.

When Disaster Strikes is a key part of gaining the knowledge requisite to survive disasters. Read it, formulate a plan tailored to your family's particular needs, and then put your plans into action. Someday, you may be very glad that you did.

We live in an uncertain world. With his writings, Matthew Stein takes away some of that uncertainty. And for that, I'm truly grateful.

—James Wesley, Rawles
(Jim Rawles is the editor of www.SurvivalBlog.com).

Acknowledgments

It is quite a large undertaking to write a comprehensive guide such as *When Disaster Strikes*. I would be dishonest if I said that I was an expert on every single topic covered by this book. I owe a debt of gratitude to the many different experts who reviewed chapters, corrected, suggested, and otherwise contributed their years of experience toward making this book a practical, useful, and comprehensive guide to emergency planning and crisis survival.

First, I would like to thank God for the inspiration and intuitional guidance that has helped me to create a far better book than I had ever imagined. Second, I would like to thank my wonderful wife, Josie, for her patience and moral support through many months of work on this project. Special thanks to my son Joshua for urging his entire family to be more self-reliant and better prepared for the turbulent times of change that are encroaching upon our world, and for his coaching, instruction, patience, and considerable expertise in the use of firearms. Thanks to my daughter, Elisha, for her love and support.

I owe a real debt of gratitude to Frank Ferris, Sensei of High Sierra Jujitsu in Reno, Nevada. Frank is a renowned instructor and sixth-degree black belt in the art of DanZan Ryu Jujitsu. His contribution to the self-defense chapter was invaluable, and I could not have asked for better models for the self-defense photographs than his students, Mike Schmidt (a black belt) and Jolie Pardeu (a brown belt). You guys did an outstanding job!

Special thanks to the following experts who contributed to making *When Disaster Strikes* a comprehensive and valuable guide. To Howard Backer, MD, for reviewing the water and first-aid chapters. To Gary Lord, Bill Conrad, and Jim Rawles (editor of www.SurvivalBlog.com) for sharing their considerable expertise and advice on the topic of firearms. To my Web designer, Jeremy O'Leary from Portland Peak Oil, thanks for your helpful suggestions, enthusiasm, and support. To the late Carla Emery for her charm, friendship, wit, and wonderful book that is a great source of information and inspiration for self-reliance. I miss you Carla!

I am very grateful for the assistance of my primary editor, Cannon Labrie, plus Susan Warner, Patricia Stone, Margo Baldwin, and the rest of the crew at Chelsea Green. Much credit must go to Karen Frances (shaded drawings with people and landscape), Merri Mckee (line-art technical illustrations), and Kristen Schwartz (edible plants) for contributing their awesome artistic talents to the illustrations.

Others who contributed measurably to this project include Andreas Kaupert (emergency preparedness); Dan Vorhis (water quality and filtration); Richard Nielsen (sprouts); John and Geri McPherson (primitive living and survival); Ralph Van Bruggen (winterizing plumbing); Hulda Regehr Clark, PhD, ND (naturopathy and herbs); Jim Humble, Dennis Richards, and Andreas Kalcker (the use of MMS for healing and water purification); David Edwards, MD (healing and homeopathy); Gary Rosen, PhD, and the late Vincent Marinkovich, MD (molds); Jim Duffy and Barry Bettman (communications/ham radio); Jeb Bateman (rocket stoves and self-reliance); Jerry Emanuelson (EMP and solar storms); and Laurie Ecklund Long, who shared her "My Life in a Box" advice and checklist. Special thanks to Andrew and Mary Hall for sharing their harrowing experiences in a tragic Australian wildfire, and to Jim Bolton, my fireman friend who graciously shared his experiences and reviewed the fire chapter.

To the rest of you who contributed measurably, but whose names I neglected to list, thank you for your help and please forgive my oversight.

Introduction

❝Complaining of a slow government response to the crisis, many survivors fled on foot and in cars, clogging secondary roads connecting Kobe with nearby Osaka. Hundreds of thousands of others packed into evacuation centers to escape the winter chill, the strain of their ordeal clearly showing. Outside one such center, a school gymnasium, an elderly man stood wrapped in a blanket, tears running down his cheeks. 'This is like after the Second World War,' he said. 'We suffered so much. I am too old to suffer the same fate once again.'❞ —"Kobe Earthquake," *Maclean's*, January 30, 1995

Most of us who own a car also purchase automobile insurance. I doubt that anyone steps into his or her car thinking, "I bet I will get into a head-on collision today!" We all hope that we never actually need to use our car insurance, but it fosters peace of mind when we know that we are covered, "just in case." Putting together a modest collection of supplies, skills, and information, falling under the loose heading of "emergency preparations," is like purchasing car insurance—it will bring great peace of mind and could make the difference between life and death, or extreme discomfort and relative ease, should that day ever come when you find yourself in the middle of a true disaster.

Put yourself in the position of a parent stuck in New Orleans when Hurricane Katrina struck. What if extreme thirst and lack of alternatives forced you and your children to drink untreated ditch water that made you sick for days with debilitating diarrhea and vomiting? How would you feel if you knew you could have planned ahead and purchased a $60 water filter, a $14 Polar Pure water purification kit, or a bottle of chlorine bleach for a couple of bucks that would have purified hundreds of gallons of water, but you never got around to it? Even if you did not have any of these water purification supplies on hand, had you known about the solar disinfection (SODIS) techniques that I teach in this book, you could have scavenged some discarded empty plastic bottles and purified adequate drinking water using just the rays of the sun. Stocking up on several bags of extra supplies, learning a few new skills, and making a brief set of contingency plans for coping with emergencies doesn't take a whole lot of time or money, but it's cheap insurance for living in today's world of rapid change, uncertainty, and turbulence.

When the lights go out for an extended period of time, what sane person would not want to provide for the health, safety, and welfare of their loved ones? This is an innate human desire that is shared by each and every one of us. In these times of great change and uncertainty, planning ahead by making a few contingency plans, and setting aside certain key provisions and supplies to deal with a variety of potential emergencies, will help put your mind at ease and could one day make the difference between life and death for yourself and your loved ones!

A Changing World

Just a few generations back, before the days of supermarkets, Costco, cell phones, and interstate highways, stocking up on supplies and developing self-reliant living skills was not considered survivalist paranoia but simply a prudent and practical approach to life in general. In those days, about 30 percent of the American workforce was engaged with farming, and the majority of U.S. citizens lived in rural areas. Today's world is far different, with less than 2 percent of us involved with farming, and only 17 percent living in rural areas (U.S. Department of Agriculture 2011). With all of our supermarkets working off computerized just-in-time delivery systems, there are no more local warehouses with a month's worth of food on hand. The complex interwoven systems that keep the wheels of our modern world greased and working so well are really quite fragile, and all it takes is one significant hiccup and the shelves will be quite bare within just one or two days' time.

America's confidence in a rosy, secure future has been shaken to its core. In the 1990s, we shared a seemingly unsinkable optimism fueled by the dot-com explosion, real estate and construction booms, low oil prices, and easy credit combined with a rapidly expanding global economy. The first decade of the new millennium was quite a different story, starting out with the double whammy of 9/11 striking on the heels of "dot-bomb." This downward slide continued with the Indian Ocean tsunami in December of 2004 and picked up speed when Hurricane Katrina struck in August of 2005. The skids were greased again when oil prices skyrocketed in the following couple of years. Even after the housing bubble burst in 2007, oil prices continued to climb, capping out at nearly $150 a barrel in July of 2008. Perhaps it was the cost of oil trading at those record-breaking prices that was the proverbial straw that broke the camel's back? In December of 2008, when the dust began to settle from the first wave of the global financial meltdown, the price of oil had plummeted to just $34 a barrel. And if the first decade of the new millennium was not bad enough, the second decade started out with back-to-back crippling earthquakes in Haiti and Chile followed by the Gulf oil spill—America's worst environmental catastrophe—and the triple disaster of a mega earthquake and tsunami coupled with a nuclear reactor meltdown in Japan.

Is it any wonder that the average American might be feeling uneasy? Are not most of us wondering what's next, and thinking that perhaps we should develop an emergency-preparedness plan, learn first aid, practice a few survival skills, and pick up several bags of critical supplies to help our families cope in the event of some kind of local disaster or lengthy power blackout? In uncertain times like these, it is comforting to know that we have the information, supplies, and critical skills at our fingertips to make the best of things in a bad situation.

This book is your guide for building a disaster-preparedness tool kit, supplies, and skill set—the key elements to your homegrown crisis and emergency insurance policy. *When Disaster Strikes* covers everything you need to know, do, and have on hand to keep yourself and family safe in the event of a crisis or disaster. Part 1 deals with basic supplies and preparations, including 72-hour survival kits, stored food, making a preparedness plan, and preparations in the home to help you cope with extended power blackouts and lack of access to central services. Part 2 focuses on a set of valuable emergency and crisis skills, techniques, tips, and tools, including first aid, water storage and purification, survival strategies, self-defense, emergency communications, and how to deal with potential pandemics and diseases when the usual medical resources are either unavailable or simply not working. Part 3 offers useful tools, techniques, tips, and checklists to help prepare for, and cope with, specific crises and disasters such as earthquakes, floods, tornadoes, hurricanes, severe winter weather, electromagnetic pulses (EMP), and nuclear events.

The best place to start is with the Preparedness Plan and 72-Hour Grab-and-Go short-term emergency survival kits detailed in chapter 2. It won't take a lot of time or money to acquire these items. The food-storage information in chapter 3 will help you stock and organize supplies to weather longer term emergencies. Chapter 4 is a useful guide for putting your house in order. The chapters in part 2 describe survival skill sets and necessary tools and materials. As for the chapters in part 3, while the skies are still sunny, I strongly recommend you consult the chapters that cover the types of disasters that may occur in your part of the country, taking the recommended precautions ahead of time, rather than waiting until a disaster has already struck.

You don't have to do everything at once, but I urge you to make the commitment to start right away. Procrastination has been the death of many a good intention! At this point in time you may feel it is only necessary to have enough supplies on hand to weather a week or two of disruption. If that situation should change, however, whether from further declines in the world situation, such as a nuclear exchange between Pakistan and India or some

Where There Is a Need, There Is a Way

"Imagine all of the Federal buildings in Washington collapsing in less than a minute killing 30–40% of our government workforce, crippling the tax collection system leaving the government no money to pay salaries or overhead. Our government, which seems to barely work at full capacity with gleaming buildings and a gargantuan budget, would come to a halt.

This is the state of Haiti today. . . . At the University Hospital, the entire second-year nursing class was crushed and died in the nursing school. Teachers and nearly all the schools were destroyed. During the five o'clock hour of the quake all the priests and seminarians met in their churches. Most of the priests, the future priests and their churches are now gone. The Universities with most of their precious intellectual capital of professors and the best and the brightest of Haiti are gone.

Now imagine New York after a similar disaster, a city of 8 million with a loss of a million citizens, with four million people living in the streets, with winter about to come and a marginally functioning government without resources to help. . . ." —Mark Hyman, "Haiti Weather Report: Mostly Foggy With Rain Storms Expected," *Huffington Post*, March 20, 2010

When a major disaster strikes, like the recent mega earthquake and tsunami in Japan or Hurricane Katrina in the United States, all the normal supply lines, utilities, and central services that we take for granted are either crippled, destroyed, or what little that is left functioning is hopelessly overloaded. When the scope of the disaster is huge, as in these cases, most of the doctors, nurses, firemen, and policemen are either injured themselves, busy caring for family members, or evacuated from the area, and those civil servants that remain will be seriously overworked and under-supplied. In times like these, the majority of survivors are left to fend for themselves for several days, and sometimes for weeks or months. Mother Nature built into each and every one of us a desire to provide food, shelter, water, and protection for ourselves and loved ones. It is the aim and purpose of this book to enable the reader to do just that!

Regardless of whether the disaster is in the "first world" or the "third world," when the scale of a disaster is huge, central services, utilities, and public-support systems are overloaded and fail. When a 6.8 magnitude earthquake struck Kobe, Japan (a country priding itself at being the most earthquake ready nation in the world), massive liquefaction of wet gravelly soils under the city resulted in far greater destruction than Japanese officials had anticipated, devastating Kobe's roads, buildings, and infrastructure. Initial relief efforts progressed at a painfully slow rate, taking as long as nine days for supplies of food, medicine, and water to reach many of the city's residents. After Hurricane Iniki ravaged the Hawaiian island of Kauai with sustained winds of 145 mph and recorded gusts of up to 175 mph, most island roads were blocked for several days with downed trees, and it took four weeks to restore electricity to just 20 percent of the island.

Many of us live in areas that are prone to natural disasters. For example, I live in the mountains of the High Sierra, near Lake Tahoe, California, in the town of Truckee, located where the infamous Donner Party resorted to cannibalism after being snowbound for months in the winter of 1846–47 while attempting to cross the Sierras on their way to central California. My town is known for its severe winter storms and deep snows, but it is also threatened by wildfires and earthquakes. Other locales may be similarly threatened by intermittent floods, hurricanes, or tornadoes, but what about the millions of people who live in the multitude of towns and cities that don't appear to face significant threats from natural disasters? Should those people be concerned with being prepared?

The Fragile Web of Today's World

“Tens of thousands of northwest Queens residents suffered through a sixth day without electricity yesterday, and any hope for a full restoration of power this weekend was shattered by new barrages of severe thunderstorms and the discovery of more extensive damage to the underground power grid. As Consolidated Edison crews struggled manhole to manhole, Mayor Michael R. Bloomberg said that 15,000 to 20,000 customers—an estimated 60,000 to 80,000 people—remained without power in darkened, sweltering homes and apartments with spoiling food, no air-conditioning or elevators and no immediate relief in sight.” —Robert D. McFadden and Winnie Hu, *New York Times*, July 23, 2006

On the surface, our modern world appears to be superabundant with an almost unimaginable array of foodstuffs and consumer goods available twenty-four hours a day at our supermarkets and superstores. Behind the facade of this consumer fantasyland is an incredibly complex system that electronically and mechanically ties, tracks, and coordinates suppliers of raw materials, farmers, miners, factories, and shippers from around the world to grow, manufacture, warehouse, and otherwise produce, stock, and sell the products that we consume everyday as we keep ourselves clothed, fed, sheltered, entertained, and employed. However, this great complexity and convenience also comes at the price of great fragility.

Clearly, if a midsummer afternoon's thunderstorm could flood manholes in New York City, severing power to nearly a hundred thousand people for a week, then a major natural catastrophe, or a coordinated terrorist attack, could cause far more significant damage and disruption. The four scenarios that follow are examples of events that would cause major disruptions in the flow of goods, services, and electricity to millions of people in the Western world. My goal is not to spread fear, but motivation. By reading these scenarios, it is my hope that you will become motivated to spend a modest amount of time, effort, and money to follow the advice and precautions given in this book. Hopefully none of the following disaster scenarios will ever occur, or if they do, perhaps we will be lucky and they will take milder forms rather than the full-blown versions that would hopelessly overload our systems of distribution of food and goods, communications, and emergency response. While contemplating these various scenarios, consider the wisdom in the old Yankee adage that says, "Hope for the best, but plan for the worst!"

Scenario 1: Pandemic

❝The era of antibiotics is coming to a close. In just a couple of generations, what once appeared to be miracle medicines have been beaten into ineffectiveness by the bacteria they were designed to knock out. Once, scientists hailed the end of infectious diseases. Now, the post-antibiotic apocalypse is within sight.❞ —Sarah Boseley, "Are You Ready for a World Without Antibiotics?" *Guardian*, August 12, 2010

Imagine a Hurricane Katrina–sized catastrophe occurring in fifty major U.S. cities at the same time, and you have some idea of the scale of disruption that a deadly global pandemic will cause. Medical centers, essential services, and government personnel would be overwhelmed. If there were no viable vaccines or pharmaceutical medicines, or if they were only available in limited quantities, most healthcare workers would desert medical facilities to care for the sick in their own homes or simply abandon the cities to improve their chances for survival. When things get really bad, most buses, trains, trucks, and planes will stop running, bringing food and fuel deliveries to a grinding halt. If this sounds far-fetched, realize that this was exactly what happened when the Spanish flu struck the United States in 1918. With a 30 percent mortality rate in American hospitals, this flu killed more people in a few months than had died in all of World War I. After first striking the United States, troop transport rapidly spread the Spanish flu spread around the world, causing an estimated 50 to 100 million deaths before it subsided in 1920. Unlike the typical influenza outbreak, where it is primarily the elderly, infirm, and young children who perish, the bulk of the Spanish Flu victims were previously healthy young adults.

However, there was a big difference between the way the world of 1918 functioned and the way the world works today. Most people would assume that today's world is far better equipped to handle a major pandemic than we were almost a hundred years ago, but that assumption is dead wrong. We are certainly more capable of rapidly diagnosing, isolating, and treating infectious diseases, but modern air travel practically guarantees that once a virulent drug-resistant strain of a deadly virus or bacteria has spread beyond a few small villages, it has burst the boundaries of easy containment and will rapidly spread around the world. When the 1918 Spanish flu struck, over half the population of the United States lived in rural areas and roughly 30 percent of the workforce was employed on farms. In those days, if trucks stopped making deliveries, you could simply walk over the hill to a local farm to buy items of food. In those days, people made and grew most things by hand. Nowadays, if gasoline stops flowing, and the electricity is shut off for extended periods because everyone left work to tend for the sick (or to keep from getting sick), the big machine of global commerce would screech to a halt!

Take the case of the swine flu pandemic of 2009—once it started to spread, there was no stopping it. Luckily, it turned out that this flu was no more deadly than your average winter's strain of influenza, but it was certainly quite virulent, infecting a large part of the world's population in a single year. If that flu had turned out to be as deadly as some people feared, we would have suffered a global meltdown like we have never seen in the modern world—totally crashing the systems that keep our food, water, and medicine flowing freely. We dodged that bullet, but with bacteria developing antibiotic resistance faster than we can develop new medicines, and viruses' ability to "gene swap" genetic material between deadly diseases with low infection rates (such as avian flu, which has a 50 percent fatality rate but is rarely transmitted between humans) and highly infectious diseases, like common human flu viruses, it is only a matter of time before the roulette wheel of natural genetic selection and mutation deals humanity a crippling blow.

When it comes to battling serious antibiotic-resistant bacteria and viruses, the news is not all bad. The good news is that there are a number of alternative medicines, procedures, and herbs that can be quite effective against antibiotic-resistant superbugs and deadly viruses. The bad news is that there is no money to be made on these alternative remedies, and since it takes many millions of dollars to run a drug or remedy through the Food and

Drug Administration (FDA) you can count on the fact that most doctors or hospitals won't know a thing about them. There is no patent protection for herbs and alternative medicines, which means that drug companies cannot secure a twenty-year monopoly (granted by owning the rights to a new patent) on these types of products, and their prices remain low and affordable. No patent protection also means there is not enough profit motive for manufacturers to sponsor expensive clinical trials to obtain FDA approval for herbs and non-patentable alternatives, and none of the "big pharma" retail outlets will stock them.

For detailed information on this topic, including important practical information on how one might fend off antibiotic-resistant bacteria and viruses, see chapter 6, "Staying Healthy in a Crisis or Pandemic."

Scenario 2: Widespread Grid Blackout Due to EMP, Solar Storm, or Terrorist Act

ɡɡA globalized world is extremely dependent upon electronic communications to operate banking, communications, health care, computers, transportation systems, and a massive electric grid serving billions of people. A super solar flare on the scale of the one in 1859 could shut down modernity for days, weeks, perhaps months depending on the size of the white solar flare eruption from within a sunspot. One could equate such a possible episode as a Cosmic Katrina-like event on a nearly global scale happening in say less than twenty-four hours and possibly affecting millions of people.ɟɟ —Jack Kennedy, "Could a Solar Storm Send Us Back to the Stone Age?" *Spaceports*, **August 9, 2010**

Imagine that you wake up one morning and your alarm does not go off. You try to turn on the lights, and they don't work either. You try to make a call on your iPhone or Blackberry, and find that the circuits are all tied up by millions of other Americans trying to use their portable battery-powered devices to access the Internet, and make long-distance calls, in their efforts to find some shred of information about what is going on. If you planned ahead, you have a hand-crank emergency radio that can access shortwave as well as standard radio channels.

After you have exhausted other alternatives, you dig out your emergency radio, crank it up, and search the channels for information. Incredibly you find that most of the local channels are either dead or broadcasting a monotonous, irritating emergency signal tone, and the few that are actually on the air using their backup batteries and generators have no clue as to what is going on. Switching bands on your radio, you start scanning the shortwave frequencies. Most of the broadcasts are in foreign languages, but eventually you come across a few in English. From listening to the broadcasts and shortwave radio discussions from people in faraway lands, it becomes clear that North America has been struck by a powerful solar storm that induced massive wire-melting currents in hundreds of the large power-station transformers across America that are absolutely critical for keeping the electric power grid functioning. Not all of the transformers and electrical devices in North America were fried, but enough damage occurred that the massively interconnected grid failed across the entire continent.

Does this scenario sound far-fetched, like it came out of some apocalyptic 2012 end-of-the-world Hollywood extravaganza? According to two major scientific government reports, *Severe Space Weather Events: Understanding Societal and Economic Impacts*, and the *Report of the Commission to Assess the Threat to the United States from Electromagnetic Pulse (EMP) Attack*, either severe solar storms or a nuclear detonation purposefully designed to create an EMP could generate such an effect. Considering the fact that some of the critical large electrical components within our electrical power-grid structure are no longer manufactured within the United States, and that the lead times on these expensive custom-made items are running one to three years, severe damage or loss of a number of these items, whether through a coordinated terrorist act, solar super storm, or EMP, could have devastating long-term consequences for our infrastructure, quality of life, and the economy.

So, how likely are these kinds of events? In March of 1989, a severe solar storm induced powerful electric currents in grid wiring that fried a main power transformer in the HydroQuebec system, causing a cascading grid failure that knocked out power to 6 million customers for nine hours. More recently, in 2003 a solar storm caused a blackout in Sweden and induced powerful currents in the South African grid that burned up fourteen of their major power transformers, blacking out power to significant portions of that country for many months (Joseph 2010). In May of 1921, a great geomagnetic storm produced ground currents roughly ten times as strong as the Quebec incident, affecting the Northern Hemisphere as far south as Mexico and Puerto Rico, and the Southern Hemisphere as far north as Samoa. It has been estimated that if an event like that one occurred today, in the United States alone it would put over 350 main grid transformers at risk of serious damage, potentially knocking out power to over 130 million people.

However, the great-granddaddy solar storm of recorded history is the 1859 "Carrington Event." During this storm, Northern Lights were seen as far south as Cuba and Hawaii, awakened hikers in the middle of the night in the Rocky Mountains because the lights were so bright they thought it was dawn, and induced currents in copper wires so powerful that telegraph lines, towers, and stations caught on fire at numerous locations around the world. Best estimates are that the Carrington Event was roughly 50 percent stronger than the 1921 incident.

If it were to happen today, the Carrington Event would almost certainly devastate the giant interconnected machine that keeps our global economy working smoothly. It would take many months, and possibly years, for things to get back to normal.

Though probably significantly smaller in area than that of a huge solar storm, the localized damage from a terrorist EMP attack could be much greater. According to the Commission Report, a nuclear blast detonated 60 miles above the earth's surface could expose roughly 1.5 million square miles to crippling EMP-field intensities. This is an area equal to about half the continental United States! Let's say a terrorist, or a rogue state like North Korea, did manage to detonate a nuclear device high above the eastern seaboard of the United States. Even if the EMP impact was far smaller than the scenario described by the Commission Report, it may well be powerful enough to paralyze the densely populated region extending from Boston through New York City all the way past Washington, D.C. Without killing a single person directly, a single suborbital nuclear detonation would wreak great havoc, potentially devastating the economy of the entire country.

Chances are slim that events like this will cause a total collapse of civilization, but they may well lead to the end of the world as we know it through extreme short-term failures of all utilities and central services for hundreds of millions of people. This would decimate financial systems and far exceed the federal government's capacity to cope with the situation, making post-Katrina New Orleans and the recent financial meltdown look like picnics, in comparison.

Scenario 3: Category 4 or 5 Hurricane Hits New York City

❝I'll be surprised if over the next five years a major hurricane doesn't hit the northeastern United States," said Joe Bastardi, an expert senior meteorologist for AccuWeather, a commercial forecaster based in State College, Pa. . . . 'After New Orleans, the worst area with respect to storm surge is Long Island and New York and the Northeast,' said Karen Clark, president and CEO of AIR Worldwide, an insurance industry consulting firm.❞ —"Ready or Not, Northeast Ripe for Big Hurricane," Associated Press, May 22, 2006.

Most people associate hurricanes with more southern climates than New York City or New England, but records show that New York City, Long Island, and the New England coast have all been pounded by major hurricanes, but

size as the Japanese mega quake of 2011 (a magnitude of 9.0), it would have been 200 times as strong. Instead of collapsing only 6 freeway interchanges, somewhere on the order of 600 or more freeway overpasses would have fallen down, and the vast majority of the buildings in the northern Los Angeles basin would have either collapsed or suffered irreparable structural damage. How do you begin to rebuild a major metro area like Los Angeles, when practically all the roads, airports, bridges, railroads, and shipyards are destroyed? Would Los Angeles become like Port-au-Prince, Haiti, with people living in tent cities for months on end, widespread deadly cholera outbreaks spread by untreated human waste, with little hope and no change in sight? Even though the 2011 Japan earthquake was centered about 80 miles (130 km) off Japan's east coast, and 240 miles (400 km) from Tokyo, this massive 9.0 magnitude quake and its ensuing tsunami wiped out several small cities, leaving a total of over 25,000 people dead or missing. Had the epicenter of this quake fallen inside a major metropolitan area, in all likelihood it would have killed, crippled, or displaced several million people.

The Perfect Storm

If these four scenarios are not enough to persuade you that the time is at hand to get your disaster plans and preparations in order, I suggest that you consider the following six trends that appear to be combining to form the perfect storm for global catastrophe, each of which is a potential civilization buster in its own right, if left unchecked. You may not agree with the scientific foundation for all of these trends, and it may turn out that scientists' concerns about one or more of these trends are unfounded, but is it not prudent to plan for the potential that one or more of these trends might significantly damage or disrupt the complex global systems that we rely upon to keep ourselves comfortably fed, clothed, and sheltered?

1. Peak Oil

Our global economy and culture are built largely upon a reliance on cheap oil. From the cars we drive, to the jets we fly, to the buildings we live in, to the food we eat, to the clothes we wear—almost everything that encompasses the fabric of our modern life is either powered by oil, built from oil, or made/grown via machines powered by oil. When the price of oil rose above $140 a barrel in 2008, the world's economy went into a tailspin—collapsing local economies, reducing consumption, and bringing the price of oil back down to a fraction of what it had been just a few months earlier. Global output of traditional crude oil peaked around 2005–6 and is currently declining.

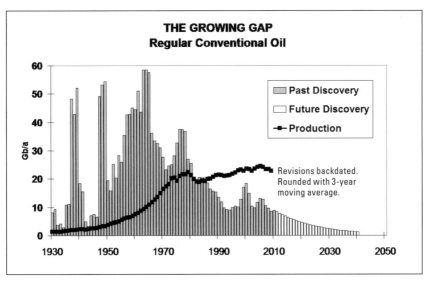

Figure 1-1. World discovery and production of oil. Source: Dr. Colin Campbell, ASPO (Association for the Study of Peak Oil)

Expensive alternative oil and oil-equivalent sources, like tar sands, deep ocean oil wells, and biofuels, have taken up the slack for the time being, but these are limited resources and their utilization is not growing as quickly as necessary to fill in the gap caused by the shrinking output from the world's mature oil fields. In 2008 the International Energy Agency (IEA) estimated the decline of output from the world's mature oil fields at a rate of 9.1 percent annually, with a drop to "only" 6.4 percent if huge capital investments are made to implement "enhanced oil recovery" technologies on a massive scale (Hoyos 2008).

Without developing energy alternatives at warp speed, or discovering and developing an entire Saudi Arabia's worth of oil every few years from now until eternity (an impossible fantasy), our world will be in a heap of trouble if and when the economy starts to pop back and supply once again falls short of demand, resulting in more oil price spikes followed by another round of financial declines (as of May 2011, there are distinct signs that this is starting to occur). Even if the global economy never returns to its pre-2008 levels, we will still be in trouble as declining supplies are projected to fall short of the current demand in this rather depressed economy.

In the mid 1960s, when discoveries of new oil reserves reached their historical peak, we were discovering oil at a rate four times faster than we were consuming it. In recent years, the tables have turned. With technology that is miles beyond what was available in the 1960s, we are discovering about one-tenth as much oil each year as we did then, and consuming it at a rate five times faster than we discover it. That's like charging $100,000 dollars on our credit cards each year, and only paying off $20,000! How long can we keep that up before we bankrupt the system? For years, governments have been official naysayers about the "Peak Oil theory." However, in April of 2010 the U.S. military issued a report saying, "By 2012 surplus oil production capacity could entirely disappear, and as early as 2015, the shortfall in output could reach 10 million barrels per day" (Macalister 2010). Over the next few months, this report was followed by similar ones issued by both the British and German militaries (Schultz 2010).

2. Climate Change

❝The outlook for global warming if the world continues its current path is a lot worse than it was just a few years ago, says new research from MIT, making it even more urgent to put in place strong policies to curb greenhouse-gas emissions. The new MIT study, like all climate studies a sophisticated computer model, projects a median temperature rise of 5.2 degrees centigrade in 2100. That's double the 2.4 degree increase projected in a 2003 study, MIT said. The range of temperature increases that are 90% likely stretches from 3.5 to 7.4 degrees centigrade [6.3°F–13.3°F].❞
—"Climate Change: MIT Study Says Temperatures Could Rise Twice as Much," *Wall Street Journal*, May 19, 2009

With a 90 percent degree of certainty, the world's top scientists believe that our planet's climate is changing at an accelerating pace, that these changes are caused by humankind, and will have increasingly severe consequences for our world. Naysayers stress the 10 percent scientific probability that man is not the cause of current climate changes, but would you board a plane if you were told it "only" had a 9 in 10 chance of crashing? It is a rare person over the age of thirty who will tell you that the weather is not quite different now from when they were a child; if nothing else, certainly far more erratic, though not always hotter.

In addition to mankind's emissions of "greenhouse gases," good climatologists also look at a wide variety of contributing interwoven factors, such as solar fluctuations, orbital variations, volcanic ash, air pollution particulates, and so on. For example, in the winter of 2009–10, a combination of cooling effects from the Northern Hemisphere's aerosol pollutants (smoke from coal power plants, industry, cars) and the sun being in a phase known as a "solar minimum" temporarily counteracted the warming effects of the greenhouse gases across the central latitudes of the Northern Hemisphere, helping to give many of those living in the heavily populated areas of Europe, North America, and Asia a winter that seemed like "the good old days." This led many to breathe a sigh of relief, siding with the climate change deniers' proclamations that global warming is a hoax foisted upon the peoples of the world by a huge conspiracy that managed to corral and censor the vast majority of the world's climate scientists from countries around the world. However, global scientific weather data for that winter showed composite temperatures well above average in the far north as well as most of the Southern Hemisphere—areas not subject to the cooling effects from the bulk of the aerosol pollutants emitted by the industrial nations of the north, and this data was in agreement with scientific climate models (Hansen et al. 2008 and 2010). After analyzing temperature data for the entire world, scientists concluded that 2005 and 2010 ended up in a tie for the hottest year on record (NOAA 2011).

Recent estimates by a team of climate scientists, including a group from MIT, calculate that even if we implemented the most stringent greenhouse gas limits currently proposed by some of the world's governments, our climate is likely to warm between 6.3°F and 13.3°F over the next century, leading to disastrous crop failures in most of the world's productive farmlands and "breadbaskets" (*Wall Street Journal* 2009).

3. Collapse of the World's Oceans

"Experts on invertebrates have expressed 'profound shock' over a government report showing a decline in zooplankton of more than 70% since the 1960s. The tiny animals are an important food for fish, mammals and crustaceans. . . . 'But, despite this experience, we were profoundly shocked to read that zooplankton abundance has declined by about 73% since 1960 and about 50% since 1990. This is a biodiversity disaster of enormous proportions.'" —"Fall in Tiny Animals a Disaster," *BBC News*, July 10, 2008

With eleven out of fifteen of the world's major fisheries either in collapse, or in danger of collapse, our world's oceans are in serious trouble. The ocean's planktons form the bottom of both the food chain and the bulk of the carbon-oxygen cycle for our planet. According to a recent British government report, the oceans have lost 73 percent of their zooplankton since 1960, and over 50 percent of this decline has been since 1990, and the phytoplanktons are also in serious decline.

Unfortunately, the coral reefs aren't doing much better than the planktons. By 2004, an estimated 20 percent of the world's coral reefs had been destroyed (up from just 11 percent in 2000), an additional 24 percent were close to collapse, and another 26 percent were under long-term threat of collapse (Allsopp et al. 2007, 10). The oceans' roll in sequestering atmospheric CO_2

and maintaining a breathable concentration of oxygen in the atmosphere is even more vital to our planet's health than the rainforests, but perhaps because the damage is occurring out of sight beneath the surface, we appear to be less concerned with what we are doing to the oceans.

4. Deforestation

❝The rainforests of the Amazon, the Congo basin and Indonesia are thought of as the lungs of the planet. But the destruction of those forests will in the next four years alone, in the words of Sir Nicholas Stern, pump more CO_2 into the atmosphere than every flight in the history of aviation to at least 2025.❞ —Daniel Howden, "Deforestation: The Hidden Cause of Global Warming," *Independent*, May 14, 2007

Over 50 percent of the world's forests have already disappeared, and much of the rest are threatened. Deforestation annually contributes approximately 25 percent of all global greenhouse gases, nearly double the 14 percent that transportation and industry sectors each contribute (Howden 2007). Additionally, the forests of the world are a critical part of the weather cycle as well as the carbon-oxygen cycle. Each large mature tree acts as a giant water pump, recycling millions of gallons of water back into the atmosphere via evaporation from its leaves or needles. It has been estimated that a single large rainforest or coniferous tree has an evaporative surface area roughly equal to a 40-acre lake. When the trees are decimated in a region, a process called "desertification" tends to occur downwind because the trees are no longer there to pump groundwater back into the atmosphere to fall back to earth as additional rainfall at some downwind location.

5. The Global Food Crisis: Soils, Weather, and Water

❝'World food prices have risen 45 percent in the last nine months and there are serious shortages of rice, wheat and [corn],' Jacques Diouf, head of the Rome-based U.N. Food and Agriculture Organization (FAO), said at a major conference in New Delhi yesterday. . . . World Bank President Robert B. Zoellick said earlier this month that nearly three dozen countries face social unrest because of surging food and fuel prices. For the countries most at risk, 'there is no margin for survival,' he said.❞ —David R. Sands, "Global Food Riots Turn Deadly," *Washington Times*, April 10, 2008

For the first time since the "green revolution" started, our world is producing less food each year, yet its population continues to rise as we lose more topsoil, arable land, and have less water for irrigation. Climate change is currently contributing more to losses than technology is to gains. In 2008 and 2009, food riots threatened the stability of many governments. In 2010 extended droughts in the breadbaskets of both China and India threatened the food supply for over one-third of the world's population.

6. Overpopulation

❝Sometime around 2050, there are going to be nine billion people roaming this planet—two billion more than there are today. It's a safe bet that all those folks will want to eat. And that's . . . an incredibly daunting prospect. Right now, an estimated one billion people go hungry each day. So add two billion more people, a limited supply of arable land, plus the fact that rising incomes will boost demand for meat and dairy products, plus the fact that many key natural resources (fisheries, say) are already being overexploited . . . and it's hard to see the situation getting better. And that's before we get into the fact that the planet's heating up, which is expected to wreak havoc on agricultural yields.❞ —Brad Plumer, "Is There Enough Food Out There for Nine Billion People?" *New Republic*, February 3, 2010

Overpopulation is the elephant in the room that few are talking about. In the last decade, we have added more people to the planet than were added between the births of Jesus and Abraham Lincoln. Around the year 1975, our world first overshot its capacity to provide for its human population, yet this population continues to grow, and we continue to live on borrowed time (Global Footprint Network 2010). One thousand years after Jesus walked the earth, human population was around ½ billion. It took another 800 years to double this population to 1 billion. It took only 130 more years for the next doubling to 2 billion in 1930. When I was a kid in 1960, world population hit 3 billion people, and it only took another 40 years to double to 6 billion in the year 2000.

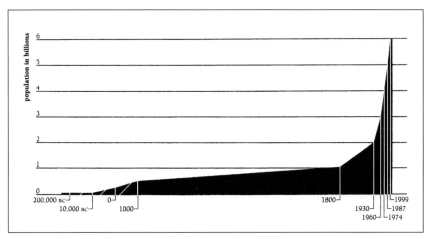

Figure 1-2. Global population growth. Source: U.S. Census Bureau

It is anticipated that the world's population will reach 7 billion in the year 2011, meaning that between the start of the year 2000 and the end of 2011 (barring some huge catastrophe that kills many millions of people), we will have added more people to the population of our world than lived on the entire planet just two hundred years ago! There is simply no way we can achieve a sustainable future unless our population stops growing and starts shrinking. Either Nature will do this for us, with starvation and plagues spreading across the planet as our natural and manmade systems fall apart, or mankind will use its intelligence and free will to proactively implement positive solutions to these issues.

Are You a Gambling Man?

❝Is it not too late if one waits until one is thirsty to begin digging a well?❞ —Old Chinese saying

So, what are the chances that any of the prior four scenarios will actually come to pass, or that the six trends will develop into this "perfect storm"? My personal opinion is that each of the four scenarios has a significant chance of occurring. I would give them somewhat less than a 50/50 chance, but far greater than the chances of coming up with a straight flush in a hand of poker, and probably better than your odds of drawing a full house. So, if you are a gambling man, and like to take lots of risks, go ahead, and play the odds that nothing will happen.

It is also my opinion that the odds are quite high (better than 50/50) for running into major disruptions along the lines of the perfect storm, and on a scale large enough that one would benefit from the advice, skills, and supplies recommended and taught in this book. In fact, given the lack of effective action from the world's governments on changing the course of even one of the six trends of this "perfect storm," I would say those odds are close to 100 percent!

The fact that you are reading this book means that you are significantly concerned for the safety and welfare of yourself and your loved ones. Now that we have established the *need* to be prepared, let's proceed to the next chapter so we can start learning the *way* to prepare!

[2]

Your Preparedness Plan

❝Inaction breeds doubt and fear. Action breeds confidence and courage. If you want to conquer fear, do not sit home and think about it. Go out and get busy.❞ —Dale Carnegie

We are living in an era of economic upheaval, super storms, record-breaking droughts and floods, international terrorism, global food shortages, and increasingly destructive earthquakes. It appears quite likely that at some point in the not-too-distant future many of us will experience significant disruptions in central services, basic utilities such as electricity, and access to whatever you desire from local stores. Remember that when electricity stops flowing, furnaces, cash registers, gasoline pumps, refrigerators, elevators, phones, and air conditioners all stop working, except for the rare facilities that are hooked up to a backup source of power. Without gas and electricity, most municipal water-treatment and waste-removal systems will soon shut down, and emergency medical services are usually quite limited. If the power goes out when temperatures are well below freezing, without a backup source of heat (or drained and winterized plumbing) the toilet bowls and pipes in most modern homes will start to freeze and will burst within one or two days.

This chapter helps you to formulate your personalized preparedness plan, and to put together the basic supplies you will need to weather short-term emergencies, such as a 72-hour "grab-and-go" survival kit and a comprehensive first-aid kit. It also provides suggestions for compiling critical information and records in one single location, so they may be grabbed on a moment's notice if an unexpected evacuation is required. The chapter ends with my top-ten list of important survival skills and strategies.

Are You Prepared?

As mentioned in chapter 1, emergency preparedness isn't about a bunch of survivalists crawling around in the woods, preparing to fight off the starving hordes in some grim, post-9/11, apocalyptic fantasy. In today's world of terrorist acts, global warming, and super storms, there is an ever-growing likelihood most of us will experience significant disruptions in the flow of electricity and goods at some point in our lives. Stocking up on a few extra supplies, learning some new skills, and making a few emergency contingency

After living in the States off and on for several years, in 2008 Andrew and Mary Hall moved back to their home in Buxton, Australia, so they could be closer to their aging parents. It was a modest three-bedroom two-bath house with exterior walls of mud brick (adobe) that helped keep the home's interior cool during the hot Australian summers. With large eaves, a metal roof, and mud brick walls, many would consider their home to be quite fire resistant, but its construction proved no match for the forces of nature that turned the neighboring towns of Buxton and Marysville into deadly infernos on Australia's tragic "Black Saturday" of February 7, 2009.

The prior week, the weather had been extremely hot, with several days recording temperatures of over 40°C (104°F). On that Saturday morning, record-breaking temperatures combined with long-term drought conditions and high winds (over 60 mph) to generate the most serious fire conditions that anyone could remember. An official "extreme fire alert" was issued along with a strict "no burning" command. Mary remembers looking at the thermometer on that day, and it read a blistering 47°C (117°F)! Around 4:30 in the afternoon, a neighbor came by and pointed out a large ominous plume of smoke rising to the southwest. Andrew dialed 000 (The Aussie equivalent to America's 911), and it just cut out. When attempts to call the fire department also failed, they decided to pack and go. Knowing that they did not have enough water and other resources to stay and fight should a major wildfire break out, Andrew and Mary's fire plan had always been to evacuate. They packed some clothes, the dog, a few files, their computers, and a couple bicycles into the car and left their home, hoping and praying it would still be standing upon their return.

Andrew and Mary headed for a friend's place with a defensible piece of property that included a swimming pool and a dammed reservoir, plus an extensive supply of fire-fighting materials such as pumps, a tractor, and backpack sprayers. Unlike Andrew and Mary's property, which backed up to a steeply wooded hillside, their friend's property was mostly grassland, making it easier to hold back a bushfire. About 10:30 pm a 3-meter (10-foot) high

plans doesn't take a lot of time or money, and it's cheap insurance that can foster peace of mind in turbulent times.

Disturbances such as floods, earthquakes, major storms, or terrorist acts can disrupt the distribution of electricity, food, fuel, goods, and services for significant periods of time. In 1998, a severe ice storm in the Northeast knocked out power for periods ranging from three days to several weeks, and many of the survivors of Japan's Kobe quake did not receive food or potable water until a week after the quake. Could you keep your pipes from freezing if your power went out for several days during a winter's cold snap?

Before the magnitude 6.9 earthquake struck Kobe, Japanese engineers and politicians thought they were better prepared for earthquake disasters than any other country in the world. Japan's freeways and buildings are theoretically designed to handle much stronger quakes than the one that struck Kobe, yet most of Kobe's downtown freeways and tall buildings either fell down during the quake or had to be torn down afterward because of struc-

wall of fire descended upon that property, and for the next eight hours family, friends, and neighbors fought to keep the flames and flying embers at bay. Exhausted, around 6:00 am they were able to catch an hour and a half of fitful sleep before braving the drive back to their home to survey the damage. At this point, they still had hopes that a favorable wind direction had spared their home. As they walked up the hill to their front yard, they saw that all but three mud brick walls had been totally obliterated. Except for the few things they had packed in their car they day before, all of their personal belongings and the tools for Andrew's bicycle repair business had been reduced to cinders and scraps of molten metal.

Andrew also had a commercial coffee roaster housed in a shed on his partner's property just outside of the neighboring town of Marysville. The entire commercial section of Marysville, except for the bakery, had also been destroyed by the fire, but miraculously, the shed that the coffee roaster was stored in, as well as their friend's home, had survived. Both were scorched by the flames, but spared the destruction that had taken all but 14 of over 400 buildings in Marysville. In spite of having lost their home, one of their businesses, and nearly all their personal possessions, they fared much better than many others in the surrounding area who had lost their lives or loved ones. On what has become known as "Black Saturday," bush fires took the lives of 173 people, wiped out whole towns, and entire families were found incinerated in their cars while trying to escape the inferno.

In addition to the details of their trials and losses, Mary also had this to say in her official statement to the local police, "I don't believe we would have done anything any differently. As far as having adequate warning, we weren't given any. Other than knowing that it was a high fire danger day, there was no real warning. I don't know that having had any other warning would have made a difference. I know I didn't hear any siren or warning sound that day." Like my friends Mary and Andrew, knowing when to stand and fight, and when to pack and run, clearly meant the difference between life and death for hundreds of folks on that blazing hot Saturday in Australia!

tural damage. This disaster was a harsh blow for hundreds of thousands of survivors who lost friends, family members, and most (if not all) of their possessions. How well would you fare if you could not purchase any food, water, or gasoline for a week? What about a month or longer? If a wildfire was barreling down on your home, and you only had a few minutes to evacuate, would you know what is most important to take, and could you gather those things together in just a few minutes?

No one really knows what the future will bring. You can't plan for all possible scenarios, but a wise person plans for several of the most likely possibilities and stores at least a few basic supplies for emergencies. This chapter will help you to evaluate your own particular needs and goals, and offers guidance to help you plan for both short-term and long-term situations. I suggest that everyone should have at least a 72-hour grab-and-go kit, plus a minimum of two weeks of food supplies on hand at all times. In the event that the world situation should rapidly degrade, whether it is due to a nuclear exchange between warring countries; escalating violence in the Middle East; a well-coordinated, large-scale terrorist act; or some other form of societal meltdown, it might become obvious that the time is at hand to open up the next chapter for quick advice on putting together rudimentary supplies to cover the basics for several months, a year, or perhaps even longer. Once a crisis hits, time will be of the essence since it won't be long before stores are wiped clean of most of the supplies you will need!

To help you organize your thoughts and guide your actions, ask yourself the following questions while making your emergency plans and building your backup supplies and skills:

- What natural hazards are there in my area? Have I taken precautions to protect my home?

- What is my potential for being caught in a significant earthquake, flood, hurricane, tornado, or wildfire? *Note:* See the appropriate chapters in part 3 for specific information pertaining to each of these hazards.

- How long do I anticipate that I might be without access to utilities and supplies?

- If the electricity goes out for an extended period of time, how will I cook, and how will I heat and light my home? How will I keep the food in my refrigerator and freezer from rotting?

- Do I have supplies and training to deal with medical emergencies if medical help is unavailable?

- If I must evacuate my home, do I have portable emergency supplies readily available to bring with me?

- In case I need to evacuate on foot, do I have a large backpack, lightweight compact camping gear, and sturdy hiking boots?

- How many people do I wish to store supplies for? What about my friends, neighbors, or relatives?

- Do I have pets that I wish to feed and care for?

- Do I have small children or infants with special needs?

- Do I require prescription medications or are there any addictions I wish to provide for in case distribution systems go down for a period of time?

Planning for the Short Term

The following information on short-term planning is designed to help you to prepare for emergencies when services are disrupted for periods of up to one week. Everyone should have enough food, water, and other emergency supplies to last for at least three days (72-hour emergency kits), and preferably two or more weeks.

I suggest making these preparations as soon as possible. It is hard to focus on this task when skies are blue and nothing is threatening, but it is usually too late once a disaster strikes or is close at hand. When the tourists come to our town in the High Sierras, just the threat of a major winter storm is enough to send swarms of people to the local supermarkets, where they stock up on food. Once the highway over Donner Summit closes to trucks for a day or two, local market shelves are quickly stripped bare (my wife and I like to refer to this as "the Donner Party syndrome").

Short-Term Preparedness Checklist

❏ Store at least one 72-hour emergency "grab-and-go" survival kit in or near your home, and condensed versions in your cars.

❏ Determine a local meeting place with a large open area, such as a park or school, where your household can gather if you are separated and do not have access to your home during emergencies.

❏ Make sure that all capable members of your family know how and where to shut off the water, gas, and electricity for your home in the event of an emergency.

❏ Stash spare keys to your vehicles somewhere on the vehicle and an additional supply of keys somewhere outside of your home (securely hidden).

❏ Store at least a two-week supply of food for your household.

❏ Store a combination of water, water-treatment chemicals, and water-purifying filters to provide for your household for at least a week (see chapter 8 for more information on filters and purification).

❏ Keep a survival manual in each car with a first-aid kit, spare clothing, and a water filter, if not a full 72-hour kit.

❏ Get proper first-aid and CPR training for all capable members of your family. See the American Red Cross for first-aid training and assistance with local emergency planning.

❏ Arrange for an out-of-state emergency contact to reach for coordination and communication. After an emergency, it may be easier to call long distance than locally, or your family may be separated and need an outside contact to communicate through.

❏ Locate your nearest emergency shelter (call your local Red Cross for this information). Practice the route to the shelter, if it's not conveniently located.

❏ Make sure that you have smoke detectors in your home. Change their batteries at least once each year.

❏ Store your important papers in one easily accessible location, preferably in a waterproof and flameproof box.

❏ Discuss your emergency-preparedness plans with all members of your household. Keep the discussion light and positive.

72-Hour "Grab-and-Go" Survival Kits

These short-term emergency kits should be readily accessible and cover the basic daily needs of your family for a period of at least three days. Please note that three days is a minimal time period (in Kobe, Japan, it was nine days before many survivors received food and water) and that you should have at least a two-week supply of food stored in or around your home. You may purchase ready-made, 72-hour kits from various survival supply outlets, or you can put together your own. Large families should probably divide up the stores between several easily grabbed small backpacks or plastic containers. One advantage of building your own kits is that you get to choose foods that you like. Remember that all foods have some kind of shelf life. *Rotate stores, and use them or lose them.* Bug-infested, rancid, or rotten food doesn't do anyone any good. Consider placing all of the following items in your 72-hour survival kit.

72-Hour Grab-and-Go Survival Kit

1. **Portable radio,** preferably one that works with no batteries, such as by a hand crank or combination hand crank and solar cells (available through survival and surplus outlets). See figure 2-1.

2. **First-aid kit** with first-aid and survival handbooks (this book covers both). Make sure that your fist-aid kit includes a couple of stretchy Ace bandages for binding wounds and sprained joints, as well as a roll of 2-inch-wide cloth adhesive first-aid tape for taping "hot spots" to prevent blisters, as well as for taping sprains and wounds.

3. **Water, water-purification chemicals, and/or purifying filter.** Enough to provide 1 gallon per person per day. Retort (foil) pouches can handle freezing in a car trunk, but most other water containers can't handle freezing without potentially bursting. Three gallons per person is heavy (25 lbs.), so I strongly suggest that you include a water filter and water-treatment chemicals. I suggest pump-type backcountry filters, such as those made by Katadyn or MSR (see fig. 2-2), that are rated to filter out all bacteria and have a carbon core to remove toxic chemicals. Also, supplement your filter(s) with purifying iodine crystals (or other chemicals), such as a "Polar Pure" water purification kit (see fig. 2-3), to kill all

Figure 2-1. Survival radio with AM/ FM and shortwave band widths plus combination battery power, solar charger, and hand-crank dynamo. Photo courtesy of Eton Corp.

Figure 2-2. MSR Miniworks fully field-maintainable water filter with ceramic cartridge and carbon core. Photo courtesy of Eastern Mountain Sports (EMS)

Figure 2-3. Polar Pure iodine-crystal water purification kit. Photo courtesy of Polar Equipment, Inc.

viruses. Pump filters that are rated for virus removal have tiny pore sizes and tend to clog quickly (a clogged filter is worthless). Sports bottle–type purifying water filters are simple, reliable, compact, and inexpensive, but clog easier and won't purify nearly as many gallons of water as the pump-type filters. I also carry a small compact Steripen in my grab-and-go kit, which is a terrific new gadget that flashes high intensity UV light to kill bacteria and viruses in a bottle of water in a matter of seconds. The downside to a Steripen is it requires clear water to reliably eliminate all the nasty organisms in your water, so all bets are off using a Steripen on dirty water unless it is filtered first to remove sediment and debris. See chapter 8 for more details on water purification and purification products.

4. **Waterproof and windproof matches** in a waterproof container, and a utility-type butane lighter (large size with extended tip).

5. **Wool or pile blankets** (avoid cotton) because they are warm when wet, and/or a sleeping bag. Also, a heat-reflective, waterproof "space blanket." Fiber-pile, mountaineering-quality sleeping bags are great, if you have the space (avoid down sleeping bags, except for extremely cold climates, because they are worthless when wet).

6. **A colloidal silver generator** (see fig. 2-4) for making a broadband

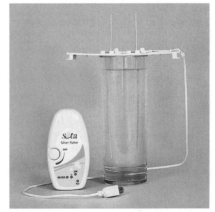

Figure 2-4. Silver Pulser colloidal silver generator from Sota Instruments. Photo courtesy of Sota Instruments

antibiotic solution that can kill all known pathogenic bacteria (if you are without access to pharmaceuticals, this could save your life someday, see chapter 6 for details). Can also be used to preserve drinking water so it won't grow bacteria, and will slowly purify water by killing pathogenic bacteria, but it takes a long time (typically several hours).

7. **Flashlight with spare batteries, or a solar-recharge flashlight.** I highly recommend that you purchase a headlamp with LED bulbs. Headlamps (see fig. 2-5) leave your hands free to carry things, or work on things. LED bulbs use a fraction of the power, are far more shock resistant, and last far longer than traditional light bulbs, so your batteries last many times longer.

Figure 2-5. Waterproof lightweight headlamp with LED bulbs, by Petzl.
Photo courtesy of Eastern Mountain Sports (EMS)

8. **Candles** (useful for lighting fires with damp wood) and light sticks (emergency light when nothing else works or explosive gases are present).

9. **Toiletries,** including toilet paper, toothbrush, soap, razor, shampoo, sanitary napkins (also good for severe bleeding wounds), a pack of dental floss (for sewing and tying things), sunscreen, extra eyeglasses, diapers, and so on.

10. **Food for three days per person, minimum.** Use foods you will eat and that store well, such as nuts, sport bars, canned vegetables, fruits, meats, dry cereals, and military-type preserved meals (available at surplus and survival stores).

11. **A Swiss Army knife,** Leatherman, or other stainless steel multi-tool knife with scissors, can opener, blades, and screwdrivers (see fig. 2-6).

12. **Map, compass, and whistle.** When you are in a weakened state, or

Figure 2-6. Multi-tool knife by Leatherman.
Photo courtesy of Eastern Mountain Sports (EMS)

have a parched throat, a whistle may draw someone's attention and save your life. In smoke or fog, a compass may be the only thing pointing you in the right direction. The dial on the compass should glow in the dark. Put a string on your compass so you can hang it around your neck for quick referral.

13. **Sewing kit with extra-heavy-duty thread.** Should be strong enough to stitch a torn strap onto your backpack (I never travel in the backcountry without a sewing kit and have had to use it several times). *Note:* May be used to suture (stitch) wounds in an emergency (soak needle and thread in boiling water first)!

14. **Towel or dishcloth.** Knives, forks, spoons, and so on. A camping "mess kit" is a compact set of utensils.

15. **Tent** and/or 50-foot roll of plastic sheeting for shelter.

16. **Extra clothing,** such as long underwear, hat, jacket, waterproof mittens, leather work gloves, rain coat or poncho, sturdy boots, and so on. Remember that cotton is very cold when wet, but wool and specialty outdoor clothing (usually polyester) wick moisture and are warm when wet.

17. **Entertainment** for kids and other special needs (prescription medicines, diapers, extra glasses, etc.).

18. **Twenty-five kitchen-size garbage bags** and lime or sewage-treatment chemicals (powdered type preferred) for garbage and toilet sewage. A few large heavy-duty garbage bags can double for raincoats, ground cloths, and shelter.

19. **Fifty feet of heavy-duty nylon string or light rope.**

20. **Record of bank numbers and important telephone numbers.**

21. **Spare checks and cash.** Many Katrina victims were caught without any cash. *Tip:* Use a bank that has widespread branch locations so their records won't disappear in a severe local disaster, leaving you with no bank-account access.

Figure 2-7. Multi-fuel backcountry stove from MSR is lightweight, compact, and fully field serviceable.
Photo courtesy of Eastern Mountain Sports (EMS)

22. **Optional items:** A compact stove with fuel, like one of the MSR multi-fuel stoves (see fig. 2-7), along with a cook set. Good for boiling water, warming hands and feet, as well as for cooking.

First-Aid Kits

Get yourself a decent first-aid kit. Each car should have a kit, and your house should have one too. Most preparedness/survival suppliers stock an assortment of first-aid kits, from simple to field-surgical quality. I stock my grab-and-go kit in a large blue tub that can be quickly thrown in a car. It includes both a large, extensive first-aid kit in a waterproof box, designed for back country river-guide usage, and a small, compact kit (fits in the palm of my hand), so I have a lightweight option in case circumstances dictate that I must evacuate on foot rather than in my car. The compact first-aid kit easily fits into my backpack, whereas the large first aid kit and the hand-crank radio will not. Here are my suggestions for a modest first-aid kit:

Basic First-Aid Kit

❑ Two Ace bandages

❑ One box of adhesive bandages (at least 12 Band-Aids) of varying sizes, with at least two 2-inch or larger square bandages

❑ Six butterfly bandages

❑ One large roll of 2-inch cloth adhesive tape (may be torn or cut to smaller widths). Useful for binding wounds, taping sprains, and taping "hot spots" to prevent blisters)

❑ Several 4-inch-by-4-inch sterile, nonadhesive dressings

❑ Three 3-inch-wide gauze rolls

❑ Two triangular bandages

❑ Triple antibiotic ointment*

❑ Mouth shield for mouth-to-mouth resuscitation (precaution against AIDS, tuberculosis, and hepatitis)

❑ Three sterile applicator sticks, cotton tipped

❑ Alcohol and/or ten prepackaged alcohol squares*

❑ Instant cold-pack/icepack

❑ First-aid manual

❑ Thermometer

❑ Safety pins and sterile needle

❑ Scissors

❏ Surgical rubber gloves (several pairs)

❏ Pain-reliever tablets (aspirin, acetaminophen, etc.)*

❏ Laxative*

❏ Antidiarrhea medication*

❏ Syrup of ipecac (to induce vomiting)*

Add the following items for a more advanced first-aid kit:

❏ Snakebite kit

❏ Emergency suture kit

❏ Splinting material (air splint, traction splint, hard splint, etc.)

❏ Tourniquet

❏ Thumb/finger splint

❏ Burn gel and "second skin"

❏ Echinacea, colloidal silver, spilanthes-usnea, and grapefruit seed extract natural antibiotics and antifungal (internal and external)

❏ Tea tree oil natural antifungal and antibiotic (external only)

❏ Single-edged razor blades and surgical scalpel kit

❏ Kelley hemostats

❏ Surgical blunt-tip and pointed scissors

❏ Silver nitrate to cauterize bleeding (powdered goldenseal herb also does a good job at stopping bleeding from wounds)

❏ Prescription antibiotics and painkillers

❏ Sterile thread

* Check expiration dates and try to rotate stock every year.

Your Life in a Box

Most people who have "lost everything" in earthquakes, fires, floods, or other emergencies will tell you that they wished they had somehow been able to save at least one box filled with critical documents and other items that would help them prove their identity, manage their bank accounts and credit cards, contact their insurance companies, reproduce family photos, and in general speed the process of putting their lives back together. The following is a checklist of items to put into a box that you can grab on a moment's notice to take with you, which will be of assistance in the process of putting your life back together, should you have to suddenly "leave it all behind." When compiling "your life in a box" using original documents, it is a good idea to make a second set of copies for storage off-site at a significantly removed location (far enough away that a single fire, flood, or earthquake should not take both locations down), such as a relative's or friend's home. The use of a "fireproof" storage file is a good idea, but realize that these containers are not totally fireproof, but fire resistant to hold back the heat of a normal fire for a certain period of time (check the box's rating) without igniting the internal contents. The use of a safety deposit box may be a good idea, but you should consider whether or not your bank might be in a potential flood zone, susceptible to earthquake damage, or inaccessible in times of disaster or crisis when you may wish to grab your "life-in-a-box." I suggest you use the following checklist to organize "your life in a box" into seven different folders with the following headings:

Life-in-a-Box Checklist

Emergency Information
❑ Make a list for each family member of any special medications, medical directives, personal important contacts, personal physician, etc.

Personal Information
❑ Birth certificates

❑ Social Security cards / Social Insurance cards (Canada)

❑ Alien cards/immigration papers

❑ Copies of driver's license

❑ Medical and immunization records

❑ Marriage certificates

❑ Military papers

❑ Ownership and registration papers and license numbers for cars, RV, boats, etc.

Legal Information
❑ Will/living trust

❑ Safe-deposit box information, location and key

❑ Durable power-of-attorney document

❑ Medical power-of-attorney document or health care directive

Insurance Policies
❑ Medical insurance

❑ Homeowner's or renter's insurance

❑ Car insurance

❑ Life insurance

❑ Burial (funeral) insurance

Real Estate

❑ Property deeds (or location of originals)

❑ Current mortgage, rental or lease documents

❑ Deed to cemetery plot (if applicable)

Investments

❑ Bank accounts, credit unions

❑ Copies of credit cards (front and back)

❑ IRA, 401(k) (United States); CRA, RRSP (Canada)

❑ Stock certificates

❑ Mutual funds

❑ Certificates of deposit

❑ Bonds

Personal Items

❑ Backup critical items off your computer onto DVDs or CDs

❑ Digital copies of family photos, certificates, etc. onto DVDs or CDs

❑ Digital copies of pictures of home, Including each room and personal possessions for insurance purposes

(Source: Adapted from *My Life in a Box: A Life Organizer* by Laurie Ecklund Long, 2009)

Top Ten Survival Skills

The following is my top-ten list of skills and strategies most crucial to personal survival in a disaster situation. I suggest you keep this list in mind while reading through the rest of this book, and while building your disaster preparation supplies and skill sets.

1. **Be prepared.** I strongly suggest that everyone put together a basic 72-hour grab-and-go survival kit (see preceding section for a full list of items). This kit should cover the basic food, water, and survival needs for you and your family for at least the critical first three days after a disaster. Most of us could survive for a month without food, but a single day without water in extreme heat is enough to kill a person. For planning ahead to cope with longer-term shortages, use the "OAR" system (organize, acquire, and rotate) to stock up on supplies you may need, and keep them up to date and viable (see chapters 3 and 4).

2. **Develop your intuition.** Most survivors credit their instincts and "gut feel" with saving their lives. Natural selection has bred the most incredible survival mechanism into man. It is called "intuition," and primitive man has relied upon it for millennia to help him to make life-and-death decisions in a split second. Unfortunately, our modern society places most of

its emphasis on the rational left-brain type of thinking, and for the most part ignores the intuitive right-brain type of thinking. In chapter 7, I teach the "Pit of the Stomach" exercise for intuitively testing potential options before making a decision. It is best to practice these skills in your daily life, when the consequences of your decisions are not usually life-and-death, rather than to wait until a crisis comes along.

3. **Have a disaster plan.** See the preceding "Short-Term Preparedness Checklist." Create a plan with your family for communicating and responding to a disaster when phone lines may be dead (select a predetermined local meeting area and out-of-town contact, know how to shut off your home's gas and electricity supply, etc.).

4. **Learn first aid.** In the back country, as well as in most natural or manmade disasters, knowing fist aid (including CPR) saves lives (see chapter 5).

5. **Go camping and backpacking.** Most people have not camped or backpacked since they were kids, or perhaps never at all. If you are in this category, start with some car camping for a few weekends. I suggest you get comfortable with car camping before graduating to overnight backpacking trips. Backpacking will accustom your body to hiking several miles at a time and carrying whatever you need yourself. When you have to carry everything on your own back, you learn quickly what is necessary, and what you can do without. If you are an inexperienced "city slicker" and are thrust into a true survival situation, the experience will probably be quite painful, and possibly deadly. My basic outdoor gear recommendations start on page 48.

6. **Know how to start a fire.** Being able to build a fire is important for cooking, purifying water, preventing hypothermia in cold climates, keeping wild animals away at night (in some areas), and signaling potential rescuers. Illustrated instructions for building fires are found starting on page 154. Having grown up camping since I was barely out of diapers, I can usually start a fire with a single match. If you don't know what you are doing, you might go through a whole box of matches and still not have a fire lit. With bone-dry tinder and practically perfect conditions, starting a fire with a flint-and-steel or a primitive "fire drill" is a difficult task that takes practice and persistence, and it's practically impossible with wet wood and tinder. Until you have practiced these skills to the point where you are certain of your ability to build a fire with simple tools, or just a single match, you may be unpleasantly surprised by your lack of success when the conditions are less than ideal and your life depends upon your ability to start a fire.

7. **Learn how to find and purify water.** Unless you are in a cold climate, a single day without water will make you quite miserable, and three days could kill. Bees and birds can lead you to sources of fresh surface water. In chapter 8, I provide instructions for purifying water using common household chemicals, and offer my specific recommendations for portable water filters and purifiers. Having designed a number of water filters (both back-

country and residential) over a span of more than twenty years, water quality and treatment are fields in which I have considerable expertise.

8. **Develop a survivor personality.** Developing the mental traits of the "survivor personality" will help you to navigate and thrive in spite of life's challenges. The best survivors are flexible, tend to keep their cool in stressful situations, don't give up, have a playful curiosity, have a good sense of humor, don't tend to "cry over spilled milk," follow their "gut feelings," and are often "bad patients" and poor rule followers. In chapter 7, I discuss these traits and how to develop your own "survivor personality."

9. **Learn the "plant edibility test."** Most people will not happen to have a guide to wild edible plants on hand when they are thrust into a survival situation. If you know how to perform the "plant edibility test" (see page 162), you will always have a safe way to test local plants for potential edibility. The full test takes a couple of days to complete, but most inedible plants will be weeded out in the first few minutes. In general, people who can forage for wild edible plants will be much better fed than others who must rely solely on primitive trapping and hunting skills without modern equipment (like a gun or fishing gear).

10. **Learn how to make a primitive shelter.** Learn how to make a "scout pit," "squirrel's nest," snow cave, and other primitive shelters. In severe weather a shelter could save your life, and at other times it will make your life far more comfortable (instructions start on page 182). A plastic tarp, a couple of large-sized garbage bags, or a compact "space blanket" will provide a welcome shield against a downpour when no other more substantive shelter is available.

This chapter won't do you much good unless you put it to use. It won't take a lot of time or money to put together a first-aid kit, 72-hour grab-and-go short-term family survival kit, and a disaster survival plan for yourself and family. Think of how wonderful it will feel to know you are able to fend for yourself and family in the event of a disaster, and perhaps even lend a hand to others who are not so fortunate (and as well prepared) as yourself!

Stored Food and Other Supplies

"Anger over spiraling world food prices is becoming increasingly violent. Deadly clashes over higher costs for staple foods have broken out in Egypt, Haiti, and several African states, and an international food expert yesterday warned of more clashes with no short-term relief in sight. 'World food prices have risen 45 percent in the last nine months and there are serious shortages of rice, wheat and [corn],' Jacques Diouf, head of the Rome-based UN Food and Agriculture Organization (FAO), said at a major conference in New Delhi yesterday. 'There is a risk that this unrest will spread in countries where 50 to 60 percent of income goes to food,' he said.

The FAO has reported popular unrest over rising food prices in Burkina Faso, Cameroon, Indonesia, Ivory Coast, Mauritania, Mozambique, Bolivia and Uzbekistan, among other countries. The Philippines, the world's biggest rice importer, moved to head off protests after global prices doubled in a year. . . . World Bank President Robert B. Zoellick said earlier this month that nearly three dozen countries face social unrest because of surging food and fuel prices. For the countries most at risk 'there is no margin for survival,' he said.**"** —David Sands, "Global Food Riots Turn Deadly," *The Washington Times*, April 10, 2008.

It used to be that people thought things like food riots, famine, and starvation were "other country's problems" and could not happen here in America. Nowadays, people are not so sure. In uncertain times, it makes prudent sense to stock up on critical items, food, and supplies for weathering long-term shortages and widespread disasters. Knowledge is power, and this chapter provides valuable information and checklists to help you prepare to handle longer-term shortages and emergencies. Topics covered include storing food and water; basic supplies and equipment; calculating how much food you'll need; food-storage tips; sprouting seeds to make fresh food; and a guide to the best camping and cooking equipment.

Long-Term Planning and Food Storage

If you are planning to store food, water, and other items to supply your household for significant periods of time (more than one month), the packaging, preservation, and nutritive quality of your food stores will be vitally important. You can purchase specialty prepackaged bulk foods from preparedness/survival suppliers (see appendix 2), or package your own foods. If you have more time than money, packaging your own supplies will be far less expensive than the prepackaged types and gives you the best chance for ensuring that your stored food is of the quality and variety that you will want to eat.

You will probably want to store a significant variety of foods preserved by a variety of methods. Traditional high-heat canning processes destroy a significant portion of the food's nutritive value, but low-heat dehydration results in a loss of only about 10 percent. Many canned foods do have the advantage of providing syrups or juices, which can be a significant source of water if you are experiencing scarcity. If you have access to a source of water, however, it makes better sense to use dehydrated foods. A pound of dry grains or beans will contain many times the calories of a typical pound of canned foods. Each pound of dehydrated fruits or vegetables is equivalent to 10 to 12 pounds of fresh, canned, or frozen produce, and a pound of dry meat is equal to about 3 to 4 pounds of fresh meat.

Stored whole grains may be sprouted to give you the nutritive value of fresh "live" food. Most whole grains and beans can be sprouted. The sprouting process converts proteins in the seeds into different essential amino acids and dramatically increases their vitamin content. For example, sprouted soybeans have 700 percent more vitamin C than the dry beans, though they have a lower caloric content. Vitamin C is a natural detoxifier, destroying damaging toxins in the body. It is essential for helping the body maintain an effective immune system and for preventing deficiency conditions, such as scurvy. However, minerals, protein, and caloric content are not improved by sprouting.

The downside to whole grains is that unless they are kept cool, they contain oils that can go rancid, thereby ruining them for consumption. A useful fact to remember is that most foods retain useful nutritive value long after they have lost their aesthetic appeal. However, foods that smell rotten, rancid, or moldy should be thrown out. Mold may be cut off the outside of cheese, apples, and meats, but moldy grain, other fruits, fats, and vegetables should be thrown out. Most molds give off aflatoxins, which are highly toxic poisons, so your living area and foods should be kept as mold free as possible.

Whole grains last much longer than grains ground into flour, because finely ground particles have far more surface area for oxidation (degradation). A grain mill, preferably hand-cranked or combination hand-and-electric powered, is useful for turning your stored grain into flour as it is required. Most long-term storage programs stress wheat storage, because properly stored wheat has an indefinite shelf life. Some wheat discovered in the pyramids was found to be viable after thousands of years. Brown rice, on the other hand, has a typical shelf life of six months to one year, which may be extended to two to three years when packaged with nitrogen or CO_2 in properly sealed containers.

Basic Supplies

Here is a checklist of supplies to pick up for stored goods to weather longer term disruptions:

❑ **Water, stored supplies, and water-purification materials.** Water is the most important commodity. You can live for a long time without food, but when physically active during hot weather, you may survive only three or four days without water. (See chapter 8 for detailed information pertaining to water.)

❑ **Wheat and other grains, flours, and beans.** These are the easiest bulk materials to store for calorie, shelf life, and nutritive value.

❑ **Grain grinder.** Buy a quality grinder for grinding grains into flour. You should have a hand-cranked or combination hand-and-power unit that works without power, but an electric grinder is much easier if you use it a lot. It is best to have one electric-powered grain mill and one that operates by hand.

❑ **Cooking catalysts and seasonings.** Includes oils, shortenings, salt, leavenings, herbs, and spices. Herbs and spices will provide essential phytonutrients and add much needed variety to the usual monotony of stored grain and beans.

❑ **Powdered milk, dairy products, and eggs.** These are good for nutritive value and variety in cooking options. These items should be professionally packaged by a reputable food-storage company, since without proper oxygen-reduced packaging, their shelf life will be drastically reduced.

❑ **Sprouting seeds and supplies.** With a couple of jars, some nylon stockings, and a variety of seeds, you can eat garden-fresh live foods for pennies a day. I suggest alfalfa seeds, any whole grains, mung beans, soybeans, lentils, and cabbage, radish, and broccoli seeds. See table 3-3 for detailed sprouting instructions.

❑ **Sweeteners.** Honey, sugar, and maple syrup are not essential, but may help sweeten an otherwise bitter experience. Honey has the advantage of being a natural topical antibiotic. It has been used for centuries on the battlefield for helping wounds to heal, and will not spoil (to reliquefy crystallized honey, open cap and heat the honey container, using caution if it's plastic, in simmering or lightly boiling water).

❑ **Canned and dried fruits, vegetables, and soups.** Store a variety of your family's favorites.

❑ **Canned, dried, or frozen meats and fish.** Store these if you will use them.

❑ **Dietary supplements.** Vitamins and minerals supplement the limited nutritional value of stored foods. I suggest using quality supplements manufactured from live foods wherever possible (check your local health food store).

❏ **Fuels, lighting sources, camping gear.** Camping gear can provide you with portable shelter and materials for living comfortably if you must evacuate your home (see "Notes on Camping Gear" in this chapter).

❏ **Medicines and first-aid kits.**

❏ **Pet food and personal items.** Don't forget the things in life that help you stay happy and centered. A couple of decks of cards and a copy of Hoyle's book of card games can break the tension and generate a lot of laughs when times are tough. Don't forget the favorite board games and a stack of poker chips too!

❏ **Open-pollinated seeds for gardening.** I recommend that you store a variety of seeds for gardening. Use open-pollinated seeds, not hybrids, so you can save seeds from your garden for future needs, if necessary. *Do not eat seeds for planting. If they are dyed a bright color, they may be poisonous. Also, they will provide a hundred times more nutrition after the harvest than if eaten first.*

❏ **Pleasure foods, including snacks, treats, sweets, and beverages.** These may not have much nutritive value, but they are great for lifting morale or giving yourself a little reward.

Calculating a Year's Food Supply

❝Store what you eat. Eat what you store. Use it or lose it!❞ —James Talmage Stevens, *Making the Best of Basics: Family Preparedness Handbook*

Because most stored foods have a limited shelf life, you are throwing money away if you do not store food that your family will eat. The day that your life depends on your food stores is the wrong time to find out you have an allergy to 90 percent of your stored food. Develop a plan of rotating through and replacing your stored food to ensure that the food does not exceed its shelf life and that you will actually eat the kinds of food that you have stored. The average American diet of 3,500 calories a day leads to obesity. When the Soviet Union collapsed and Cuba lost its main source for food imports, the average Cuban diet slipped from 2,908 calories in 1989 to 1,863 calories in 1995, and most Cubans lost about 20 pounds (Pfeiffer 2006). The following food-storage quantities are for one typical adult American male, for one year, consuming roughly 2,600 calories per day. Divide these numbers by 12 for a one-month supply and by 52 for a one-week supply. Since not everyone has the same food requirements, refer to table 3-1 to estimate how much food you should store. Totaling the values will give you the equivalent number of typical adult males, which you will multiply by the figures for the various foods (see example below table). Make your own adjustments based on family members, such as counting a teenage female with an unusually large appetite the same as a teenage male (equal to 1.4 typical adult males).

Food-Storage Quantities for One Average Adult Male for One Year

❏ **Grains—375 lbs.** You will probably want to store a variety of grains, including whole wheat, pasta, oats, corn, rice, barley, and so on. Due to its longevity, most long-term storage plans focus on wheat. Brown rice goes rancid in six months to a year (but lasts longer if stored with CO_2 or nitrogen), but white rice can keep for many years if stored properly. Whole grains can be sprouted, increasing their food value.

❏ **Legumes—60 lbs. (dry).** This includes many different varieties of beans, peas, lentils, seeds, and so on. Soybeans offer very high protein content, but it is a good idea to store several other legumes for taste and variety.

❏ **Milk, dairy products, and eggs—60 lbs. (dry).** Nonfat dry milk keeps longer than dried whole milk. Dehydrated eggs and powdered milk greatly expand your cooking possibilities. Also, you can make a variety of cheeses from powdered milk.

❏ **Meat and meat substitutes—20 lbs (dry).** Dried vegetarian meat substitutes and freeze-dried meats are very light. They are best cooked into stews and soups for extra flavor.

❏ **Fruits and vegetables—10 to 30 lbs (dry).** Traditionally, dehydrated fruits and vegetables are much less expensive than freeze-dried.

❏ **Sweeteners—65 lbs.** These include sugar, honey, syrups, and so on. Honey is preferred for its nutritive and antibiotic values.

❏ **Fats, oils, and shortenings—22 lbs. (2 gals. liquid plus 6 lbs. shortening).** Includes butter, margarine, powdered butter, shortening, cooking oil, nut butters, and so on. Hydrogenated processed oils are nonnutritive, but last for years (bacteria can't eat them, and our bodies can't do much with them either). Cold-pressed oils, such as olive and safflower, provide essential fatty acids that your body needs to metabolize foods, but do not last as long. Storing a combination of mostly cold-pressed unprocessed oils plus a smaller portion of hydrogenated oils offers a blend of good nutrition and longevity.

❏ **Sprouting seeds and supplies—20 to 50 lbs.** These provide live foods and essential vitamins and are great for variety and nutrition. For best results, use untreated organic whole grains, beans, and seeds. I suggest alfalfa seeds, all types of whole grains, mung beans, soybeans, lentils, and cabbage, radish, and broccoli seeds. (See later in this chapter for sprouting instructions.)

❏ **Leavenings.** Include approximately ¾ lb. dry active yeast, 1 lb. baking powder, and one box of baking soda. Dry active yeast is a living organism and has a shelf life of only one and a half to three years, but baking powder and baking soda are chemical compounds that will keep indefinitely.

❏ **Miscellaneous foods and seasonings.** These include spices, cocoa powder, seasoning sauces, condiments, vitamins, minerals, other nutritional supplements, and so on. Include at least 8 lbs. of salt.

❏ **Multivitamins (with minerals).** Include 365 (one a day).

CALCULATING FOOD REQUIREMENTS (in typical equivalent adult males)*

Food Factor	Equivalent Adult Males
Multiply the number of adult males × 1.0	_____
Multiply the number of adult females × 0.85	_____
Multiply the number of teenage males × 1.4	_____
Multiply the number of teenage females × 0.95	_____
Multiply the number of male children (aged 7–11) × 0.95	_____
Multiply the number of female children (aged 7–11) × 0.75	_____
Multiply the number of children (aged 4–6) × 0.6	_____
Multiply the number of infants (aged 1–3) × 0.4	_____
Total:	_____

*For example, if the members of your family consist of: 1 man (1.0), 1 woman (0.85), 1 boy between ages 7 and 11 (0.95), and 1 other child between 4 and 6 (0.6), your family should store the amount of food needed by the equivalent of 3.4 men. So, 325 lbs. of grain × 3.4 (adult male equivalents) = 1,095 lbs. of grain to feed your family of four for one year. (Source: Adapted from James Talmage Stevens, *Making the Best of Basics: Family Preparedness Handbook*, Gold Leaf Press, 1997)

Storage Tips

The main culprits responsible for destroying your food stores are time, moisture, heat, oxygen, mold, and pests. Poor food selection and improper packaging can compound the problem. Time is always working against you. Try to store what you normally eat, so you can rotate stocks. Do not store dented cans or other goods with damaged packaging. Molds can grow in low-moisture environments and are extremely toxic. *Do not eat moldy foods or food from bulging cans—sickness or death may result.*

Keep stored foods cool, clean, dark, and dry. Try to keep them below 70°F. The optimum storage for most nonfrozen foods is 35°F to 40°F. Shelf life decreases by 50 percent for each 20°F increase, even for canned foods. Moisture, food, oxygen, and above-freezing temperatures are the key ingredients insects need to grow. A few bug eggs, once they hatch, can rapidly destroy a sealed container of dry food, if they have an adequate supply of oxygen and moisture. Sunlight also contributes to the degradation of many stored foods.

Store foods in manageable sizes of containers. If you are packaging food yourself, I recommend no. 10 cans (approximately 1 gallon) or the 5-gallon size. Garbage cans will not keep critters out without airtight liners, are heavy to move, and you risk losing large amounts of food from a single contamination.

Commercial foods are generally free of pests, but paper packaging will not keep pests out for long. All goods packaged in paper, or other flimsy materials, must be repackaged for long-term storage.

Mice, rats, cockroaches, and beetles are "dirty" pests that carry diseases. The foods they have spoiled should be discarded. Weevils, found in many flours and grains, are "clean" pests and are not harmful if consumed.

You can freeze containers of food to destroy living insects, but this will not usually kill their eggs. Refreeze the container after thirty days to destroy bugs that have hatched. Freeze in an upright or chest freezer (not the freezer section of a standard kitchen refrigerator) for 72 hours at 0°F or lower.

You can heat dry food in an oven to destroy living insects, but this method may also kill "live" food. Pour infested foods into shallow pans to a depth of ½ inch and bake for 15 to 20 minutes at 150°F. *Caution:* Foods will scorch if left in the oven for too long.

Do not store food containers directly on concrete floors, because moisture will wick from the floor. Stack on wood slats for ventilation and reduced moisture.

Use dry ice, vacuum packaging, oxygen absorbers, or nitrogen packaging to reduce oxygen levels, kill pests, and increase the longevity of stored dry foods. You can package foods yourself using these methods (except for nitrogen packing, which requires commercial equipment), or purchase prepackaged foods from preparedness/survival suppliers.

You can dust grains, legumes, and so on with diatomaceous earth to kill bugs when they try to eat your stored food. Diatomaceous earth, available from most garden-supply, hardware, and building-supply stores, is deadly to bugs but nontoxic for humans and animals. It is a good source of silica (helpful for mending bones and joints) and is formed from the shells of single-celled diatoms. These diatom skeletons contain microscopic sharp edges, which wreak havoc with little critters' insides, but have no harmful effects on humans. Insert 1¼ cups of diatomaceous earth for each 5 gallons of food, then shake, stir, and roll the container until all the contents are thoroughly dusted. Diatomaceous earth is easily rinsed from stored food prior to cooking.

Caution: If you rely on frozen food for long-term storage, ensure that you have an adequate source of backup power to prevent losing your food stores to a long-term power outage.

Dry-Ice Fumigation

A good way to repackage dry foods and protect them from pests is with dry-ice fumigation. Dry ice is frozen carbon dioxide. A properly sized block of dry ice, placed on the top or bottom of a container of dry foods, will gradually evaporate (dry ice melts straight into gas through a process called sublimation). As it evaporates, the heavier-than-air carbon dioxide floats the lighter air out the top of the container. Bugs cannot live in an atmosphere of carbon dioxide. Dry ice can be stored for a short while in an ice chest (use no regular ice or liquids with the dry ice) and is available at most supermarkets and restaurant supply stores. Wrap it with newspaper for handling. Break it into appropriately sized chunks with a hammer and chisel or screwdriver. See table 3-2 for the basics on dry-ice fumigation.

Caution: Do not handle dry ice with your bare hands. Contact with bare skin immediately results in frostbite!

If frost crystals are present on the surface of the dry ice, wipe clean with a cloth to prevent the introduction of extra moisture into your food. Press the lid down gently, leaving a small gap for air to escape. After 20 to 30 minutes, check to see whether the dry ice has fully evaporated. If it has, seal the container. For the bottom-of-the-bucket method, seal the container after 20 to 30 minutes. If the lid pops off, or the container bulges, crack the lid open and try again in 5 minutes.

Caution: A bulging container may burst.

Note: For the dry-ice method to be effective for the long term, the container must be airtight.

TABLE 3-2. BASIC DRY-ICE TREATMENT GUIDE			
Container size	**Food quantity (lbs.)**	**Dry ice required (oz.)**	**Expansion space**
Metal containers			
no. 10 can	3–5½	1	¼″
5 gal.	15–35	2–3	½″
25–30 gals.	100	8	½″
Plastic containers			
1 gal.	3½–7	1	¼″
4 gal.	13–30	4	½″
5 gal.	15–35	4	½″
(Source: Stevens, *Making the Best of Basics: Family Preparedness Handbook*, 1997)			

Vacuum Packaging

Vacuum packaging removes the oxygen and excess moisture from dry foods, killing critters and extending shelf life. A simple, but only partially effective, vacuum-packing method is to pack food in plastic bags and suck as much air out of the bags with a soda straw as you can prior to sealing the bags. Heat sealers are the most effective vapor barrier, with zip locks a second best. Moderately priced electric and hand-operated vacuum pumps are available for vacuum-packing goods in jars, cans, and bags for long-term storage.

Mousetraps and Rat Poison

Don't forget to buy a bunch of mousetraps and Decon (or similar rat poison) to protect your food stores. The mousetraps that work best for me are the traps with a food-scented yellow-plastic bait paddle. I find that mice can't resist the trap when I spread a little peanut butter on its bait paddle, and the wide paddles are so easily tripped that mice almost never escape with the bait. Be careful if you use poison, because it can also poison children, and if your cat eats a poisoned mouse, your cat will be poisoned too. We personally rely upon traps, and don't use poisons. Poisoned rats and mice have a tendency to crawl into hidden, tucked away places to die, and until their bodies fully rot or dehydrate, the smell is quite nauseating! In a survival situation, mouse- and rattraps provide a quick and easy way to supplement your food supply, at least until all the neighbors get so hungry that there are no more rats or mice to be found anywhere!

Shelf-Life Guide

The following list is for foods stored at room temperature (70°F). If stored at different temperatures, adjust shelf life per above mentioned guidelines. The ideal storage temperature for most nonfrozen foods is around 35° to 40°F. Remember, whenever possible, to keep cool, dark, and dry (CDD). Once a container is opened, the contents may not last long. I suggest dating containers with a grease pen, so you can change markings if the container is opened or reused. Many dry or canned foods will last longer than their official shelf life, but *can't be relied on* to last longer.

Here is a guide to food longevity:

- **Very long life.** Under the right conditions, these materials will last a very long time, possibly longer than you live. Honey, sugar, salt, soy sauce, apple cider vinegar, black pepper, Worcestershire sauce, and properly packaged wheat berries fall into this category.

- **Five to ten years.** Most dried legumes and most whole grains are in this category, as are dehydrated cheese, instant coffee, vacuum-packed coffee, baking powder, powdered eggs, and frozen butter.

- **Up to five years.** Processed (partially hydrogenated) liquid vegetable oils, Crisco shortening, cornmeal and corn flour, and nonfat powdered milk.

- **Two to three years.** Bouillon cubes, cornstarch, white rice, powdered gelatin, white wheat flour, white flour pasta (dry), tapioca, textured vegetable protein (TVP), hydrogenated peanut butter, catsup, canned salmon and sardines, most dried fruits, and most other canned foods except for meats, some fish, and fruits. Sprouting seeds, such as alfalfa, mung, soybean, wheat, and so on, will keep for two to three years.

- **Up to eighteen months.** Canned meats, canned seafood (halibut, mackerel, tuna, and shrimp), unshelled raw nuts, dry active yeast, bag-packaged snack chips, cake mixes, dry puddings, herb teas, black teas, bottled juices, most seasonings and extracts, jams and jellies, canned non-citrus fruits (blackberries, blueberries, cherries, pears, peaches, plums, etc.), cranberry sauce, pickles, canned rhubarb, and sauerkraut.

- **One year.** Canned nuts, packaged dry breakfast cereals, rolled oats (oatmeal), bottled dressings, mayonnaise, natural liquid vegetable oils, candy bars, bottled juices (grapefruit, pineapple, apricot, and orange), canned citrus fruits, and natural nut butters.

- **Six months.** Most store-packaged food in boxes, fresh potatoes (keep cool, dark, and dry), granola, shelled raw nuts, and unshelled roasted nuts (Stevens 1997, 22–34; Spigarelli 2002, 97–127; Danks 1998, 73).

How Long Does Stored Food Really Last?

The previous list offers general shelf-life figures that you can count on for planning purposes. However, people always wonder how long stored food really lasts. Who better to answer this question than the Mormons? Ever since the early members of the Mormon Church nearly starved in their first winter in Utah, food storage has been an important tradition for many Mormons. The Department of Nutrition, Dietetics, and Food Science at Brigham Young University (BYU) in Ogden, Utah, has made a science out of the study of food storage. BYU researchers have worked with panels of consumers to taste-test and evaluate a variety of long-term stored foods.

The taste and nutritive quality of long-term stored foods depends upon a variety of factors, including quality of packaging, storage methods, and storage temperatures. In spite of these variables, the information gathered by the BYU testing and evaluation program provides valuable insight into what the "real shelf life" might be for long-term stored foods. A few of the results are summarized as follows (Godfrey 2009):

- Freeze-dried foods tend to be good for 20 to 30 years.

- Whole-grain wheat and white rice, packaged to remove oxygen and stored at room temperature or cooler, are usually good for 30-plus years.

- Beans, dried apples, macaroni, potato flakes, and oats are good for up to 30 years.
- Properly stored nonfat dried milk is good up to about 20 years.
- Baking powder will store for many years, and baking soda will keep indefinitely.

My mother was a pack rat of sorts, and rarely threw anything away if she thought it might be edible or useful "someday." Without a doubt, I have eaten a lot of food that was well past the "use by" date. As a child I remember cleaning out cans from our root-cellar shelves that were bulging, and some of them were super light, the contents having long before rotted through the can walls and the liquid drained out. When in doubt, throw it out. If a can is bulging, leaking, or "spits at you" when you first pierce the can with an opener, get rid of it! Dented cans are prone to corrosion failure long before their undamaged twins, so don't waste your money on bargain-basement canned foods that are dented or close to their expiration date.

Root Cellars and Other Cold Storage

Light and heat are the enemies of most stored food. A root cellar is the traditional way of storing fresh foods for use throughout the winter. Even canned foods last far longer when stored at lower temperatures. The shelf life of canned foods is doubled for each 20°F decrease in storage temperature (Stevens 1997, 41). Ideal storage temperatures for most nonfrozen foods are 35°F to 40°F. Most fruits and vegetables shrivel rapidly unless they are kept in a moist environment, so either store them in cartons layered with moist sawdust, burlap, sphagnum moss, and so on, or keep cold-storage areas moist by spraying water on the floor at regular intervals. Too much moisture causes rot, so make sure that moisture is not condensing on the ceiling and produce. Root cellars offer a means of storing "live" food for use throughout the winter. Unlike fresh fruits and vegetables, dry fruits, vegetables, seeds, nuts, and grains must be kept as dry as possible, so they should be kept in sealed containers or in a separate, dry, cold-storage area.

Freezing is simple, quick, and easy, but has higher energy costs than other preservation methods and requires a steady source of power (or an extremely cold winter). Deep freezers can keep food for years, but the regular frost-free home freezer is only good for about six months. Propane refrigerators and freezers are a good option in remote locations, in solar homes to take the load off solar panels, and where power outages are frequent.

You can build an efficient root cellar in the basement of your house, in the outside stairway to your basement, in a pit outside, or aboveground in an insulated structure. The keys to success are temperature and moisture control, and effectively keeping critters away from your stores.

A handy basement root cellar can be made by walling off an unheated corner of the basement with insulated stud walls (see fig. 3-1). Building the walls on a double runner of pressure-treated wood sills allows for wetting down the floor without rotting the walls. If possible, pick a north wall for one of the walls of the root cellar. A window or some type of screened ventilation pipe is required to vent stale air and allow cooler air into the

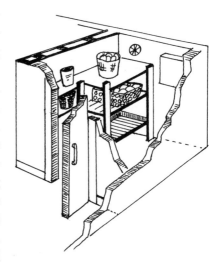

Figure 3-1. In-home root cellar.

root cellar. Do not insulate the exterior walls. You are using the thermal mass of the earth (at about 55°F) and the colder north-wall outside temperatures to help keep your root cellar optimally cold. Place a reliable thermometer inside the root cellar and one outside the window or vent. Open and close the vent/window to try and keep the cellar temperatures between 35°F and 40°F. Place slats under wooden crates stored on the floor to allow for air circulation and prevent rot.

You can make an inground root cellar when a basement is not available (see fig. 3-2). The main things to watch for are water infiltration/drainage, pest barriers, and adequate insulation from the top to prevent freezing. Some people bury garbage cans or old refrigerators. In severe climates, the storage container should be insulated from above with hay bales, rigid styrene foam panels, or at least one foot of loose snow.

Low-tech, aboveground storage can consist of a hay-bale shack or vented "mounds" to keep food stored through the winter months (see figs. 3-3 and 3-4). Both methods rely on the latent heat of the earth and a thick layer of topside insulation to keep produce cold but not frozen. If vented, the vent should be capped during extremely cold weather. Unfortunately, mice and gophers

Figure 3-2. Inground root cellar.

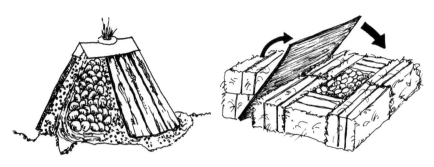

Figure 3-3. Aboveground
storage: vented mound.

Figure 3-4. Aboveground
storage: hay-bale shack.

may enjoy the great nest and food supply that these methods provide, so regular inspection is a must.

Sprouting: Your Own Mini-Garden on a Windowsill

Seeds are one of nature's most perfect foods. They contain all the nutrients necessary to sustain the growth of budding seedlings until the seedling has developed a root system large enough to sustain growth from soil sources. One of the few foods more perfect than raw seeds is sprouted seeds. The sprouting process decreases the carbohydrate and increases the vitamin and protein content in these "live" foods.

Sprouting is a simple process, and the equipment is very inexpensive. You can sprout seeds in your own home, creating a low-cost source of fresh vegetables all year long. All you need for starting your indoor sprout garden is a 1-quart glass jar, untreated whole seeds, a piece of nylon stocking (or cheesecloth, screen, nylon mesh, etc.), and a rubber band or canning-jar seal to hold the mesh over the jar. Richard Nielsen's company, Life Sprouts, sells organic sprouting seeds and supplies, including an excellent covered combination crisper and sprouting tray.

Though most nutritious in their raw form, sprouts can be sautéed, stir-fried, boiled, or cooked into almost any dish. In just a few days, sprouts provide a source of garden-fresh vegetables any time of the year. Nearly all seeds can be sprouted, including most whole grains and legumes. Grains and legumes are probably the most compact and inexpensive type of food that can be stored for emergency preparedness.

A Sprouting How-To

Caution: Potato and tomato sprouts are poisonous. Do not sprout commercial seeds for planting, because these are usually treated with a poisonous fungicide.

Seed	Quantity per quart jar	Soak time (hours)	Rinses per day	Average number of days to sprout	Harvest length (inches)
Adzuki bean	½ cup	6–12	3–5	2–5	½–1½
Alfalfa	2 tbsp	3–8	2–5	3–6	½–2
Almond	1 cup	10–12	2–3	2–5	when split
Amaranth	12 tbsp	none	3–4	2–3	¼
Barley	1½ cups	5–10	2–4	2–4	0–¼
Cabbage	3 tbsp	7–10	2–3	3–5	½–¾
Cabbage, Chinese	3 tbsp	4–7	2–3	3–5	1–1½
Clover	1½ tbsp	4–8	2–3	3–5	1–2
Corn	1½ cups	8–12	2–3	2–3	¼–½
Garbanzo (chickpeas)	1 cup	8–12	3–4	2–4	½
Kidney beans	¾ cup	8–12	3–4	2–4	½–1
Lentil	¾ cup	5–10	2–4	2–4	¼–1
Lettuce	3 tbsp	3–7	2–3	3–5	1–1½
Millet	1½ cups	4–8	2–3	2–4	⅛–¼
Mung bean	½ cup	6–10	3–4	3–5	1–3
Mustard	3 tbsp	5–8	2–3	3–5	1–1½
Oats	1½ cups	3–5	1–2	1–2	0–¼
Pea (not split)	2 cups	7–10	2–3	2–3	¼–½
Peanut	1 cup	8–12	2–3	3–5	¼–1
Pinto bean	1 cup	8–12	3–4	3–4	½–1¼
Pumpkin	1½ cups	5–10	2–3	2–3	⅛–¼
Quinoa	⅓ cup	3–5	2–3	1–2	¼–1½
Radish	3 tbsp	5–8	2–3	3–5	¼–1½
Rice	1½ cups	10–20	2–3	2–4	seed length
Rye	1 cup	6–10	2–3	2–3	¼–½
Sesame	1½ cups	6–10	3–4	2–3	seed length
Soybean	1 cup	10–20	5–6	3–6	½–2
Spinach	3 tbsp	5–8	2–3	3–5	½–2
Sunflower (hulled)	1 cup	2–6	2–3	½–3	½–2
Triticale	1½ cups	6–10	2–3	2–3	¼–½
Wheat	1 cup	6–10	2–3	2–5	¼–½

TABLE 3-3. SPROUTING GUIDE

(Sources: Stevens 1997, 198; Emery 1998, 114)

1. Measure the seed batch according to the sprouting guide in table 3-3. Use only untreated whole seeds, preferably organic (available at health food stores). Inspect and pick debris out of the seeds.

2. Place the seeds in a quart jar (or sprouting tray) half-filled with warm water (preferably unchlorinated). Cover the jar with nylon stocking (or cheesecloth, screen, etc.) and put the rubberband in place.

3. Soak overnight or as directed in table 3-3. Drain and rinse with cool water (always rinse with cool water). If you use tap water, let the water sit in an open container for a few hours before using, to get rid of the chlorine.

4. Keep the jar warm and covered with a dark cloth, or keep it in a cabinet, while germinating. For greener sprouts, give them more light as they grow, but usually keep them out of direct sunlight. For whiter sprouts, keep them out of the light. Experiment to find how you think they taste best.

5. Rinse and drain well two or three times a day (or as recommended in the guide) to keep sprouts from spoiling or souring.

6. Sprouting time is a matter of personal taste, but peak nutritive value is reached in two to three days. Sprouts can be kept in the refrigerator for a week. Freeze them if you wish to store for longer periods.

7. Some people recommend that you lightly steam bean sprouts to destroy toxins found in raw beans (Stevens 1997, 198).

Notes on Camping Gear

If you ever need to evacuate your home and emergency shelters are either full or unavailable, camping gear can make a big difference in your comfort and mobility. This section offers suggestions for selecting practical, high-quality camping equipment.

Tents

Your tent is your shelter from the elements. What kind of weather do you anticipate you might encounter? Low-cost dome tents are available from major discount stores and price clubs. They will do an adequate job when the weather is not severe, but will keep you awake in moderate winds due to flapping fabric, and will probably fall apart in winds over 40 mph. Specialty backcountry stores stock four-season tents, which will hold up under significant snow loads and high winds. Expedition tents, proven in arctic conditions and the Himalayas, will hold up under hurricane-force winds (provided they are anchored to something that does not blow away), and can provide shelter when roofs are blowing off buildings, though they provide little protection from flying debris. Naturally, they cost several times what the cheap discount tents cost. Expedition tents (see fig. 3-5) do not have the comfort and head-

Figure 3-5. Expedition-quality tent from North Face holds up to extreme weather.
Photo courtesy of Eastern Mountain Sports (EMS)

room of low-cost family tents, which are adequate for moderate weather conditions. Several top-quality brands of tents that I can recommend are Wild Country, Sierra Designs, Bibler, North Face, Gauruda, and Walrus.

If you are living in your tent for extended periods, pitch your tent in the shade, or shade your tent with a tarp that you are willing to sacrifice. After a couple of seasons in the sun, most synthetic materials will lose their strength and shred easily.

Clothing

Wool and the new synthetic piles are warm when wet. Synthetic pile sheds water quickly and dries fast. Cotton clothing is terribly cold when wet, and is referred to as "death cloth" by my friends in Yosemite Search and Rescue. A good set of long underwear, made from wool, silk, or one of the synthetic moisture-wicking materials, can make a huge difference in keeping you warm. When your body is covered but your head is not, you will lose most of your heat through your head, so get yourself a warm hat that covers your ears. If the weather is severe, you should have a thick balaclava, which is a knit hat that can be pulled down to cover your face and neck. In addition, your head should be covered with a hood or another hat to add an extra layer over the ears. A breathable waterproof jacket or a waterproof poncho is a must for keeping yourself dry. Breathable waterproof fabrics such as Gore-Tex should have factory-scaled seams. Specialty backcountry stores and many camping/surplus stores carry these items.

Sleeping Bags

A good sleeping bag will keep you warm, even in severely cold temperatures. Down has long been known for providing the greatest warmth with the least weight, but it is totally worthless when wet. When used over long periods of time in subfreezing temperatures, down collects frozen condensation from body moisture and gradually loses its insulating value. The new fiber piles, such as Dupont Hollofill, are not as light or resilient as down, but remain warm when wet. You can dunk a fiberfill sleeping bag in an ice-cold river, wring it out with your hands, then climb right inside to get warm.

Caution: Check the temperature ratings on the bag that you are buying and add a 10°F to 20°F safety margin unless you are a warm sleeper. The ratings are notoriously optimistic.

Mummy-style bags are more constricting, but allow you to cover your head and are much more efficient insulators than traditional, inexpensive rectangular sleeping bags. Discount stores carry fiberfill bags, but specialty backcountry stores will have the best selection.

Tip: When I was a kid, we did not have money for expensive down sleeping bags, and it was before the days of modern synthetic down-alternative fiberfill materials. In those days, we camped with flimsy summer-weight Dacron sleeping bags that our parents had procured by redeeming "green stamps" from the grocery stores. In spite of the lack of proper backcountry gear, we were quite happy snow camping on the sides of Mount Washington so we could challenge ourselves on the super steep ski slopes of Tuckerman's Ravine. We managed to snow camp with our flimsy gear by bringing along an extra wool blanket and wrapping ourselves in the blanket inside our lightweight sleeping bags. When the nights were extremely cold, we would also go to sleep wearing our long underwear, insulated ski pants, sweaters, and sometimes even our ski jackets. We were kids, and we loved roughing it. We never knew what we were missing until we got older, found part-time jobs, and were able to buy down bags and real backcountry gear for ourselves. If we could "make-do" like this, so can you!

Insulated Sleeping Mats

A good insulating pad is important for both comfort and warmth. Without extra insulation under your body, most of your body heat will be lost into the ground, especially if you are camping on snow. Stiff, closed-cell foam pads are lightweight and excellent for insulation, but are not the best for comfort. Traditional air mattresses are cheap, but not as warm as closed-cell foam and are often unreliable. A great modern invention, developed by Thermarest, is the nylon-covered, self-inflating camping pad with an inner foam layer. The foam gives shape to the air mattress and prevents internal convection air currents from robbing heat from your sleeping body. These mats are comfortable, lightweight, and provide excellent insulation. They are usually available at discount stores and price clubs, but you will find a better selection in specialty backcountry stores. When snow camping, I like to combine a short closed-cell foam pad (can't puncture or deflate, and won't compress under your hips and shoulders to make a cold spot), placed under my midsection, along with a full-length self-inflating pad, for outstanding thermal insulation combined with good comfort.

Backpacks

If the need arises, a large-capacity pack (at least 4,000 cubic inches, and preferably over 5,000 cubic inches) can help you transport your gear, food, and water on foot. The traditional frame pack, with a rigid welded frame of tubular aluminum, is best for carrying maximum loads. Personally, I prefer the mountaineering-style soft packs, with internal molded or bendable frames, because they allow more freedom of movement for traveling over rough terrain, plus they stuff better into car trunks or other tight places. Whether you choose an internal or external frame model, a good, comfortable, padded hip belt is essential to take some of the load off your shoulders. Proper fit is also important. If the pack is too long or short for your torso, you will have a hard time adjusting the hip belt and

Figure 3-6. Mountaineering-style soft pack with internal frame from Osprey Packs. Photo courtesy of Osprey Packs

shoulder straps to distribute the load properly. Some recommended manufacturers of mountaineering packs are Osprey, Dana Designs, North Face, Arc'teryx, and Lowe Alpine. Specialty backcountry stores will have the best selection.

Camp Stoves

For pure convenience, two- or three-burner Coleman-style stoves (see fig. 3-7) are hard to beat, but they are bulky, heavy, and inefficient. For occasional use, and if you are planning to use your stove inside your house, propane fuel stoves

Figure 3-7. The two-burner propane or white-gas stove is convenient to use.
Photo courtesy of Eastern Mountain Sports (EMS)

are the most convenient and emit the least fumes. If you use your stove for an extended period, you will find that white gas (Coleman fuel) is much cheaper and more compact than the propane canisters used on propane stoves. For portability, efficiency, and reliability, the hands-down backcountry choice is one of the MSR stoves (pictured in fig. 2-7). Their multi-fuel models can run on white gas, kerosene, and other fuels. All MSR stoves can be dismantled without tools and can be serviced with simple repair kits. Since Primus now makes several stoves that are very similar to MSR, it appears that the original MSR patent has expired. Coleman stoves are available at most outlet and surplus stores, but MSR stoves are mostly available at specialty backcountry suppliers.

Cookware

Cast-iron Dutch ovens and frying pans are great for cooking over an open fire. Dutch ovens are shallow, heavy-duty covered pots designed to be placed directly on hot coals. Some models have a wide brimmed cover to retain a layer of hot coals on top to promote even heating from all sides. Heavy-duty, cast-iron pots spread the heat of a fire evenly, but are too heavy for most backpacking needs. For backpacking, I prefer lightweight spun stainless steel cookware. It weighs about the same as aluminum cookware, but does not leave traces of aluminum in your food (aluminum has been linked to Alzheimer's disease). It's not a bad idea to have both heavy-duty and lightweight cookware on hand—one set for your backpack and one set for your home or car.

Footgear

For support, durability, warmth, and heavy-duty use, it's hard to beat a full-grain leather boot with a Vibram-type, rubber-lug sole. These types of boots are heavy and should be worn for several days to break them in (and harden your feet) prior to leaving on a backcountry trip. Leather boots must be preserved and waterproofed with an appropriate boot grease or synthetic sealer. New, modern lightweight hiking boots can provide waterproof materials and support with considerably improved comfort and reduced weight, but will not usually offer the durability and protection of a heavy, full-grain leather boot or a heavy-duty plastic boot designed for mountaineering. For protection from extreme cold and travel across snow, the common Sorel-type boot is a good choice. This type of boot has a removable, heavy wool felt liner, an upper of heavy fabric or leather, and a lower outer rubber boot with a steel shank.

I recommend trying on boots and climbing shoes to be sure of a good fit, rather than purchasing them from a mail-order catalog. Blisters from badly fitting boots can cripple your attempts to travel on foot. Always bring mole-skin (a fuzzy adhesive-backed pad for protection against blistering) and cloth athletic tape (duct tape will work in a pinch) along in your pack, and please *do yourself a favor by dealing with sore spots before they turn into blisters.* Rotate socks to keep your feet dry and comfortable. Unlike cotton, wool or Orlon synthetic sporting "ski" socks will keep feet relatively warm and comfortable when wet. For multiday snow-country travel, I bring along a supply of thin grocery-store produce bags. I wear these under my socks to form a vapor barrier and prevent sweat from wetting my socks and causing cold feet by wetting my boots from the inside-out. They also help prevent blisters by adhering to your skin and slipping against the socks.

Note: Since many women are prone to wearing shoes that look good but are poor for walking any kind of distance, they should keep a pair of comfort-able multi-season boots in the car.

Planning for the Long-Term Future

Planning for the long haul depends on the possible futures you wish to plan for. If you are planning for the possibility that central distribution systems may break down for extended periods of time, then this book provides a good start, but you should expand your self-reliance and survival skills, materials, and library by picking up many of the books and materials listed in the appendices. Appendix 1 provides a list of recommended books. Appendix 2 provides a list of recommended resources to help readers plan and prepare for both emer-gency survival and long-term self-reliance that could be invaluable should a major long-term upheaval occur. It will take many tools, supplies, skills, hard work, and spare parts to maintain a somewhat modern existence in the event of the long-term loss of central services.

[4]

Home Is Where the Hearth Is

'Mid pleasures and palaces though we may roam,
Be it ever so humble, there's no place like home;
A charm from the sky seems to hallow us there,
Which, seek through the world, is ne'er met with elsewhere.
Home, home, sweet, sweet home!
There's no place like home, oh, there's no place like home!
—**John Howard Payne,** *Home Sweet Home*

Home truly is where the "hearth" is. It is where we cook our meals, raise our children, and spend much of our free time. In times of trouble, most of us will probably weather the storms within the comfort of our own home. This chapter covers the equipment, tools, and techniques necessary for securing backup sources for heating, cooking, lighting, and power, enabling people to "weather the storms" from the comfort of their own home when the power goes out for an extended period. Subjects include backup sources for heating and cooking, including propane and wood; different kinds of stoves for cooking and heating; backup light sources and lanterns; a detailed section on how to hook up a generator to power your home's critical items during a blackout; and what to do when the toilet won't flush.

Special Considerations: The Elderly, Infirm, Children, and Pets

Make sure that you plan ahead for the needs of any children, elders, or other people with special needs. A time of crisis will be stressful for everybody, but the effects of being cooped up and deprived of your normal routines tend to be especially difficult for children and the elderly. Be sure to stash a supply of important medications, diapers, entertainment needs, special foods for picky eaters, comfort foods, pet foods, and so on, that might help make a tense situation just that much more relaxed. Even if you have to fake it, try to reassure your children that you have things under control and know what you are doing. Communicate with your children. Kids especially will need a lot of assurances, physical contact, and emotional support during stressful times when their routines are broken and their daily existence is far removed from what they have come to know as their "normal life." Try to be honest and keep children and elders informed, but don't burden them with all the fears and concerns that may be running through your head during a time of crisis. Don't forget to plan for the family pet. In times of crisis, pets can offer tremendous solace and are great natural-born stress relievers.

Use wisdom, compassion, and restraint. The amazing thing is that when you hold your head up, straighten your back, and stand tall, giving the impression of self-confidence and that you have the situation under control, you will actually feel more confident and in control. Body language, including body posture, and your actual feelings and the state of your mind are all linked together. When you consciously choose a positive, strong body language that says "I am confident and in control" you will actually begin to feel that way.

Backup Sources for Heating and Cooking

For most people, the simplest and easiest forms of backup heat for basic cooking will be a propane- or gasoline-powered portable camping stove. As noted in chapter 3, for pure convenience, two- or three-burner Coleman-style stoves are hard to beat; though too bulky and heavy for backpacking, they are perfect for car camping or backup home use. The backyard propane grill

Figure 4-1. Kerosene cookstove by **Perfection.** Photo courtesy of Lehmans

Figure 4-2. Portable kerosene space heater.
Photo courtesy of Sengoku Portable Heaters

is an invaluable tool in the event of a disaster, so don't forget to stock up on extra propane cylinders. For occasional use, and if you are planning to use your stove inside your house, propane-fuel stoves are the most convenient and emit the least fumes, but do consume oxygen and potentially give off carbon monoxide, which is a toxic odorless invisible gas, so if you do use a portable stove inside your home you must open a window at least 1 inch and should operate the stove close to the open window.

If you use your stove for an extended period, you will find that white gas (Coleman fuel) is much cheaper and more compact than the propane canisters used on propane stoves. If you bring your Coleman-style propane stove to a local propane distributor, most of these places are able to build a custom hose adaptor for running your camping stove off the larger multi-gallon refillable propane cylinders, which are far more economical than the small throw-away cylinders.

Portable kerosene heaters have provided generations of Americans with a reliable source for backup space heating (see fig. 4-2), and can be a lifesaver when the power is out. Even though modern kerosene space heaters burn much cleaner than their old-fashioned predecessors, and do not give off fumes nearly as noxious as they used to, they still release enough fumes to cause problems for some people.

Caution: When using a fuel-burning portable stove for indoor cooking or space heating that is not vented to the outside with a chimney or some kind of vent pipe, you must take extreme caution to prevent carbon monoxide (CO) poisoning! When in use, make sure you crack a window or door approximately 1 inch for ventilation, and never sleep in a room with a charcoal brazier or kerosene heater running.

Carbon Monoxide and Space Heater Safety Precautions

Carbon monoxide (CO) is a colorless, odorless, poisonous, invisible gas that is a byproduct of incomplete combustion, and is formed whenever fuels are burned, such as charcoal, kerosene, alcohol, gasoline, coal, and propane.

According to the Centers for Disease Control (CDC), carbon monoxide poisoning results in roughly 15,000 emergency room visits, and 500 unintentional deaths in the United States each year (King 2007). The problem is that CO binds to the hemoglobin in your red blood cells more easily than does oxygen, so the victim of CO poisoning essentially dies from lack of oxygen. Since you can't see, smell, or taste CO, it is incredibly and insidiously dangerous, and for this reason it is wise to install CO detectors (or combination CO and smoke detectors) inside your home. Code approved heating appliances installed inside a home vent their combustion gases to the outside via a chimney or some kind of vent pipe to help keep combustion gases, including CO, out of the home.

Carbon Monoxide and Other Space Heater Considerations:

- A non-vented fuel-burning heating apparatus is not supposed to be used inside enclosed spaces. Typically you should crack a window or door approximately 1 inch in the room where the fuel-burning appliance is located. One rule of thumb is to allow at least 1 square inch of ventilated gap for each 1,000 BTUs of fuel consumption, so a 10,000 BTU kerosene space heater, like the one in figure 4-2, would require a minimum of 10 square inches of window or door gap.

- A clear or blue flame is clean burning with minimal CO generated. A yellow flame generates significant CO. Because of their small size, candles are not usually a problem (unless you are burning dozens at a time), but appliances that burn with a yellow flame are dangerous.

- Check your chimney and stove flues for proper venting. A vented appliance with a clogged flue can kill (think bird's and rat's nests in the chimney)!

- Never sleep in a room heated by a fuel-based non-vented space heater. Charcoal braziers and kerosene space heaters are famous for killing people in their sleep during cold snaps.

- Keep flammables (curtains, books, clothing, etc.) at least 3 feet away from the front of space heaters. The hotter the space heater, the greater the fire danger.

- Space heaters typically come with a BTU rating, which describes the heater's output, and a square-footage rating. The square-footage rating is for average construction, and is a very subjective rating prone to wide fluctuations. If your home is older and poorly insulated, or the outside weather is extremely cold, the heater will not warm as large of an area as its rating might indicate. When comparing heaters, the BTU rating gives an apples-to-apples comparison, unlike the square-footage rating, which is subjective and varies considerably between manufacturers.

Signs of Carbon Monoxide Poisoning:

- Headache
- Nausea
- Dizziness
- Shortness of breath
- Muscle pains
- Disorientation
- Unusually bright red lips (common, but not always)
- May feel like the flu, but you feel better when outside or away from the home
- Often effects pets and elderly, or those with a heart condition, before others
- May effect all household members at same time, rather than passing from one to the next like a typical flu

Treatment for Carbon Monoxide Poisoning:

- Get victim into fresh air immediately!
- Contact emergency personnel, if available, and perform CPR if necessary.
- Treatment may require supplemental oxygen, either by oxygen mask or hyperbaric oxygen therapy in a pressurized oxygen tent.
- Find and correct problem leading to CO poisoning.

Heating with Wood

As a backup source of heat for cooking, melting snow, and keeping your home warm and toasty when the power goes out, it is hard to beat good old-fashioned wood. When Benjamin Franklin invented the first enclosed woodstove, he felt it was too important an invention to patent, so he gave the design for his "Franklin Box" to the world. Prior to this time, people kept themselves warm by standing in front of open fireplaces that send most of their heat up the chimney and only radiate a small portion of the heat back into the room. An open fireplace constantly sucks large volumes of cold outside air into the house to replace the hot air that flows out the chimney.

The original Franklin Box probably cut wood consumption by three-quarters and made for better-heated homes with fewer drafts. Modern EPA-rated woodstoves have considerably improved burning efficiencies beyond that of the simple Franklin Box. Rather than dumping a significant portion of your energy up the chimney in the form of thick wood smoke, new stoves encourage secondary-burning processes in different areas

Figure 4-3. Clean-burning woodstove features. Illustration courtesy of Aladdin Hearth Products, manufacturers of Quadra-Fire woodstoves

of the combustion chamber. In each of these combustion zones, some of the heat that would have escaped up the chimney of conventional woodstoves is instead captured and transferred to your home. In this way, the maximum heating value is extracted from your fuel with minimal environmental impact. EPA-rated, highly efficient woodstoves burn roughly one-half the fuel of traditional noncertified woodstoves.

Do yourself and your neighbors a favor and replace your old woodstove with a modern, clean-burning, EPA-rated model. The bottom line is that efficient woodstoves keep your air cleaner, minimize chimney maintenance, and require fewer trips to the woodpile!

Efficient Woodstove Features

- **Baffle plate.** At the top of the combustion chamber, a horizontal metal plate, called a "baffle plate," performs two functions. First, it retards the flow of hot, smoky combustion-chamber air as it rises toward the chimney. Second, an insulating layer (usually rock wool) on top of the plate helps to keep this plate extremely hot so that it can ignite unburned gases for secondary burning before they flow up the chimney as smoke.

- **Secondary air jets.** A set of secondary air jets provides a regulated flow of air to the area under the baffle plate to encourage complete secondary burning of the smoke in the upper zone of the combustion chamber. This smoke mixes with the fresh air from the secondary jets and ignites as it hits the hot baffle plate. If done right, all the visible smoke is burned within the woodstove.

- **Ducted outside air intake.** A significant amount of air is required to burn wood. This air has to come from someplace. The most efficient woodstoves allow for ducting the air intake to draw air directly from outside your home. If your stove draws air from inside your home, cold outside air will filter through the windows, doors, and cracks to replace the heated house air that flows up your chimney.

- **Catalytic secondary combustion.** Some stoves rely on a catalytic element in the top of the stove to accomplish secondary burning. Although catalytic stoves can burn with excellent efficiencies, most folks prefer high-efficiency non-catalytic models because they tend to require less maintenance and are not prone to smoky back-draws when starting a fire, which can be a problem with some catalytic models.

- **Convection fan.** The efficiency of most stoves is improved by adding a blower system to transfer more heat from the stove to your home. Long, turbine-type fans quietly move more air than the noisier and less expensive propeller-type fans. A nifty recent invention, which is particularly handy in homes with a limited supply of power, is a fan attached to the woodstove and powered by a thermoelectric generator that uses the heat from the stove to generate electricity to drive the fan.

The Rocket Stove

The principles of the rocket stove were originally developed by Dr. Larry Winiarski back in the early 1980s. The intention was to develop a clean-burning efficient source of heat for cooking purposes in third-world countries where fuel sources are often hard to come by, and where a major factor in local deforestation is the use of wood for cooking and heating. Rocket stoves can burn relatively small amounts of fuels such as twigs, grasses, and dung for boiling water and cooking, and have earned numerous humanitarian awards for the improvements they have brought to the lives of poor people in places like Honduras, Ethiopia, Malawi, and Uganda. The use of rocket-stove principles has expanded into efforts to provide low-cost high-efficient space and hot-water heating.

So, if you wish to burn a fuel efficiently and cleanly for cooking and/or heating, here are Larry Winiarski's rocket-stove design principles (Still 2002):

1. Insulate, particularly the combustion chamber, with low-mass, heat-resistant materials, such as perlite or rock wool, in order to keep the fire as hot as possible and not to heat the higher mass of the stove body.

2. Within the stove body, above the combustion chamber, use an insulated, upright chimney of a height that is about two or three times the diameter of the chimney before directing heat to any active surface (griddle, pots, etc.).

3. Heat only the fuel that is burning, i.e., leave the bulk of the fuel sticking out of the stove's combustion area and burn just the tips of sticks (or other materials) as they enter the combustion chamber. The object is to *not* produce more gases or charcoal than can be cleanly burned at the power level desired.

4. Maintain a good air velocity through the fuel. The primary rocket stove principle and feature is using a hot, insulated, vertical chimney within the stove body that increases draft.

5. Do not allow too much or too little air to enter the combustion chamber. We strive to have stoichiometric (chemically ideal) combustion: in practice there should be the minimum excess of air supporting clean burning. In other words, there should be enough air to burn cleanly (essentially zero smoke), but not too much to burn the fuel more rapidly than necessary, or to cool the heating surface with excessive air flow, so you may wish to choke the draft to the point where the fire smokes a little, then open it up just until the smoke disappears.

6. The cross-sectional area (perpendicular to the flow) of the combustion chamber should be sized within the range of power level of the stove. Experience has shown that roughly 25 square inches will suffice for home use (6 inches in diameter or 5 inches square). Commercial size is larger and depends on usage.

7. Elevate the fuel and distribute airflow around the fuel surfaces. When burning sticks of wood, it is best to have several sticks close together, not touching, leaving air spaces between them. Particle fuels should be arranged on a grate.

8. Arrange the fuel so that air largely flows through the glowing coals. Too much air passing above the coals cools the flames and condenses oil vapors.

9. Throughout the stove, any place where hot gases flow, insulate (use rock wool, perlite, or something similar) from the higher mass of the stove body, only exposing pots, etc., to direct heat.

10. Transfer the heat efficiently by making the gaps as narrow as possible between the insulation covering the stove body and surfaces to be heated, but do this without choking the fire. Estimate the size of the gap by keeping the cross-sectional area of the flow of hot flue gases constant.
Exception: When using an external chimney or fan the gaps can be substantially reduced as long as adequate space has been left at the top of the internal short chimney for the gases to turn smoothly and distribute evenly. This is tapering of the manifold. In a common domestic griddle stove with external chimney, the gap under the griddle can be reduced to about ½ inch for optimum heat transfer.

A simple rocket stove can be made from a metal 5-gallon bucket, one adjustable 4-inch, 90-degree stovepipe elbow, an 8-inch-long piece of 4-inch stovepipe for the exhaust-side chimney, and a 7-inch-long piece of 4-inch stovepipe for the horizontal combustion chamber (see fig. 4-4). Cut holes in the 5-gallon bucket's cover and side to accommodate the pipe, and use a noncombustible insulating material such as vermiculite, rock wool, or perlite, to support and insulate the stovepipe inside the bucket. All it takes is a little paper and a few sticks for your rocket stove to become a roaring, clean-burning cookstove. Keep feeding the sticks into the combustion chamber

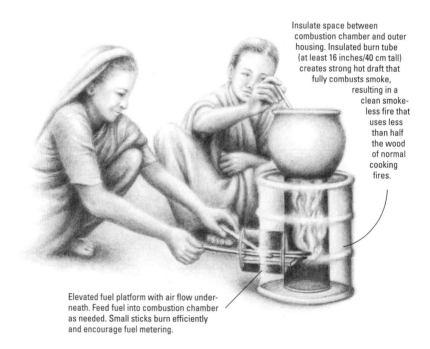

Insulate space between combustion chamber and outer housing. Insulated burn tube (at least 16 inches/40 cm tall) creates strong hot draft that fully combusts smoke, resulting in a clean smoke-less fire that uses less than half the wood of normal cooking fires.

Elevated fuel platform with air flow underneath. Feed fuel into combustion chamber as needed. Small sticks burn efficiently and encourage fuel metering.

Figure 4-4. Rocket stove.

for as long as you wish to keep the stove burning. If necessary, knowing the design principles of the rocket stove, you could design and build a heating or cooking stove using a wide variety of found or scavenged materials. You may purchase a factory-built rocket stove for personal use, or for donation to a needy third-world community, at http://www.stovetec.net.

Solar Ovens

Solar ovens offer simple fuel-free solutions for cooking, and for sterilizing/pasteurizing water, using just the rays of the sun. You can use a solar oven to cook anything that can be cooked in a crock pot, including stews and casseroles. You can even bake bread and muffins in a solar oven. Their main drawbacks are that they are not much good for browning foods, don't work on cloudy days, and take more time and patience to cook a meal, so they require planning ahead. On the plus side, you can prepare a meal in the morning, set it out to catch the afternoon sun, and come home to a slow cooked hot meal ready to eat in the evening.

The simplest solar oven is basically an aluminum-foil-covered cardboard box that is tilted toward the sun and covered with a sheet of glass, or Plexiglas, to let the sun in while also holding the heat inside. More complex designs include flat or parabolic reflectors to capture more of the sun's rays than are captured by a simple box. There is a fine article by Joe Radabaugh in *Backwoods Home* magazine that has plans and instructions for how to make a simple yet elegant and efficient solar oven for less than $10 that can

Figure 4-5. An assortment of solar ovens. Photo courtesy of Jennifer Stein Barker

be found at http://www.backwoodshome.com/articles/radabaugh30.html. Other designs abound on the Internet, or you can purchase a readymade solar cooker from most solar supply houses.

Backup Sources for Power

Without electricity, our air conditioners, furnaces, credit card machines, gasoline pumps, elevators, water heaters, refrigerators, computers, electric lights, and cash registers cease to function. A few hours after the power goes out, most long-distance automotive traffic runs out of gas and grinds to a halt. In the event of a prolonged power failure, our gas and water utilities will also fail. Even pellet stoves will not operate with electricity. Most gas-powered water heaters and stoves will still operate, though some may need a match to light the burners if their flame igniters are electric. When the power goes off for more than a few hours, generators can provide short-term, low-cost backup power that will help keep your lights on, your furnace going, and prevent the food in your freezer from rotting. Generators are noisy, smelly, inefficient, and require regular maintenance, including full rebuilds after surprisingly low numbers of hours in use, but they sure do come in handy when the power goes out!

Installing a backup renewable energy system is a terrific idea, but they can be quite pricey. They are quiet, clean, and environmentally friendly. Most modern renewable energy systems operate seamlessly with little maintenance, and keep on running year after year. Large-scale off-grid systems that are sized to operate an entire large home strictly on renewable energy typically include a large backup battery storage bank, and tend to be quite expensive. Renewable energy systems with large battery banks run in the range of $25,000 to $100,000. Smaller, more affordable scaled-down systems can provide a backup source of electricity that will make a huge difference during extended blackouts, though you won't be able to run all of your appliances at the same time, like you can when the grid is operating. For

Figure 4-6. Compact portable solar power pack with battery storage and AC/DC inverter.
Photo courtesy of SolMan

example, I have a single 300-watt solar panel mounted on my 21-foot travel trailer that keeps a couple of heavy-duty six-volt golf-cart batteries charged. During sunny weather, this system provides enough power to operate a few lights, my laptop, a stereo, and the fan on my trailer's propane furnace, but when skies are cloudy it needs a couple of hours of recharging from my small generator every day or two. Figure 4-6 shows a portable solar panel with a built in battery backup power supply and an inverter to run basic low power 110 VAC appliances, such as computers, a few lights, a refrigerator, etc.

The details and instructions for providing a renewable energy system for your home are beyond the scope of this book, but may be found in some of the recommended references in the appendix.

About Generators

When shopping around for generators, consider the following questions:

1. Is your generator for occasional backup usage, or might it be a primary source of energy for long periods of time? Whole-house generators to provide long-term off-grid power will be considerably larger and more expensive than smaller, more portable generators for occasional backup power and multipurpose use, plus they will consume quite a bit of fuel over a surprisingly short period of time (and can be shockingly expensive to operate).

2. Will your generator be hard-wired into your home's electrical system? If so, it should be installed by a qualified electrician to meet electrical codes that require a transfer switch to disconnect your home from the grid whenever the generator is operating (more on this later). Whole-house generators are quite expensive, and may be installed to automatically and seamlessly disconnect your home from the grid, and switch into generator operation, whenever the grid goes down.

3. What is the size of the power loads that you wish to run with your generator (see table 4-1 for a listing of typical electrical power loads for common appliances)?

Small, relatively lightweight portable generators, like the Honda EU2000i and the equivalent Generac IX 2000 two-kilowatt (kW) generators, commonly found in use on travel trailers and by car-campers across America, are powerful enough to operate a few lights, a refrigerator, and a computer, but do not provide enough power and/or voltage to operate electric hot-water heaters, electric stoves, or most air-conditioning units (see fig. 4-7).

The plus about having a small portable generator, either instead of, or in addition to, a larger generator is twofold. First, the 2 kW Honda and Generac units are very quiet, and they can run continuously in the background with little irritation to yourself and your neighbors. Secondly, they are quite

Figure 4-7. Generac IX 2000, a popular lightweight portable generator. Photo courtesy of Generac Power Systems

economical to operate the low-power appliances that people tend to find most important during a blackout. My 2 kW Honda EU2000i can run at ¼ of its rated continuous capacity (400 watts) for about nine hours on a single gallon of gas. My 4 kW jobsite generator is about ten times as loud, and will consume about 4 gallons of gas over the same period when run at 50 percent load (2 kW), and the Honeywell HW7500E generator will consume about 8.5 gallons of gas at 50 percent load (3.75 kW). A quick calculation shows that in order to run this 7.5 kW backup generator for ten hours a day for a period of two weeks, you would need to store 130 gallons of gasoline, and fill its tank at least twenty times! However, if I ran fewer appliances and circuits, I could provide the same ten hours a day of backup power to my home using my small quiet 2 kW generator, and it would only consume approximately 16 gallons of gas—a much more affordable and easily stored amount of fuel.

Larger portable "jobsite" generators provide more power, typically on the order of 4–10 kW, and usually include both 110 VAC and 220 VAC output plug sockets, but are bulkier and heavier than the small units. Though still considered "portable," these generators are heavy (on the order of 100–250 lbs.) and usually require at least two persons to lift onto a truck bed or hand carry any kind of distance (see fig. 4-8). Many of these units come equipped

Figure 4-8. Medium-duty portable jobsite-size generator. Photo courtesy of Generac Power Systems

with wheelbarrow-style wheels for easier handling. Some of the more expensive and larger models in this category come equipped with their own trailer for easy towing with a pickup truck or SUV.

When purchasing a portable generator in the 5 kW–15 kW range, one thing to consider is whether you want a diesel- or gasoline-powered unit. Diesel will be much more economical when run for long hours, but it has the drawback of needing to winterize the fuel for cold-weather use, and its cold-starting issues. Unless it has been conditioned with a winterizing fuel additive, standard diesel fuel starts to crystallize and clog the fuel filter when temperatures hit 15°F (–9.5°C), and turns into an unusable gooey gel as temperatures approach 0°F (–18°C). Even with winterized fuel, getting your diesel generator to start in frigid temperatures can be a nightmare, so if you live in a cold climate, your backup diesel generator might fail to start during severe winter weather, just when you need it most!

Heavy-duty "whole-house" generators are on the order of 12 kW to 25 kW in size, and are sometimes mounted on a trailer, but are usually permanently mounted on a foundation inside either a small out-building or an insulated utility room to contain the noise and keep the generator sheltered from the elements (see fig. 4-9). These large generators usually operate on propane or natural gas, but may come equipped with multi-fuel options. Due to the high volume of fuel consumed by large generators when operated for extended periods of time, you definitely don't want to be driving back and forth to a gas station to fill 5-gallon containers of gasoline to keep a large-sized generator operating continuously. Most generator installations in this category are plumbed directly to either a natural-gas line, a large propane tank, or a large diesel fuel tank.

Figure 4-9. Heavy-duty "whole-house" style generator. Photo courtesy of Solar Wind Works

Hooking Up Your Generator

Caution: Used improperly, electricity can kill! If you are unsure about how to properly hook up your generator, seek qualified professional help.

Small Portable Generators and the "Extension Cord" Method

The simplest and safest way to use your small portable or jobsite generator (approximately 1 kW–10 kW) is to run your appliances directly using extension cords and outlet strips to add more plug sockets if needed. This way of using your generator is fairly safe, provided that you keep your electrical plugs and connections dry and out of the weather, but can lead to a "rat's nest" of power cords running throughout your house, and can be a fire hazard if you overload your power cords. Realize that these small generators have limited capacity—far less than the capacity of the typical home electrical system, so you will need to pick and choose which appliances you will run at one time on your generator. For example, my Honda UE2000 portable generator is rated for continuous loads of 13.3 amps at 120 volts AC (VAC), which is about 1.6 kW, and can handle peak loads of 2 kW. To determine the load of the appliances you wish to run, you can add up either the amps (electric current) for each appliance, or the wattage of each appliance.

Power, also known as "watts" is simply the current (amps) multiplied by the voltage for each appliance. One kW is one "kilowatt," which simply means 1,000 watts. For example, the tag on my refrigerator says it is rated for 6.6 amps at maximum load, which means it uses a maximum of 6.6 amps × 120 volts = 792 watts. So, if I want to run my refrigerator off my Honda 2 kW generator (2 kW is equal to 2,000 watts), then that leaves me 2000 watts – 792 watts = 1208 watts of available generator capacity left over to run other things, such as light bulbs, computers, and televisions. My desktop computer is rated for 6 amps at 120 VAC (6 × 120 = 720 watts) and my refrigerator is 792 watts (720 + 792 = 1512 watts so far), so that means I could run my refrigerator and my desktop computer plus no more than eight 60-watt lightbulbs off my Honda 2 kW generator. Since the plug-in adapter power pack to run my laptop computer is rated at only 90 watts, if I chose to run my laptop instead of my desktop computer, plus my refrigerator, that would total only 882 watts, leaving me 1118 watts left over for running things like lights, a stereo, a small TV, etc. Now, if I replaced my old 60-watt incandescent lightbulbs with 15-watt compact fluorescent (CF) light bulbs (they give off light equivalent to 60-watt incandescent bulbs), I could run four times as many CF bulbs on the same amount of power, which makes a huge difference when you are operating your home off the limited power supplied by a small generator! Long-lasting super-efficient LED light bulbs that screw into normal 110 VAC lightbulb sockets are relative newcomers in the home lighting market. They used to be prohibitively expensive, but are now coming down in price to the point where they are starting to give compact fluorescents serious competition. Currently a 9-watt LED bulb gives off light that is equivalent to a 15-watt CF and a 60-watt incandescent bulb, plus some of the new LED bulbs are dimmable (unlike CF bulbs), so the new LED bulbs will allow you to stretch your limited generator or renewable-energy-system power even farther than before!

To help you figure out what your generator or backup renewable energy system is capable of powering, table 4-1 illustrates how much power it will

TABLE 4.1 TYPICAL APPLIANCE POWER CONSUMPTION

Appliance	Watts/hour	Appliance	Watts/hour	Appliance	Watts/hour
Coffee pot	200	Table fan	20–25	Compact fluorescent	
Coffee maker	800	Electric blanket	200	incandescent equivalents	
Toaster	800–1,500	Blow dryer	1,000	40 W equiv.	11
				60 W equiv.	16
Popcorn popper	250	Shaver	15	75 W equiv.	20
Blender	300	Waterpik	100	100 W equiv.	30
Microwave	600–1,500	Computer		Electric mower NA	1,500
Waffle iron	1,200	laptop	20–50	Hedge trimmer	450
Hot plate	1,200	pc	80–150	Weed eater	500
		printer	100		
Frying pan	1,200	Typewriter	80–200	¼" drill	250
Dishwasher	1,200–1,500	Television		½" drill	750
Sink waste disposal	450	25" color	150	1" drill	1,000
Washing machine		19" color	70	9" disc sander	1,200
automatic	500	12" bw	20	3" belt sander	1,000
manual	300	VCR	40	12" chain saw	1,100
Vacuum cleaner		CD player	35	14" band saw	1,100
upright	200–700	Stereo	10–30	7¼" circ. saw	900
hand	100	Clock radio	1	8¼" circ. saw	1,400
Sewing machine	100	AM/FM car tape	8	Refrig/freezer, conventional	
Iron	1,000	Satellite dish	30	20 cf (15 hrs.)	540
Clothes dryer		CB radio	5	16 cf (13)	475
electric NA	4,000	Electric clock	3	Sunfrost	
gas heated	300–400	Radiotelephone		16 cf DC (7)	112
Heater		receive	5	12 cf DC (7)	70
engine block NA	150–1,000	transmit	40–150	Vestfrost refrig/freezer	
portable NA	1,500	Lights		10.5 cf	60
waterbed NA	400	100 W incandescent	100	Freezer, conventional	
stock tank NA	100	25 W compact fluor.	28	14 cf (15)	440
Furnace blower	300–1,000	50 W DC incandescent	50	14 cf (14)	350
Air conditioner NA		40 W DC halogen	40	Sunfrost freezer	
room	1,000	20 W DC compact fluor.	22	19 cf (10)	112
central	2,000–5,000			Vestfrost refrig/freezer	
Garage door opener	350			7.5 cf (8)	50
Ceiling fan	10–50				

Note: NA denotes appliances that would normally be powered by nonelectric sources in an RE-powered home.
(Source: *Solar Electric Design Guide*, Golden Genesis Corporation 1999)

take to run a variety of appliances. Simply make a list of each appliance, and next to that appliance list its watts/hour power-consumption figure, and add these figures to find your total power-consumption value. For appliances where multiples might be powered simultaneously, such as lightbulbs, be sure to multiply the power usage by the number of individual items that may be powered at a single time. After you add up the power consumption values for each appliance, you may decide to explore options where only certain combinations of appliances are powered at the same time, so as to not overload your generator capacity.

If all of this sounds a bit confusing, don't worry too much, because modern generators are usually equipped with a safety overload circuit breaker that will pop whenever you try to run more appliances than your generator can handle. If the on-board circuit breaker keeps popping, either there is a short circuit in one of your appliances, or you are attempting to run too many appliances at the same time and you need to disconnect some of them.

Caution: If your generator does not have an on-board overload protection circuit breaker, then you must be extremely careful not to exceed the rated capacity of your generator!

Medium-Sized Generators and the "Manual Transfer Switch" Method

Medium-sized generators run from the smaller "jobsite" generators (see fig. 4-4), like my 9-horsepower 4 kW gasoline-powered generator, to the large models such as the 15-horsepower 7.5 kW (9.4 kW at temporary peak load) model HW7500E made by Honeywell. These generators typically offer both standard household-style 120-VAC outlet sockets and high-amperage "screw lock" 240-VAC sockets. Standard North American household wiring is powered by two opposite phased 110-VAC main lines coming into the home. These two oppositely phased 110-VAC lines provide the two "hot" legs of your home's 220-VAC circuits (the red and black wires) that carry power to major 220-VAC appliances such as electric water heaters, kitchen ranges, and large air-conditioning units.

Note: If the following discussion means something to you, congratulations! If not, please play it safe and keep it simple. Plug a power strip and/or extension cords into your generator to power your appliances, and leave it to the professionals to hook up anything more complicated.

The advantage of hooking your generator directly into your home's power system is that you can avoid the clutter and physical hazard created by running power cords thorough open windows and hallways to hook into different appliances, and simply use your home's electrical system and switches to power your lights, refrigerator, TV, computers, furnace, etc. However, electrical codes require that whenever a generator is hooked into a building's electrical system, the connection must pass through a "transfer switch" to guarantee that when the generator is powering your home, the home will be disconnected from the grid (see fig. 4-10).

A transfer switch is an electrical device to ensure that whenever electrical contact is made between the generator and the home's electrical system, a circuit breaker simultaneously breaks the electrical connection between the home and the power grid, and vice versa. This ensures that your generator will not electrify the grid in your neighborhood, possibly electrocuting someone working on local grid wiring, expecting that there would be no power running through the local power lines. Additionally, since there is no way that your small generator could power the entire neighborhood, your home must be disconnected from the grid whenever your generator is hooked into your home's electrical system.

For manual transfer switches applicable to powering your home from a modest-sized backup generator, there are two main categories of transfer switches. The option that gives you the most flexibility is to have an electrician install a large-capacity transfer switch, commonly known as a "transfer panel" (see fig. 4-11).

Figure 4-10. Generator plugged into an outdoor power-outlet box that is wired to a transfer switch next to a load center located in the garage. Illustration courtesy of Reliance Controls

Figure 4-11. Power-center manual transfer panel. Photo courtesy of Reliance Controls

Option 1, Manual Transfer Panel

This transfer panel must be the same size capacity as the main power panel for your home. For example, my home has a 200-amp main breaker, so if I were to use this option, I would need to have my electrician install a 200-amp transfer panel right alongside my home's 200-amp main panel load center. The electrician would run the heavy-gauge wires directly from my electric meter into the transfer panel, then back from the transfer panel to the bus bars (the bus bars are what all the circuit breakers inside the load center are attached to) inside of

Figure 4-12. A 30-amp outdoor power-inlet box. Photo courtesy of Reliance Controls

Figure 4-13. A 30-amp twist-lock power cord. Photo courtesy of Reliance Controls

my home's 200-amp main panel load center. He would also run a heavy-gauge set of wires from the transfer box to a power-inlet box (see fig. 4-12) that is connected to the backup generator via a heavy-duty extension cord (see fig. 4-13) with special 220-VAC plugs to fit the power box on one end, and the outlet socket on the generator at the other end.

The advantage of using this option (transfer panel), is that when the switch in the transfer panel is set to the generator position, the power from my generator is supplied to my home's entire main load center, and I have the option of switching any one of my home's circuit breakers either "on" or "off." This means that I can use my generator to power any circuit inside my home that I choose. However, please realize that your backup generator has a much smaller power output than the capacity of all of the circuits in your home, so you will need to use discretion and understanding when you decide which circuits to activate, and which to turn off. Using my modest-sized 4 kW generator for example, means that at 220 VAC (to power my home's 220-VAC load center), I only have a maximum continuous output from my generator of about 20 amps, and in fact my generator has a 20-amp-rated 220-VAC outlet socket. Looking at my home's load center, I see a 30-amp 220-VAC circuit for an electric stove, and a 50-amp 220-VAC circuit for my an electric hot-water heater, and my generator does not have adequate power to supply these circuits, so I know that I must switch the circuit breakers for these items to the "off" position.

In general, you should also switch any other high-amperage circuit breakers (those breakers labeled with a number greater than 15 or 20 amps) in your home's electrical subpanel to the "off" position, since your modest-sized generator will not have the capacity to power these large loads. These include all of the 220-volt breakers that are commonly identified by a joining bracket that ties two small side-by-side breakers to each other. The disadvantage of this option (transfer panel) is that it really isn't a suitable do-it-yourself job—I highly recommended that you enlist the services of a qualified electrician for this type of installation.

Option 2, Manual Transfer Switches

This option does not have all the convenience of the transfer panel, however, it is more easily installed by the do-it-yourself home handyman. In this option, a manual transfer-switch box is installed directly alongside the home's main load center. Instead of the entire incoming power for the home being run through the box, as is the case with the transfer panel, individual circuits are run from the load center to the transfer switch box. Inside the transfer-switch box are toggle switches for controlling dedicated home circuits. Each toggle switch has three positions: generator, line, or off. Similar to the transfer panel, the installer would run a heavy gage set of wires from the transfer-switch box to a power-inlet box (see fig. 4-12) that is connected to your backup generator via a heavy-duty extension cord (see figs. 4-13 and 4-10) with special 220-VAC plugs to fit the power box on one end, and the outlet socket on your generator at the other end.

The disadvantage of this system is that the installer must choose beforehand which specific circuits are to be controlled by the transfer switches. For this reason, this option does not have as much flexibility as the transfer panel to allow for on-the-spot decisions as to which circuits are to be powered up by the backup generator. In some cases this may be an advantage, since a qualified installer is probably better qualified than many end users to make the proper decision as to which circuits could (and should) be electrified, given the specific capacity of the generator to be used.

If you connect a 220-VAC output from your generator to the 220-VAC trunk line in your home, it will power all the circuits of your home that have not been turned off at the subpanel breaker box. If you connect a 110-VAC circuit from your generator to the wiring of your home, it will only power the circuits drawing from one of the two oppositely phased 100-VAC trunk lines entering your home, and the circuits drawing from the other oppositely phased 110-VAC main line will be dead.

Figure 4-14. A six-circuit manual transfer-switch box. Photo courtesy of Reliance Controls

Large-Sized Generators and the "Automatic Transfer Switch" Method

Large stationary "whole-house" generators are usually mounted on a concrete foundation inside a small outbuilding, or well-insulated utility room, that provides protection from the elements as well as sound insulation to reduce the level of noise coming from the generator (see fig. 4-9). In general, large generator installations of this type will be installed by qualified professionals and will include an automatic transfer panel to provide for seamless automatic startup and switching from grid connection to power from the generator system in the event of a grid failure.

A mid-range alternative that works quite well for many people is to install a compact, air-cooled, exterior, hard-plumbed, and hard-wired backup generator system, such as one of the models from Generac Power Systems (see fig. 4-15). When combined with their load-management system that monitors generator output and avoids overload situations by automatically shedding power to high-current devices (such as air conditioners, hot-water heaters, and electric stoves) whenever demand exceeds generator capacity, and returning power to those items when overall demand drops, these systems can power an entire home using a smaller, more cost-effective generator that will be also be more fuel efficient than larger systems, even when they are operated for extended periods of time. Generator systems such as these are typically plumbed directly into a home's natural-gas or propane lines, circumventing the tedious task of transporting large quantities of gasoline or diesel fuel to keep a portable generator operating for a significant period of time.

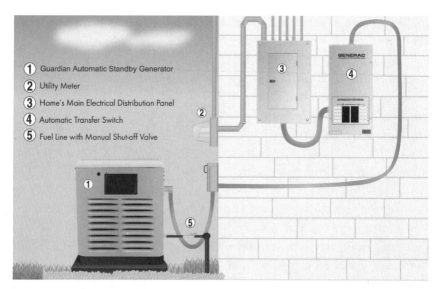

Figure 4-15. A compact hard-plumbed and hard-wired exterior mounted backup generator system with automatic transfer switch. Photo courtesy of Generac Power Systems

Generator Safety

1. Generators must not be run in enclosed areas lacking proper ventilation. Like a car, generator exhaust includes carbon monoxide, which is a poisonous, odorless gas that will kill you if the exhaust vents into an enclosed living space!

2. If you connect your generator directly into your household wiring, this must be done properly with a code-approved transfer switch to ensure that no one gets hurt and that your insurance policy is not invalidated due to a non-code-approved installation.

3. Some people have been known to make their own custom "male-to-male" plug extension cord to hook the female electrical outlet of their generator directly into a female plug outlet on their home. *This is not a code-approved way of providing power to your home, and is very dangerous, so I must advise against this technique!* It is dangerous for two reasons. The first is that when this special homemade adapter cord is plugged into an operating generator, the male plug on the other end is "hot," meaning it could electrocute someone if they accidentally make skin contact with the male plug contacts protruding from the opposite end of the cord (imagine a child innocently unplugging an extension cord from a wall socket and then touching the "hot" prongs of that plug with his hand!). The second is that electrical codes require that generators hooked into residential housing must be hardwired through a special switching circuit that automatically disconnects the residence from the local power grid whenever an operating generator is engaged at the residence, to prevent sending power to the neighborhood grid and possibly electrocuting someone working on the local power lines.

Backup Light Sources

Candles are a simple, cheap, readily available backup source of light, but can be a fire hazard, and, if you have ever tried to read by candlelight, you will know that a single candle does not put out a lot of light. A candle lantern will make your candles more wind and weather proof, pretty much eliminating the fire hazard, and makes their light much more useful via the use of a built-in reflector.

For regular usage, an old-fashioned oil

Figure 4-16. A portable oil lantern by Dietz. Photo courtesy of Lehmans

Figure 4-17. A portable propane-powered lantern.
Photo courtesy of Eastern Mountain Sports (EMS)

lamp offers much brighter light than a candle, can last for two weeks on a single filling of oil, and will cost much less to operate than burning through dozens of candles. Oil lamps come in numerous styles and sizes that offer low-cost nonelectric lighting solutions for backup and off-grid applications (see fig. 4-16).

Classic propane or gasoline-powered camping lanterns (see fig. 4-17) provide an excellent source of bright light for both off-grid and backup applications. In these types of lanterns, the burning fuel causes a silk mantle to glow brightly, giving off an extremely bright light. Make sure that you stock several spare mantles, because once a mantle has been lit for the first time, it becomes extremely fragile and small shocks to the lantern may cause the mantle to fracture, requiring its replacement with a new one. Electric lanterns using either LED or compact fluorescent bulbs are energy efficient battery-powered devices that provide long-lasting alternatives to traditional candles, oil lamps, and mantle-type lanterns. A couple of excellent suppliers for basic self-reliant supplies and tools, such as these backup sources for light and heat, are Lehman's (www.lehmans.com) and the Cumberland General Store (www.cumberlandgeneral.com).

Protecting Your Plumbing During a Winter Power Outage

Typical residential furnaces and wood-pellet stoves require a supply of electricity to operate the fans and blowers they need in order to function properly, so most homes in America will not stay warm for very long once the power goes out. Without a backup source of heat, such as a woodstove, when it is extremely cold outside, the plumbing inside the typical North American home may start to freeze just a few hours after the power goes out. See details in chapter 15 for important information on winter survival tips plus how to drain your pipes and winterize your plumbing fixtures to avoid damage from freezing.

Sanitation Notes

The luxury of hot and cold running water, and flush toilets, is one of those things that most people take for granted until they have to do without them for a while. When water resources are tight, there is an old saying that may be quite appropriate, "When it's brown, flush it down, but when its yellow, let it mellow." Many people do not realize it, but even when the water system is shut off, you can still flush a toilet by pouring a bucket of water into the toilet bowl. If you have a nearby pond or creek, the bucket flush may be a valid option.

If you do not have any water for flushing, or the sewage system won't drain anymore (after a few hours with no electric power to drive sewage pumps, the sewers in many locations will stop draining), the use of a 5-gallon bucket, or a backyard trench, will be a whole lot more appealing than overloading your bathroom fixtures. In a group situation, putting up some kind of privacy shield will be well worthwhile, and will help avoid other issues such as constipation on the part of people who are too embarrassed to "do their business" in front of others. Try to dig a trench a couple of feet deep, so you can fill it in when it reaches a little less than a foot from the top. A handful of lime or fireplace ashes sprinkled on top of the poop will help keep the flies and odor down. When the sewage system goes down, all that uncovered poop in a metro area can quickly lead to a serious health and sanitation issue.

When toilet paper runs out, the classic standbys have been Sears catalogs, phone books, leaves, moss, and corn cobs. When those run out, plan B includes the bucket of water with a wash rag, and remember to keep your left hand under the table! From experience, I can tell you that snow does a good job too, but it sure is cold.

[PART TWO]

Emergency Medicine, Survival Skills, and Tools

5

First Aid

I can't emphasize strongly enough the value of basic first-aid training. You never know when you might face an emergency situation where the knowledge of first aid could make a huge difference in someone's life. This chapter is not intended to replace a first-aid manual and first-aid training. I recommend that you pick up a copy of the *Red Cross First Aid and Safety Handbook* and that you take the Red Cross advanced first-aid course. I believe that every able-bodied adult should take CPR (cardiopulmonary resuscitation) training, or a more advanced training, such as for emergency medical technician (EMT) certification.

A few basic first-aid principles and instructions are presented in this chapter in the event that you find yourself in an emergency and this book is the only text you have. I repeat: *This chapter is not a first-aid manual.*

Initial Evaluation

Survey the Scene
The very first thing to evaluate in an emergency is your safety. As a rescuer, it does you and the victim little good if you are injured or killed during the rescue. Assess potential dangers, such as oncoming traffic, rockfall, live downed power lines, poisonous or flammable fumes, and so on, and take adequate precautions to ensure the safety of both rescuers and victim. The general rule is to move a victim only if you absolutely have to. Ask the bystanders or victim(s) what happened.

The ABCs of first aid are airway, breathing, and circulation. If any of these fail, death is certain. *Call for help immediately!* Feel free to ask bystanders for assistance, and don't hesitate to send one of them off to call 911 for emergency medical services (EMS) while you attend to the victim.

In the case of multiple victims, quickly evaluate the status of each victim to determine where to expend your efforts and resources first. Life-threatening injuries require immediate attention, whereas less critical injuries may be able to wait. If someone is obviously fatally injured, spend your time on another victim who might benefit from your efforts, but even when things look terrible, try not to give up. Hypothermic and cold-water drowning victims have been revived after unbelievably long periods of time (hours, not just minutes), and many accident victims have been kept alive for hours using CPR.

Consent and Liability

When approaching an accident victim, shout for help, and then identify yourself, quickly explaining that you know first aid and that you are there to help. It can happen that a person just looks like they need help, but may be drunk or simply resting in an unnatural-looking position. Sticking to these procedures can save you embarrassment, justifiable outrage, or a hard fist in the face.

Note: If the victim is aware and mentally capable, you must receive his or her consent before you begin treatment. For minors (under eighteen), obtain the permission of the guardian. If a parent or guardian is not available, the law says that you have "implied consent," meaning that it is assumed the parents would have wanted you to help their child had they been present.

If the victim is conscious and aware, talk to him or her about the extent of the injuries before proceeding. Use your judgment, but always try to do no further harm. For example, using CPR on an injured person whose heart is still beating could cause serious injury, but if the heart is not beating, CPR is probably the victim's only chance for survival. Nearly all states have Good Samaritan laws to protect lay citizens from liability, as long as they did not do something grossly negligent or deliberately harmful.

ABCs of First Aid

Treatment of the trauma victim starts with the ABCs: *airway, breathing,* and *circulation.* If any of these fail, the victim is in a life-or-death situation, and intervention is essential.

- **Airway**: The air passage must be clear of fluids and obstructions so the victim can breathe.
- **Breathing**: To survive, a person must breathe.
- **Circulation**: The blood must circulate for the victim to survive for more than a few minutes. There must be a pulse, and severe bleeding must be stopped.

Treatment Priority

Assess the situation and move yourself and the victim(s) out of danger if necessary. Use the following priority list to determine what and whom to treat first.

1. Restore and maintain breathing and heartbeat. Without these, death is certain and quick.
2. Stop the bleeding.
3. Protect wounds and burns.

4. Immobilize fractures.

5. Treat shock.

Unconscious Victim

Follow this sequence to evaluate an unconscious victim's ABCs:

1. **Shake and shout.** Check for consciousness. Tap or gently shake the victim. Ask, "Are you OK?" If not OK, shout for help.

2. **Check for neck or back injury.** If you suspect a neck or back injury, try to evaluate the ABCs without moving the victim. Moving a person with a spinal injury always entails a risk of severing the spinal cord.

3. **Position the victim.** If you do not suspect a spinal injury, carefully roll the victim onto his or her back. Grasp the shoulder and hip, supporting the neck and head as well as you can, while you try to roll the body as a unit.

4. **Open the airway.** Use the "head tilt/chin lift" technique. Place one hand on the victim's forehead and two fingers under the bony part of the chin. Lift the chin and push on the forehead to tilt the head back.(*Caution:* If a spinal injury is suspected, open the airway with a chin lift only. Do not tilt the head, unless absolutely necessary.)

5. **Look, listen, and feel for breathing.** Watch the chest to see whether it is rising and falling. Place your ear beside the victim's mouth to listen for the sounds of breathing and feel for breath against your cheek. Chest movement alone does not mean there is breathing.

6. **If the victim is breathing.** Check for bleeding and continue your evaluation.

7. **If the victim is not breathing.** Give two rescue breaths (mouth-to-mouth resuscitation) by pinching the victim's nostrils,

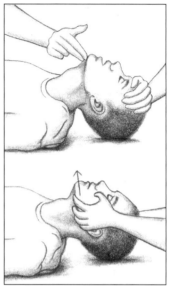

Figure 5-1. *Top,* Head tilt/chin lift procedure for opening the airway; *bottom,* jaw thrust maneuver for suspected spinal injury.

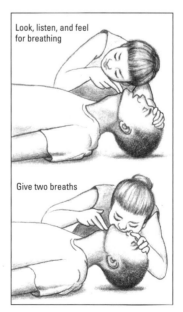

Look, listen, and feel for breathing

Give two breaths

Figure 5-2. Rescue breathing.

taking a deep breath, sealing your lips around the victim's mouth, and giving two full breaths. In the case of a small child, it may be easiest to cover both the nose and mouth with your lips. If the breaths do not raise the chest, tilt the head back further and try two more rescue breaths. If the chest does not rise, sweep your finger through the victim's mouth, lift the chin, and tilt the head further back before trying two more rescue breaths. If the head tilt and finger sweep does not clear the airway, begin abdominal thrusts (Heimlich maneuver) to try to dislodge whatever is blocking the airway.

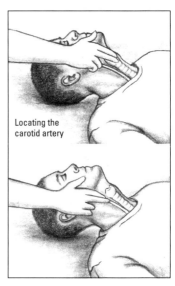

Locating the carotid artery

8. **Check the circulation.** Put your index and middle fingers over the windpipe, and slide them down alongside the neck muscle; feel between the windpipe and the neck muscle for a pulse. Check for a pulse for 5 to 10 seconds. *If the victim has no pulse, begin CPR.* If there is severe bleeding, it must be controlled. If there is a pulse, but no breathing, continue rescue breathing.

9. **If the victim has a pulse and is breathing.** Continue monitoring ABCs and give first aid for other injuries or illness.

10. **If the victim has a pulse but is not breathing.** Continue with rescue breathing, giving one breath every 5 seconds and checking for a pulse once each minute (every 12 breaths). Continue until the patient recovers, you are relieved by EMS, or until too exhausted to continue.

Figure 5-3. Checking for pulse at the carotid artery.

11. **The recovery position.** If an unconscious victim is breathing and has a pulse and no spinal injury, the safest position is the recovery position.

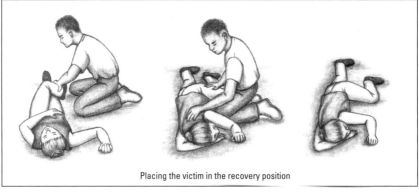

Placing the victim in the recovery position

Figure 5-4. The recovery position.

Unconscious victims have little or no control over their muscles and can easily choke on their tongue, vomit, or other fluids. Roll the victim onto his or her side and toward the front, bending and propping one arm and one leg to prevent the person from lying face down. Keep the head tilted down and to the side, allowing fluids to drain, and open the jaw to inspect the mouth to be sure that the tongue is lying flat and not against the back of the throat. Loosen tight clothing.

Remember

- Never lay an unconscious victim flat on his or her back, except to begin CPR or rescue breathing.
- Never give fluids to an unconscious victim.
- Never tilt an unconscious victim's head forward with a pillow.

CPR

Cardiopulmonary resuscitation (CPR) is one of those things you hope that you never have to use. When the heart stops, CPR may be the only thing that can prevent death. To properly learn CPR, you must take a course from a certified instructor using a CPR demonstration dummy. Too much force will break ribs or cause other serious internal injuries, while too little force will be insufficient to pump the blood through the victim's heart. The CPR dummy gives feedback to help you get a feel for the proper timing, head tilt, and the amount of force to apply for CPR compressions. Do yourself and your loved ones a favor: get yourself certified in CPR by the American Heart Association or American Red Cross. A summary of the procedure for CPR is included for your reference.

Caution: Do not attempt CPR solely on the basis of these guidelines (without proper training) unless no CPR-trained person is present and the victim has no pulse—in other words, unless there is no alternative. For a more detailed description of the first five steps, see the previous procedures for "Unconscious Victim."

1. **Shake gently and ask, "Are you OK?"**
2. **If there is no response, shout for help.**
3. **Position the victim.** Roll the victim onto his or her back on a firm, flat surface. Roll the body as a unit, supporting the head and neck. Try to keep the head at the same level as the heart.
4. **Position yourself.** Kneel next to the victim, halfway between the chest and head.
5. **Check the ABCs:**

- Open the airway. Use the "head-tilt/chin-lift" technique.

- Breathing. Kneel alongside the victim and check to see whether he or she is breathing. Look, listen, and feel for signs of breathing.

- Circulation. Use one hand to keep the head tilted. With the fingers of the other hand (not the thumb), feel between the windpipe and the neck muscle for a pulse at the carotid artery. Check for 5 to 10 seconds. If the victim has no pulse, begin CPR. *Time is critical!*

6. **Call EMS.** If possible, send someone else to call EMS (emergency medical services). Alert EMS to the status of the ABCs.

7. **Position your hands.** Using your fingers, locate the notch at the bottom of the ribs where they join the sternum (breastbone), a few inches straight above the belly button. Place your index finger on the notch and your middle finger right above it. Using your middle finger and index fingers as a spacer, place the heel of your hand two fingers above the notch, at the center of the breastbone. Remove your two fingers from above the notch, and place the palm of this hand on top of the one on the breastbone.

8. **Chest compressions.** With arms straight and shoulders directly over your hands, lock your elbows and lean over the victim to use your body weight to compress the victim's breastbone 1½ to 2 inches. Keep your fingers raised to compress the breastbone and not the ribs. Compress the chest at a rate of 80 to 100 compressions per minute, stopping every 15 compressions to open the airway and give two rescue breaths. Count out loud with each compression so you do not lose track of the number. Release the pressure, but do not lift your hands between compressions or otherwise allow your hand position to shift. Don't let the heel of your hand slide down over the tip of the breastbone, and keep your fingers away from the chest. *Caution:* Excessively forceful or misplaced compressions can cause fractures and injuries to internal organs. [**Special instructions for children and babies**: Babies require very little force. Use light pressure with two fingers at about 100 times per minute. Small children will usually only require medium pressure from the heel of one hand, not two as used for adults. Use cycles of one breath and five compressions

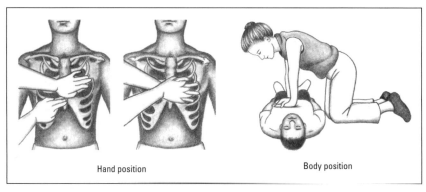

Hand position   Body position

Figure 5-5. CPR position.

for 10 cycles between pulse checks. Depress the child's breast 1 to 1½ inches per compression. Compress an infant's chest only ½ to 1 inch per compression.]

9. **Two rescue breaths.** Use head tilt/chin lift to open the airway, then give two rescue breaths, watching to make sure that the chest rises with each breath.

10. **Four cycles, then check.** Use the two-finger technique to reposition your hands with each set of compressions. Recheck the pulse after every four sets of 15 compressions and two rescue breaths.

11. **If the victim regains a pulse and is breathing.** Continue to monitor ABCs, while checking for and treating other injuries.

12. **If the victim regains a pulse but is not breathing.** Continue rescue breathing at the rate of one breath every 5 seconds. Listen for breathing and recheck pulse every 12 breaths (count out loud between breaths).

13. **If the victim has no pulse, continue CPR until:**
    • Breathing and pulse return.
    • The rescuers are exhausted.
    • The rescuers are in danger.
    • The victim fails to respond to prolonged resuscitation (how you define "prolonged" depends on the circumstances; prolonged CPR is most likely to be successful in hypothermia cases).
    • The rescuers are relieved by medical professionals.

CPR is not magic. There are situations in which it should *not* be attempted, including:

• A lethal injury (death is obvious).
• A dangerous setting in which rescuers' lives are in danger.
• Chest compressions are impossible, such as in cases where the chest is frozen or crushed.
• When there is any sign of life (breathing, heartbeat, pulse, movement).
• The victim has stated, in writing, that he or she does not want to be resuscitated.

Heart Attack

Heart attacks can be fatal, and anyone experiencing severe chest pains should seek medical attention and be treated as if he is having a heart attack, even if he seems to be an unlikely candidate for a heart attack. Most heart attacks involve discomfort in the center of the chest that lasts for more than a few minutes, or goes away and comes back. The discomfort can feel like uncomfortable pressure, squeezing, fullness, or pain. The truth is that many heart attacks start slowly, as a mild pain or discomfort. If you feel such a symptom, you may not be sure what's wrong. Your symptoms may even come and go. Even those who have had a heart attack may not recognize their symptoms, because the next attack can have entirely different symptoms from prior ones.

Most heart attack victims have one or more of the following symptoms:

- Chest pains, ranging from a dull ache to a crushing sensation. The pain sometimes radiates to the jaw, shoulder(s), or arm(s).On occasion, people may have a heart attack without feeling chest pains.
- Difficulty breathing, gasping, and/or shortness of breath.
- Sensation of irregular heartbeat, or palpitations.

The above symptoms are often accompanied by one or more of the following symptoms:

- Excessive sweating.
- Dizziness or a lightheaded feeling.
- Nausea, vomiting, or other feelings typically associated with indigestion.
- Pale or bluish lips and skin.
- Cool clammy skin.
- Shock and/or unconsciousness.

First Aid for Heart Attack

- Call EMS.
- If victim is unconscious, look, listen, and feel for breathing and check for pulse. Start CPR if no pulse, and rescue breathing if no breathing but pulse. Check for medical alert tag/bracelet.
- If victim is conscious, calm and reassure victim.
- Encourage the victim to rest in a comfortable position, but do not force to lie down as it may be more difficult to breath while lying down.
- Loosen clothing around victim's neck, chest, and waist. Keep victim warm and inactive.
- Continue to monitor ABCs, and stay with victim until medical personnel arrive.
- If CPR is required, and you are in or near a public building (school, library, government building, sports facility, etc.) that may have an automatic external defibrillator (AED), send someone else to look for and retrieve the AED while you continue with CPR.

Using an Automatic External Defibrillator (AED)

An AED is a portable electronic device that automatically diagnoses certain potentially life-threatening cardiac arrhythmias and then automatically treats them through defibrillation, the application of electrical therapy (regulated shocks) that stops the arrhythmia, allowing the heart to reestablish an effective rhythm. It is preferable that someone has training in the use of an AED, but if not, don't be afraid to use the AED since they are designed for simple use by the layman and they come with clear graphical instructions. Most states protect untrained AED users from liability via "good Samaritan" laws. The use of an AED could be a lifesaver! Once attached and activated, it will instruct the user as to which action to perform next (continue with CPR, apply shock, discontinue CPR, etc). The approximate procedure is as follows:

1. Switch the AED on, then attach the two pads to the victim's chest per Figure 5-6. One pad goes under the victim's right collar bone and the other along his left ribcage. The AED should have a clear picture denoting these locations.

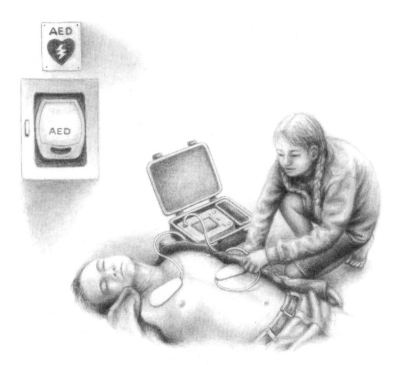

Figure 5-6. Application of AED.

2. Have everyone stand clear while the AED analyzes the victim's heartbeat.

3. The AED will advise if a shock is necessary. Everyone must stay clear, and not touch victim while AED is both analyzing and when it is applying cardiac shocks. If advised to shock the victim, push the "shock" button on the AED and stand clear (some AEDs apply shocks automatically without pushing the button). Most AEDs advise users via audible commands, but some supplement these audible commands with visible directions detailed on a display panel.

4. Continue to follow the AED's directions. It will probably direct you to apply CPR for another couple of minutes before reanalyzing the victim's heartbeat.

5. If victim resumes breathing, discontinue use of AED and keep victim calm and inactive until EMS arrives.

Survey for Injuries and to Control Bleeding

Do a quick head-to-toe survey for wounds and fractures. Try to control bleeding by applying direct pressure to wounds with any bulky, clean material—use your shirt if nothing else is handy. Use the cleanest material available to reduce the chance of infection, but stopping severe bleeding is far more important than worrying about infection. Elevate the wounded limb to reduce the blood pressure to the wound. Do not change dressings if blood-soaked, but add new dressings on top of old ones. Tie dressings in place with strips of cloth or roll bandages to maintain pressure. Bright red blood spurting from a wound is arterial. Oozing, dark blood is probably from a vein. Arterial bleeding, especially from the scalp, neck, groin, or shoulder, can be difficult to control and can rapidly lead to life-threatening shock. If direct pressure and elevation are not enough to stop the bleeding, add pressure-point techniques to help control severe bleeding.

Pressure Points

Arm

For arm injuries, the pressure point (for the brachial artery) is located on the inside of the arm, halfway between the elbow and the shoulder, between the upper muscle (biceps) and the lower muscle (triceps). Cup your hand around the arm, applying firm pressure with all four fingers and squeezing the artery against the arm bone.

Leg

For severe bleeding from an open leg wound, apply pressure on the femoral artery, forcing it against the pelvic bone. This pressure point is on the front

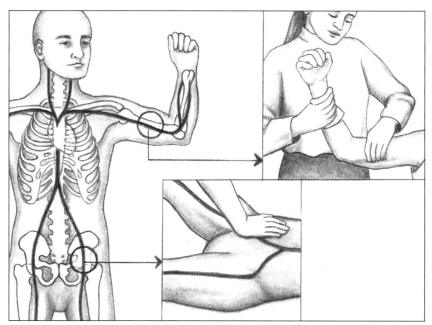

Figure 5-7. Arm and leg pressure points.

of the thigh just below the middle of the crease of the groin where the artery crosses over the pelvic bone on its way to the leg. To apply pressure on the femoral artery, quickly place the victim on his or her back and put the heel of your hand directly over the pressure point. Then lean forward over your straightened arm to apply pressure against the underlying bone. Apply pressure as needed to close the artery. Keep your arm straight to prevent arm tension and muscular strain. If bleeding is not controlled, it may be necessary to compress directly over the artery with the flat of the fingertips and to apply additional pressure over the fingertips with the heel of the other hand. Alternately, to control severe bleeding from a leg wound, push your fist into the abdomen at the level of the navel and press firmly. This compresses the aorta against the spinal column and will control the flow of blood into the legs while you apply a bulky bandage.

Tourniquets

If there is a detectable pulse, severe bleeding must be controlled, but tourniquets are dangerous *and should be used only as a last resort.* Don't use one unless you are willing to write off the limb to save the victim. The only acceptable positions for tourniquets are around the upper arm, just below the armpit, and around the upper thigh. Tourniquets should be made from material that is at least 2 inches wide. If string or wire is used, the tourniquet must

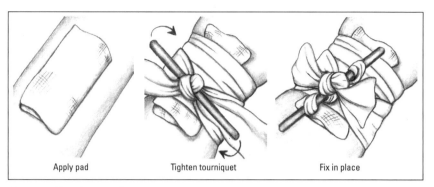

| Apply pad | Tighten tourniquet | Fix in place |

Figure 5-8. Tourniquet application.

be padded with a strip of heavy material. If a tourniquet has been applied, loosen the tourniquet every 20 minutes to allow some circulation to the limb (only if this won't cause too much blood loss). Tourniquets should always remain visible, never covered by dressings, blankets, and so on. If a tourniquet is applied, the fingers or toes on the appropriate limb should remain uncovered to allow for visual inspection for discoloration and swelling.

Wounds

The danger of infection is always present with any wound. Soap is antiseptic, and it will help to reduce the chance of infection if a wound is washed with soap and clean water. Fresh urine is almost always sterile, and can be used to cleanse a wound in the absence of clean water. Antiseptics are handy to reduce the chance of infection, but will cause further tissue damage if used inside deep wounds. Honey is mildly antibacterial and has been used for thousands of years to prevent infection and speed the healing of battlefield wounds. Colloidal silver is also antibacterial and will not harm human tissue.

Abrasions

The main danger from abrasions is the possibility of infection. Clean the wound with soap and antiseptic and cover with a clean dressing. Wash hands in sterile water, and boil non-sterile dressings to sterilize.

Incisions

Incisions, or cuts, generally bleed enough to clean the wound, and are not as prone to infection as abrasions. Minor wounds can be closed with butterfly bandages or stitches (sutures).

If a wound gets infected, it may be necessary to undo some of the stitches or lance the wound to allow it to drain. To stitch a wound, use only a steril-

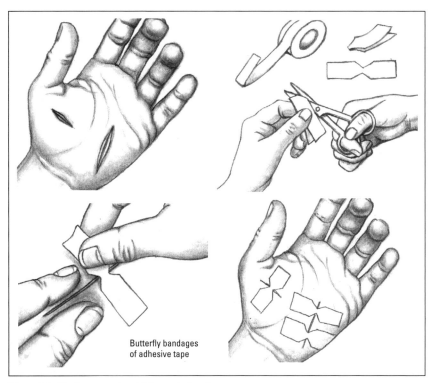

Figure 5-9. Closing wounds with butterfly bandages.

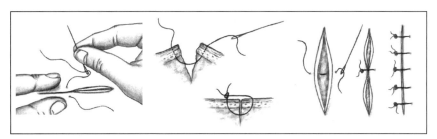

Figure 5-10. Suturing a wound.

ized needle and thread. Draw the edges of the wound together and begin stitching at the center of the wound. Tie off each stitch individually, before moving on to the next stitch.

Puncture Wounds

Because puncture wounds generally do not bleed enough to flush out dirt and germs, they are prone to infection and should be watched carefully for signs of infection (tenderness, red, puffy swelling, discharge with pus, fever). If available, emergency medical personnel should remove foreign material and treat all deep puncture wounds.

Abdominal Wounds

Any deep abdominal wound should be considered serious due to the potential for significant injury to internal organs and internal bleeding. Give no food or water, unless it takes longer than two days to reach medical care. Allay thirst with a damp cloth in the mouth (use IV for fluids, if available). Do not try to stuff bowels back inside the abdominal cavity, but cover with cloths soaked in lightly salted, boiled water. Make sure that you keep cloth coverings moist. Seek immediate medical attention.

Warning: Do not give an enema or purge, because this may cause death.

Head Wounds

Minor head wounds often bleed a lot and look more serious than they are, but all significant head wounds should be examined carefully owing to the potential for injuries to the brain. Injuries to the brain can affect breathing and circulation. Any time a person is knocked unconscious, he or she must be observed carefully for at least twenty-four hours. Dilated pupils, severe and unrelenting headache, nausea, prolonged dizziness, or blood from the ears and nose are all potential signs of serious head injuries. Remove false teeth and carefully monitor the ABCs. Blood or straw-colored fluids seeping from the ear or nose may indicate a skull fracture. Do not block the drainage of these fluids, as this may cause brain damage from internal pressure buildup. If there are no signs of neck or back injury, place the victim in the recovery position, with the leaking side down to help fluids to drain.

Chest Wounds

Puncture wounds in the chest may result in a collapsed lung. If you hear a sucking noise or see bubbles coming from a chest wound, immediately cover the wound with the palm of your hand, then seal around the wound with a dressing made from plastic wrap or aluminum foil. Coat the dressing with petroleum jelly or antiseptic ointment to help it seal to the skin. If available, tape the dressing edges, except for one corner, to improve the seal, yet allow for excess air to vent outward.

1. Monitor ABCs.
2. Do not give fluids.
3. Call EMS.
4. Do not move the victim unless absolutely necessary.

Choking

The symptoms of choking are easily recognized—clutching at the throat, staring eyes, face contorted. If the person is coughing or making significant breathing sounds, his or her own efforts to clear the blockage stand a better chance than your intervention, which might cause the blockage to lodge more deeply. Remember that a person who is choking can hear you even though she or he is unable to speak. Ask the person if he or she is choking. *If the person is unable to answer, and there are no breathing sounds or only a high-pitched squeaky noise, the blockage is life threatening. Begin abdominal thrusts (Heimlich maneuver) immediately.*

Heimlich Maneuver (Abdominal Thrusts)

1. Stand or kneel behind the victim and wrap your arms around the midsection.

2. Make a fist with one hand and grab the outside of the fist with the other hand. The thumb side of the fist should be touching the victim's belly, just above the belly button and well below the breastbone.

3. With elbows out, vigorously thrust your fist upward into the victim's belly, attempting to force air through the windpipe to blow the obstruction from the windpipe.

4. After four abdominal thrusts, try four sharp blows between the shoulders to dislodge the obstruction followed by more abdominal thrusts. Do not give up! Be prepared to give artificial respiration if the victim passes out.

Note: You can perform abdominal thrusts on yourself with your fists or against an object, such as a chair or stump.

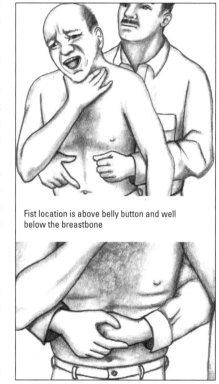

Fist location is above belly button and well below the breastbone

Figure 5-11. Heimlich maneuver.

Bandages and Dressings

Dressings are typically sterile, gauze-covered cotton pads placed directly on wounds to stop bleeding and to keep the wounds clean. They often have a shiny protective coating on one side to keep the dressing from sticking to the wound and to facilitate daily dressing changes. Do not touch the surface of sterile dressings before applying to wounds. Roll *bandages* are usually made from gauze, crepe, or stretch material (Ace bandage). Bandages can be improvised from any clean cloth material, such as sheets or clothing. Large triangular bandages, with short legs of one yard or more, are versatile. Use large triangular bandages for arm slings, head wounds, binding splints, and so on. Bandages should be tied just tight enough to hold dressings in place and stop bleeding, but not so tight that they cut into the flesh or restrict circulation. Tie bandages with a square (reef) knot. Check fingertips and toes for numbness or bluish color, which indicates restricted circulation from bandages that are too tight.

Shock

Be on the lookout for shock in any accident victim. Virtually any serious injury or illness can lead to shock. When trauma or severe illness threatens the flow of oxygen and blood to the body's tissues, the body responds with a counterattack, known as shock. When in shock, the body constricts blood flow to nonessential organs in an effort to conserve blood and sustain life. Shock can be life threatening, even though the injuries that caused the shock would not normally cause death.

Symptoms of Shock

- Skin pale or bluish, cold to the touch, and possibly moist or clammy.
- Weakness, dizziness. Victim may be apathetic and unresponsive due to lack of oxygen to the brain.
- Rapid pulse (usually greater than 100), often too weak to be felt at the wrist but perceptible at the carotid artery on the side of the neck where the windpipe joins the muscle, or at the femoral artery at the groin.
- Restlessness, anxiety, or confusion. Decreased alertness.
- Nausea, vomiting.
- Rapid, shallow breathing.
- Intense thirst.

Trauma specialists talk about the "golden hour" in treating shock victims.

If shock is not reversed within one hour, the patient may die, no matter what actions are taken.

Treatment for Shock

1. Check the victim's ABCs. Perform CPR or control the bleeding, if necessary.

2. Lay the victim on his or her back in the "shock position": legs flexed at the hips, knees straight, feet elevated 12 inches, and head down. This promotes the return of venous blood to the heart and enhances the flow of arterial blood to the brain. *Warning*: Do not lay the victim in the shock position if you suspect head, neck, or back injuries, or if the victim is having breathing problems.

3. Give treatment for the underlying illness or injury.

4. Keep the victim comfortable. Loosen tight clothing and conserve body heat by bundling in blankets or a sleeping bag. *Do not add heat from an external source,* as this will swell capillaries in the skin and draw blood from vital organs.

5. *Do not give fluids by mouth.*

6. Move the victim out of danger if you have to, but avoid rough handling. Check vital signs (ABCs) every few minutes, including pulse and breathing rate and pattern. Restlessness and agitation may be signs of worsening shock.

7. Make arrangements for rapid medical evacuation. *Time is of the essence!*

Fractures and Dislocations

Dislocations occur when a joint is overstressed to the point where the bone pops out of location (the joint is "dislocated"). Usually dislocations are accompanied by tearing and rupturing of the soft joint tissues. A fracture occurs when a bone is overstressed to the point where it breaks. It is often hard to tell whether a bone is fractured or dislocated, but the first-aid treatment for both is usually the same. Fractures are divided into two types. In the case of an open fracture (also known as a compound fracture), the broken bone ruptures the skin. The bone may be sticking out of the wound, or it may retract back inside the flesh. Open fractures are very serious injuries, because they are easily infected and can lead to bone infections and gangrene, which are difficult to treat and may result in amputation if treatment is unsuccessful. Injuries that appear to be dislocations may actually be fractures near a joint, and should be immobilized and treated as fractures.

In general, it is recommended that untrained personnel do not try to reposition dislocations or fractures. However, if you are in a remote location, or if you are sure that emergency medical services will not be available for several hours, you should try to pop a dislocated joint back into position, or tension and reposition a fractured limb. You must use your judgment on this one. The Red Cross manuals state that fractures and dislocations should be immobilized in the position they are found in, to minimize the risk of further damage while trying to reposition the joint or break. Wilderness medicine manuals will tell you that you should attempt to reduce (relocate or "pop" back into joint) a dislocated joint as soon as possible after the injury, or swelling and muscle spasms will make this task nearly impossible and will make rescue far more difficult. Similarly, setting a fracture (realigning the break prior to splinting) may cause more damage if done improperly, but if properly handled will reduce the risk of further injury by:

- Preventing a closed fracture from becoming an open (compound) fracture
- Reducing bleeding and pain at the fracture location
- Reducing the risk of shock complications
- Making it easier to apply an effective splint

If you do choose to align a fracture ("set" or "reduce" the fracture), you must apply tension to the fractured limb both while the splint is applied and while in the splint. Without tension, muscle contractions may cause the fractured bone sections to pull beside each other, resulting in further injury due to the cutting of internal tissues on sharp bone fragments.

General Guidelines for Treating Dislocations and Fractures

1. Check the victim's ABCs.

2. Keep the victim still. Movement of fractured limbs could turn a closed fracture into a compound fracture or cause damage to internal tissues. *Do not move the limb or attempt to "set" the fracture.* Movement may cause severe tissue damage from razor-sharp edges of fractured bones.

3. If there is an open fracture, or you suspect there may be a fracture below an open wound, take extreme precautions against infection and contamination. Do not wash the wound, but cover the wound with sterile dressings and immobilize the limb. *Do not breathe on, or probe, the open wound.* Do not try to set the limb (unless you have no access to emergency medical services in the near future).

4. Splint or sling the affected area in the position you found it. Include at least the joint above and below the injury when immobilizing the injured area. Splint the break with some kind of firm material, such as boards,

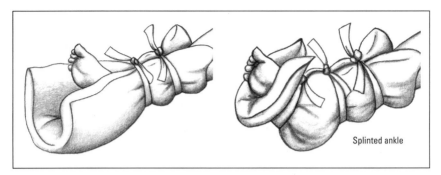

Splinted ankle

Figure 5-12. Ankle splint.

tree branches, ski poles, broomsticks, umbrellas, and so on. If rigid materials are unavailable, you can use rolled-up newspapers or rolled towels, or you can tape or tie a limb to the body or another limb (that is, strap the broken leg to the good leg). Pad the splint with some kind of soft cushioning material such as towels, moss, or rags between the victim's flesh and the hard splints. Tie the splint in at least two places above and two places below the injury, but not directly on top of the injury. *Always treat wounds before splinting.*

5. Treat for shock. Lay the victim flat, elevating the feet and keeping the head down, *unless you suspect a head, back, or neck injury.*

6. Call EMS.

Special Precautions for Fractures

1. **Pelvis and thigh.** Fractures to the pelvis and thigh are serious injuries that can rapidly turn life threatening. If possible, do not move the victim, but get immediate medical attention. If the victim must be moved, use the clothes-drag technique rather than lifting or carrying.

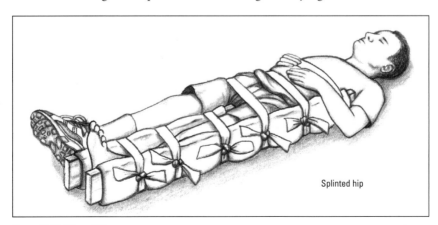

Splinted hip

Figure 5-13. Hip splint.

2. **Neck or back.** If a spinal injury is suspected, call EMS immediately, and do not move the victim unless in danger. If you must move the victim, use the clothes-drag technique (see page 107 for a description). If the neck is injured, it is imperative that the neck be immobilized with a neck collar, sack of earth, or some other obstruction to movement. You may improvise

Figure 5-14. Stabilizing the head and neck.

a collar from a rolled towel or newspaper, among other items. If a neck fracture is suspected, *do not allow the victim to move her or his neck!* If the victim must be lifted or rolled over, get several people to assist so the victim may be rolled or lifted as a unit, with no twisting to the spine or neck.

3. **Skull.** Blood or straw-colored fluids seeping from the ear or nose may indicate a skull fracture. Do not block the drainage of these fluids, as this may cause brain damage from internal pressure buildup. If there are no signs of neck or back injury, place the victim in the recovery position, with the leaking side down to drain. Cover wounds lightly with sterile dressings if a fracture is suspected. Dilated pupils, dizziness, difficulty breathing, nausea, unclear thinking, vision problems, unconsciousness, and severe, unrelenting headaches are signs of potential brain injury. Monitor the ABCs and call EMS.

Reducing Dislocations

When traveling in the wilderness or when emergency medical services are hours away, try to pop dislocated joints back into place ("reduction"). Do not wait too long, or else swelling and muscle spasms will make this task difficult or impossible. Gently probe the area to try to ensure that the dislocation is not actually a fracture.

- **Fingers** are easy to relocate. Simply grasp the fingertip and pull steadily outward until the joint pops back into place. After relocation, tape the injured finger to an adjacent finger for support.

- For **shoulders**, try to position the victim lying flat on her or his stomach with the arm hanging down over an edge. Either hang a weight of 10 to 15 pounds from the wrist for 10 minutes, or pull steadily downward on the victim's wrist until the shoulder pops back into place. Separated shoulders are often confused with shoulder dislocations. Separated shoulders are usually caused by falls directly onto the shoulder, which tears some of the tissue connecting the collarbone to the shoulder. If you detect a "spongy" feel while gently probing the collarbone, the injury is probably a separation and should be treated by immobilization with a sling. After reduction, support the arm with a sling.

- **Elbows** are more difficult to treat, and you may not be able to get the elbow to relocate while you are in the backcountry. Check pulse and circulation in the fingers. Have the victim lie on his or her belly, draping the injured elbow over a padded ledge or edge so the elbow bends 90 degrees and the forearm hangs straight down. Grasp the wrist and pull downward while another rescuer pulls upward on the upper arm just above the elbow. Rocking the forearm back and forth gently may assist the process. Recheck pulse and circulation in the fingers. After relocating the elbow, splint as if it were fractured.

- **Hips** are tough, but if successfully relocated, will prevent further damage to the hip joint and sciatic nerve. Lay the victim on his or her back and, keeping the knee bent at a right angle, lift the leg until the thigh is pointing straight up. Have an assistant hold the victim's hips down while you straddle the victim. Grasp just below the knee and pull firmly upward, slowly twisting the leg a little to the right and left until the hip pops back into place. It takes considerable force to counteract the strong thigh muscles. After reduction, splint the injured leg to the other leg.

Sprains and Strains

Sprains

Sprains are injuries to the joints, usually accompanied by soreness and swelling, which indicates that internal tissues have torn. Severe sprains can be more debilitating, more painful, and take longer to heal than simple fractures. Standard treatment is covered by the acronym RICE—rest, ice, compression, and elevation. Stay off the injured limb. Apply cold compresses for the first 24 to 48 hours. Do not apply ice directly to the skin, but insulate ice packs with a towel or folded cloth. After two days, massage and hot soaks (or alternating hot and cold soaks) will boost blood circulation and

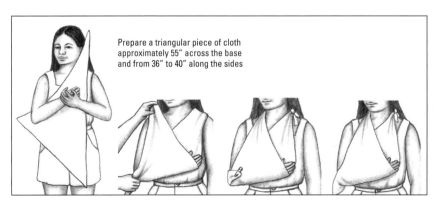

Prepare a triangular piece of cloth approximately 55" across the base and from 36" to 40" along the sides

Figure 5-15. Arm sling.

speed healing. Elevating the limb and compressing the area with a snug Ace bandage wrap will help control swelling. Tincture of *Arnica montana* and Traumeel cream, a homeopathic remedy, will usually promote and accelerate the body's natural healing processes. These remedies are also good for bruises and most other traumatic injuries.

Immobilization is key to treating severe sprains and connective tissue tears. It used to be that doctors jumped in right after a serious tearing injury with invasive surgery to reconnect torn ligaments and tendons using pins, stitches, and staples. Years later, these artificial connections tend to cause problems with arthritis and joint degeneration. Researchers have found that the natural intelligence of the body's healing mechanisms usually does a better job of reconnecting these tissues, provided that the injury is immobilized for an appropriate period of time.

Strains

Muscle strains ("pulled" muscles) can be very painful. Apply cold compresses at once, and elevate the limb to control swelling. If pain begins to recede, apply heat after 24 hours. If the muscle does not improve in one to two days, seek medical attention.

Heat-Related Trauma

Heatstroke

Heatstroke is a life-threatening condition that occurs when the body's heat-regulating mechanisms are overloaded and simply stop working. When the body stops sweating due to heat stroke, brain damage or death may rapidly occur, so it is absolutely critical that the victim's body temperature is rapidly reduced. Signs and symptoms are hot, red skin; very small pupils; and elevated body temperature. If the person was exercising, they may still be wet with sweat, but often there is a peculiar lack of sweat. Body temperature will be above normal, and if it exceeds 105°F, brain damage and death may occur.

Call EMS immediately, get the victim out of the sun and heat, soak the body in a cool bath if available, or keep the victim wet and fan to promote cooling. Care for shock, and give nothing by mouth until EMS arrives.

Heat Exhaustion

Heat exhaustion is much more common and less dangerous than heatstroke. Heat exhaustion typically occurs when people are working hard or exercising in hot, humid conditions where the person's sweat is not sufficient to adequately cool the body. Fluid loss due to dehydration, usually from heavy sweating, causes a decrease in blood flow to vital organs, resulting in a form of shock.

The signs and symptoms of heat exhaustion are cool, pale, and moist skin; heavy sweating; dilated pupils; headache; nausea; dizziness; and vomiting. Body temperature should be near normal.

Get the victim out of the sun and heat, cool the person immediately, and treat for shock. Use cold packs (placing a towel between the skin and cold pack), a fan, a cool bath, wet towels and sheets, etc. Lay the victim on his or her back with elevated feet and give a half glass of water every fifteen minutes (if the person is fully conscious and can handle it without vomiting). The person should feel much better within a half hour.

Bites and Stings

Animal Bites

The main concern with animal bites is infection. Thoroughly cleanse the wound and apply disinfectant or antibiotic ointment and dressings. Rabies is always a possibility with animal bites. Felines, canines, apes, raccoons, and other mammals may carry rabies. If bitten, the person should always be examined by the appropriate medical services, even if some time has passed and the wound has healed. Once rabies progresses to the point where there are symptoms of nervousness, light sensitivity, and aversion to water, it is usually fatal.

Snakebites

Except for the brightly colored coral snake (red, black, and yellow, or white rings with a black nose), all poisonous snakes leave two large holes from their fangs, along with smaller holes from their other teeth. Most snakes are not poisonous, but can generate a significant wound with their bite. Venomous snakebites require first aid and medical treatment.

- Call EMS. Identify the type of snake, if known, so the proper antivenin can be prepared in advance of treatment. Try to kill the snake and take it along for identification.

- Keep the victim calm, quiet, and inactive. Have the victim lie down and keep the bite below the heart.

- Wash the wound and apply antiseptic.

- *Do not* cut the wound and try to suck the venom out. If you have a snakebite kit, you can use the suction cups or suction syringe.

- *Do not* apply a tourniquet or cold compress to the wound.
- Monitor the ABCs and treat for shock, if necessary. Remove rings and bracelets that might cause problems if the limbs begin to swell.
- Seek medical treatment.

Spider Bites

Treat spider bites in the same way as snakebites. The most serious spider bites in the United States are from the brown recluse and black widow spiders. Unless the person bitten is elderly or a small child, the bites from these spiders are usually not fatal, but they can make you very sick and lead to flesh loss.

The black widow has a very shiny, black patent-leather look with a large abdomen and a bright red hourglass-shaped marking on the underside of its belly. The bite may not even be noticed, or may feel like a small pinprick followed by tingling and numbing of the hands and feet. Symptoms may progress into severe back and stomach cramps, sweating, vomiting, headaches, and seizures. Ice at the wound site can ease the pain somewhat. Seek medical attention as soon as possible; there is an antidote for severe cases. Most people recover within twelve hours without treatment (Weiss 1997, 116).

The bite of the brown recluse spider can cause serious tissue damage if left untreated. The body of the brown recluse is about ½ inch long and has a dark, violin-shaped marking on the top of the upper section of its body. Initial mild stinging is followed by itching and burning, and then blistering and ulceration at the bite area. Fever, chills, nausea, and vomiting may follow within one to two days. Seek medical attention; there is an antivenin that can halt or prevent tissue damage (Weiss 1997, 117).

Tarantulas are scarier looking than they are dangerous. Their bites can be painful and should be treated for possible infection.

Tick Bites

❝Lyme disease is now the most common tick-transmitted infection, with an estimated 5,000 to 15,000 new cases in the United States each year. The majority of people with Lyme disease do not recall the precipitating tick bite.❞ —Eric A. Weiss, M.D., *A Comprehensive Guide to Wilderness and Travel Medicine*

Ticks typically hang around on blades of grass and other vegetation until a host rubs against them. They crawl onto the host and wander around until they find a spot, then dig their head into the skin for a blood feast (usually when the host is at rest). If you tear a tick off the host, typically, at least part of its head is left buried in the skin. Tick bites often lead to infection and may require a quick surgical procedure if a cyst has formed around an imbedded tick head. The preferred removal method is to grasp the tick body with a pair of tweezers, getting as far under the head as possible without puncturing or rupturing the tick's body. Gently lift up and back until the tick releases its grasp and pulls free from the host (this may take a few minutes of steady pressure). Traditional methods, such as coating the tick with fingernail polish or petroleum jelly or burning the tick with a hot object, can force the tick to release from the host—but these methods increase infection risk from the tick regurgitating potentially infectious fluids into the host's bloodstream. Tick bites can cause infection or introduce diseases such as Lyme disease or Rocky Mountain spotted fever.

The deer tick, which is responsible for the spread of Lyme disease, is so small that it is almost never seen or noticed. The bite is often followed by a flu-like fever and typically develops a "bull's eye" rash up to several inches in diameter centered on the bite, which usually disappears on its own within a month's time. About 20 percent of Lyme disease victims develop further long-term symptoms, such as severe arthritis, heart problems, and neurological difficulties sometimes resembling multiple sclerosis. Lyme disease is treatable with antibiotics and has been treated successfully with colloidal silver (see the *Micro Silver Bullet,* by Dr. Paul Farber).

Stings

Bees, wasps, hornets, and scorpions can cause severe reactions in some people. In the case of a scorpion, try to kill the scorpion (and bring it along) for identification, because some varieties can be extremely poisonous. The sting from the small straw-colored bark scorpion (1 to 2 inches in length, with slender pinchers) is potentially lethal. Look for neurological symptoms, such as twitching, drooling, numbness, blurred vision, and seizures. Seek immediate medical attention.

Benadryl can be helpful for reducing the symptoms of swelling and itching associated with many insect bites and stings. Try to remove bee stingers with a scraping action, as pinching a stinger with tweezers may drive more venom into the sting. Multiple stings or an allergy to stings can cause a severe reaction, known as anaphylactic shock, a life-threatening conditioning in which the throat swells shut, blood pressure falls, and unconsciousness may ensue. In this case, call EMS and seek immediate medical attention. Check for a medic alert bracelet. A person with severe allergies usually carries a kit with emergency medicine for dealing with this kind of emergency.

Eyes

The eye is very delicate, complicated, and easily damaged. When in doubt, always seek medical attention. If foreign material is irritating the eyes, try to wash it out with an eyecup, by holding the eye open in a bowl of water, or lying the victim on his or her side and dribbling water from a glass across the eye. While washing the eye, use your thumb and forefinger to hold the eyelid open, since the natural reaction is for the eye to clamp shut. Room-temperature sterile saline solution is the best flushing solution for the eyes, but clean freshwater will do if saline solution is not available. Use lukewarm or cold water—*never use hot water!* The standard procedure for chemical irritants in the eyes is to flush the eyes for fifteen minutes with water, and then seek medical attention. You may be able to dislodge foreign debris by pulling the upper eyelid outward and scraping its inner surface over the short eyelashes of the lower lid. A soft, clean cloth may be gently dragged across the eyeball to snag particles of debris. Do not use cotton or tissue paper.

First Aid for a Foreign Object in the Eye

- If the object does not move freely, do not attempt to remove it.
- Call EMS.
- Prevent the victim from rubbing the eye and causing more damage.
- Cover both eyes, so the victim will not cause more damage by moving the eyes around.

Moving Injured People

If the victim is in physical danger, or is in a remote location, it may be necessary to move him or her. Whenever there is a potential spinal injury, the victim must be immobilized and the utmost care must be given to minimize or prevent movement of the back or neck (see fig. 5-16). Ideally, several qualified medical personnel will be available to lift the victim onto a backboard

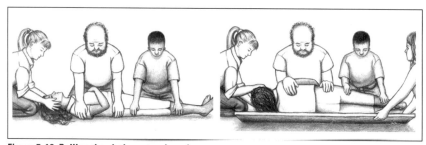

Figure 5-16. Rolling the victim onto a board.

or Stokes litter, where the person will be strapped down to prevent movement. In reality, you may have to improvise and do your best with whatever materials are available. If a spinal injury is suspected, immobilize the head and neck at all times, and always roll or lift the body as a unit (see fig. 5-17).

Clothing Drag for Single Rescuer

If you must move a victim by yourself owing to immediate danger, use the clothes drag to drag the person, face down or face up, out of danger. Crouch by the victim's head and grab the clothing by the shoulders, using your forearms to stabilize the head and neck. Keep your lower back straight, to minimize back strain. Walk backward to drag the victim out of danger. With a helper, you can position the victim on a blanket and use the blanket for a modified clothes drag.

Multi-Helper "Stretcher" Rescue

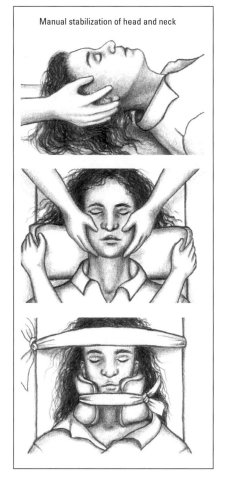

Manual stabilization of head and neck

Figure 5-17. Stabilizing head and neck for board carry.

Whenever possible, recruit others to help move the injured. The more helpers, the easier it will be. Four people is a good number for moving victims short distances over easy ground. Over rough ground, three per side and one at each end makes the carry less tiring and helps minimize the chance of dropping the stretcher if one person trips. Rotate crews every ten minutes over long stretcher hauls. In the event of a suspected spinal injury, the use of a rigid board (such as a door) is preferred over a flexible stretcher made from two poles and a blanket.

If the victim is lying flat, lift the victim as carefully as possible onto the board. Always position one person at the head to cradle the head and neck while lifting. Most of the weight will be in the shoulders and torso, so place most of your strength and attention on these areas.

If the victim is not lying flat, place the board against the person's back, parallel to the body. Roll the victim as a unit, never twisting the spine, onto the board and gently lower the board to the ground. Always have one person attending to the head, cradling the head and neck as the victim is rolled.

In the case of a potential spinal injury, immobilize the head and neck with rolled-up towels, blankets, bags of sand, and so on, and strap in place. If you have none of these materials, a helper must stabilize the head with forearms and hands.

One- and Two-Person Carries

Extra help is not always available when it is necessary to move an injured person out of danger or to transport him or her to emergency medical services. In these cases it may be necessary to perform a one- or two-person

1. Grasp the patient's wrists and stand on the patient's toes and pull

2. Pull the patient over a shoulder

3. Pass an arm between the legs and grasp the arm nearest you

Figure 5-18. Fireman's lift.

carry. Use extreme caution with all one- or two-person carries to prevent injuring your back. Try to keep your back relatively straight, and lift mostly with your legs. The classic *fireman's lift* (fig. 5-18) is particularly effective where speed is critical, distances are short, and there is no apparent spinal injury.

The two-person, wrist-catch seat carry (fig. 5-19) is a comfortable shorter-distance carry.

Over longer distances, the *backpack* (fig. 5-20) or *sling carry* (fig. 5-21) will be much less tiring and easier on both victim and rescuer than the *fireman's lift*.

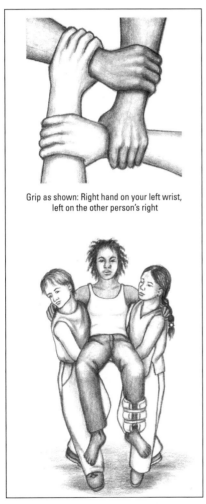

Grip as shown: Right hand on your left wrist, left on the other person's right

Figure 5-19. Two-person wrist-catch seat carry.

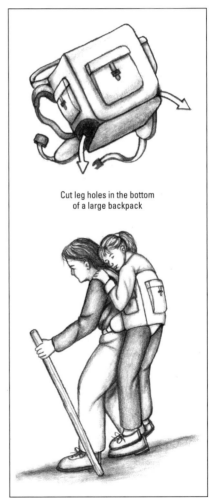

Cut leg holes in the bottom of a large backpack

Figure 5-20. Backpack carry.

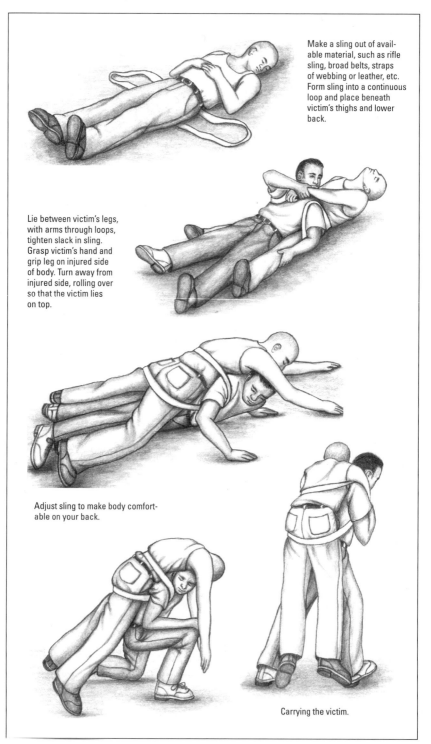

Make a sling out of available material, such as rifle sling, broad belts, straps of webbing or leather, etc. Form sling into a continuous loop and place beneath victim's thighs and lower back.

Lie between victim's legs, with arms through loops, tighten slack in sling. Grasp victim's hand and grip leg on injured side of body. Turn away from injured side, rolling over so that the victim lies on top.

Adjust sling to make body comfortable on your back.

Carrying the victim.

Figure 5-21. Sling carry.

Emergency Childbirth

This section provides some of the most basic instructions for dealing with emergency childbirth. See Elizabeth Davis' excellent *Heart and Hands: A Midwife's Guide to Pregnancy and Birth* or *Where There Is No Doctor* by David Werner et al. for more detailed instruction and advice. When my wife was pregnant with our daughter, we read several books on the subject and found some very interesting statistics. The United States has the highest percentage of hospital births and caesarean sections in the entire world. We also have one of the highest infant mortality rates among the developed countries. Apparently, in most cases, low-risk births happen faster and with fewer complications at home under the care of a qualified doctor, nurse, or midwife, than in the harsh environment of a hospital. Many hospitals have taken this into consideration and now offer "birthing centers" with a more relaxed, homey atmosphere. Whenever possible, enlist the assistance of qualified medical personnel, and have the backup insurance of a medical facility available in case of complications.

Signs of Impending Delivery

- Regular contractions, at intervals of two minutes or less between the start of each contraction.
- Strong urge to have a bowel movement.
- Rupture of the amniotic sac ("breaking of the water") may happen while the mother is attempting to go to the bathroom. Usually the baby comes shortly after the sac ruptures, but sometimes may not come for a few days. In this case, it may be best to have the labor induced in a hospital to avoid infection.
- Strong urge to push. Often the mother yells that the baby is coming.

Stages of Labor

The first stage lasts from the beginning of strong contractions until the baby has dropped into the birth canal (launch position). The mother should drink a lot of fluids and try to keep the bowels evacuated. An enema may be helpful to evacuate the bowels. The mother should wash her buttocks and genital area with soap and water. Birthing supplies should be readied if the birth will be at home. The first stage typically lasts from ten to twenty hours (but it may last several days) for a woman's first birth and five to ten hours for subsequent births.

Caution: Births can happen very quickly, like my daughter's, which took less than two hours from the start of labor.

Make sure you have plenty of clean sheets or other bed coverings (newspaper will do in a pinch) and change them as soon as they get soiled. If the mother has a bowel movement, wipe from front to back. Have a sterile unopened razor blade or a pair of boiled scissors on hand for cutting the cord. The midwife should not massage the belly and the mother should not push during this stage. Deep, slow breathing can help to ease the pain. Walking helps to speed the delivery and labor.

The second stage starts when the baby has dropped into the birth canal and finishes when the baby is born. This stage is often easier than the first stage and is usually finished within a couple of hours. Cleanliness is of the utmost importance. Hands should be washed frequently in sterile water, and surgical gloves should be worn if available. For normal births, the midwife or attendant should never insert hands or fingers into the birth canal, as this is the major cause of severe infections in the mother. The mother should push hard with each contraction until the child's head shows about 3 inches across. At that point the mother should try not to push too hard and should breathe with short fast breaths. This helps to avoid tearing the vaginal opening.

The third stage lasts from the birth until the placenta (afterbirth) has been expelled and bleeding has stopped or reduced to a trickle. This usually happens between five minutes and one hour after the birth.

Warning: If there is severe bleeding or the placenta does not come out, seek medical attention immediately.

Emergency Childbirth Supplies

- Flashlight in case of poor lighting or power outage.
- Plastic sheet, tarp, or large garbage bags to place under the mother on top of the bedding.
- Clean sheets, towels, newspapers, and so on to place under the mother and on top of the plastic sheet. Change as soon as soiled. Have at least three extra, clean, dry towels on hand.
- Sanitary napkins (several).
- A rubber suction bulb for suctioning the newborn's mouth. A turkey baster with a fine tip will do in a pinch.
- Sterile gauze dressings.
- Sterile gloves.
- Sterile razor or scissors for cutting the umbilical cord.
- Two pieces of sterile string, such as shoelace, for tying the umbilical cord. Boil in water for 10 minutes to sterilize. *Do not use thread because it will cut through the cord.*

- Receiving blankets and diapers for the newborn.
- A container for the placenta (afterbirth). A plastic bag will do.

Delivery

Keep everything as clean as possible before, during, and after the delivery. Use no antiseptics. Soap and clean water are best. Remove jewelry and watches and scrub hands, including under the fingernails. Wear sterile gloves, if available. Remind the mother to pant or take long deep breaths, because this helps the baby to emerge slowly, with less chance of tearing the vaginal opening.

1. *Do not* try to delay the birth in any way, such as by crossing the mother's legs or pushing the baby back inside.

2. *Do not* allow the mother to go to the toilet. The sensation of having to have a bowel movement means the baby is coming. Spontaneous bowel movements in the final stages are normal. Wipe the mother front to back (always away from the vagina) and immediately remove soiled cloths.

3. *Do not* pull the baby from the vagina.

4. The baby's head usually emerges first, but not always. If something else appears first—the buttocks (breech birth), a shoulder, or a hand, for example—the chances for birthing complications are significantly increased.

5. *To help reduce tearing*, when the crown of the head shows a few inches, have the mother stop pushing. Panting and deep breathing will help her to overcome the desire to push and gives her skin more time to stretch. The midwife can support the skin between the vagina and the anus with the palm of one hand, while gently pressing on the baby's head with the other hand, to keep the head from emerging too fast and tearing the mother's flesh.

6. Tear any membrane covering the baby's face.

7. If the umbilical cord is wrapped around the baby's neck, hook it with your finger and gently but quickly slip it over the baby's head. If it is too tight to flip over the baby's head, it must be tied and cut or the child will suffocate or bleed to death.

8. Support the baby's head in the palm of your hand. Once the head is free, the rest of the body delivers quickly. Be ready for the baby to be extremely slippery. Suction the mouth and nostrils with the bulb, or clean with a clean, dry cloth. *Caution:* Sometimes the baby will have had a bowel movement in the womb. When the water breaks, this will appear as a dark green, almost black liquid. If the baby breathes this material (meconium) into his or her lungs, the baby may die. If there is evidence of meconium in the mother's amniotic fluid or on the baby's face and mouth, it must be completely suctioned out of the baby's nose and mouth before the baby begins to breathe. Once the baby's head is free, have the mother proceed very slowly to allow time for suctioning. Seek immediate medical attention, if available.

9. If an arm comes out first, the mother may need an operation to birth the baby.

10. If the buttocks come first (breech), the birth may be easier with the mother in a crouching position on all fours. If the head is stuck, try pushing down on the mother's lower abdomen to help push the head out from the inside. Have the mother push hard, *but never pull on the body of the baby.*

After Delivery

1. Hold the baby face down, with the feet higher than the head, to allow fluids to drain. If you have a suction bulb, gently suction the child's mouth and nose. The baby may be blue but should turn pink a few minutes after starting to breathe.

2. *If the baby is not breathing,* tap the bottom of the baby's feet a few times and massage the baby's back with a clean towel. If the baby is not breathing within 1 minute of birth, try a couple of quick rescue breaths, then gently begin mouth-to-mouth resuscitation.

3. When the baby cries or is breathing normally, lay the baby on the mother's breast and encourage the baby to nurse. This will help stimulate the mother's uterine contractions for expelling the placenta. Make sure there is no tension on the umbilical cord.

4. The umbilical cord should not be cut immediately. Immediately after birth, the cord is fat and blue. *Wait* until the cord has stopped pulsing and has become thin and whitish in color, then tie the cord firmly in two places using sterile cord (not thread). Tie one spot in the cord about 4 inches from the baby's end, and the other spot about 8 inches from the same end. Cut the cord in between the ties with a sterile razor blade or sterile scissors, and immediately cover the baby's end of the cord with clean cloth or sterile gauze. To protect the child from infections, the cord should be allowed to dry and should be kept dry.

5. Keep the mother and baby warm. The mother will continue to have contractions to expel the placenta, which should happen between 5 minutes and an hour after birth (but sometimes it takes several hours). If the placenta is slow in coming, feel the womb (uterus) through the mother's belly. If it is soft, firmly massage the womb until it contracts (gets hard) to expel the placenta. Inspect the placenta. If it appears to be missing large chunks, you may be faced with a serious medical emergency due to severe bleeding.

6. Wash the mother and give her plenty of warm fluids.

Staying Healthy in a Crisis or Pandemic

❝A gene that makes bugs highly resistant to almost all known antibiotics has been found in bacteria in water supplies in New Delhi used by local people for drinking, washing and cooking, scientists said on Thursday. The NDM 1 gene, which creates what some experts describe as 'super superbugs,' has spread to germs that cause cholera and dysentery, and is circulating freely in other bacteria in the Indian city capital of 14 million people, the researchers said. 'The inhabitants of New Delhi are continually being exposed to multidrug-resistant and NDM 1-positive bacteria,' said Mark Toleman of Britain's Cardiff University School of Medicine, who published the findings in a study on Thursday. . . .

It first emerged in India three years ago and has now spread across the world. It has been found in a wide variety of bugs, including familiar pathogens like Escherichia coli, or E. coli. . . . 'We would expect that perhaps as many as half a million people are carrying NDM 1-producing bacteria as normal (gut) flora in New Dehli alone,' Toleman said. Experts say the spread of superbugs threatens whole swathes of modern medicine, which cannot be practiced if doctors have no effective antibiotics to ward off infections during surgery, intensive care or cancer treatments like chemotherapy. . . .

'We are at a critical point in time where antibiotic resistance is reaching unprecedented levels,' said Zsuzsanna Jakab, the WHO's regional director for Europe. 'Given the growth of travel and trade in Europe and across the world, people should be aware that until all countries tackle this, no country alone can be safe.'❞ —Kate Kelland, "Scientists Find Superbugs in Delhi Drinking Water," Reuters, April 7, 2011

Fifty years ago, with the discovery of penicillin and other modern antibiotics, followed by the successful eradication of smallpox through a vigorous worldwide program of vaccination, it appeared that devastating plagues were a thing of the past. Recently, however, scientists have sounded ominous warnings that bacteria and viruses appear to be gaining ground on the human medical technologies that we had once thought would soon conquer all diseases. In this modern age of emerging antibiotic-resistant superbugs coupled with worldwide jet travel, the specter of deadly global pandemics has once again raised its ugly head.

This chapter offers practical information about herbs, alternative medicines, and self-treatment devices you may wish to stock in your personal self-healing arsenal. The "Top-Ten List of Healing Remedies" will give you an excellent starting point. The herbs and alternative treatments covered in this chapter could be the key elements that you and your family will need to stay healthy in times of disaster or pandemic, or perhaps they may be useful in helping someone you know to heal from the increasingly common misfortune of infection by antibiotic-resistant bacteria. I am not a doctor, and I am not telling anyone how to cure any illness, but simply sharing information on my own and others' experiences. When you are sick, you should always seek qualified medical attention.

Top-Ten List of Healing Remedies

For inclusion in your pandemic survival kit, here are my top ten recommended items:

1. MMS (miracle mineral solution). I suggest you stock up on a hefty supply of sodium chlorite and citric acid, the two simple raw ingredients (plus water) for making MMS. Make sure you have glass bottles for storing the MMS, and droppers or plastic dropper bottles for dosage and application.

2. A colloidal silver generator for making homemade colloidal silver solutions. It is a good idea to keep a nebulizer on hand for inhaling a colloidal silver mist when dealing with lung infections.

3. Several small squeeze bottles of grapefruit seed extract (available at most health food stores).

4. A blood electrification device for the Beck Protocol. *Note:* The Sota Instruments model "Silver Pulser" does both colloidal silver generation and blood electrification. You may also wish to add a magnetic pulser and a drinking water ozonator so you will be equipped for all four elements of the full Beck Protocol.

5. Elderberry extract (available at most health food stores).

6. Spilanthes-usnea extract (available at most health food stores).

7. A multi-remedy homeopathic medicine kit.

8. One or two gallons of 10 ppm "ASAP" nano-particle silver solution (also sold under the trade name "Silver Biotics"), plus at least two tubes of ASAP gel ointment, made by American Biotech Labs.

9. Several courses of Cipro (or similar) pharmaceutical antibiotics, if you can get a prescription or otherwise have access to antibiotics.

10. At least twenty surgical masks plus a pack of surgical throw-away gloves. The masks will not protect you from infection, but will help one to reduce the risk of spreading infection to others through coughing or sneezing.

Viruses and Bacteria

In general, viruses do not respond to antibiotics, and the few antiviral pharmaceuticals that have been developed may have little or no effect on most new strains of viruses. Many people do not realize that typical antiviral drugs, such as Tamiflu, should be taken within twenty-four hours of the onset of flu symptoms in order to be effective, and show little or no positive effect if taken more than foty-eight hours after symptom onset. It can take decades to develop vaccines for specific viruses. For example, after spending billions of dollars on research, scientists have yet to produce viable vaccines for the viruses responsible for AIDS, Ebola, and hemorrhagic dengue fever. A recently discovered trait shared by most viruses, that has quite frightening implications, is their capacity for "gene swapping"—the ability to share genetic material between different strains, potentially resulting in mutations that combine the deadly properties of one strain with the contagious properties of another.

Experts are gravely concerned that this could happen with the extremely deadly H5N1 strain of avian flu, and it appears that this is what has already happened in the case of the less deadly 2009 Mexican strain of swine flu virus, commonly referred to as the H1N1 swine flu. DNA analysis performed on specimens from Spanish flu victims, taken from 1918 tissue samples that were preserved in wax, indicate that the Spanish flu was originally an avian flu virus that mutated into a swine flu virus before mutating into a human flu virus. According to the CDC, the new strain of swine flu that showed up in Mexico during the spring of 2009 contained gene sequences from North American and Eurasian swine flu, North American bird flu, and North American human flu, and was quite similar to the 1918 Spanish flu, but nowhere near as deadly.

Thus far, we have managed to dodge the bullet both with the avian flu and the H1N1 swine flu. All attempts to contain the H1N1 flu strain via quarantine failed, as it rapidly spread around the world, qualifying as a true "pandemic." However, this strain of flu virus turned out to be only slightly more lethal than even the average winter flu strain, and less contagious, so even though hundreds of thousands of people got sick, no more people died (approximately 0.03 percent fatality rate) than during an average flu season. The concern is that if a super deadly strain of influenza, such as the H5N1 avian flu, were to gene swap with a highly infectious human strain of flu, it could create a new flu strain having the high mortality rate of H5N1 (on the order of 50 percent or more) combined with the highly infectious and easily transmitted traits of more common flu strains. Experts believe it is not a question of "if" this will ever happen, but "when" the Russian roulette game of viral gene swapping comes up with a "winning" combination that wreaks havoc on human society. When that day comes, all hell will break loose!

In addition, a significant and growing threat is cultivated right here in the United States on our modern factory farms. Some bright researchers figured out that farm animals fed subclinical doses of antibiotics grow faster than animals that eat regular feed, get sick less often, and fewer animals are lost to disease. This has been a boon to the pharmaceutical industry (40 percent of U.S.-made antibiotics are fed to animals), but it is also contributing to the end of "the Age of Wonder Drugs." Since bacteria reproduce at 500,000 times the rate of humans, natural genetic selection has made antibiotic-fed farm animals (and our own bodies after we ingest the antibiotics contained within the flesh of these farm animals) into perfect breeding grounds for growing super-microbes that are resistant to modern medicines.

When Jim Hensen, the beloved inventor of *The Muppets*, succumbed to a pneumonia-like infection from an antibiotic-resistant form of strep (group A beta-hemolytic streptococci), the best doctors and antibiotics that money could buy were unable to save his life. In the fall of 2008, Miss Brazil (Mariana Bridi da Costa), who took seventh place in the 2008 Miss World Pageant, was on the top of her world. Raised in abject poverty, she was well on her way to supermodel stardom, and it seemed as if her future was bright and limitless. In late December, she was hospitalized and treated for a urinary infection.

On January 3, 2009, she was transferred to Dorio Silva Hospital in "septic shock," a serious medical condition caused by infection-induced inflammation. The culprit was the bacteria *Pseudomonas aeruginosa*. This variety of bacteria has shown a tendency to rapidly develop drug resistance to new antibiotics, and even though it is now responsible for roughly 10 percent of all hospital-induced infections, there is little known about what causes this disease. In spite of receiving treatment with the most advanced antibiotics, Mariana Bridi's disease spread throughout her body. The spreading infection resulted in necrosis, which is the deadening of tissues caused by septicemia with its resulting lack of blood flow to organs and tissues. In an attempt to save her life, they amputated her hands and feet, then placed her on a respirator, but she died anyway.

As the above-mentioned cases portray, the specter of antibiotic-resistant bacteria is truly frightening, but the good news is that there are many alternative medicines, herbs, and treatments that can be quite effective in the fight against a wide variety of viruses and antibiotic-resistant bacteria, to which mainstream high-tech Western medicine has little or nothing to offer. The bad news is that 99 percent of the doctors in our hospitals are not trained in these alternatives, and don't have a clue about what to do when their pharmaceutical high-tech medicines fail to heal. If you wait until a pandemic starts, you will have at best just a slim chance for locating an available health practitioner familiar with alternative herbs, medicines, and methods. In the words of Robert Saum, PhD, the typical attitude among most of his medical colleagues in this country is, "If I didn't learn it in medical school, it can't be true."

Treating Antibiotic-Resistant Super Bugs

When it comes to antibiotic-resistant bacteria and deadly viruses, so-called alternative medicine, including herbs, homeopathy, and a variety of other treatments, may well be your most effective tools for treatment and prevention. In the summer of 2001, my wife, Josie, suffered from an antibiotic-resistant urinary-tract infection that was probably caused by the same strain of antibiotic-resistant *E. coli* that reportedly plagued women across the country (Torassa 2001). We spent nearly $2,000 on doctors and multiple courses of three different antibiotics, including three full courses of the infamous Cipro, but the infection returned every time we tried to discontinue the Cipro, which was the only antibiotic that had any positive effect.

After nearly two months of unsuccessful medical treatment, Josie was finally able to kick the infection in less than one week's time, once she resorted to self-treatment with a combination of grapefruit seed extract (from the health food store) and large quantities of homemade antibiotic colloidal silver solution (roughly one quart a day).

The Low-Tech Medicine Cabinet: Simple, Effective Remedies and Supplements to Have on Hand

Here are some of the more effective self-help remedies that I recommend you keep on hand. They are readily available in your local supermarket, drugstore, health food stores, or online. See *Prescription for Nutritional Healing,* by James F. Balch, MD, for more complete dose and application information on many of these remedies and supplements. A few of the remedies and procedures mentioned in the following list are, in my opinion, so valuable that I have added full sections with detailed descriptions for those procedures and remedies, immediately following this list.

Caution: For serious conditions, seek out a qualified medical physician, herbalist, and/or naturopathic doctor.

Aloe vera gel. The juice from the aloe vera plant has been scientifically proven to improve the healing of burns. It is also good for healing cuts and scrapes (it is not antibiotic or antiseptic) and as a nutritional supplement. Use the live plant by cutting off a leaf and squeezing the gel from the leaf directly onto the wound. Alternatively, buy the gel or juice at a health food store.

Arnica montana. Arnica is an herbal remedy available in a tincture or extract or in homeopathic preparations. It is a useful remedy for boosting the body's healing response to traumatic injuries, such as sprains, fractures, and bruises.

Astragalus. One of the most highly regarded herbs used in Chinese medicine, astragalus is an efficient immune-system booster. The recommended dosage is 10 drops of the extract taken in water daily (Renders 1999, 203). Taking it during the flu season is recommended, if there is something "going around," or if you are suffering from cancer, AIDS, or other immune-deficiency diseases. Do not take astragalus if you are already suffering from a fever. Many herbal immune-system boosting combinations, available at health food stores, are based on astragalus.

Calendula. Used as a cream, it is an effective salve for skin irritations and rashes, including eczema. This cream can promote the healing of stubborn skin splits and wounds that are not responding to normal treatment. Taken internally (25 to 75 drops, one to four times per day), it supports the immune system and has both antibacterial and antiviral properties.

Colloidal/ionic silver. The medicines that hospitals use to fight skin infections on severe burn patients are all based on the active component of silver. Colloidal/ionic silver is a broadband antibiotic solution that has been used against a myriad of harmful protozoa, bacteria, and viruses, though users indicate that it may require significant quantities (on the order of 2 cups to a quart a day) to successfully treat serious illnesses. It is available in health food stores (expensive!) or can be made for just pennies a day with a simple commercial or homemade colloidal/ionic silver generator. See the "Colloidal and Ionic Silver" section in *When Technology Fails* for more information.

DMSO. DMSO, short for dimethyl sulfoxide, is a nontoxic solvent that can be used promote the rapid absorption and transmission of MMS and other supplements directly through the skin (to fight infections, heal injuries, etc.). It is also very good at providing nearly instant relief from tendon inflammation and joint pain. I have heard that many Tour de France bicycle racers carry a small tube of DMSO inside their tire-repair kits, in case they need a little something extra to help them cope with painful tendons during the extreme physical ordeal of the Tour. It is also commonly used on racehorses to soothe sore legs and tendons. I can think of many instances in a crisis situation where DMSO could provide a valuable boost for your survival. DMSO is available at many health food stores and on the Internet (more on DMSO later in this chapter).

Echinacea. A traditional Native American medicinal herb, echinacea has become a part of mainstream self-help medicine. It is now available at most drugstores, since its antiviral and antibacterial properties have been scientifically documented, though a recent medical study, reported in the *New England Journal of Medicine,* has cast doubts on its efficacy. Take a dropperful of the extract twice daily for short-term use or use as directed in one of the many different commercial healing herb combinations (Renders 1999, 212). Echinacea is often combined with goldenseal for fighting flu. Do not use echinacea for over three weeks at a time, for it has the potential to cause bladder irritation

Elderberry. This herb has excellent antiviral properties, and has been referred to as the "medicine chest" of country people. Laboratory studies on Sambucol, an Israeli-made elderberry extract, have shown the product to be effective against human, swine, and avian flu strains. Unlike Tamiflu, the well-known antiviral pharmaceutical Sambucol and other elderberry extracts have no negative side effects.

Epsom salts. Epsom salts are useful for adding to water for hot-soak infection treatments, and for adding to enema water. A low-cost material, Epsom salts are available at all drugstores and many supermarkets.

Garlic. A true "wonder herb," garlic has powerful antibiotic and antibacterial properties as well as tremendous nutritional antioxidant value. Whereas the number of active ingredients in penicillin is one, at least thirty-five active ingredients have been identified in garlic, making it much more difficult for bacteria to grow resistant to garlic than to penicillin. Crush the whole cloves and use directly on fungal infections and on wounds to prevent infection or gangrene. Taken internally, it has been found effective against various tumors, tuberculosis, cholera, typhus, and amoebic dysentery. It has been used effectively against many different viruses and antibiotic-resistant bacteria as well as intestinal parasites. Use raw, fresh cloves, as powdered garlic loses most of its potency. *Caution:* Cooking destroys most of garlic's potency, but your friends may not stick around after a serious raw garlic treatment!

Goldenseal. Goldenseal is one of the most popular herbs of all time. It has powerful antifungal and antibacterial properties against organisms such as *Candida* and *E. coli.* The powdered root has strong cauterizing properties and can be used directly on wounds to reduce or eliminate excessive bleeding.

Grapefruit seed extract (GSE). Like garlic, GSE is another true "wonder herb," exhibiting powerful antibiotic, antiviral, antifungal, and antibacterial properties. It has been used successfully to battle numerous diseases and ailments, including Lyme disease, *Candida*, *Giardia*, amoebic dysentery, many kinds of parasites, athlete's foot, ringworm, gum disease, herpes, colds, flu, and some forms of arthritis. We have used GSE to successfully fight illnesses that did not respond to colloidal silver. The liquid form is bitter and may be diluted in juice to make it more palatable. The typical treatment is 10 to 15 drops of GSE liquid concentrate diluted in juice, taken three to four times daily (Sachs 1997, 78). Its high antibacterial action combined with low toxicity makes GSE a great alternative to regular antibiotics as a topical treatment for wounds. Mix a half-ounce of GSE with 8 ounces of distilled water and apply to wounds with a spray bottle. Drinking water may be disinfected using 10 drops of GSE concentrate per 6 ounces of water. Allow water to stand for 15 minutes before drinking. For more information on specific treatments and the efficacy of GSE, see *The Authoritative Guide to Grapefruit Seed Extract* by Alan Sachs.

Homeopathic medicine. Homeopathy appears to stimulate the body's own immune system in ways that Western science still doesn't fully understand. For a reasonable price, you can buy homeopathy kits that contain 10 to 30 common remedies for treating a wide variety of ailments. Sometimes homeopathy works wonders when other medicines and remedies fail.

Honey. A natural antiseptic, honey has been used on the battlefield for treating wounds since ancient times and as recently as World War I. Some physicians claim that wounds treated with honey heal faster than those treated with modern antiseptics.

Hyssop. Though little used in the West, hyssop is another powerful herb, exhibiting strong antiviral and antibacterial properties. One of the few herbs that has been proven effective against active tuberculosis, hyssop is often prescribed by Chinese herbalists for lung ailments. In today's world, where there is a constant threat that antibiotic-resistant tuberculosis might blossom into a global pandemic, I suggest keeping a supply of hyssop on hand.

MMS. MMS is short for "miracle mineral solution" (formerly known as "miracle mineral supplement") and is a simple chemical combination that has taken the world by storm. Credited with over a hundred thousand rapid (commonly in just four hours) cures of malaria, returning hundreds of deathly ill African AIDS victims to active healthy lives, and thousands of cures for a multitude of other ailments ranging from chronic fatigue to various cancers, Lyme disease, and hepatitis C, I consider MMS to be a vital part of my personal pandemic survival kit. It also purifies drinking water, which is the only legal application for MMS in the United States. See the "MMS" section later in this chapter for more details.

Neem oil. The National Research Council (NRC), Washington, D.C., considers neem to be "one of the most promising of all plants. . . . [It] may eventually benefit every person on this planet." Like garlic, neem appears to be another "wonder herb" with tremendous antiviral, antifungal, and antibacterial properties. It is used in herbal cosmetics, medicines, shampoos, and for organic pesticides/fungicides.

Oregano oil. Oil of oregano is another broadband super-herb with powerful antioxidant, antiviral, antifungal, antiparasitic, and antibacterial properties. It is traditionally used for treatment of wounds, headaches, sinusitis, lung infections, colds, intestinal worms, athlete's foot, and so on. More recently it has been found to be effective in fighting chronic *Candida* (yeast) infections. It may be taken internally or applied topically. I like to supplement my diet by taking one or two oregano oil capsules each day.

Parasite herbs. Take black walnut tincture, clove capsules, and wormwood capsules to deparasite yourself and your pets. There are a number of herbs commonly known as "wormwood," but studies show that *Artemisia annua* (one of the wormwoods) is also very effective in treating malaria, being 90 percent more effective than chloroquine (Naiman 2008). For more details, see the section on "Dr. Clark's Herbal Parasite Cleanse" in *When Technology Fails*.

Parasite zapper. Build a low-cost electronic "zapper," or buy one from the Dr. Clark Research Association (see appendix 2) or one of several other sources available on the Internet. Searching the Internet for "zapper" combined with "Hulda Clark" will turn up several different suppliers, since Dr. Clark did not patent this technology, but gave it to humankind as a gift.

Caution: If you plan to build your own zapper, check the Internet for a correction to the wiring connections described in Dr. Clark's earlier editions of *The Cure for All Diseases*. This mistake has been corrected in all of her more recent publications.

St. John's wort. Sometimes called "nature's Prozac," St. John's wort is mostly known for its antidepressant and mood-enhancing properties. It is also an immune-system booster with antiviral properties. A typical dose is 10 drops of the liquid extract once daily (Renders 1999, 242). Do not take it if pregnant, because it may cause increased photosensitivity and can cause adverse reactions with some prescription drugs (contact your physician before combining it with pharmaceutical antidepressants or other drugs).

Super-antibacterial/antifungal lotion. I found the following concoction works well against toenail fungus that no longer responds to over-the-counter

TABLE 6.1 Herbal substitutes for common pharmaceuticals

Ailment	Pharmaceutical	Herbal options
Acne	Retin-A, Tetracycline	Tea tree oil (external), calendula
Allergies	Synthetic antihistamines	Garlic, stinging nettle, Ginkgo biloba
Anxiety	Ativan, Xanax, Klonopin	Hops, kava-kava, valerian
Arthritic pain	Tylenol and other NSAIDs*	Cayenne (external), celery seed, ginger, turmeric
Athlete's foot	Griseofulvin	Tea tree oil, garlic, coffee grounds (all external)
Boils	Erythromycin	Tea tree oil, slippery elm (both external)
Body odor	Commercial deodorants	Coriander, sage
BPH (benign prostatic hyperplasia)	Hytrin, Proscar	Saw palmetto, evening primrose, stinging nettle, Pygeum africanum, Serona repens
Bronchitis	Atropine	Echinacea, garlic
Bruises	Analgesics	Arnica, St. John's wort, yarrow, plantain (all external)
Burns	Silvadene cream	Aloe vera gel (external), calendula
Colds	Decongestants	Echinacea, ginger, lemon balm, garlic
Constipation	Laxatives	Flaxseed, psyllium, cascara sagrada
Cuts, scrapes, abscesses	Topical antibiotics	Tea tree oil, calendula, plantain, garlic (all external)
Depression (mild)	Prozac, Elavil, Trazodone, Zoloft	St. John's wort
Diarrhea	Imodium, Lomotil	Bilberry, raspberry
Dysmenorrhea (painful menstruation)	Naprosyn	Kava-kava, raspberry
Earache	Antibiotics	Echinacea, garlic, mullein
Eczema (itchy rash)	Corticosteroids	Chamomile
Atopic eczema (allergy-related rash)	Corticosteroids, sedatives, antihistamines	Evening primrose
Flu	Tylenol	Echinacea, elderberry
Gas	Mylanta, Gaviscon, Simethicone	Dill, fennel, peppermint
Gingivitis (gum inflammation)	Peridex	Chamomile, echinacea, sage
Halitosis (bad breath)	Listerine	Cardamom, parsley, peppermint
Hay fever	Antihistamines, decongestants	Stinging nettle
Headache	Aspirin, other NSAIDs*	Peppermint (external), feverfew, willow bark
Heartburn	Pepto-Bismol, Tums	Angelica, chamomile, peppermint
Hemorrhoids	Tucks	Plantain, witch hazel, calendula (all external)

Hepatitis	Interferon	Dandelion, milk thistle, turmeric
Herpes	Acyclovir	Lemon balm
High cholesterol	Mevacor	Garlic
Hives	Benadryl	Stinging nettle
Indigestion	Antacids, Reglan	Chamomile, ginger, peppermint
Insomnia	Halcion, Ativan	Chamomile, hops, lemon balm, valerian, evening primrose, kava-kava
Irregularity	Metamucil	Flaxseed, plantain, senna psyllium
Lower back pain	Aspirin, analgesics	Cayenne (external), thyme
Male pattern baldness	Rogaine	Saw palmetto
Migraine	Cafergot, Sumatriptan, Verapamil	Feverfew
Motion sickness	Dramamine	Ginger
Nail fungus	Ketoconazole	Tea tree oil, garlic (both external)
Night blindness	Vitamin A	Bilberry
PMS	NSAIDs*, diuretics, analgesics	Chaste tree, evening primrose
Rhinitis (nasal inflamation)	Cromolyn, Vancenase	Echinacea
Shingles	Acyclovir	Cayenne (external), lemon balm
Sprain	NSAIDs*	Arnica, calendula
Stress	Diazepam	Kava-kava, valerian
Tinnitus (ringing ears)	Steroids	Ginkgo
Toothache	NSAIDs*	Cloves, willow bark
Urinary tract infection	Sulfa drugs	Cranberry, stinging nettle
Vaginitis	Clindamycin, Flagyl	Garlic, goldenseal

*NSAIDs are nonsteroidal anti-inflammatory drugs.

(Source: Adapted from "Nature's Medicine—The Green Pharmacy," by James A. Duke, PhD, *Mother Earth News* [December/January 2000], pp. 22–33)

pharmaceutical medications. It is very powerful, very effective, and very malodorous. First, mix equal parts of tea tree oil and neem oil. Next, crush an equal part of fresh garlic cloves and throw into the solution. The tea tree oil keeps the neem oil liquid and preserves the crushed garlic cloves, drawing active components out of the garlic cloves and into the oil.

Tea tree oil. This powerful antifungal and disinfectant is used topically (do not take internally) for skin infections, itchy scalp, and fungal infections such as athlete's foot. This oil is very penetrating and will penetrate through the skin to heal sealed-over infections, boils, and pimples. Tea tree oil is one of the few liquids that can seep through toenails. It may be applied directly to sores in the mouth, lips and nose, though do so sparingly, as some people find it irritating to sensitive tissues. I sometimes combine tea tree oil with other oils and herbs to lend its more penetrating properties to the rest of the concoction.

Traumeel cream. This homeopathic ointment is great for speeding the healing of bruises, muscle aches, and sprains. Rub the ointment into the affected area. Based on *Arnica montana* combined with about a dozen other homeopathic remedies, it also comes in liquid and tablet form.

Usnea. Another powerful tool in your medical survival kit, this extract from a lichen has strong antibiotic, antiviral, and antibacterial properties. Usnea is used both internally and externally. It is often combined with spilanthes or echinacea. Apply the tincture directly to external infections, and/or take 30 to 40 drops of the tincture with water, twice a day.

Vitamin C. Vitamin C is a powerful antioxidant, immune-system booster, natural detoxifier, and necessary body nutrient for tissue health and wound healing. Nobel Prize–winner Linus Pauling suggests daily ingestion of 2 to 9 grams (spread into several doses throughout the day) for cancer prevention and optimum health. A more conservative daily dosage is 500 to 1,000 milligrams (Renders 1999, 197). Powdered Vitamin C is handy for sprinkling in foods and liquids to detoxify mold aflatoxins and many other toxic substances. Sprinkle powdered Vitamin C into purified water to remove the taste of iodine, chlorine, or other water treatment chemicals.

Vitamin E. Vitamin E is a powerful antioxidant useful for maintaining the health of the circulatory system and the skin. The benefits of Vitamin E could fill several pages. I like to break open capsules to spread on healing wounds to help speed the healing process and minimize scar tissue. A dose of 400 IU is good for combating the effects of toxins in everyday foods (Renders 1999, 114).

Miracle Mineral Solution (MMS)

In the world today, the leading killer of mankind is malaria, a disease that is usually overcome by this solution [MMS] in only 4 hours. This has been proven through clinical trials in Malawi, a country in eastern Africa. In these trials, MMS has never failed to kill the malaria parasite in an infected human. More than 75,000 malaria victims have taken the Miracle Mineral Solution and are now back to work and living productive lives.

After taking the Miracle Mineral Solution, AIDS patients are often disease free in several weeks, and other diseases and conditions simply disappear. If patients in hospitals around the world were treated with this Miracle Mineral Solution, over 50% of them would be back home within a week.

For more than 100 years, clinics and hospitals have used the active ingredients in this solution to sterilize hospital floors, tables, equipment and other items. Now, this same powerful germ killer can be harnessed by the immune system to safely kill pathogens in the human body. Amazing as it may seem, when used correctly, the immune system can use this killer to attack only those germs, bacteria, and viruses that are harmful to the body. It does not affect the friendly bacteria in the body or any healthy cells.

. . . Well, you might ask; that may be OK for the people in Africa, but what will it do for me here in America? Well, it overcomes colds in an hour or so, overcomes flu in less than 12 hours, overcomes pneumonia in less than 12 hours, cures more cancer than any other treatment by hundreds of times, cures hepatitis A, B, and C. It cures appendicitis, rheumatoid arthritis, and a hundred other diseases.**"** —Jim Humble, from *The Miracle Mineral Solution of the 21st Century*

If you listen to the proponents of Miracle Mineral Solution (MMS), it would appear that this combination of two simple and inexpensive chemicals is as close to a "cure all" remedy as one might imagine. I don't claim to have personally witnessed any miraculous cures with MMS. Both topical and oral doses of MMS failed to heal a stubborn toenail fungus that was not touched by more than a dozen pharmaceutical remedies that I had tried over the years, and which has been kept under control through the use of several strong herbal remedies. However, I have spoken with others who have healed serious conditions, including crippling arthritis, using MMS where pharmaceuticals have failed to heal.

Caution: If you choose to self-medicate with MMS, you are essentially experimenting on yourself. There are no guarantees, and there are no recognized medical studies in the United States to prove its efficacy for healing any disease whatsoever!

The following is a brief summary of information about MMS—what it is and how to use it.

How to Make MMS

The current "best practice" for making MMS is to make a 28 percent solution of water and sodium chlorite (this is the MMS itself) to be activated just prior to usage by mixing with an activator solution composed of 50 percent citric acid and 50 percent water. These two solutions are mixed together, drop for drop, in a one-to-one ratio, in specific concentrations to make an activated solution of MMS that may be used for either water purification or for various healing protocols. When MMS and its activator solution are mixed together, chlorine dioxide, a powerful oxidizing agent, is released into the solution, and it is the chlorine dioxide that is responsible for both the water-purifying properties of MMS as well as its reputed healing properties.

Some instructions involve making a 10 percent citric-acid solution, or using fresh lemon or lime juice, as an activator, but these concentrations of activator required using 5 drops of activator for every 1 drop of MMS, which can be quite tedious and time consuming when counting out 100 drops of activator for a 20-drop MMS solution. If none of the above activators are available, vinegar may also be used as an activator, with 5 drops of vinegar for every 1 drop of MMS, but the results are less consistent than with either lemon juice or citric-acid solutions.

Note: If this all seems too complicated, you may simply buy your MMS from Internet sources preformulated in two plastic bottles (MMS and activator) with dropper caps for easy application.

When the 50 percent citric-acid activator is used, the 1:1 mixture must stand for at least thirty seconds after mixing to allow for complete activation/reaction before dilution with water for use in one of the various protocols. When the 10 percent citric-acid activator, lemon juice, lime juice, or vinegar is used, the 1:5 activated mixture must stand for at least three minutes after mixing to allow for complete activation reaction prior to dilution with water for use in one of the various protocols. The weaker 10 percent activator solutions take longer to fully react with the sodium chlorite MMS solution than the stronger 50 percent solution. After activation, the longer the mixture sits before it is diluted with pure water, per one of the following protocols, the more chlorine dioxide gas will be generated and bleed off into the surrounding air, rendering the solution less potent when it is mixed with water, so it is best to dilute the activated MMS concentrated solution with water per one of the protocols as soon as the required waiting period (thirty seconds or three minutes, depending on the activator strength) has elapsed.

Caution: Prior to consumption or application to the skin, all activated MMS solutions should be diluted with water according to one of the various MMS protocols.

To prepare one 4-ounce bottle of 28 percent MMS solution (water purification drops):

Step 1: In a small glass or ceramic bowl, add 3 ounces of warm (approximately 150°F) pure water. Either use distilled water or water purified by reverse osmosis filtration (R/O).

Step 2: Slowly stir in 4 level teaspoons of pure sodium chlorite flakes. Stir with a non-metallic spoon to help dissolve the sodium chlorite flakes, then cover to eliminate light (especially direct sunlight), which causes an adverse reaction in the sodium chlorite.

Step 3: Let the solution sit for three hours or more. This will be a saturated solution, so expect some undissolved particles to settle to the bottom of the bowl.

Step 4: Pour liquid from bowl into a clean glass bottle (preferred) or plastic (PET-1-type plastic) bottle, and discard undissolved crystals. Label the bottle with "MMS." A dark brown- or green-colored bottle is preferred, so as to protect the MMS concentrate from the degrading effects of light.

Caution: Do not store MMS concentrate in bottles with a rubber dropper cap, since chlorine dioxide gas exuded by the solution will cause the rubber dropper to expand and to burst over time.

To prepare one 4-ounce bottle of 50 percent citric-acid activator solution:

Step 1: In a small glass or ceramic bowl, add 2 ounces (¼ cup) of warm (approximately 150°F) pure water. Either use distilled water or water purified by reverse osmosis filtration (R/O).

Step 2: Slowly stir in 2 ounces (¼ cup) of powdered citric acid (purchase online or from a pharmacy). Stir with a non-metallic spoon to help dissolve the citric acid.

Step 3: Pour liquid from bowl into a clean glass bottle (preferred) or plastic (PET-1-type plastic) bottle. If necessary, add water to equal a total of 4 ounces of liquid (½ cup). Label the bottle with "50 percent citric acid."

Standard Protocol 1000

Protocol 1000 is basically taking 3 drops of activated MMS each hour, diluted in water or juice, for eight hours a day, over a period of three weeks. Many people find it easiest to mix up an entire day's supply of diluted MMS once in the morning (typically in either a 1-liter or 1-quart glass jar), and drink it in small doses spaced throughout the day. You may stop the protocol sooner if dealing with minor issues that clear up quickly, or serious diseases like malaria that respond rapidly to treatment with MMS. As the MMS starts to kill pathogens in the body, it releases toxins into your bloodstream that your body will try to purge if the toxic level gets too high, so you may feel nausea or diarrhea (this is called a "Herxheimer reaction"). If one is feeling very sick, then start with 1 drop an hour or even ½ drop and hour, but then begin taking more if you feel that you can. The rule is, if the drops seem to be making you feel worse (nausea, diarrhea, etc.), take a smaller dose, and if they are not making you feel worse then take a little bit more the next hour, but never more than 3 drops an hour.

No one person reacts exactly the same as another. For example, a friend of mine got to 3 drops in a single dose, taken once a day, when he was struck with a severe case of diarrhea and quit taking MMS altogether. Much better to go slow and stick with the program, than to go fast and quit! In general, slow and safe is the prudent way to go, but the decision about how fast to proceed is purely a personal one.

In my own case, I quickly grew impatient with the slow progress of increasing my dose by a single drop once a week, so after a couple of days I opted for increasing the dose by a drop with each new dose. I never did experience nausea or diarrhea, but must admit that when I exceeded about 10 drops of MMS in a single dose diluted in a half glass of water, the taste was pretty bad (I can usually handle drinking herbal concoctions that many others might not tolerate), so I did opt for adding juice to my activated MMS mixture, which made it a much more palatable and pleasant experience.

The way you accomplish the Protocol 1000 activation can be done in four different ways, any one of which is acceptable. First, add your number of MMS drops to a clean dry glass, then activate as follows:

1. Add 1 drop of 50 percent citric acid for each drop of MMS that is in your glass, swirl or shake to mix, wait twenty seconds, then add a half to a full glass of water or juice, then drink. This is the preferred method.

2. Add 5 drops of 10 percent citric acid for each drop of MMS in the glass, and then shake or swirl to mix, wait three minutes, add a half to a full glass of water or juice and then drink.

3. Add 5 drops of full-strength lemon or lime juice for each drop of MMS in the glass, shake or swirl to mix, wait three minutes, add a half to a full glass of water or juice and then drink.

4. Add 5 drops of vinegar for each drop of MMS in the glass, shake or swirl to mix, wait 3 minutes, add a half to a full glass of water or juice and then drink (the vinegar activator is the least consistent and therefore the least preferred method).

Note: Vitamin C (ascorbic acid) is an "antidote" for MMS, and will neutralize the effects of MMS, so do not add MMS to orange juice, or any other juice with added vitamin C/ascorbic acid. Apple, carrot, prune, and pineapple juice work well (preferably fresh), but ensure that no added vitamin C is in their ingredients.

Important instructions: You must not make yourself sicker than you already are. Do not cause yourself a lot of nausea, or pain, or diarrhea. When you notice any of these symptoms coming on take less MMS. Try not to stop taking MMS, just take less. Go from 2 drops an hour of activated MMS to 1 drop an hour. If you are already taking only 1 drop an hour, then take

½ drop and hour, or even ¼ drop an hour. Do not cause yourself diarrhea if you can avoid it by taking less MMS. Pain, diarrhea, nausea, and other discomforts tend to slow healing and recovery. On the other hand, if you are not having adverse reactions to the MMS, try to increase the amount of drops you are taking until you are taking 3 drops an hour, but do not go over 3 drops an hour, unless you have a life-threatening illness, in which case you should use the Protocol 2000.

Note: For information on the MMS Protocol 2000, and in-depth information on all other facets of MMS, I strongly suggest you visit Jim Humble's Web sites at www.jimhumble.biz or www.miraclemineral.org, where you may also download his E-book, *The Miracle Mineral Solution of the 21ˢᵗ Century.*

MMS Comments, Notes, and Precautions

In general, MMS is more effective when taken in smaller doses every hour or two, rather than in large doses taken once or twice a day. Exceptions to this rule are when dealing with parasites, such as worms or malaria, or battling a poisonous bite or food poisoning, in which case large doses, such as 15 drops at a time, tend to be more effective. Here are several precautions and considerations pertaining to the use of MMS:

- Store MMS in a secure place away from children.
- Do not allow children to use MMS unsupervised.
- For children, it is recommended to start slow and work up to a maximum of 1 drop of MMS per hour for every 25 pounds of body weight, applied at these concentrations according to the rest of the Protocol 1000.
- *Do not ingest MMS full strength!* Dilute as suggested in the protocol.
- Use only glass or plastic containers. If using plastic, the preferred plastic is PET (recycling symbol "1"). *Do not use or store MMS in metal containers!*
- It is recommended that you do not take MMS one hour before or after eating and/or taking supplements. The desire is for the MMS to oxidize the pathogens and toxins in your body, not your food and supplements. Do not take vitamin C, or foods/drinks containing significant vitamin C, within two hours before or after taking MMS.

Antidote: If you experience an unacceptable reaction to MMS, such as nausea or diarrhea, a reliable antidote is to drink 1,000 or 2,000 milligrams of powdered or crushed vitamin C dissolved in a glass of water. Another MMS neutralizer is bicarbonate of soda. Take a level teaspoon of bicarbonate of soda, or an Alka-Seltzer tablet, in a glass of water. *Do not take the vitamin C antidote along with the bicarbonate of soda antidote—use one or the other!*

Colloidal and Ionic Silver

❝The heightened alarm comes in response to a federal report indicating that the bacteria Methicillin-resistant Staphylococcus aureus, or MRSA, are responsible for more deaths in the United States each year than AIDS.❞ —Ian Urbina, *New York Times*, October 19, 2007

Imagine a powerful antibiotic agent that attacks more than 600 harmful bacteria, protozoa, molds, yeasts, and viruses that you can make yourself any time and any place for just pennies a day. This is what proponents of colloidal and ionic silver claim it to be. They tout it as a solution to antibiotic-resistant bacteria, such as MRSA, and possibly devastating future plagues. Colloids are solutions of particles that are so tiny that they remain suspended in a liquid without settling to the bottom of their container, and colloidal silver is a solution of water with tiny suspended particles of silver. Ionic silver is a solution with extremely tiny electrically charged particles of silver that are on the order of the size of individual molecules. According to some proponents of ionic silver, it is the charged particles of silver that are primarily responsible for the healing and antibiotic properties in both of these related solutions. Since colloidal silver is the more common term, rather than saying colloidal/ionic silver, I will simply refer to these solutions as "colloidal silver."

Caution: There is a rare medical condition, known as argyria, which is caused by the ingestion of large amounts of silver, typically in the form of the silver salts and nitrates that were common in patent medicines of the 1800s and early 1900s. Argyria is a cosmetic condition that is physically harmless, but results in an undesirable bluish tint in some parts of the body. The recent news headlines about a "blue man" suffering from argyria makes it clear that it is possible to overdo it with colloidal silver. Apparently, this man had been suffering from a bad case of dermatitis, and had treated it for over a decade both by drinking large amounts of colloidal silver daily, supposedly a quart or more per day, and also rubbing colloidal silver on his skin every day (Fox News 2007). Proponents of ionic silver state that the particles of silver in this type of solution are so small, and the actual amount of silver in these solutions is so tiny, that the chance of getting argyria from the consumption of ionic silver is practically nonexistent. From 1900 to 1950, when most cases of argyria were reported, silver-based medicines typically contained large concentrations of silver nitrates or silver chlorides and were not based on colloidal or ionic silvers, which are typically effective using far smaller net amounts of silver. At any rate, I suggest that you proceed cautiously when ingesting significant quantities of colloidal or ionic silver on a regular basis.

Making Your Own Colloidal Silver Generator

In the early 1900s, colloidal silver was very expensive, but in recent years a physicist (Bob Beck) came up with a simple method for making it. A modern colloidal silver generator is about as complex as a flashlight. Making colloidal silver simply involves placing a DC voltage across two chunks of pure silver (a cathode and an anode) immersed in pure water. Supposedly, 33 volts is the optimum voltage, but 27 volts from three 9-volt batteries works fine. If these are not available, you could get by with two 12-volt solar panels wired in series for a total output of 24 volts. This setup would generate colloidal silver at a slower rate.

See figure 6-1 for a sketch of how to hook up your own colloidal silver generator. Connect three 9-volt transistor-radio batteries in series (+ terminal to – terminal to + terminal, etc.) using readily available 9-volt battery clip-on terminals. Wire a 24-volt lightbulb in series with the batteries, then connect it to a mini-jack for easy use. The lightbulb performs two functions. First, it is your battery indicator, which should shine brightly when you touch the two alligator clips or silver wires to each other (if it does not light at all, or very dimly, when you touch the clips to each other, then you should replace

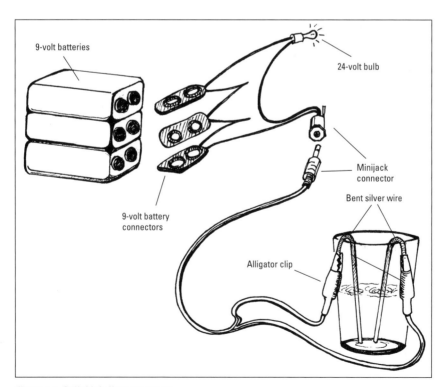

Figure 6-1. Colloidal silver generator

your batteries). Second, it provides a load to the batteries, so you don't drain them dead after a minute or two if the silver wires are accidentally touching while making the solution. Connect one wire from your battery pack and one from the light bulb to a mini-jack socket. Tape your battery pack together and mount your lamp, battery pack, and mini-jack socket into an appropriate box. Split the wires from the mini-jack plug and connect them to two alligator clips. Cut two 6-inch lengths of 99.99 percent pure silver wire (14 or 16 gauge works well) and bend the ends into ½-inch hooks for hanging over the edge of a glass. Purchase the electrical materials at Radio Shack, Walmart, Intertan, and so on. Silver wire of 99.9 percent purity is available from jewelry supply stores and some craft stores, or you may purchase the pure silver wire, silver generator kits, and complete silver generators from Sota Instruments at www.sota.com.

Using Your Colloidal Silver Generator

- Most people stress the use of distilled water, though some people say that reverse-osmosis-filtered water will do, provided that the source water is low in total dissolved solids. Pour distilled water into a glass (avoid plastic, since colloidal silver has a tendency to bind to some plastics).

- Regardless of what you may have heard previously, *do not add salt to your solution.* Salt will combine with some of the silver ions to make silver chloride, which is less effective against bacteria (purportedly hundreds of times less effective than ionic silver), is mildly toxic (silver chloride is 300 times less toxic than silver nitrate, which is a powerful antiseptic used in eyedrops for infants), and puts added silver into your system that has inferior healing properties.

- Hang the two pure silver wires over the edge of your glass into the water, and clip the two alligator clips to the outside ends of the wires (see fig. 6-1). Plug the mini-jack connector into your box. The lightbulb should be dark or glowing very faintly. If glowing brightly, either the wires are touching or the water contains significant impurities and should not be used. Separate the wires in the solution by 1 to 2 inches.

- If the generator is working properly, after about ten to twenty minutes there should be tiny bubbles forming on one or both of the wires. If these are not visible, touch the wires together to check the battery and/or connection (the bulb should shine brightly). Ionic silver solutions should be clear or have a gold tint to them. The particles of ionic silver are too small to be seen except with an electron microscope. Colloidal silver is made from silver particles that are microscopic in size, look like wisps of smoke emanating from one of the silver electrodes, and will usually have a gray or silver tint to the solution. Sota Instruments states that tests on solutions made using distilled water and their current-limiting "Silver Pulser" ionic silver generator indicate that this setup will make one cup of roughly 5 ppm ionic silver per hour of usage (i.e., four hours for 4 cups of 5 ppm ionic silver at room temperature, starting with distilled water). In his article, "Colloidal Silver: A Closer Look," Peter Lindemann says that the homemade colloidal silver generator of figure 6-1 should make 8 ounces of a 3–5 ppm colloidal silver solution in about twenty to twenty-five minutes at room temperature (Lindemann 2006).

- Dosage is a matter of personal preference and experience. As a preventative, some people suggest drinking a tablespoon or two daily. For serious illnesses, some people suggest drinking daily one to four 8-ounce glasses of 5 ppm solution. According to calculations based on an equation at silver-facts.com, the safe daily lifetime dosage for a 150-pound man is roughly ½ cup per day of 5 ppm colloidal silver (silverfacts.com 2007). After each use, clean the silver wires with a harsh plastic pot scrubber.

- For external use, silver solution may be applied to Band-Aids and compresses or sprayed onto burns and affected skin areas. A handy silver salve kit for making a useful antiseptic/antifungal balm from colloidal silver is available at www.elixa.com/silver/ointment.

- Best-quality 9-volt batteries will last a very long time. It is preferable not to use rechargeable batteries as they usually only produce approximately 7.6 volts. An alternative to using three or four 9-volt batteries is to purchase a 30-volt converter that can be plugged into a wall outlet.

- Silver colloidal solutions are light sensitive. Store them in brown glass bottles (beer, wine, root beer, or prune-juice bottles) out of the sun and fluorescent light, or in a dark cabinet. Do not store in the refrigerator or near microwave or magnetic fields. Do not store in plastic or metal containers. Wash and rinse bottles thoroughly, with a final rinse using colloidal silver solution. If capping a bottle with plastic or metal, be sure the cap does not touch the colloidal silver solution. If the solution is put into an eyedropper bottle, the dropper stem should be glass.

Solutions of Metallic Silver Nano-Particles

American Biotech Labs (ABL) has developed a patented process for multivalent nano-particle metallic-silver solutions that have gone through extensive independent laboratory testing showing they are extremely effective, safe, and very stable for long-term storage. On a molecular level, the ABL products are significantly different from the rest of the pack of common colloidal silvers, and they are backed by scientific studies and medical trials, validating their products' effectiveness against a variety of viruses. The effectiveness of homemade and commercial colloidal silvers against a wide variety of bacteria has been well documented, but I have yet to see a reputable study showing their effectiveness against viruses. However, on more than one occasion I have successfully used ABL's ASAP gel to quell a budding cold sore, and none of the other dozen or so remedies I had previously tried were able to accomplish this task. For me, this accomplishment verified the effectiveness of ABL's nano-particle silver products at deactivating at least some types of viruses.

ABL's silver products are being used successfully in African clinics to rapidly and cost effectively heal malaria (even drug-resistant varieties), and have been shown in clinical studies to be quite effective against most known pathogenic bacteria and viruses, including HIV and avian influenza. Testing at the National Institutes of Health (NIH) laboratory at the Utah State University has determined the proper prophylactic use of ABL's ASAP silver solutions necessary to improve live animal survival rates by 100 percent, when these animals were injected with lethal doses, directly into the lungs, of the most powerful and lethal avian flu virus strain known to man (70 percent mortality rate). NIH tests determined that two teaspoons taken orally, administered twice a day, should do the trick, but ABL's Keith Moeller says he personally drinks more like 2 tablespoons two to three times a day to play it safe, and that he and his family never get any of the flus that are going around when they maintain this regimen.

According to ABL's Dr. Gordon Pedersen, when one is suffering from an illness, the recommended procedure is to immediately ingest 4 ounces of their 10 ppm silver ASAP solutions, then follow this with 2 tablespoons four or five times daily until well. In addition, for surface wounds or infection, Dr. Pederson recommends applying their ASAP silver gel several times a day, and for lung ailments recommends inhaling 10 ppm silver solutions for a minimum of thirty minutes per day via the use of a nebulizer. A number of doctors have reported great success healing MRSA infections by combining oral doses of ASAP solution with topical application of ASAP gel applied several times a day to infected areas.

In my personal experience, large quantities of homemade colloidal silver may be more effective in some cases than small quantities of ASAP solution. However, since ASAP is generally effective at far smaller doses than homemade colloidal silver, the long-term daily ingestion of ABL silver solutions at their recommended dosages should present no risk for developing the rare cosmetic condition of argyria. For this reason, if I were suffering from a significant medical condition caused by bacterial, viral, or fungal infection, I would seriously consider the use of an ABL product. For further information check out ABL's Web site at www.americanbiotechlabs.com.

The Beck Protocol

Bob Beck, DSc, an inventor and physicist, invented the modern Xenon electronic flash bulb when he was just a teenager. When Beck was in his mid fifties and his health was failing, his doctors told Beck that a sedentary lifestyle, poor diet, and old age had simply caught up with him and there was very little he could do about it. Scouring through hundreds of medical journals and books, Beck uncovered groundbreaking medical research outlining procedures that had proven quite effective in clinical studies, yet had never seen commercial realization. Beck used his creative genius to develop a set of simple electronic devices and procedures that enable people to apply these medical innovations simply and cost effectively in the comfort of their own home. His combination of devices and procedures are now known as "The Beck Protocol," which Beck refused to patent, but gifted to the world. Many people who had been seriously ill with a multitude of chronic and deadly diseases, ranging from AIDS/HIV to hepatitis C, fibromyalgia, and stage 5 cancers, have offered glowing testimonials to the effectiveness of this relatively simple protocol.

The Beck Protocol consists of the following four self-administered treatments:

1. **Blood electrification**: Based upon groundbreaking research at the Albert Einstein College of Medicine (disclosed in patent 5188738) showing that pulsed microcurrents of electricity would affect bloodborne viruses and bacteria in ways that prevented these organisms from being able to multiply and grow, Beck developed an innovative, low-cost device that accomplished the same process simply and easily by passing microelectric currents through the blood inside the user's wrist veins where they pass close to the skin's surface, via electrodes that are wetted with a salt solution as they are held snugly in place by an elastic wristband.

2. **Ionic colloidal silver**: After reading about the groundbreaking research from orthopedic surgeon Dr. Robert Becker, in which he discovered that tiny charged particles of silver killed all known pathogenic bacteria while boosting the body's bio-electric healing mechanisms, Beck invented the simple modern colloidal silver generator that makes ionic colloidal silver using 9-volt batteries, distilled water, and pure silver wire.

3. **Magnetic pulsing**: After working with his blood-electrification invention, Bob Beck realized that there were organs of the body that did not receive a high flow of blood, and that these organs could benefit if they were directly stimulated with microelectric currents. He invented an electromagnetic pulse-generating device that stimulates microelectric currents directly inside organs and glands located within the body via the mechanism of electromagnetic induction.

4. **Ozonated water:** Beck found that many people, himself included, experienced fatigue and other flu-like symptoms after they started drinking colloidal silver and doing the blood electrification. It was proposed that this was caused by toxins released when the body's foreign organisms were killed. Beck found that drinking highly ozonated water, made by bubbling ozone through drinking water, helped the body eliminate these toxins and avoid the flu-like symptoms.

For more information on the Beck Protocol, see *When Technology Fails* or visit www.bobbeck.com. You may purchase all of the experimental Beck Protocol instruments and supplies at Sota Instruments (www.sota.com).

Hypnosis for Pain Control and Healing

Hypnosis can be a valuable tool for pain control and relief from allergies, stomach problems, skin problems, migraines, in addition to facilitating the rapid healing of a wide variety of other conditions. In the 1860s, the British surgeon James Esdaile reported that he had performed hundreds of successful, pain-free surgeries using hypnosis for anesthesia. The journalist F. W. Sims once watched Esdaile amputate the leg of a woman using no anesthesia. Amazed by how little the wound bled and how still the conscious woman lay, Sims wrote, "During the whole operation, not the least movement or change in her limbs, body, or countenance took place: she continued in the same apparently easy repose as at first, and I have no reason to believe she was not perfectly at ease."

When my wife took her professional hypnotherapist training, one of the other students in her class related this remarkable story: Patty and her husband, Joe, were cutting firewood in a remote location. Joe's chain saw slipped and cut deeply into his thigh, severing a major artery. Blood was spurting everywhere, and they were many miles from any medical services. Maintaining a cool head, Patty decided to try a hypnosis technique that she had heard about. Speaking in a soft monotone, she quickly induced a light trance in Joe, then gave him the hypnotic suggestion that the severed arteries in his leg were squeezing shut and that the blood flow was turned off, like the flow of water from a faucet. Amazingly, the leg stopped bleeding! They were able to walk to their truck and drive for half an hour until they reached the hospital. When they arrived at the hospital, the surgeon expressed concern that the wound had not bled enough to cleanse the chainsaw gash and therefore left a significant chance for severe infection. At his recommendation, Patti removed the hypnotic suggestion to allow the wound to bleed. Immediately, the wound began spurting startling amounts of blood. The surgeon said that he had never seen anything like that in all his years of medicine. Normally, without a tourniquet, this kind of severe bleeding would have cost the life of her husband before they could have reached the hospital. The other amazing thing about this story is that Patty had no prior training in hypnotic techniques at the time of the accident.

In a disaster situation, where access to anesthesia and high-tech medical facilities may be severely limited or nonexistent, hypnosis could be an invaluable tool for pain control and to boost both the speed of healing and the success rate for a wide variety of physical conditions. Detailed instructions on hypnotic methods are beyond the scope of this text, but if this topic interests you, I suggest you pick up a copy or *When Technology Fails* and read the practical "how-to" instructions for hypnotic inductions and basic techniques. The same chapter of *When Technology Fails* that contains information on hypnotic inductions and methods also provides considerably more information on herbal treatments, and other alternative healing modalities, than I am able to cover in this chapter of *When Disaster Strikes*.

I am not a doctor, and I am not suggesting you turn your back on regular medical diagnosis and treatments. A wise course of action is to become familiar with several of the alternative therapies and herbs that have proven themselves by helping thousands of people to heal, many times only after high-tech Western pharmaceutical-based medicine had failed them. Since my primary concern is with getting and staying healthy, and not with performing scientific studies on myself or my loved ones, I tend to go for the "shotgun" approach (combining multiple alternatives). However, when combining therapies, use caution, since some herbs may have harmful interactions with certain pharmaceutical drugs, and other treatments, such as MMS, may oxidize and destroy other remedies, such as colloidal silvers, if consumed at the same time.

I suggest you have a variety of these recommended materials on hand, including pharmaceutical antibiotics (if you have a source for them), in the event that Western pharmaceutical medicines are not readily available, or are simply not working.

7

Emergency Survival

££It's easy to imagine that wilderness survival would involve equipment, training, and experience. It turns out that, at the moment of truth, those might be good things to have but they aren't decisive. Those of us who go into the wilderness or seek our thrills in contact with the forces of nature soon learn, in fact, that experience, training, and modern equipment can betray you. The maddening thing for someone with a Western scientific turn of mind is that it's not what's in your pack that separates the quick from the dead. It's not even what's in your mind. Corny as it sounds, it's what's in your heart.JJ —Laurence Gonzales, from *Deep Survival: Who Lives, Who Dies, and Why*

We all hope that the world will keep on working well, disaster will never strike our town, clean water will always flow out of our tap, the lights and heat will always come on at the flip of a switch, and that we will always be able to buy all the food and gas we need whenever we so desire. Most of us will probably never face a crisis without a home, or at least some kind of roof over our heads. However, real life rarely replicates a TV sitcom, is usually somewhat unpredictable, is often downright messy, and can be ruthlessly unforgiving. This chapter provides a condensed survival manual to help people cope with those times when life gets truly messy and you suddenly find yourself without access to goods, central services, and perhaps even shelter. Topics covered include basic survival strategies and using your intuition; assembling a survival kit; developing a survivor's personality; locating and purifying water in a survival situation; starting a fire; foraging for edible plants, bugs, and other critters; hunting, trapping and fishing; building a shelter; and making snowshoes, rope, and simple tools.

Your personal survival in harsh physical conditions and other emergency situations involves more than simply applying the right techniques. A synergistic combination of skill, intuition, action, wisdom, good judgment, training, preparation, and the most important factor of all—the determination to survive—will give you the best chance for success. It pays to be both mentally and physically prepared for survival. The mentally prepared person has a "can do" attitude, sees problems as obstacles to surmount, and has learned basic skills for dealing with survival situations. The common personality traits of survivors are just as useful for adapting and thriving under the changing conditions of modern society as they are for dealing with emergencies. Physically prepared people tend to have supplies on hand to deal with emergencies and respect their bodies enough to maintain some kind of physical conditioning, so their bodies can perform when needed.

Being prepared is about being mentally and physically prepared to cope with things that you hope and pray will never happen. With luck, you will never need any of the information in this chapter, but just in case, here it is.

Survival Strategies

Twenty years ago, I nearly made a tragic mistake while trekking solo through the High Sierra Mountains during a severe snowstorm. I started this trip dressed in a wool sweater and a pair of pile pants. Heavy snow and high winds settled in about a half hour after leaving the trailhead. I was moving quickly, and my body temperature stayed pretty warm for most of the next hour. Initially, I delayed putting on additional clothing because I wanted to avoid overheating and consequently drenching my clothes with sweat. As I got wetter and colder, I delayed because I knew that as soon as I stopped moving and took my pack off my sweaty back, the icy winds would make me feel miserably cold. I was hoping for a break in the winds, but they only grew stronger. When I finally stopped to put my gloves and coat on, I realized that I had a serious problem. Even though my body core felt just a little cool, I was shocked to find that my hands had chilled to the point where they were numb and nearly useless. They felt like lumps of clay. The winds had picked up to about 60 miles per hour, blasting snow onto my hands and face. I realized that it was absolutely critical that I get myself into protective clothing, but my fingers were unable to work the zippers, straps, and buckles on my pack. After fifteen minutes, using my teeth and near useless hands, I managed to open my pack and remove my mittens and coat. During this time, I started to shiver violently, but I knew that if I gave up, I would lose my fingers to frostbite and might perish in the snow. I managed to slip my coat on, but it took another ten minutes of warming my hands in my armpits before I could work my mittens over my fingers. I am an experienced mountaineer. It was very sobering to see how close I had come to disaster through procrastination and ignoring a few simple signs!

That day, I committed two common blunders that nearly led to my demise. First, *I failed to react quickly to rapidly changing conditions*, and second, *I failed to conserve my resources*. In emergencies, it is often vitally important to *conserve what you have*. In this case, I failed to conserve body heat. In spite of the wind and snow, I was moving rapidly and felt that I was generating enough body heat from exercise, but I was wrong. Many people facing emergencies squander their resources in the first few hours. Expecting a speedy rescue, they thoughtlessly consume their available food and water supplies before the reality of their situation sets in. Wasted resources can also include fuel, physical energy, health, and dry clothing. It is usually easier to conserve the resources at your immediate disposal than to find new ones.

The original twenty-eight survivors of the 1972 airplane crash in the Andes Mountains (made famous by the book and the movie *Alive*) also squandered their resources in the first few critical days of their epic struggle to survive. Expecting a speedy rescue, they freely ate and drank from the plane's supplies. Up until the third night, they failed to conserve precious heat and energy, allowing the icy winds to blow unchecked through the plane wreck. It was several days before they decided to ration food and water. Their food ran out on the tenth day, and after that some starved, while the rest sooner or later resorted to cannibalism. Finally, realizing that no one was going to find them, two of the survivors spent eight days climbing and hiking out of the mountains to a remote ranch, where they were fed and the authorities were notified about the crash site, where a number of survivors were still hanging on to life sheltered by the wreckage of the plane. Of the original twenty-eight survivors, only sixteen made it out alive.

Rex Lucas, in *Men in Crisis: A Study of a Mine Disaster*, relates similar wasteful actions in the first two days of a mining disaster. Trapped 12,000 feet underground in a major mine collapse and expecting a speedy rescue, the survivors freely drank from their canteens and wasted valuable physical reserves trying to dig themselves out. On the third day, once they realized that rescue might take many days, they began conservation efforts that allowed them to survive for several more days until they were rescued.

Basic Strategies

First Things First

Quickly scan the situation. If you are in immediate bodily danger, you must deal with this first, and you might have to act with lightning speed. But, if you have the time, don't rush into a decision. In *Survive the Savage Sea*, Dougal Robertson credits his wife's quick thinking with saving his family's life. After whales rammed a large hole in their sailboat, Dougal wasted precious time examining the hole in their hull, but his wife used their remaining three minutes to gather the necessary survival gear into their life raft. Expect that there is some positive action that you can do, and be willing to consider *any* possible action or reaction that might promote your survival.

Don't Panic

In an emergency situation, try to remain calm, but do not become paralyzed. Action will most likely be required to see you through your ordeal, but it must be the right kind of action. When you are unable to think clearly, it is a poor time to make major decisions. It is important not to waste precious energy and resources doing the wrong things or going to the wrong places. When you are tense and bound by fear, try breathing deeply and repeating a simple word or phrase, such as "stay calm" or "God is good." From decades of extreme rock climbing, I have observed that when my breathing is shallow and tense, my muscles are also tense, and I waste my energy by fighting one muscle against another. By consciously controlling my breathing through forcing myself to breathe deeply, I can send a wave of energy and relaxation to my arms and legs, helping me to overcome the debilitating effects of fear. From numerous survival accounts, it is quite clear that a large percentage of survivors resorted to prayer, even if they didn't believe in God. Praying, focusing on rhythmic deep breathing, or reciting a simple "mantra" (a short, simple word or set of words) can help to calm the endless stream of tortuous thoughts blazing through a tormented mind, returning your mind to some semblance of peace, where it stands a chance of hearing the quiet voice of intuitional guidance or of making a decent rational decision.

Conserve What You Have

The assumption that help will be along soon has been the downfall of many. Conservation includes body heat, dry clothing, water, food, fuel, medicine, and so on. Try to tap nature's resources for food and water before using your own reserves. Seek shelter *before* you are cold and wet. In survival situations people frequently underestimate the need for rest. Adrenaline tells you to go, go, go, but the truth is that you need to take your time, conserve your strength, energy, fluids, and warmth. Operate at about 60 percent capacity, if possible, and rehydrate regularly when water is available. If you are sweating at cold temperatures, you are probably working too hard and will burn out quickly.

Be Realistic

Rambo types are often the first to go. Use a healthy mix of positive attitude and determination to survive, tempered by realistic appraisal of pitfalls and dangers. When lost, don't panic. Backtrack, if at all possible. On a number of occasions, I have salvaged a wrong turn in the backcountry through backtracking (researchers have found that few people who got seriously lost ever backtracked), and on other occasions when I found I had taken a wrong turn several miles back, I calmly assessed the situation and sometimes altered my route based on where I now found myself, even though it was not according to my original plan. Better to accept a mistake, change plans and deal with it, than to plunge foolishly forward.

Use Your Intuition

Intuitive hunches have been credited with saving many a person's life. On the other hand, there are a lot of people, myself included, who wish they had followed their intuitive hunches. In 1981, Debbie Kiley and four other members of the crew hired to sail 1,000 miles to deliver a large sailboat to its owner were cast adrift in a small raft for five days at sea when the sailboat sank during a hurricane. While drifting in shark-infested waters without food, water, or adequate clothing, three of the five crew members succumbed before Kiley and the other remaining crew member, Brad Cavanagh, were rescued. When author Laurence Gonzales asked her what advice she had for others, she replied, "Trust your gut. I had misgivings about the trip all along. It just didn't feel right. So I have just one piece of advice for people: Your gut tells you what to do. Believe it. I didn't, and a lot of people are dead, and I have to live with it. Also, never forget that you can't depend on anybody. You really have to have it within yourself to do it."

Don't Give Up

Survivors are not saints who never doubt and never have moments of weakness where they give up hope. But at some time during their ordeal, most survivors relate that they had an epiphany, a moment when they felt certain that they would survive their ordeal, and that this moment gave them added strength to battle their inner demons and regain control over negative defeatist thoughts.

Compact Survival Kit

Be prepared. The following basic survival kit is small enough to slip into the top pocket of a knapsack or a coat pocket. It fits into a 2-ounce tobacco tin or other small case, and its weight is hardly noticeable. Polish the inside of the case to a mirror finish for signaling. Check the contents of the case regularly, to replace items that have exceeded their shelf lives. Tape the box seams with duct tape to waterproof the container.

- **Matches.** Fire can be started by other means, but matches are the easiest. Waterproof matches are useful, but bulkier than ordinary stick matches. You can waterproof ordinary matches by dipping them in molten candle wax. Break large kitchen matches in half to save room for more matches. Include a striker torn from a book of paper matches.

- **Bic lighter.** A small compact cigarette lighter can make stating a fire immensely easier.

- **Candle.** Great for helping to start a fire with damp wood, as well as for a light and heat source. Shave it square to save space in your kit.

- **Flint with steel striker.** Flint will last long after your matches are used up. You must find very dry, fine tinder to start a fire with sparks from a flint. Solid magnesium fire-starter kits are an excellent improvement on the traditional flint with steel. Using a knife to scrape magnesium shavings from the magnesium bar, you light the shavings with a spark from the flint, and they burn hotly to help ignite the tinder.

- **Magnifying glass.** Useful for starting a fire with direct sunlight or for finding splinters.

- **Needle and thread.** Choose several needles, including at least one with a very large eye, which can handle yarn, sinew, or heavy thread. Wrap with several feet of extra-strong thread.

- **Fishhooks and line.** A selection of different hooks in a small tin or packet. Include several small, split-lead sinkers and as much fishing line as possible.

- **Compass.** A small, luminous-dial compass (for night reading). Make sure that you know how to read it and that the needle swings freely. A string is handy for hanging it around your neck for regular reference.

- **Micro-flashlight.** A keychain LED-type (light-emitting diode) lamp, such as the Photon Microlight II, is useful for reading a map at night or following a trail when there is no moon.

- **Brass wire.** Three to five feet of lightweight flexible brass wire, or fine braided steel wire from a bead shop. Wire is useful for making snares and repairing things.

- **Flexible saw.** These come with large rings for handles that can be removed to allow it to fit into your kit. While using the saw, insert sticks through the end loops for more useful and comfortable handles. Coat the saw with a film of grease or oil to protect it from rust.

- **Survival knife.** For overnight backcountry travel or as part of your car kit, I would also carry a stout knife with about a 6-inch blade. If the knife has a folding blade, it should have a heavy-duty blade lock. It should be strong enough to use as a pry and to split branches and cut hardwoods without damage. You may need a knife to fabricate crude tools, such as a bow and drill for starting a fire without matches. A variety of "survival" knives are available; they are capable of cutting various materials, including thin sheet metal, and will do nicely. If the knife has a fixed blade, it should be covered in a sheath that it can't easily cut through. Some knives come with a small sharpening stone in the sheath, which is a nice feature.

- **Condom.** When placed in a sock or other cloth for protection and support, this makes a good emergency water bottle.

- **Compact medical kit.** Vary the contents depending on your skill and needs. Pack medicines in airtight containers with cotton balls to prevent powdering and rattling. The following list, which is a rough guide, will cover most needs.

  - *Mild pain reliever.* Pack at least ten of your favorite aspirin, ibuprofen, Tylenol, or other pain reliever.

  - *Diarrhea medicine.* Immodium is usually favored. Take two capsules initially, and then one each time a loose stool is passed.

  - *Antibiotic.* For general infections. People who are sensitive to penicillin can use tetracycline. Carry enough for a full course of five to seven days. Use echinacea or grapefruit seed extract from the health food store, if prescription antibiotics are not available.

  - *Antihistamine.* For allergies, insect bites, and stings, use Benadryl or equivalent.

  - *Water purification tablets.* Much lighter and more compact than a filter. For use when you can't boil your water.

  - *Potassium permanganate.* Has several uses. Add to water and mix until water becomes bright pink to sterilize it, a deeper pink to make a topical antiseptic, and a full red to treat fungal diseases, such as athlete's foot.

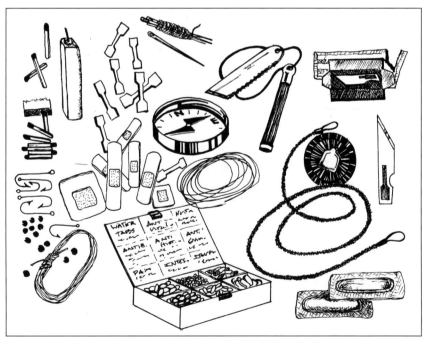

Figure 7-10. Compact survival kit.

- *Salt tablets.* Salt depletion can lead to muscle cramps and loss of energy. Carry five to ten salt tablets.
- *Surgical blades.* At least two scalpel blades of different sizes. A handle can be made of wood, if required.
- *Butterfly sutures.* To hold edges of wounds together.
- *Band-Aids.* Assorted sizes, preferably waterproof, for covering minor wounds and keeping them clean. Can be cut to make butterfly sutures (adapted from Wiseman 1996, 16).

Developing a Survivor Personality

❝The best survivors spend almost no time, especially in emergencies, getting upset about what has been lost, or feeling distressed about things going badly. . . . Life's best survivors can be both positive and negative, both optimistic and pessimistic at the same time.❞ —Al Siebert, *The Survivor Personality*

The struggle for survival is a fascinating and inspiring subject, forming the basis for many of the most memorable books and movies. Psychologist Al Siebert's personal fascination with survivors began when he received his military training from a group of veteran paratroopers. His teachers were legendary members of the 503rd Airborne Infantry Regiment. They had lost nine out of ten members in combat in the Korean War. Siebert found that these "survivors" were not the crusty, yelling drill sergeants that he had anticipated. They were tough, yet showed patience. They had a good sense of humor and were likely to laugh at mistakes. They were positive, yet also looked at the downside of things. They didn't act mean or tough, even though they could be as mean and tough as anyone. Siebert noticed that each of these men had a type of personal radar, which was always on "scan." He realized that it was not dumb luck that had brought these men through their ordeals, but a synergistic combination of qualities that tilted the odds in their favor. Al believes that we can all benefit in our daily lives by nurturing and developing these positive character traits within our own personalities.

Typical Survivor Personality Traits

- **Flexibility.** The number-one trait to which many survivors attribute their success is the ability to adapt to the situation.
- **Commitment to survive.** When conditions are extremely difficult, it takes a strong will and commitment to survive. Jewish Holocaust and Bataan Death March survivors tell tales of watching their friends lose the will to

My father-in-law, Joseph Jussen, was a resistance fighter in World War II and a Dutch soldier during the Indonesian revolution. He was credited with saving many Jewish, Dutch, and Indonesian lives with numerous courageous acts of resistance and sabotage. In the first part of 1943, Joseph was captured while driving a truckload of smuggled food for the resistance, and accused of being a saboteur and an "enemy of the people." Such accusations were usually followed by execution. He was imprisoned, and routinely tortured, for a period of six and a half months as they attempted to crack his spirit and force him to release the names of his friends in the underground. When he passed out, they would revive him with buckets of ice water and begin the torture again. Faithfully Joseph stuck to his story that he worked alone and had no accomplices, because he knew that if he cracked, he would be sentencing his friends and comrades to a similar fate of torture and death. In an effort to break his spirit, on three separate occasions he was placed in front of a firing squad and shot with blank cartridges. Joseph never gave up. Finally, when they realized that they could not break him, he was sentenced to death in a public trial held by the puppet government under the control of the Nazis. A friend of Joseph's was sitting in the audience during the trial. He caught Joseph's eye and winked at him. On the day scheduled for his execution, several resistance fighters disguised as Nazi officers boldly walked into the prison where Joseph was held and requested to "take the prisoner to the yard for execution." When he got to the prison yard, instead of the anticipated firing squad, they surprised Joseph by hoisting him to the top of the tall prison yard wall. Joseph leapt to the sidewalk below, breaking both ankles, and was carried into a waiting getaway car. The authorities posted his picture throughout the area, so for the next year, until the liberation of Europe by Allied Forces, he was unable to show his face in the light of day.

survive. Under these harsh conditions, once the drive to survive was lost, they usually lasted a short while, ranging from a few hours to a few days.

- **Staying cool.** Survivors have the ability to stay calm, or regain calmness, so they can think clearly and intuitively "feel" their way to a correct choice, without being hampered by emotions that have run amok.

- **Playful curiosity.** Survivors usually like to know how things work. They show a playful curiosity that helps them adapt to changing circumstances.

- **Sense of humor.** The ability to laugh helps people manage under the worst conditions. My father-in-law survived being captured and tortured by the Nazis. Later, as a Dutch marine in the Indonesian revolution, he survived while more than three-quarters of his company was killed. Throughout his life he maintained a great sense of humor and loved nothing more than to make people laugh. His favorite saying was, "Make you happy!"

- **A mixture of opposites.** The typical survivor is not always either hot or cold. Survivors have the ability to blend optimism with pessimism, so they can see the faults in a plan, but are not paralyzed by negativity. They combine humor with seriousness, self-confidence with a critical eye, and so on.

- **Intuition.** At some point in our lives, we have all had demonstrations of the power of intuition. The rational mind makes decisions based on the available information, which is always imperfect at best. Intuition appears to give us the ability to move beyond the limits of time and space, to "see around corners" that the rational mind can't breach.

- **"Get over it."** Most survivors don't waste a lot of time lamenting mistakes and losses. They move on and deal with the situation, unhampered by paralyzing regrets and disappointments.

- **"Bad patients."** Bernie Siegal, founder of Exceptional Cancer Patients, observed that survivors who beat the odds against cancer and other life-threatening diseases were usually "bad patients." These patients typically questioned their doctors and took an active role in their recovery, whereas "good patients" did just as they were told, questioned very little, and often died right on schedule.

- **Rule followers.** Like the "bad patients," survivors are generally not good "rule followers." Many of the victims of the 9/11 World Trade Center collapse were told by security guards that the second tower was safe and to return to their offices. Others were told by firefighters to stay put until they returned and escorted them out. In his book, *Deep Survival*, Laurence Gonzales tells the story of Julianne Koepcke, a seventeen-year-old teenage girl who survived the mid-flight breakup of an airplane over the Peruvian rain forest. Ill equipped and without any survival training, she took eleven days to find her way out of the jungle to a hunting cabin and rescue. During the same period of time, a dozen adult survivors of the same crash "followed the rules," stayed put, and died while waiting for rescue (Gonzales 2004, 172–74).

Intuition: A Survivor's Powerful Ally

We think conscious thought is better, when in fact, intuition is soaring flight compared to the plodding of logic. Nature's greatest accomplishment, the human brain, is never more efficient or invested than when its host is at risk. Then, intuition is catapulted to another level entirely, a height at which it can accurately be called graceful, even miraculous. Intuition is the journey from A to Z without stopping at any other letter along the way. It is knowing without knowing why. . . . Some people say about rape, for example, "do not resist," while others say "always resist." Neither strategy is right for all situations, but one strategy is: Listen to your intuition. I do not know what might be best for you in some hazardous situation because I don't have all the information. Do not listen to the TV checklist of what to do, or the magazine article's checklist of what to do, or the story about what your friend did. Listen to the wisdom that comes from having heard it all by listening to yourself. —Gavin de Becker, *The Gift of Fear and Other Survival Signals That Protect Us from Violence*

From climate change, to terrorism, to an economy clouded by the peak in global oil production, we all face a future filled with uncertainty. Whatever actions and strategies we may have used successfully to guide our lives and businesses over the past few decades may not continue to work in this next period of rapid change. Clear intuitive messages can provide the extra guidance needed to navigate the murky waters of an uncertain future. I like to call it *the intuitive edge*, and many businessmen take high-priced seminars from intuitive experts to improve their "gut feel" and the accuracy of their business decisions.

Intuition is a powerful ally, especially in dangerous situations. Intuition is one of nature's gifts to us. It is a beautiful example of how natural selection has biologically programmed into human beings an incredible survival mechanism to protect the organism (us) in times of trouble. Intuitive hunches have been credited with saving many a person's life, and with guiding numerous entrepreneurs and investors on their road to success. I'm sure that nearly all of us can remember times when we received strong intuitive guidance about something. If we listened to that guidance, we usually found that we were glad we did. If we didn't listen, we may have been "burned" in some kind of painful life lesson.

This "inner compass" inside each and every one of us provides the ability to simply know what to do, without having to "figure it out," because in ancient days when human beings were being chased by a saber-toothed tiger, or confronted with a snap decision on the battle field, they did not have time to "figure things out," so they had to rely upon their own innate sense to guide them to make the best snap decision in no more time than it takes to blink an eye. Those humans who did not have access to this inner compass, well, they simply did not make it, and their genes died out.

In our modern high-tech world we are taught to ignore our feelings and intuition and to follow cold hard facts and rational reasoning. This works just fine when there is adequate information for our computer brains to calculate the optimal decision. The problem is that in a typical crisis or survival situation, there is often a distinct lack of information for the rational mind to make a fully informed decision. You know that you can't trust the decisions your rational mind is making when it keeps changing its mind every minute or two. Once you observe this happening inside your own head, it is imperative that you quiet this mind that "can't make up its mind," and activate that inborn intuitive-based inner guidance system.

The difficulty in dealing with intuitive messages is to distinguish between the different inner voices. Which is speaking? Is it the voice of fear, ego, fantasy, or true inner guidance and wisdom? Many times I have allowed my strong rational mind to overrule my inner messages, only to regret later listening to this mind that thinks it always knows everything. Through trial and a lot of error, I have developed the following simple technique for quieting the rational mind and intuitively "testing" the outcome of a potential action:

Testing Your Intuition—"Pit of the Stomach" Exercise

❝The intuitive mind is a sacred gift and the rational mind is a faithful servant. We have created a society that honors the servant and has forgotten the gift.❞ —Albert Einstein

Note: The "pit of the stomach" exercise might well be the single most valuable technique taught in this book—it could quite literally be a "lifesaver"!

First, decide which potential paths of action are your prime choices.

Second, take several deep, slow breaths to calm your mind and alter your consciousness. As you do this, offer a simple prayer asking for guidance. The simple act of intentionally asking a higher power for guidance opens up your being to a seemingly magical, and oftentimes miraculous, intuitive internal guidance system. Focus your attention on the pit of your stomach, behind your belly button. Keep breathing deeply until you find that your stomach muscles are totally relaxed and your mind's thoughts are quieted.

Third, once you find that both your thoughts and stomach muscles are calm and relaxed, make a mental picture of one of the potential actions, paths, or decision. Check for physical reactions in your stomach area. If you have an expanded, relaxed feeling in the pit of your stomach, then your pictured action is probably a good path to follow. It should be an "Ahhhh" feeling. If you get a clenched, tight feeling in your gut, or a queasy, nauseous, sickly feeling, it's probably a good idea to avoid the pictured action. If you get nothing, either the choice is unimportant, or you simply are not intuitively in touch with it.

Fourth, repeat the process for each of the other potential course(s) of action, first calming yourself, then picturing the course of action and sensing the feeling in the pit of your stomach to determine which course is best.

Water

Requirements

Water is essential for survival. Most of us could live for several weeks without food, but for only about three to four days without water under average conditions, and in extreme heat we would be in serious trouble after a single day. The typical adult requires about 2 quarts of drinking water per day under normal conditions and 1 to 3 gallons per day in hot-weather conditions. Usually 1 gallon per adult per day is enough for drinking and some limited

In 1984, while climbing El Capitan in Yosemite Valley, we hauled the standard two quarts of water per person per day for three days of rock climbing. We baked in the sun for three days of a record-breaking heat wave. By the time we drank our last mouthful of water around noon on day three, we were already severely dehydrated. At times temperatures exceeded 100°F on the south-facing rock walls, with no shelter or shade. My throat hurt terribly and my mouth and throat were almost as dry as the back of my hand. Whenever I tried to talk, my tongue would stick like glue to the roof of my mouth and I would start to gag and retch. By the end of day three, our need for water exceeded our need for rest, so we climbed into the night, joining forces with the party above us, who had also run out of water. Around midnight, we reached the top and found a trickle of fresh water feeding a couple of large puddles where we guzzled water to our heart's content. I can assure you, beyond a shadow of a doubt, if you are as thirsty as we were on that day, you will drink from the most scummy, disgusting duck pond or ditch water, if that is all you have at hand. Personally, I would feel terrible if my family had to drink untreated water from a putrid duck pond after a disaster, when I could have planned ahead and purchased a simple pump-type water-purifying filter from any back-country or surplus supply store.

washing, but if you live in a desert location, or a hot humid climate, 2 or 3 gallons per person per day is a better figure to use for your water calculations.

Recommended Emergency Measures

- Any surface water in the United States may be contaminated, and should be boiled or otherwise purified prior to drinking.

- Bring water to a full boil. At any elevation, by the time water has reached the boiling point, it has killed all living organisms, except for prions. Prions are responsible for mad cow disease, scrapie, and other related illnesses. They appear to be formed of proteins, are not living organisms in the traditional sense, are not destroyed by traditional heat-sterilization methods, and may be found in the nervous systems of infected animals.

- Floods and earthquakes often contaminate public water systems. When in doubt, boil or otherwise purify tap water until authorities say the water is fit for drinking.

- If warned of an impending crisis, store water in as many containers as possible, including sinks and bathtubs.

- Hot-water heaters and your home's piping are good sources of stored water. Turn off the gas or electricity to your hot-water heater before draining it. If the water contains sediment, do not discard it, but allow the sediment to settle. To drain household piping, turn on the uppermost faucet slightly, to release suction in the system, and drain from the lowermost faucet (or other plumbing connection).

- Your body needs water to digest food. If you have little or no water, limit your intake of dry foods to the bare minimum.

Dehydration

Avoid dehydration, because it will sap your body strength, but ration your water usage if you have a limited supply. Signs of dehydration include thirst, fatigue, dizziness, dry mouth, headache, loss of appetite, dark-colored urine, and sleepiness. If you need physical energy to deal with your situation, you must do your best to find and conserve water.

Conserving Water

- If traveling in hot country, stay in the shade as much as possible. Avoid midday travel. Travel at night, if possible.

- Wear loose clothing because it will provide an insulating layer of air, which will help to reduce evaporative water losses by maintaining high humidity close to the skin.

- Do not go shirtless. It will feel cooler, but you will lose more water through evaporation and may sunburn. Severe sunburn can lead to a toxic condition known as "sun poisoning."

- Move slowly and avoid overexertion. Try to breathe through the nose—you will lose less water than by breathing through the mouth.

- Drink in small sips, not big gulps.

- Sucking on a small pebble, twig, or blade of grass can help generate saliva and minimize the discomfort of thirst.

- The human body seeks to maintain a certain level of humidity at the skin surface. In cold, dry climates, this results in the daily loss of significant amounts of water, since the body is slowly pumping water into the air at all times. Mountaineers often use "vapor barriers" to minimize water consumption and the use of fuel to melt snow for water. Vapor barriers are created by wearing waterproof clothing and using plastic bags as inner sock liners. In subfreezing temperatures, and especially when using down sleeping bags, the use of a vapor-barrier sleeping-bag liner helps to prevent the daily loss of the sleeping bag's insulating value due to the condensation of perspiration into its outer layers.

- Do not waste potable water to cool yourself or wash clothing. Wash in untreated water, if available and not polluted. You can spread clothes out in direct sunlight to deodorize and disinfect, at least to some degree.

For more information on finding, storing, and treating water, see chapter 8.

Fire

Your ability to start a fire is important for staying warm in cold climates, for cooking food, and for sterilizing water. I'll start with simple instructions for city folks on building a campfire with matches and paper, and then proceed through the more Spartan methods, ending with the difficult process of starting a fire by rubbing two sticks together.

Note: I have been camping and building fires in the backcountry since I was a little kid. I am usually able to start a fire with a single match, but I have seen people who do not know how to build a fire go through an entire box of matches and still not have a fire going. For me, building a fire with a flint and steel, or a primitive fire drill, is an extremely difficult process, even with bone-dry tinder. I suggest you practice some of these techniques and don't blindly count on that "cool survival fire-starter flint" that you bought in some store to save your you-know-what when you are wet and cold and trying to start a fire.

Starting a Fire with Matches

Materials

I like to separate my materials into piles by size. Start by gathering a couple of handfuls of tinder, about a third of a shopping bag's worth of kindling, at least a half shopping bag's worth of small sticks (½ to 2 inches thick), and at least a shopping bag's worth of thicker wood (2 to 12 inches thick).

Tinder

Any kind of material that takes very little heat to start it on fire can be used for tinder. Paper makes great tinder, if you have matches. If you don't have matches and are attempting to build a fire with a spark (see "Starting a Fire with Flint and Steel" below), you will need extra-fine dry tinder. Dry pine needles, fine dry grasses, shredded paper, birch bark, dried moss, bird down, mouse nests, cotton balls, wood shavings, pulverized dry pinecones, and fibrous inner cedar bark make good tinder.

Kindling

Kindling must catch on fire within a few seconds from burning tinder, yet burns for only a few minutes to ignite the larger pieces of wood. Dry pine needles, still stuck to branches, are perfect. Small twigs, ⅛ to ¼ inch thick, are also excellent. Test the sticks to see whether they are dry or wet. If the sticks can be bent and twisted without snapping, they are wet and will not do for kindling. If all available kindling is wet, you can still burn green pine needles or else you must find standing wood, which can be split with an axe or shaved down to find a dry core. You can make "feather sticks" for kindling from larger sticks of wood by carving many shallow cuts with a knife to create fine, curved shavings protruding from the side of the sticks.

Positioning the Fire

Build your fire in a protected spot, especially if the area is windy. If it is exceptionally windy, you may have to dig a trench for your fire or build it on the leeward side of a fallen tree or large rock. If the ground is swampy or the snow is deep, you may have to build your fire on a platform of green logs covered by dirt.

Caution: Do not use stones from a riverbed or porous stones around or under a fire. These stones can explode when heated due to internal steam pockets.

Building the Fire

If you have paper, crumple a couple of sheets, build a small pile of fine kindling on top of the paper, then light the paper in several places. If you don't have paper, use two handfuls of extremely fine, dry tinder instead. Make sure you don't smother the tiny flames of the beginning fire with a pile that's too big or too tightly packed, or by stacking larger wood too quickly onto the fire. As the kindling catches on fire, pile on more kindling and gradually add thicker chunks of wood. Make sure the fire gets enough air circulating through it. Either build your fire in a crisscross fashion or lean the wood against itself in a tepee-like cone shape (see fig. 7-2), to ensure that there are plenty of gaps between the wood for air circulation. A well-built fire, with dry wood and plenty of gaps for air circulation, will not smoke much.

Figure 7-2. Crisscross- and tepee-style fires.

Starting a Fire with Flint and Steel

Flint is a naturally occurring stone that yields heavy sparks when struck by a knife or other sharp stones. Artificial flints do the same thing and may come with a saw striker, which creates lots of good sparks. Starting a fire with the spark from the flint requires patience, shelter from wind, and very fine, dry tinder. Strike sparks into your tinder (see fig. 7-3), and gently blow on a spark resting in the tinder until it grows into flames. Continue building your fire following the previous set of instructions. A modern improvement on flint and steel is a commercial magnesium block with a flint. Using a knife, shave a pile of fine magnesium filings from the side of the block. When struck by a spark from a flint, magnesium filings rapidly burst into tiny hot flames, helping to ignite the tinder. You may wish to pick up a "Blast Match" for your survival kit, which is a handy fire-starting device that casts a multitude of heavy sparks by rapidly raking the sides of a thick artificial flint, making the job of starting a fire without a match or butane lighter considerably easier.

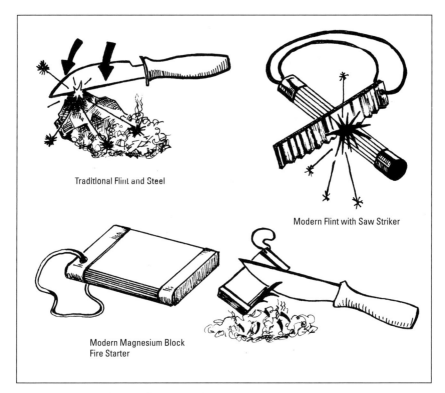

Traditional Flint and Steel

Modern Flint with Saw Striker

Modern Magnesium Block
Fire Starter

Figure 7-3. Starting a fire with flint and steel.

Starting a Fire with Bow and Drill

A fire can be started by rapidly spinning a wooden "drill"—under pressure—against a notch in a board (see fig. 7-4), until enough heat is generated to create a small coal, which is dropped into tinder and fanned into fire. This is not easy, but it's about a hundred times easier than starting a fire with a hand-spun stick.

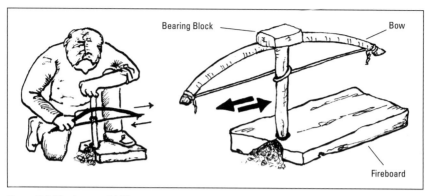

Figure 7-4. Fire bow and drill.

Bow

Use any stick, preferably curved, and roughly ½- to ¾-inch thick by 30 inches long. With your knife, make a shallow groove around each end (about an inch from the ends) to make a spot to tie your bowstring. Use a hefty, strong string or leather thong (not rope) to tie the bow. Braided leather thongs or ⅛- to ¼-inch nylon cord work well as bowstring. Typically, plant fiber cordage must be doubled back on itself and corded a second time to make it strong enough for the bowstring on a fire-drill bow. The string may stretch as you work the bow. Tie the bowstring with a little slack to allow for the string to wrap around the drill. Experiment with different string tensions and with using your fingers to tweak the string for more or less tension while using the bow.

Drill

Usually the drill and the fireboard will be made from the same material, though the choice of wood for the fireboard (also known as hearth board) is most critical. For a fire drill and hearth board to make fire, they must be very dry and they must generate an extremely fine powder when spun together. Try to pick freestanding wood with the bark weathered away, because wood lying on the ground usually picks up ground moisture. If your pieces of wood generate coarse, gritty wood shavings, you should find another chunk of wood. The best woods are usually softwoods that are not very resinous. Resins such as those found in most pines, spruce, and firs tend to act like a grease, making it difficult or impossible to get enough friction going to make a fire. Some recommended varieties of wood are cottonwood, aspen, yucca, birch, and poplar. Other woods that work, but not as easily, include box elder, elderberry, and willow.

Note: Even pieces of the recommended varieties will not work well if they are moist or resinous or generate coarse shavings.

The drill should be about ½ to ¾ inch in diameter and about 6 to 10 inches long. The wood should dent somewhat under your thumbnail, being neither too hard nor extremely soft. Round the drill end for the fireboard and trim the corners of the drill end for the bearing block at about 45 degrees.

Fireboard

The exact dimensions of the fireboard are not important but, like the drill, the type and condition of the wood are critical. The fireboard should be long enough to steady with your foot and significantly wider than the drill; about 1½ to 2 inches wide by a couple of feet long works well. In a real-life situation, you will use a fireboard many times, until its entire length has been used up. Using your knife, split an appropriate branch for fabricat-

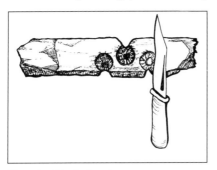

Figure 7-5. The fireboard.

ing your fireboard. Shave down the round side until it's about ½ inch thick, and then square up the sides. By rotating your knife tip, make a shallow depression in the fireboard just over one-half the diameter of the drill from the board edge. This depression must hold the drill as it spins. Cut a narrow V-notch from the edge of the board to the center of the depression you just gouged into the fireboard. This V-notch will collect bits of wood shavings, which eventually smolder as you work the drill (see fig. 7-5).

Bearing Block

You can use many different materials for the bearing block. The main requirements are that the materials be hard and slippery. A one-ounce shot glass, a smooth stone with a depression, a chunk of bone, a knot of resinous softwood, or a knot of hardwood works well. Make a shallow hole in the bearing block to capture the end of the drill. If it's made of wood, a little ChapStick, some Crisco, or animal fat will help to lubricate the bearing block. Make sure you don't contaminate the fireboard end of your drill with the lubricant.

Tinder

Almost any dry, fibrous material will work for tinder. The inner bark of cedar is great, and cottonwood works well, as do many dried grasses. Roll these around between your fingers until they are shredded fine like a cotton ball.

Make a small bird's nest out of your tinder, with a depression in the middle to catch the glowing ember. Set it to the side on a piece of bark, so you can carry it when it bursts into flame without burning your hands. Make sure that you have kindling and dry wood ready, too. Unlike matches, a second chance with a bow drill involves considerable effort.

Procedure

Place a piece of bark under the fireboard notch to catch the ember and to insulate it from the ground. Wrap the bowstring in a single full loop around the drill. Kneel down with one foot firmly standing on top of the fireboard next to the V-notch. Get comfortable, because this will probably take twenty minutes or more. Apply pressure with the bearing block, and start rotating the drill with a full back-and-forth stroke of the bow. Very little will happen until the drill seats itself into the cavity on the fireboard; at that point it will develop considerably more friction and start to smolder. Once the spark inside the dust pile is clearly smoldering, relax and lift the spark on its bark bed, dumping the spark into your bird's nest of tinder. Blow on the spark until the tinder bursts into flame. Congratulations, you have made fire!

Starting a Fire with a Hand Drill

This is tough, but doable. Prepare the tinder, kindling, and fireboard as above. The fireboard should be a little thinner, perhaps as thin as ¼ inch. The drill should be about ¼ inch in diameter and about 30 inches long. Dried cattails are a favored drill material. Persistence, tough hands, and lots of rapid drilling with steady downward pressure are the keys to success. Use the full length of your hands and apply downward pressure as you spin the drill between your hands (see fig. 7-6). Some people are able to flutter their hands up the drill, while maintaining the drill

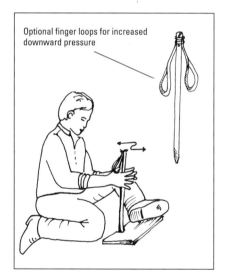

Optional finger loops for increased downward pressure

Figure 7-6. Using a hand fire drill.

spin, to prevent it from cooling down as they shift their hands to the top of the drill to begin another round of downward pressure spins. If you find that you must stop drilling to shift your hands, do so as quickly as possible to minimize cooling. Thumb loops of string or a leather thong attached to the top of the hand drill can help you start a fire faster by applying steady downward pressure as you spin the drill.

Starting a Fire with a Fire Plough

Cut a lengthwise shallow groove in an 18-inch fireboard made from soft, non-resinous wood that is at least 1½ inches wide (see fig. 7-7). Prepare your tinder and kindling in the same way as for starting a fire with a bow drill. Using a hardwood or other non-resinous stick, drive the stick back and forth under considerable pressure to generate friction, sawdust, and eventually a spark.

Figure 7-7. Using a fire plough to start a fire.

Food

Most people can live for weeks without food, but long-term survival depends on finding and preparing a variety of foods. If you lived in the middle of a rabbit paradise or trout heaven, you would eventually starve to death if you just ate either rabbit or trout, since they wouldn't provide you with all the vitamins and minerals necessary for long-term sustenance, and they are low in fat and calories. This section gives you some basic guidelines and suggestions. If you are stuck without food for extended periods, intestinal cleansing will help you to feel better and to work at a surprising level of functionality. I once ran for 11 miles through the High Sierra Mountains on the last day of a ten-day fast, and my energy level was remarkably good.

The theory behind fasting was explained to me as follows: When a body is digesting food, it does a poor job of cleaning toxic wastes and deposits out of its different systems. A fast gives the autonomic nervous system, which controls digestion and other automatic processes, the chance to focus on internal cleansing. A fast gives the body a chance to "spring clean" and helps it to return the immune system to peak performance. In addition, the fasting body scavenges raw materials from places such as cholesterol deposits, tumors, and calcified deposits in the joints for use in other parts of the body. Normally the body's natural cleansing cycle dumps toxins into the colon in the morning. In the afternoon, if you are fasting, the body will be hungry and will try to absorb what it can from the colon. Unless the colon is cleansed, the body will reabsorb toxins, which may produce headaches and nausea. Because you are not eating anything to push the toxins out of the colon, you should do an enema or drink some bulk nonnutritive fiber, like psyllium, to cleanse the colon.

I heard this story from a man who taught survival classes in Arizona. He talked about the experience of a group of college-age men and women taking part in a wilderness survival class in which they had to forage and hunt for all of their food and water for three days, using their bare hands or what simple tools they could fabricate from found materials. He said that their experience was pretty typical of what most participants experience in their classes. On the first day, the group divided into men and women. They each discussed their game plan. The men's group decided to focus on hunting and trapping to find their daily food, while the women's group chose to pursue foraging for their sustenance. After the first day, none of the men had been successful at hunting or fishing for food, while the women had found a few berries and edible roots. Both groups chose to continue with their individual game plans. By the morning of the third day, the men's group had not managed to kill a single animal for food and hungrily shared the roots and other edible plants that the women's group had to offer them.

In August 1954, ten members of the Swedish Vegetarian Society marched 325 miles from Göteborg to Stockholm to publicize the health benefits of the fast and to demonstrate its relative safety. After marching an average of 32.5 miles per day for ten days straight, eating no food and drinking nothing but springwater, the fasters arrived in Stockholm in excellent health and remarkable physical condition (Garten 1967, 83). If you are ever stuck without food for a prolonged period of time, remember these results. Cleanse your colon, and you may be able to perform remarkably well for prolonged periods without food.

Basic Guidelines

- Don't spend more energy looking for food than you get from food.
- Avoid scurvy, which is caused by vitamin C deficiency. Scurvy is characterized by swollen or bleeding gums, followed by weakness and bruises or wounds that won't heal. For a natural source of vitamin C, chew on wild rose hips or green pine needles (or make a tea out of them). The bright green, fresh pine-needle tips are the most palatable. Vitamin C plays an important role in the immune system and is a natural detoxifier.
- If you are dehydrated, do not eat unless the food contains a significant amount of water. Since water is required to digest and metabolize food, when you are suffering from severe dehydration, if you eat food that contains no moisture, the consumed food will not provide you with a source of energy and will only make the dehydration worse.
- In most locations, there will be some kind of vegetation that you can eat to sustain yourself. The trick is to identify and prepare the local edible vegetation.
- Trim moldy areas off food before eating. My mom used to say, "It's just penicillin," but don't you believe it. Molds manufacture aflatoxins, which

are extremely poisonous substances. Penicillium is one of the few molds not harmful to most humans. Discard grain that shows signs of mold.

Plants

I highly recommend that you pick up a field guide to edible plants in your area (see appendix 1). A brief guide to nineteen common edible plants is included later in this chapter. Edibility is the first consideration when foraging. There are many thousands of edible plants in North America, and the following test can be used to determine the edibility of unknown plants. Only one person should test each plant. If stomach problems arise, drink lots of hot water for relief. If necessary, induce vomiting by sticking your finger down your throat or swallowing some charcoal.

Caution: Do not assume that a plant is safe to eat because birds, insects, or animals have eaten it. Many plants that are poisonous to humans serve as food sources for certain animals, birds, or insects.

Edibility Test

Since most of us will not be fortunate enough to have a guide to wild edibles in our back pocket when a disaster strikes, this plant edibility test could save your life someday. When properly executed, the plant edibility test enables a person to safely test any wild plant for its edibility.

Caution: Don't skip any of the following steps—go slow and be thorough.

- Do not use the edibility test for mushrooms. Mushrooms must be positively identified. Improperly identified mushrooms may taste fine but prove deadly in small amounts.
- Do not eat plants with milky sap, except for dandelions.

1. **Smell.** Crush some of the plant. If it smells like almonds or peaches, it probably contains the common plant poison hydrocyanic acid. Reject plants with this smell.

2. **Skin irritation.** Crush a small portion and rub some of the juice onto the skin of a sensitive area, such as the inside of your arm or thigh. If you experience any discomfort, rash, swelling, or burning sensations, reject this plant. Oxalic acid, a common plant poison, can be recognized by the sharp dry stinging or burning feeling it leaves on the skin or tongue.

3. **Mouth test.** If the test plant passed the skin test, cautiously proceed with the mouth test. At the first sign of burning, irritation, swelling, stomach ache, nausea, dizziness, or other ill effects, spit it out and reject this plant. First, crush a little bit of the plant and place a small amount on the lips for at least 10 seconds. Next, place a pea-sized portion in a corner of the mouth for 10 more seconds. Move this portion to the tip of the tongue for another 10 seconds. Hold it under the tongue for 10 more seconds. Chew

and then hold in the mouth for about 15 minutes total. Spit it out, and then wait for 5 hours.

4. **First-swallow test.** If there are no ill effects after 5 hours, chew and swallow one teaspoon-sized bite. Wait 10 hours, drinking and eating nothing else during this period.

5. **Second-swallow test:** Eat about ⅓ cup of this plant. Wait 24 hours. If there are no ill effects, consider this plant edible. When in doubt, go slow!

Tree Bark

Animals and starving people have survived through the winter months solely by eating the inner live layer of tree bark (cambium layer). You can eat it raw, cook it like spaghetti, or dry and grind it into flour. It can be added to stews for nutrition and to give the stew some body. Peel off a large section of tree bark, keeping the extra for later use. Do not cut bark from more than halfway around the tree, or you might kill it. The light-colored layer of inner bark is the edible portion; sometimes it has a green hue. The more edible barks are aspens, birch, willows, slippery elm, tamarack, maples, spruces, pines, and hemlocks. The buds and shoots of these trees are also edible, except for tamarack and hemlock, which are poisonous.

Caution: All parts of the carrot-family plant known as hemlock, a herbaceous biennial with a smooth green stalk, finely divided lacey leaves, and clusters of small white flowers, are extremely poisonous, even though it looks very inviting and similar to wild celery or parsley. The young shoots can look quite a bit like carrot tops. Poison hemlock is a green leafy plant that can grow 5–8 feet tall (1.5–2.5 meters) and is not even remotely related to the evergreen family of hemlock trees. Hemlock was the infamous poison drunk by Socrates after being condemned to death. All contact with the poisonous hemlock plant should be avoided!

Grasses

Grasses are edible. The best parts to eat are the soft white stems just below the surface of the ground. Make sure it's really grass that you are eating, and do not eat grass that has been sprayed. Some grasses and other plants have tiny hooks on their stems and leaf edges that will irritate the digestive tract and should be avoided.

Seeds and Grains

All grass seeds are edible, but some other seeds are poisonous. Use the edibility test on unknown seeds. Tasting will do you no harm, but do not swallow any seed that is bitter, burning, or otherwise unpalatable.

Caution: Discard all grains from clusters that are blackened or carry black, enlarged bean-like grains. These grains are infected with ergot mold, a powerfully toxic substance.

Roots and Tubers

The starch granules in most roots and tubers are insoluble in cold water. Most edible roots and tubers should be cooked, since cooking ruptures the starch granules and makes them more digestible.

Seaweed

Most sea vegetables are edible, except for some thin thread-like seaweeds. Collect seaweed from below the high-water line, and do not eat if from polluted waters. They are rich in vitamins and minerals, but many have a strong fishy taste. Soak in fresh water to remove salt and improve the taste. Eat seaweed raw or cooked into soups and stews, or dry it for later use. Fresh seaweed spoils quickly.

Foraging for Food

After a long winter, our ancestors usually ran outside and picked a fresh salad from the first green shoots of spring. After living on salt pork, dried beans, and old roots from the root cellar, fresh greens were a welcome change. One spring, I remember going hunting for a wild spring delicacy called "fiddleheads" (young fern shoots). We found what we thought were fiddleheads, brought them home, steamed a batch and gave them a try. They were awful! They made your mouth pucker and your throat gag. Not knowing any better, we had picked the furry kind of fern shoot, instead of the "furless" fern shoots. The next week, we found some of the right kind of fiddleheads, and they were sweet, tender, and delicious.

Warning: Never eat any wild plant unless you have 100 percent positive identification that it is edible, or you have taken the time to complete the three-day plant edibility test described above. A small bite of certain plants is enough to kill an adult.

Brief Guide to Wild Edible Foods

There are thousands of edible varieties of plants in North America. Some edible plants are truly delicious, but many considered edible taste bad and are primarily useful only in survival situations. A few of the more common and tasty wild edible plants are listed below. I suggest that you pick up one or two "real" guides to edible plants in your geographical region. Samuel Thayer's two books, *Natures Garden* and *The Forager's Harvest*, provide an excellent introduction to foraging. They focus in great detail on perhaps a couple of hundred edible wild plants, providing great detail about locating, identifying, harvesting, and preparing them. Steve Brill's *Identifying and Harvesting Edible and Medicinal Plants in Wild and Not So Wild Places* is another excellent start. It is entertaining, practical, and offers varied cooking suggestions and recipes, though it lacks the detailed color photographs from various seasons that are included in Thayer's books.

A good plant guide will also warn you about potentially poisonous "look-alike" plants that might be confused with the one that you think you are identifying. Harvesting wild edible plants can be fun and will help you make your diet more complete by adding more vitamins, minerals, and trace elements than are found in typical grocery store veggies. (For a list of recommended edible and medicinal plant guides, see the recommended reading in appendix 1).

Acorns. Acorns are the nuts from about fifty-five varieties of native oak trees. Gathered in the fall, acorns were traditional staple foods for several indigenous peoples. They were stored in baskets and crushed or ground into flour for cooking. In my local area, grinding depressions, where indigenous peoples ground their nuts into meal, are a common sight on the granite slabs adjacent to lakes and rivers. Some varieties of

Figure 7-8. Acorns.

acorns are sweet and may be used without special preparation, but bitter varieties require treatment to remove excess tannic acid prior to eating. To remove bitterness, shell the acorns and boil in water until the water turns brown. Drain and repeat until the water stops changing color. If boiling is not an easy alternative, wrap nutmeats in a cloth and soak in a clear running stream for a few days until they taste sweet. Soaking acorn mush to remove bitterness takes less time than soaking the whole seed. Acorn meal makes excellent pancakes and muffins.

Black mustard, field mustard, and others. These weeds grow more or less anywhere in fields and disturbed areas. Most mustard leaves are best when harvested young in the spring, but some in the mustard family are good throughout the summer. Seeds can be harvested, ground, and mixed with vinegar, like commercial mustard. Young basal rosette looks similar to dandelions, only there is no milky sap. This is a tangy treat if you like strong

Figure 7-9. Black mustard.

Figure 7-10. Bulrush.

Figure 7-11. Burdock.

flavors. There are no poisonous look-alikes.

Bulrush. Like cattails, bulrushes provide a source of year-round food. Found in wet, marshy areas and shallow waters of lakes or ponds. Identified by long, non-branching stems, with a spiky cluster of flowers. Young roots and shoots can be used as a vegetable. Older roots can be pounded to remove fibers and then ground into flour.

Burdock. Burdock grows throughout the United States on roadsides and in fields and disturbed areas. The large broad leaves look a bit like rhubarb leaves (and rhubarb leaves are poisonous), so be careful. The leaves are bitter tasting, but the first-year plant's long taproot tastes like a delicious cross between potato and artichoke heart. The root may be harvested until the second year flowering, when it becomes inedible. Peel roots, slice to break fibers, and then boil or sauté. Burdock root has excellent nutritional and healing properties for the skin and kidneys, and for overall health. Young flower stalks may be peeled and eaten raw or boiled. Burdock flowers with purple to pink crests grow into sharp, hooked, little burr balls that are either annoying or great toys, depending on your point of view.

Cattail. Another staple of indigenous peoples, cattails are still used for food throughout the world. Find cattails in shallow waters of swampy areas. You can dig up roots in early spring to find delicious sprouts that can be eaten raw. Young summer stalks, up to 2 to 3 feet tall, may be peeled for their tasty core (known as "Cossack asparagus"), which is eaten raw, steamed, or boiled. Young buds can be picked before pollen ripens and boiled like mini corn on the cob. Roots can be harvested in the fall through spring. Dig, dry, and peel, and then pound into flour. Pounded roots may be soaked and then decanted to render starchy material. Poisonous look-alikes are the stalks and roots of wild irises, so be sure to identify stalks by the presence of old cattails. Pollens can be harvested as a flour or flour extender.

Chicory. Like its close relative the dandelion, chicory is a staple green in many countries and has a long taproot. When young, the leaves look like dandelion leaves with the addition of irregular hairs on most of the leaves. When it matures, the resemblance to the dandelion disappears as it grows a tall hairy flower stalk with numerous sky-blue fringed flowers. Widespread, chicory is found in fields and other disturbed areas. Harvest leaves and shoots early in spring. Older leaves may require boiling and water changes, if bitter. The taproot is rather bitter, but makes a good caffeine-free coffee substitute when roasted at 250°F for two to four hours until brown, and then ground.

Curled dock, yellow dock, and sour dock. In early spring, this plant is easily recognized by its rosette of long, narrow leaves—up to 2 feet long—with curly edges. It grows throughout the country in fields, disturbed soil, and near water. Early spring leaves are delicious steamed and may be acceptable raw, but should be washed first. For later harvests, boil the leaves with multiple water changes to reduce bitterness. In summer, the flower stalk may be peeled and steamed as a vegetable. With much difficulty, the seeds may be threshed and ground into flour. Dock was a staple green during the Depression. The taproot is too bitter for eating, but is a useful medicinal herb for skin and liver conditions.

Dandelion. The common dandelion is quite a versatile and delicious plant. It is found throughout the country in open fields and disturbed areas. The young leaves are excellent as salad greens, and are more nutritious than any you can buy in the grocery store. Peel young roots

Figure 7-12. Cattail.

Figure 7-13. Chicory.

Figure 7-14. Curled dock.

Figure 7-15. Dandelion.

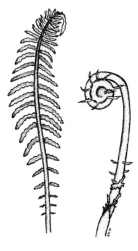

Figure 7-16. Fiddleheads.

Figure 7-17. Lamb's-quarter.

and eat raw or slice thin and boil. If leaves or roots are bitter, boiling in a couple water changes improves the taste. Dip the blossoms in fritter batter and fry in oil, like tempura veggies.

Fiddleheads (bracken and ostrich ferns). Collect young ferns in mid-spring, before the round "fiddlehead" has started to unfurl (up to about 8 inches tall). Wash to remove fur or inedible scales. I found the not-so-furry ostrich ferns much sweeter and not bitter like the furry bracken ferns. Perhaps it was just due to local effects or the age of the fiddleheads? Steam or boil fiddleheads to remove mild toxicity. Large quantities of mature bracken have been known to poison cattle. Fiddleheads are an expensive delicacy in upscale restaurants. Please leave a few fiddleheads in every cluster, as they will not return if you harvest the whole lot.

Lamb's-quarter, goosefoot. "Along with dandelions and watercress, lamb's-quarter is one of the most nutritious of foods" (Brill 1994, 47). Being widespread, tasty, long-seasoned, and easily identified, lamb's-quarter is a prime candidate for the beginner to learn to identify. This plant has little or no odor, so if the plant you pick has an odor, it's not lamb's quarters and may be poisonous. Leaves are alternating, almost triangular, with a blunt tip and jagged edges. Leaves may develop a white tinge, but they remain perfectly edible. Harvest young shoots up to 10 inches tall, or tender new growth until late fall. This plant is a good potherb, although it shrinks by about two-thirds when cooked.

Pigweed (amaranth). Similar to lamb's-quarter (which is sometimes also called pigweed), but with smoother, more elongated leaves. Use young leaves as a lettuce substitute. Harvest seeds and grind for flour. Seeds have more nutrition and higher protein than grains. Amaranth was a key staple cultivated by the Aztecs for its seeds. Pigweed concentrates nitrates, so use sparingly if taken from fertilized fields.

Pine trees. Harvest pine nuts in the fall from hard, green pine cones. Open the cones in the heat of a fire to reach the pine nuts buried inside. "Open" cones have probably already dropped their nuts. Pine nuts from the pinion pines were once a staple food for the indigenous peoples in Nevada. One of the ways that the U.S. government used to force these tribes to move off their land and onto reservations was to destroy the pinion pines, thereby removing one of their major sources of wild food. Pine needles can be boiled in water to make a tea rich in vitamin C, and in a survival crunch, the inner bark can be eaten.

Figure 7-18. Pigweed.

Plantain. Plantains are identified by their distinctive parallel veins, running the length of the leaves. This plant is another weed common to fields and disturbed areas. Leaves grow in a basal rosette and the plant grows a long, green, central flower stalk. Harvest young greens and new growth for salads or as a potherb. After mid-spring, the leaves become very fibrous and are mostly good for vegetable stock or as survival food. Harvest seeds for storage and sprouts.

Figure 7-19. Pinion pine.

Purslane. Cultivated in ancient times, purslane is now mostly seen by gardeners as a pesky weed. Both the seeds and the greens are very nutritious. This plant has succulent-like, smooth, fleshy leaves, often reddish purple, and tends to lie flat in thick mats. Pinch or cut leafy tips June through September. Purslane shoots are excellent cooked or raw in salads. This weed likes fields and disturbed areas, and has spread across the country. It has no poisonous look-alikes.

Figure 7-20. Plantain.

Ramps (wild leeks). Similar to its close cousins, wild onions and wild garlic, ramps are found ranging from the Great Lakes to New England and south to the mountains of Georgia. Wild

Figure 7-21. Purslane.

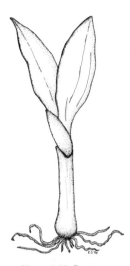

Figure 7-22. Ramps.

Figure 7-23. Rose hips.

Figure 7-24. Sheep sorrel.

leeks thrive in partially shaded, moist, rich woodlands, often under maples. They have the long leaves with parallel veins, similar to many poisonous members of the lily family. Crush a piece of one leaf and smell for the characteristic strong onion odor. Plants that smell like onions are not poisonous. In early spring, they look much like smaller versions of grocery store leeks, before the leaves shrivel and are replaced by a slender stalk with an umbrella-like cluster of small white flowers. When a few of the small, three-lobed seed clusters survive the fall, they point to an underground winter supply of delicious bulbs. Harvest green leaves in the spring, or the bulbs any time of the year. Use as flavoring in soups and stews, or sauté like onions.

Rose hips. Wild roses are found in many different varieties across the United States. Their fruits are a fantastic source of vitamin C. The larger fruits can be quite good raw, although you may want to avoid the bitter seeds. Many people collect rose hips for a delicious tea. They may be boiled and strained to make a sauce with the consistency of applesauce.

Sheep sorrel. An excellent green, sheep sorrel is one of the few wild plants that does not get bitter as summer comes along. It is distinguished by its elongated arrowlike leaves with "ears" that resemble the front view of a sheep's head, and is found in fields and disturbed areas or areas of poor soil. There are no poisonous look-alikes, but this plant sometimes grows along side the poisonous vines, nightshade and bindweed, that also have arrow-shaped leaves. Sheep sorrel leaves are tangy, tart, and kind of lemony. Mix them in salads with blander greens.

Watercress. "Along with dandelions and lamb's-quarter, watercress is one of the most nutritious of foods" (Brill 1994, 256).

Watercress is another Eurasian-introduced, cultivated green-turned-weed that has spread across America. It is usually found in clear running water, such as springs and small creeks. Wild watercress looks like the store-bought variety and is excellent in salads, sandwiches, and cooked like spinach. Collect young growth nearly all year, but it is best in the spring and autumn. Each sprig of leaves grows alternating off the main stalk and contains paired leaves with a single central leaf at the tip. It flowers in clusters of small, white, four-petaled flowers about ⅕ inch across and produces slender, capsule-shaped, ¾-inch-long seeds. The look of the watercress in my local spring varies considerably with the season. In early spring, the leaves sprout with dense, closely spaced, fleshy leaves that lay on the surface of the water. In early summer, shoots rise up out of the water, bearing thin, widely spaced leaves and flowers that look more like the illustration. It is very delicious with a slight peppery taste.

Figure 7-25. Watercress.

Wild onion. Wild onions are found throughout the United States, except in the hot and dry areas. They are found on the plains, hills, and mountains, usually in open areas, and all have the characteristic onion or garlic smell. Its bulb is usually reddish purple, and the plant has tall slender stalks with a typical allium cluster of flowers. Avoid all onion look-alikes that do not have a strong onion smell when the leaves are crushed, because they may be poisonous.

Figure 7-26. Wild onion.

Poisonous Plants to Avoid

Some poisonous plants to look out for are listed below. A few of these plants are also listed as medicinal herbs, but they are poisonous when eaten in quantity. Both *Edible Wild Plants: A North American Field Guide* by Dykeman and Elias and *Edible Native Plants of the Rocky Mountains* by Harrington contain illustrated guides to some of the common poisonous wild plants.

Table 7-1 Common Poisonous Plants		
American false hellebore	Anemone (wind flower)	Angel's trumpet (Datura)
Arrowgrass	Azalea	Baneberry (pretty white or red berries)
Bleeding heart	Bloodroot	Bouncing bet
Black locust	Butterflyweed	Castor oil plant
Celandine poppy	Christmas rose	Chokecherry
Cocklebur	Columbine	Corn cockle
Crocus	Daffodil	Daphne
Deadly nightshade	Death camass	Desert rose
Dieffenbachia	Dutchman's pipe	European bittersweet
Foxglove (Digitalis)	Frangipani (Plumeria)	Horse chestnut
Horsetail	Horse nettle	Hyacinth
Iris	Jack-in-the-pulpit	Jimson weed
Jessamine	Larkspur (annual delphinium)	Laurel
Leafy spurge	Lily, flame	Lily, glory
Lily of the valley	Lobelia	Lupine
Marvel of Peru (Mirabilis)	Marsh marigold	Mayapple (except fruit)
Mistletoe	Monkshood	Morning glory
Mountain laurel	Narcissus	Oleander
Poinsettia	Poison hemlock	Poison ivy
Poison milkweed	Poison oak	Pokeweed
Poppy, horned	Poppy, Iceland	Poppy, Somniferum
Privet	Purple cockle	Rhododendron
Rhubarb (leaves)	Rosary pea	Skunk cabbage
Snowdrops	Solomon's seal	Star of Bethlehem
St. John's wort	Tobacco	Water hemlock
Wild black cherry	Wisteria	Yew
(Sources: Emery 1998, 400; Harrington 1998, 8–52; Elias 1990, 258–273; Runyon 1995, 5)		

Hunting and Trapping

The bow and arrow is probably the most effective of the traditional low-tech hunting weapons, and is not too difficult to make.

Bow

Seasoned, resilient, long-grained woods are best for bow making. English longbows were traditionally made from yew trees, but fir, cedar, hickory, juniper, oak, white elm, birch, willow, hemlock, maple, and alder will usually do. "Green" wood bows tend to lose their strength or crack after a couple of weeks, needing replacement. For short-term survival, crude bows of many different green woods will suffice. For durable bows, select strong, straight, resilient, knot-free young saplings such as yew, greasewood, ironwood, hickory, or ash. For the bow stave, select one or two supple limbs, about 1½ to 2 inches thick in the middle, and free of knots and branches. Fire-killed standing wood has already been seasoned. Test the flex of your chosen wood and discard if it shows any signs of cracking. Depending on the stiffness and spring of the wood, either shave flats in the center section of each stave and

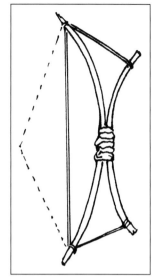

Figure 7-27. Double bow.

fasten two curved staves together for a double bow (see fig. 7-27) or shape the stave so that it is about 2 inches thick at the handle, tapering uniformly to ⅝ inch thick at the ends (see fig. 7-28). Notch the ends for the bowstring. Repeatedly greasing and heating a carved bow in front of the fire over a period of several days will deter cracking and make it more durable. The best strings are made from sinew or rawhide, but you can use any strong string or make your own cordage from animal fur, hair, or plant fibers. Rather than twisting extra-thick clusters of plant fibers, stronger bowstrings are made by braiding or twisting together multiple strands of finer cordage to make thicker cordage. When not in use, loosen the bowstring to save the bow's power. Once a bow has lost its power, throw it away and make another one. A cloth or piece of leather strapped to the inside of your forearm can help prevent chafing from the bowstring.

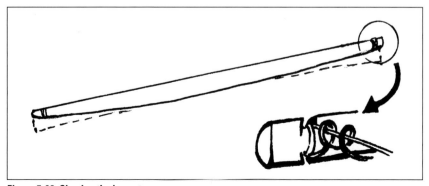

Figure 7-28. Shaping the bow stave.

Arrows

Any straight wood will do for arrows, but birch and willow sucker branches sprouting from the base of tree trunks work particularly well. Make arrows about ¼ inch in diameter and the length of your arm. Notch one end for the bowstring to catch on (the "nock"). Some type of fletching should be attached about 2 to 3 inches in front of the nock to stabilize the arrow and ensure a reasonably straight and long-distance flight. Split feathers work best for fletching, but paper, cloth, or even split leaves will do. Attach three or four feathers to the shaft. The simplest arrowhead is a sharpened and flame-hardened wooden point. For larger game and more durability, fashion arrowheads from sheet metal, stone, or bone. Attach the arrowheads and fletching to the arrow shaft using fine cordage. Wet sinew works best, because it shrinks and sticks to itself as it dries. Seal the binding with boiled pine pitch to prevent unraveling.

Traps and Snares

Using traps is a very effective way of catching animals for food, but may result in prolonged suffering for the trapped animal. Traps are not selec-

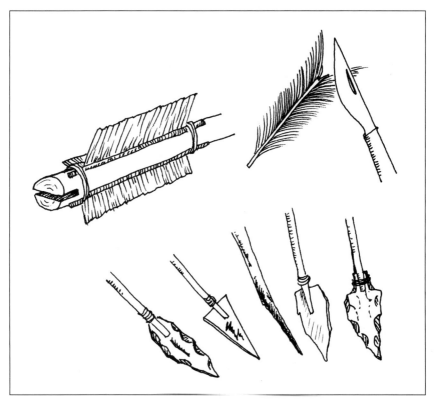

Figure 7-29. Traditional arrows.

tive. They can kill the neighbor's dog or harm an unsuspecting human who stumbles into them, so use traps only in survival situations and dismantle your practice traps when finished. Set traps in areas near abundant food or a water source that animals frequent. Look for animal scat and signs of feeding to locate a good spot for your trap. Fabricate and test your trap in camp before setting it at the trap location. Disturb the area around the trap minimally and spend as little time there as possible. Animals have a keen sense of smell. You might want to mask your scent by holding your trap materials in the smoke of a fire before setting them or by rubbing them with crushed, nonpoisonous leaves. Smoke on your hands can also cover your scent when you handle the traps. Baited traps are usually effective in semi-open areas. Baitless traps are best set in animal runs where vegetation and natural features force animals to follow a narrow path. Many animals are smarter than you might think, so make traps look as natural as possible. Leave bark on branches, and mask carved areas by darkening them with smoke or smearing dirt on the fresh cuts.

There are many designs for traps and snares, but most are variations on a few basic themes that are illustrated as follows. Traps typically try to strangle, dangle, or mangle the prey.

Figure-Four Deadfall
This classic deadfall trap does not use cordage and can be made to any size (see fig. 7-30). Three sticks are carved and stacked to support a massive weight, such as a large rock, log, group of lashed logs, and so on. An upright stake is driven into the ground to support the entire mechanism. The bait bar is notched in the center and at the far end. The center notch hooks a flat on the middle zone of the upright stake, while the end notch of the bait bar catches the locking arm. A notch in the locking arm pivots on the chamfered end of the upright stake. The deadfall weight is balanced against the locking arm, dropping the deadfall weight when the bait bar is tugged. To figure the

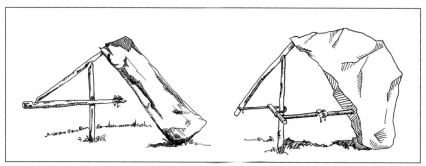

Figure 7-30. Figure-four deadfall.

proper spots for notching the various parts, lay them flat on the ground and mark the notch locations.

Rolling Snare

There are numerous variations on the rolling snare (see fig. 7-31). Baitless varieties are placed next to an animal run, where a passing animal will stick its nose through the snare noose and trigger the trap. Baited varieties are set in semi-open areas where passing animals will go for the bait. A forked stake, or notched peg, is driven into the ground for an anchor. A second forked stick, or notched peg, is tied to cordage attached to the top of a springy sapling. The sapling is bent down, and the trigger is hooked under the notch in the anchor stake. A loop of cordage makes a loose, wide, open noose that is held open across the game run via small twigs stuck in the ground. A passing animal triggers the snare and is held in the air by the noose.

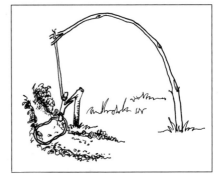

Figure 7-31. Rolling snare.

T-Bar Snare

The T-bar snare is a baited snare, similar to the rolling snare (see fig. 7-32). Start forming a circle of stakes by driving two notched stakes into the ground. Form the rest of the circle with plain vertical stakes. The bait bar hooks into the notches on the first two anchor stakes. Flatten the tops of the bait bar just enough so that it catches in the anchor stakes and holds horizontal under tension. The vertical stakes force the game to reach its head through the snare noose to reach the bait bar. Carve the notches in the anchor stakes and the flats on the bait bar so that a slight upward tug on the bait bar releases the snare.

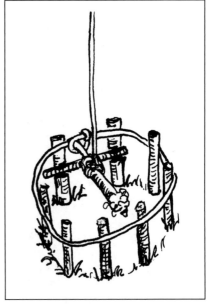

Figure 7-32. T-bar snare.

Mice and Rats

Don't forget to use your mouse and rat traps to help provide a relatively easy source of food, at least until the rest of the neighborhood catches on to the fact that while they are out hunting for big game that has made itself scarce, you are sitting at home feasting on tasty little varmints.

To be honest with you, I don't claim to be a gourmet chef when it comes to rats and mice. According to Cody Lundin, a famous wilderness survival instructor, mice are best thrown directly on the coals of a fire, and turned a few times to singe their fur. At this point, they will swell up and you can split them open to get rid of their guts, saving the heart, lungs, and liver, if you wish. Cook a bit longer on the coals, until the tail arms and legs pretty much burn off and you have about three bites of decent food per mouse. Apparently during the summer months arctic wolves feast on dozens of mice every day. If they can do it, so can you!

Cody says that rats are particularly yummy. Small rats can be cooked like mice, but the large ones (more like cat sized) should be skinned and gutted prior to roasting on an open fire. Once gutted, wash the carcass with clean water, if available. You can eat the organs too, just not the entrails (meaning the stomach and intestines).

Skinning and Cleaning

Mammals should be bled, and all animals must be gutted to avoid rapid spoilage. Birds should be plucked, saving their feathers for use as bait, insulation, arrows, or for tying fishing flies. You can usually leave the skin on birds, but skin lizards and other animals, being careful not to damage the pelt if it is to be used for something else. Blood is a rich source of vitamins and minerals and can enrich and thicken stews.

When cleaning an animal, take care not to puncture the entrails or scent glands. Use your eyes and nose to alert you to signs of disease in the organs (funny color and smell) and discard them if there is any question of their quality. If you have any skin cuts, take precautions to prevent infecting yourself from the animal.

Cleaning Procedure

1. Hang larger animals by the rear legs, with ropes tied just above the knees, and cut the large neck vein (jugular) to bleed thoroughly. If the blood is not drained, the meat will spoil quickly.

2. On males, tie off the penis to avoid getting urine on the meat. Remove the scent glands, which might taint the meat. Some deer have scent glands located on their rear legs, just behind the knee.

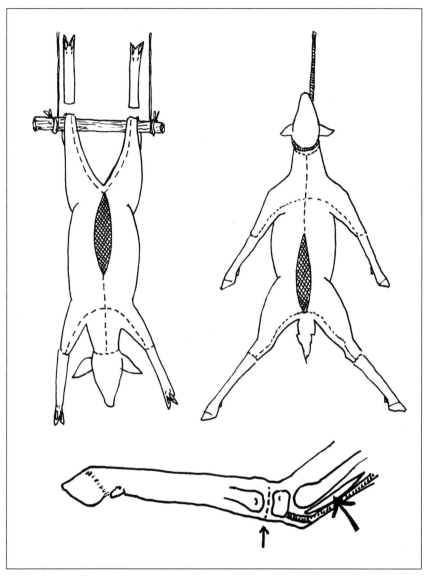

Figure 7-33. Knife cuts for skinning and gutting larger animals.

3. Cut a ring through the skin around each leg and arm by the knee joint.

4. Cut down the inside of the rear legs from the knee to the crotch, making a circle around the genitals.

5. Make a shallow incision through the skin from the tail all the way up the belly to the chin. Pointing the knife's sharp edge outward and working your fingers behind the blade will help keep it from cutting too deep.

6. Make cuts on the inside of the forelegs to the chin.

7. Peel the skin from the flesh. To keep from damaging the pelt, use your knife minimally while peeling.

8. Pinch the flesh in front of the anus and sex organs, and then make a shallow incision into the abdominal cavity. Using the fingers to guide your knife, open the abdominal cavity all the way to the windpipe and gullet, being careful to avoid piercing the entrails. The bulk of the internal organs will spill out and may be inspected and stored for use. The anus should be clear, showing daylight through it.

9. Provided the weather is cool, hanging the carcass for several days will tenderize the meat, and harmful parasitic bacteria will die. Keep flies off the meat. Protect your meat from predators and scavengers.

Fishing

You will find that fish generally bite most frequently early in the morning around sunrise, just before sunset, and just before the onset of a storm. On sunny, hot days, the fish generally head toward deeper water or seek shelter in the shade of fallen trees or riverbanks. On cold days, they often warm themselves in shallow pools. You can catch fish with your bare hands, nets, traps, baskets, baited hooks, spears, and arrows. Take your time to observe the fish and what they are eating. Bait that is the same as what the fish are eating, or closely resembles it, often works well.

For bait, try grasshoppers, flies, meat, berries, fish eggs, worms, minnows, and grubs. If the bait is still alive and wriggling, it is usually more effective. You can tie bits of feathers and tufts of fur onto hooks to make your own

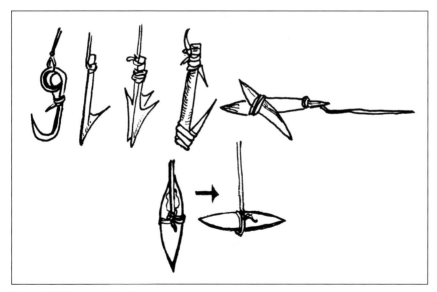

Figure 7-34. Homemade hooks.

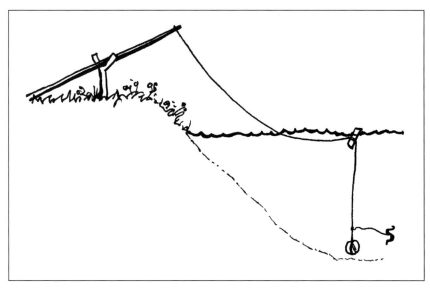

Figure 7-35. Fishing line with float and weights.

fishing "flies." Artificial lures can be carved from wood to simulate minnows, or you can make your own "spinners" by attaching a shiny bit of foil or metal above the hook in such a way that it moves and reflects light, simulating light flashing off a minnow as it swims. Attach a weight and a float to the line to position live bait at the desired depth, where the fish are hanging out. Lines can have multiple hooks and bait at different depths to improve your chances by fishing several levels at once. Crude floats could be made from some wood or a piece of animal intestine inflated with air.

Catching Fish by Hand

This takes patience, unless there are tons of fish, such as when the salmon are spawning. Wade into the water and stand very still. Fish will often come up to your legs and nibble on your leg hairs. Slowly lower your hands into the water and allow the fish to come near. Have your hands near the bottom. If the fish is big, try to grasp the fish by the gills and throw it out of the water onto the shore. If the fish is small, just try to scoop quickly and throw it onto the shore. Late in the summer, in the High Sierra of California, friends of mine have fished like this to their hearts' content when large numbers of fish were trapped in shrinking pools as creeks were running dry.

Spearing Fish

When fish congregate in shallow waters, spear fishing is relatively fast and easy. A barbed, double-pronged, forked spear is far more effective at catching and holding fish than a single-tipped spear. The addition of a central fork to make a trident spear increases efficiency and is worth the extra effort. Fire-harden wooden tips by rotating them in a flame until they sizzle and brown, but do not allow them to char. Check for hardness by creasing with your thumbnail.

Fishing with Nets

If you have a good source of plant fiber, such as dogbane, milkweed, hemp, or yucca, you can make your own fishing nets. Attach a net to a hoop on a pole, stretch it across a narrows in a fast-moving creek, or fish from a boat.

Insects, Grubs, and Worms

Insects can be a valuable source of necessary protein in emergency situations. Pound for pound they have more food value than vegetables and are usually much easier to hunt and gather than mammals. Since they may contain harmful parasites, insects should be cooked before eating. Boiling is the safest method, but roasting in hot coals or on a hot rock will suffice if no pots are avail-

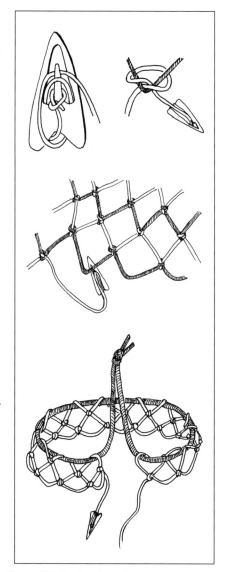

Figure 7-36. Handmade netting.

able. To make them more palatable, you can chop them finely, or dry and grind them up before adding to soups or stews. Some varieties of grubs can taste like cheese or sweets and are considered delicacies in certain parts of the world. Look for grubs in rotting stumps or under peeling tree bark.

Caution: Brightly colored insects, including their caterpillars, are usually poisonous.

Ants

Most ants have a stinging bite containing formic acid, which is quite bitter and odorous. Cook these ants for at least six minutes to destroy this poison.

Caterpillars

If hairy, you can squeeze to remove head and guts. Discard the hairy outside.

Grasshoppers, Crickets, and Cicadas

Remove the head, wings, and legs before roasting or boiling. The legs have fine barbs, which will irritate your stomach. Gather in the morning, when they are cold or sluggish, or trap them by laying out a wool blanket at night in a meadow. Barbs on their legs will catch in the wool, like burrs stuck to a sweater. Roasting or boiling will kill any parasites in your grasshoppers.

Worms

Worms are an excellent source of food for robins and humans. Starve them for a day, or squeeze them to get the dirt out of their bellies. Try drying them and grinding to a powder to make them more palatable.

Slugs and Snails

Avoid sea snails and any snails with bright shells, especially tropical ones (possibly poisonous). Starve them for a few days to remove any toxins from the food they have been eating.

Shelter

In severe climates, some kind of fabricated shelter from the elements will be essential for your survival. In more moderate climates, a shelter may not be necessary, but can make your daily life a lot more pleasant and comfortable. This section will cover several rudimentary shelters that you can build from foraged materials. A good shelter can keep you dry and warm, even in torrential rains or subfreezing weather. A plastic tarp will make the job of keeping the rain out of a primitive shelter a hundred times easier than trying to accomplish that task using just bark and grasses (thatch). Mountaineers and soldiers will often "bivouac" outside using just their rain poncho covering most of their body and perhaps stuffing their feet inside their backpack for a little extra warmth and protection from the elements.

Location

- **Water.** Try to locate your shelter near a good water supply, but above high-water marks and never in a dry streambed or wash. Stay at least 30 yards from your water source to avoid polluting it. If insects are a problem, stay away from stagnant water, especially wet, boggy areas.

- **Building materials and fuel.** Choose a location where you can find building materials and fuel nearby so you are not hauling them a long way.

- **Visibility.** If you are seeking rescue, make sure you are visible and not too near a noisy river that might obscure the sounds of rescuers approaching.

- **Natural shelter.** Utilize natural bluffs, fallen trees, caves, ridges, and so on for protection from the wind and rain.

- **Comfort.** The site should be flat enough and smooth enough for comfortable sleeping. Before pitching a tent, it's a good idea to lie on the ground first to see how the spot feels.

- **Drainage.** Make sure that the site will drain. Avoid hollows that can turn into ponds in the rain. Trenches can help to divert small streams in a downpour, but you can't move a pond.

- **What to avoid.** Don't try to build a shelter on hard, rocky ground. Check the area for stinging ants, bee nests, and so on, and avoid high wind areas, such as hilltops and ridge tops (unless you want high winds to keep insects away). Avoid areas with danger of falling rocks or large dead branches from overhead trees. Valley bottoms and hollows can collect cold, frosty air at night.

Squirrel's Nest

This is the simplest of survival shelters. It's a drag to get in and out of, so you should really make something else if you will be using it more than once. The basic idea is to heap as much dry debris as you can into a pile, and then crawl into it to stay dry and warm. Use leaves, pine boughs, bark, and so on. The debris is your sleeping bag, so the thicker it is the warmer you will be. To insulate yourself from the ground, make sure you have an insulating layer under you as well as on top. Without a poncho or tarp on top, it won't be very effective at keeping you dry in a rainstorm.

Building on Fallen Trunks and Trees

It is usually easier to start a primitive shelter from an existing feature. A fallen trunk makes an excellent support for a simple lean-to (see fig. 7-37). Shingling is an important part of primitive structures, and can be made from any materials that will keep rain from penetrating your shelter. Shingling can consist of thatch, bark, sod, or sticks and dirt. The basic idea is to make enough layers of overlapping sloped materials so that water runs down the outside

Figure 7-37. Fallen log shelter.

without penetrating the structure and getting you wet. Traditional thatch is made from bundles of straw with the straw strands all oriented in the same direction. The capillary action of water causes rain to flow along the straw strands, rather than penetrating through the straw, and is very effective at keeping rain outside of a shelter when the thatch bundles are laid in overlapping shingle fashion.

Scout Pits and Coal Beds

It takes considerable effort, but you can spend a comfortable warm night in a "scout pit," even when it's very cold outside (see fig. 7-38). First, dig a trench about 2 feet deep by 2 feet wide and a few feet longer than your body length. Build a fire in the trench that covers the entire length. After the fire has roasted the ground for an hour or two, cover the coals with several inches of dirt. Bridge the top of the trench with a layer of sticks and cover with leaves for insulation, finishing with a layer of dirt. Crawl in and enjoy the warmth of the heated ground. If the trench is big enough, you can use it a second time by heating rocks in an outside fire and dragging them in at night to heat your scout pit. One alternative

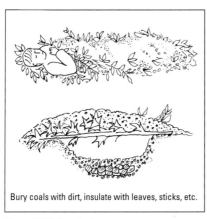

Bury coals with dirt, insulate with leaves, sticks, etc.

Figure 7-38. Scout pit.

is to build a fire in a shallower trench, 6 to 12 inches deep. When the fire is down to coals, cover the coals with a few inches of dirt, followed by debris insulation. You can pull some of this insulation over you for a preheated squirrel's nest shelter. If you have a tarp, place it underneath your body, to act as a vapor barrier for protection from ground moisture due to steam rising from the heated earth.

Snow Shelters

Snow is a good insulator and can protect you from fierce winds and bitter cold. If your clothing is cotton, or otherwise poorly designed for snow country, beware of getting yourself wet while constructing your snow shelter. Unless you are traveling in the Arctic, with wind-packed snow and little contour to the land, you will probably be better off constructing a snow cave or a shelter under the boughs of a tree than trying to construct a traditional igloo. Create a raised platform for sleeping on, with a lower area to collect the coldest air. Insulate the sleeping platform with pine boughs, when available, to keep yourself relatively warm and dry.

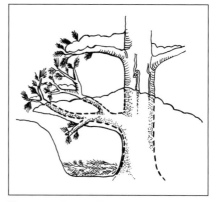

Figure 7-39. Tree-well snow shelter.

Caution: You must provide ventilation in snow shelters. Your body heat will eventually raise the inside temperature above freezing to the point where it glazes over the inside of a snow cave. You can suffocate without a hole for ventilation (I suggest a fist-sized hole).

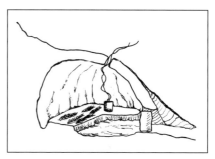

Figure 7-40. Snow cave.

If you can't find a firm snowdrift or a suitable tree well (see fig. 7-39) for your snow cave, you can pile soft snow into a heap, trample it some, and let it firm up for a couple of hours before digging it out to make a snow cave. Make sure that you carve the ceiling into a curved dome shape to prevent sagging and collapse of the ceiling (see fig. 7-40).

Emergency Snowshoes

Boughs of flexible spruce branches with a healthy supply of green needles will suffice for snowshoes in an emergency. Use string or green branches to tie boughs to your feet. Weaving a second or third branch into the boughs ties individual branches together for better flotation and more stability. With a roll of duct tape or string, you can make a decent pair of pine bough snowshoes in a short period of time. The task will be tougher if you must rely solely on green branches for holding the snowshoes onto your feet.

Cordage

Primitive living can be greatly enhanced with cordage, which is just a fancy term for string, twine, and rope. Cordage is handy for thatching your roof, lashing together branches for your shelter, stringing a bow, sewing your garments, making nets for fish, snaring animals, and so on. Many indigenous societies have been literally held together with string. You can make cordage from a variety of materials, including hair, fur, hides, narrow strips of cloth, and a multitude of plant fibers.

Recommended Plant Fibers

For many thousands of years, native peoples have gathered and spun plant fibers from thousands of different plants. Their cords have made ropes strong enough to hold elephants and carry suspension bridges across hundred-foot-wide gorges in the Himalayas. Archaeologists have discovered 10,000-year-old fishing nets that are still intact. Any strong flexible plant can make cordage. The following list is for starters, but use the "fiber test" to ensure that the plants you are working with are adequate for cordage. Some of the plants on the list can work well only at certain times of the year or under certain conditions. Common plant fiber sources are listed below.

- **Leaf fibers:** Yucca, cattail, reeds, iris, agave, and palmetto.
- **Dry outer bark:** Bulrush, sage, willow, and cattail.
- **Wet inner bark:** Aspen, cottonwood, sage, juniper, willow, cedar, mesquite, walnut, cherry, slippery elm, and hawthorn.
- **Bast fibers:** Soft fibers located between the outer bark and a woody stem on many common weeds, such as dogbane, milkweed, hemp, stinging nettle, evening primrose, flax, fireweed, hollyhock, and wild licorice. Dogbane is commonly acknowledged as one of the best fibers for cordage.
- **Roots:** Spruces, poplar, and lupines.
- **Whole plants:** Rushes, cattail, sedge, and various grasses (most grasses are weak when dry).

Fiber Test

- Tie a knot in a small bundle of fibers to check for flexibility. If it breaks, the fibers are too brittle.
- Spin a small length of twine. Pull on the twine to check for strength. Good fibers for cordage grip together when spun tightly, but fibers that are too slippery and smooth will not hold together.
- Remember that some fibers are stronger wet, while some are better dry. You may be able to make adequate cordage for a fire drill from green grasses that break once they dry.

Preparing Fibers

Different fiber types must be prepared in different ways. Leaf fibers, such as yucca, are usually best harvested green. Bast fibers, such as hemp and dogbane, are best processed dry, but the plants can be harvested green and then bundled to dry before processing (allow for ventilation so they don't rot).

Bast Fibers

Start by trying to scrape off the papery outer bark with a knife held perpendicular to the stalk (if the plant is dry and the outer bark is cracked, skip this step). Buff the stalks over your pant leg to remove what's left of the outer bark. Use a smooth rock or a wooden mallet/chunk to gently crack/split the stalks, without cutting the fibers. You are trying to split the fiber sheath and remove it from the woody core. Using your fingers, bend the fibers and peel out sections of the woody core. Roll the fibers back and forth between the palms of your hands to separate the fibers and clean the remaining bits of bark and woody core out of the fiber bundle. Chunks of this stuff will weaken your cordage and leave it messy looking.

Yucca and Agave

These and other similar tough leaf fibers are usually processed most easily when green or after they have been soaked for a while. Yucca and agave make very strong cordage and can be used to make packs, sandals, and more. Generally, the long leaves will be pounded to split the fibers from the fleshy parts. Soaking the pounded leaves can remove alkaloids, which can be irritating to the skin. Use a knife or the smooth edge of a stone to scrape the fleshy parts from the fibers. Roll the fibers between the palms of your hands to further clean and separate the fibers.

Retting

Some plant and bark fibers are most easily processed through "retting"—soaking and letting them partially rot to facilitate separating the fibers and/or their substrates. Retting might take as short a time as one or two days, but can also take as long as two weeks. The retting process uses bacteria in the water to eat away the fleshy binders that hold the fibers together.

Spinning Fibers into Cord

In general, more twists per inch make for stronger and stiffer cordage. For ease of handling, most hand cordage is spun from two strands of fibers at a time (see fig. 7-41), but you can spin from three or more, if you wish. You can spin cords into ropes by the identical process, or you can "plait" (braid) three strands into rope (see fig. 7-42). Since hand-twisting makes for the tightest, cleanest, strongest cordage, it is best for things like bowstring, where performance is critical. Leg-rolling is faster (see fig. 7-43), but not as tight, so primitive cordage that requires a high volume of spun materials, such as rope and netting, is usually made by leg-rolling.

Figure 7-41. Twisting fibers to make two-ply cordage.

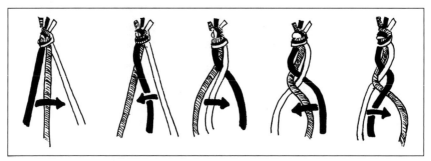

Figure 7-42. Braiding cordage into ropes.

1. **Start:** Tie the end of your fiber bundle in a knot and split the bundle into two roughly equal bundles. Alternately roll both ends of the bundle between your thumb and forefingers until it kinks in the middle.

2. **Spin:** Slip the knotted end over something to hold it or bite the kink in the center of the fiber bundle to hold it in your teeth. Spin two strands of fibers tightly, both in the same direction—either clockwise or counterclockwise.

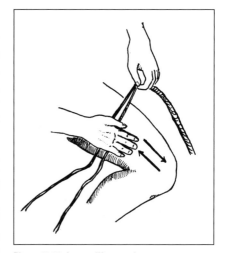

Figure 7-43. Leg-rolling cordage.

3. **Spin and twist:** Now, twist both of your spun fiber bundles into cord. The direction of twist is critical. Twist the fiber bundles in the opposite direction from the way each bundle was spun. Good tension, tight spinning, and the proper directions of spin and twist are what hold the fibers in cordage.

4. **Repeat:** Keep working your way down a few inches of cord at a time. Splice in fibers as you need them.

Splicing

Unless you are making short cords from a long bundle of fiber, you will need to add fibers by splicing. It's best to blend in splices by staggering and thinning the fiber ends in the splice and the ends of the cord bundle so that they blend together well. Unravel the ends of the cordage until the fibers are roughly parallel, and then place the splice bundle next to the cordage ends. Twisting the fibers locks the splice fibers to the existing cordage fibers. Splice fibers to either side of two-ply cordage, or bend the splice bundle and splice into both

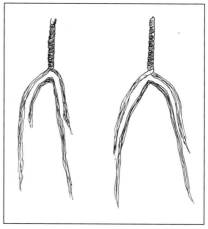

Figure 7-44. Splicing fibers into hand-rolled cordage.

sides of the cordage at the same time. Stagger the splices to prevent weak spots in the cordage (see fig. 7-44).

Simple Tools

You may find yourself surprisingly proud of your first efforts to fashion a piece of bone, stone, or wood into a usable tool.

Discoidal Stone Knives

Probably the simplest way to get a knife, without access to modern tools, is to make a discoidal knife (see fig. 7-45). Start with a fine-grained glassy rock, such as quartzite or basalt, preferably oval shaped. Obsidian, which is volcanic glass, breaks into sharper edges than the finest metal scalpels and razor blades. Strike this rock (call it a "cobble") against a larger rock (an "anvil") to bust off a sharp flake or disc of rock from the end. Riverbeds often contain many fine-grained, rounded stones suitable for making into stone knives. Once you

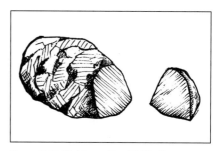

Figure 7-45. Making a discoidal knife.

have broken one disc off the cobble, it is usually easier to break the cobble into more sharp flakes.

Cautions about Working with Stone

It is essential to wear safety glasses or goggles when working with stone. Flying shards can damage your eyes or even blind you. Additionally, the dust from stone cutting contains tiny particles with sharp edges that act like tiny knives, settling into lungs and creating scar tissue and cumulative damage. Breathing too much stone dust over a period of years can lead to silicosis (similar to asbestosis). Do your stone cutting and grinding outside, protect your lungs with a dust mask, and wash the particles out of your clothing. Cut stone is sharp, so protect your skin and keep plenty of Band-Aids around when learning these arts. Of course, in a survival situation, simply do your best to protect your skin and eyes without modern safety goggles or gloves.

Flint Knapping

Flint knapping is the art of chipping away at a stone to make it into something useful with a sharp edge. I'm no expert, and will just give you a few guidelines. Both *Primitive Wilderness Living and Survival Skills* and *Primitive Technology: A Book of Earth Skills* have decent sections on flint knapping. John and Geri McPherson, authors of *Primitive Wilderness Living and Survival Skills*, have an instructional flint knapping video called *Breaking Rock*. For more information on this subject, you might also try *Flintknapping: Making and Understanding Stone Tools* by John C. Whittaker, or *Flintknapping: The Art of Making Stone Tools* by Paul Hellweg.

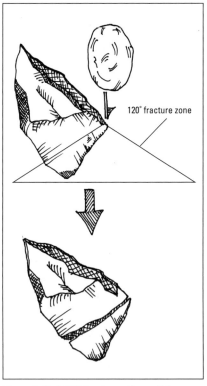

True flints can be hard to find in most locations, but most cherts, jaspers, agates, quartz, and so forth will work as long as they are fine-grained and fracture with sharp edges. When flint knapping, the main principle to remember is that

Figure 7-46. A 120° fracture of large flakes.

stone tends to break into a wide cone, at roughly 120 degrees from the line of impact (fig. 7-46). Most people would intuitively guess that the stone would break roughly in line with the impact, so you must modify your blows to a shallower angle to account for the breaking angle. Chose a hard, round stone for your hammer stone, which you will pound against the flint to remove flakes. Fist-sized hammer stones are easy to handle.

Because a somewhat squared flat platform is the best edge to hit against to remove good, clean flakes from your base material, you may need to spend some time squaring the edge of your stock between hammer blows. Stock can be squared by grinding against other stones or lightly chipping the edge. Fine flakes can be removed from flint edges by applying pressure with a sharply pointed stick or pointy bone, such as an antler. Called *pressure-flaking*, this method is often used for finishing or sharpening up edges (fig. 7-47). To avoid splitting the brittle flint flakes while pressure-flaking, try supporting the flint on a thick piece of leather.

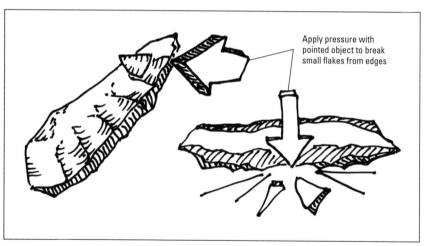

Apply pressure with pointed object to break small flakes from edges

Figure 7-47. Pressure-flaking small flakes from edges.

Bone Tools

Bone is more easily ground and shaped and is less brittle than stone. Though not as sharp, nor as deadly for bringing down large game, bone arrowheads are more durable and less likely to fracture than flint arrowheads. Antlers and thighbones of larger animals make good stock for bone tools. To use thighbones, start by cutting the heavy ends off with a saw or stone knife, then split the bone lengthwise with a sturdy knife. Grind the bone into the desired shape by abrading it against a rough piece of rock, such as sandstone or granite.

Further Study and Practice

This chapter provides an excellent overview and introduction to wilderness survival and primitive-living skills, but to become truly proficient in these areas requires decades of experience. I highly recommend that you continue building your survival library and skill set by learning from those who have made the study and practice of primitive living and wilderness survival both a lifestyle and a lifelong passion. Only a handful fall into this category and even fewer are able to present their teachings in an easily assimilated format. For more information on the schools, videos, and other teaching materials from highly respected masters of primitive living and survival, such as Cody Lundin, John and Geri McPherson, Les Stroud, Thomas J. Elpel, or Robin Blankenship, see the resource appendix at the back of the book, under the heading of "Survival and Primitive-Living Skills."

8

Water: Requirements, Purification, and Storage

"'I called as I approached, asking if she was okay,' wrote Ranger Amber Nattrass in a park report. 'She was waving frantically and screaming, "My baby is dead, my baby is dead."' In the SUV, Nattrass found Sanchez's lifeless 6-year-old son Carlos on the front seat. 'She told me they walked 10 miles but couldn't find any help (and)... had run out of water and had been drinking their own urine,' Nattrass wrote. 'She turned down a wrong road,' Nattrass said in a recent interview. 'She said she was following her GPS unit.'**"**
—Tom Knudson, "Death by GPS in the Desert," *Sacramento Bee*, January 30, 2011

Water Requirements

Water is absolutely essential for human survival; it plays a part in all of the body's biochemical reactions. Most of us could survive for several weeks without food, but in average conditions we would only last three to four days without water, and we would be very miserable for all but the first of those days.

Water requirements vary depending on activity level and temperature. When you eat dehydrated foods, you will require more water under any set of conditions. The absolute minimum for survival is about one quart of drinking water per day, with little or no activity and cool conditions. Two quarts of water per day will usually sustain moderate activity at an acceptable level of comfort, under moderate conditions with minimal urination (you will feel somewhat dehydrated). In fact, the standard hospital maintenance level for adults is 2.5 liters (roughly 2.6 quarts) of intravenous fluids per day to maintain comfort and good kidney function, without any physical activity.

More than 1 quart of water every hour can be required to perform heavy physical labor under extremely hot conditions. When I was working on a construction site in Hawaii, I drank over 1 gallon of water for every eight-hour shift, and that was barely enough! In general, 1 gallon of water per adult per day is enough for drinking and some limited washing (sponge-bath style). This is a good figure to use when calculating water for storage.

Stocking Up for Emergencies

Grocery stores typically run out of bottled water in the first few hours after a public water system fails. I recommend that all households store at least

5 gallons of drinking water to cover short-term glitches in public water systems. An adequate two-week supply of water would be 14 gallons per person. A 55-gallon plastic drum of stored drinking water does not take up much space in the corner of a garage and would provide a family of four with a two-week emergency supply of drinking water in case of an earthquake or other disaster.

Note: Be sure to protect water in storage containers from freezing, and stock chemicals (or purifying filters) to treat water in these containers, as untreated water will grow bacteria over time.

Home-bottled chlorinated tap water should be changed every month, treated before use, or preserved to prevent bacterial growth. Use commercial water preservatives or two to four drops of household bleach per quart of clean potable water to preserve stored drinking water. If stored water is tightly sealed, taste it monthly or chemically test for residual chlorine, and treat again if the chlorine has disappeared. If the container is not sealed, re-treat every few days during usage periods. Preparedness/survival suppliers sell food-grade plastic drums, smaller water containers, and water preservatives such as the Katadyn Micropur products, which preserve home-bottled water for long-term storage.

Guidelines for Coping with Disaster

In a disaster situation, *conservation counts, because your life may depend on it.* Use rivers, lakes, or ponds for washing (provided that they are not severely polluted) to conserve potable water for drinking. If you are aware of an impending natural disaster, such as a hurricane or tornado, or you have just survived a significant earthquake and your house is still intact, take the following precautions:

- **Immediately fill your bathtubs, sinks, and other available containers with water.** This will provide your household with a short-term supply of clean, potable water.

- **Conserve stored water.** There is a supply of clean, potable water in the toilet tanks, hot-water heater, and piping in your house.

- **Tape off all toilets.** When you notice that the tap water has stopped flowing, conserve the water in your toilet tanks (the tanks, not the bowl, contain potable water) and immediately notify the occupants to not flush the toilets. *Caution:* Do not drink the toilet-tank water if you use an automatic toilet cleaner (it turns the water blue).

- **Drain your water heater.** Unless you plan before an incoming storm, by filling bathtubs and basins with potable water, your water heater will be the single largest reservoir of potable water left in your home when the utilities go down, so conserve this resource and use it wisely! Water heaters are supplied with a vent located near the top of the tank and a drain near the bottom of the tank. Open the top vent (pull on the little lever on the spigot) and drain the tank into containers as needed. If there is dirt and sediment in the water coming out of the tank, *do not discard this water.* Simply allow the sediment to settle and drink the water off the top. *Caution:* Turn off the gas or the electric power to your water heater before draining, or you will damage the heater.

- **Shut off the utility water supply to your house if there's reason to believe the public water supply may have been contaminated.** Otherwise, you risk contaminating the usable water in your plumbing.

- **Drain the pipes in your house.** These typically hold a gallon or two of water, maybe more, which can be drained into containers by slightly opening a high-point tap and draining from a low-point tap.

Water Contaminants

Water systems face . . . challenges in some of the new, hard-to-kill bacteria that crop up with growing frequency. Among the most feared is *Cryptosporidium*, the parasite that polluted Milwaukee's water in 1993, killing 111 people and sickening more than 403,000. It was the worst case of waterborne illness in modern U.S. history. The city's treatment system at the time wasn't good enough to kill the bug, which can evade conventional filters and is resistant to chlorine, most systems' main defense. — Peter Eisler, "Powerful New Pollutants Imperil Drinking Water Supply," *USA Today*, October 12, 1998

Important: All surface water sources in the United States should be considered unsafe to drink without treatment.

Just because water is clear, smells good, and tastes good does not mean that it is safe to drink. When I was a child, I often went hiking in the mountains of New England. We drank eagerly from all the sweet-tasting streams and creeks along the trailside. It was a treat to drink from these unchlorinated, natural water sources, and we never gave it a second thought. Forty years later, I will not drink from these same sources without first running the water through a portable filter, chemically treating it, or boiling it to remove or kill organisms such as *Giardia* or *Cryptosporidium*. The water still looks and tastes the same, but these organisms can live in clear, clean water. In the High Sierra of California, it is estimated that about 50 percent of the wild animal feces contain traces of *Giardia*. Surface waters in agricultural areas are usually even more severely infected with *Giardia* and *Cryptosporidium* than the mountainous regions, since livestock are major carriers of these pests.

Western nations have developed vast systems of water purification, storage, and distribution designed to protect us from traditional waterborne diseases, but waterborne diseases and parasites continue to plague most of the population of this planet, particularly in the third world. In typical disaster situations, modern systems for purifying and distributing clean water often fail. In these situations, to protect your health, you must purify your own water. Basic information on contaminants is presented here so that you will better understand the limitations of particular water-treatment options. Subsequently, a variety of water-treatment options are presented, and I offer my personal recommendations on particular brands and types of water treatment.

Types of Contamination

Bacteria

Bacteria, commonly called "germs," are single-celled organisms; they are spread by wind, water, person-to-person contact, animal feces, and contaminated food. You can't be sure that any surface water is free of harmful bacteria, even when it is crystal clear and there are no signs of human habitation. Some examples of harmful waterborne bacteria are cholera, *Campylobacter jejuni*, salmonella, and some varieties of *E. coli*. They multiply by cell division when they are in a "friendly" host environment, which provides them with food and temperatures suitable for growth. Given a positive growth environment, like feces-polluted water or a human body with a compromised immune system, one bacterium cell may multiply into millions within just a few hours. Signs of bacterial infection usually show up from six hours to three days after exposure.

Bacteria are killed by boiling, ultraviolet sterilization, ozone, or chemical treatment, provided the treatments are applied at the proper concentration and temperature and for the proper length of time. Bacteria are tiny, on the order of 0.3 microns to several microns in size, and visible only under a powerful microscope. One micron is a millionth of a meter long. To give you a better idea of how tiny a micron is, realize that a single human hair is about 76 microns thick. Filters rated at 0.2 microns or less are usually effective against bacteria, but bacteria can grow through some filter media over a period of time.

Caution: Not all filters perform equally well. See the "Portable Water Filters" section following.

Protozoa

Protozoa, such as *Giardia* and *Cryptosporidium*, are single-celled animals. Unlike bacteria, they are able to move themselves around, and don't just sit there waiting for something external to push them around. They are microscopic but relatively large (3 to 10 microns), which makes them considerably easier to filter out of your drinking water. However, they have the capacity to transform themselves into a cyst, which is a form that is very tough to kill chemically with traditional iodine and chlorine water treatments. When these little animals get into a harsh environment, such as one that is too cold or has no food (like clean water), they change into cysts. A cyst cannot move itself around or feed itself, but it can passively survive in harsh environmental conditions that would kill most bacteria. The cysts remain dormant waiting for a positive growth environment, such as the intestinal tract of an animal or polluted water. In a positive growth environment, protozoa change back to the active form and begin to eat and multiply. Protozoan infections usually take considerably longer to show symptoms—from a week to several months. Boiling and ultraviolet sterilization will kill protozoa and their cysts. Protozoan infections can be extremely difficult to treat once they have become entrenched in the body.

Viruses

Viruses are different organisms altogether. They are much smaller than bacteria, on the order of 0.004 to 0.06 microns (Wilkerson 1992, 72) and are much harder to filter out. Viral contamination of drinking water is not as problematic as bacterial or protozoan contamination, but waterborne outbreaks are not uncommon. Viruses are so small that they may be visible only through the use of an electron microscope. Viruses multiply by invading the cells of a host organism and "stealing" some of the genetic material of the host cell to reproduce the virus. This process usually destroys the host cells and reproduces the virus. Some common harmful waterborne viruses are hepatitis A, polio, and Norwalk virus. Over the past few years, the Norwalk virus has been in the news quite a bit for showing up in the water systems of a number of cruise ships and seriously sickening several thousand passengers (Sardone 2007). Proper iodine and chlorine chemical treatments, as well as boiling, ozone, and UV sterilization, will kill viruses. Waterborne viruses are usually spread by human feces. Unlike bacteria, viruses generally do not cross from animals to humans, so the chance of getting viral infections in pristine remote locations is rather small, unless there has been a viral outbreak in the local human population. Viruses usually, but not always, attach themselves to larger particles, which can be effectively filtered out by standard microbial filters, so these types of filters offer significant protection against viruses even though their pore size is far larger than the size of the virus.

Parasites

Parasites live off the bodies of host organisms for at least part of their life cycles. Parasites may be microscopic, such as malaria or trichinosis. Single-celled animals like *Giardia* and *Cryptosporidium* can be considered parasites. Some parasites are several inches long, such as liver flukes, or several feet long, such as intestinal tapeworms. Parasites remain the scourge of many millions of people throughout the third world and infect a surprisingly large percentage of the Western world. Research scientist Hulda Regehr Clark believes that twentieth-century solvents tend to collect in some of the organs of our bodies and make them unusually good hosts for a variety of parasites (Clark 1995, 332). According to Clark, these solvents, and the parasites they nurture, contribute significantly to high rates of cancer. In the West, most parasites appear to be picked up through contact with house pets or while preparing raw meat. In the third world, parasites are often spread by eating raw meat or through poor sanitation and lack of water treatment. Usually parasites do not kill their hosts, but sap health, body strength, and vitality. (See any of Dr. Clark's books or chapter 9 in *When Technology Fails* for low-tech solutions to parasite infections.)

Parasites are killed by boiling, chlorine dioxide treatment, and UV sterilization, but may survive iodine and traditional chlorine treatments if they are in cyst form. Their relatively large size makes them easy to filter out of contaminated water. All known parasites are filtered out of the water by filters rated at 2 microns or less.

Chemical and Radioactive Contaminants

Potentially harmful chemical contaminants in our drinking water include heavy metals, such as arsenic and lead from industrial pollution or naturally occurring deposits in deep well water, organic compounds from various industries or chlorine treatment of surface water, and nitrates and pesticides from modern farms. In some parts of the world, pollutants also include radioactive contamination from the refining of radioactive materials or industrial accidents, such as the partial meltdown of the reactor at Chernobyl.

Organic compounds are large molecules that consist of chains of carbon and hydrogen atoms with various other atoms attached to them. The modern world has invented huge numbers of organic compounds and refined and concentrated many other naturally occurring organic compounds. Some examples of these are gasoline, solvents, pesticides, latex paint, and plastics.

When chlorine combines with organic debris, like dead leaves, it makes carcinogenic (cancer-causing) compounds called trihalomethanes (THMs). Boiling your water will kill microorganisms but will usually have no effect on chemical or radioactive pollutants. Distillation will kill all kinds of microorganisms, but simple distillers will not remove volatile organic compounds since they evaporate and condense along with the water vapor. To remove volatile organic compounds, more advanced distillers include either fractional distillation or an activated carbon cartridge to remove these pollutants. The common reverse osmosis (RO) systems, which include activated carbon filters, will remove most organic compounds and heavy metals (see the section on water treatment).

Disinfecting Your Water

Contrary to popular opinion, clear, sparkling water is often unsafe for drinking. Even springwater may not be safe. Deep-water springs from gravel or sand sources are usually safe, but may be contaminated by runoff from agricultural fertilizers, septic systems, sewer lines, and so on. Springs emerging from rock crevices can be exit points for underground streams carrying pollutants from far-off sources. When unsure about the source of your water, it is safest to boil, chemically treat, or filter the water through a certified water filter.

Boiling all your daily drinking water is time and energy consuming, and will not remove bad tastes, odors, or toxic chemicals. Most chemical treatments leave an aftertaste and should be used with care to ensure the proper concentration and contact time for the temperature of application, plus they will not remove toxic chemicals or bad tastes and odors. Traditional iodine and chlorine water treatments, except for the relatively new two-part chlorine dioxide water treatment products (trade names Aquamira, Micropur, and MMS), do not provide guaranteed protection from *Cryptosporidium* cysts, which have been found to survive a twenty-four-hour soak in undiluted household bleach. Portable filters can rapidly process surface water into potable water and, if they have a carbon block inside the filter, they will remove bad tastes, odors, and many chemical contaminants, but some filters may not purify as well as their labels lead you to believe. When your water source is highly questionable, the safest method for portable, fast, reliable water disinfection is to combine either chemical or UV treatment with bacteriological filtration, or to simply use the chlorine dioxide–based products, which will kill all organisms in five to fifteen minutes. Recommended methods for sterilizing and disinfecting water are summarized below.

Heat Sterilization

Water sterilization by boiling is preferred over any method of chemical disinfection. This time-honored method is safe and a sure thing, because disease-causing microorganisms cannot survive the heat of a sterilizing boil. The CDC (Centers for Disease Control and Prevention) recommends that you boil water at a vigorous rolling boil for at least one minute at sea level. At altitudes above 6,000 feet, they recommend three minutes of rolling boil, since water boils at lower temperatures as the altitude increases. Some references (Wilkerson 1992, 71) state that, regardless of elevation, the boiling temperature and the time to reach that temperature are sufficient to kill all pathogenic organisms. Since milk is pasteurized at 160°F, I tend to agree with those experts who say that by the time water has reached a full boil, regardless of elevation, it has long since killed any living organisms, except for prions (mad cow disease, scrapie, etc.), which are rare and are in a totally different class (not really an organism, per se) and can survive steam sterilization. Boiled water can be used after cooling (do not add ice, which may be contaminated), but it takes considerable time and fuel to boil all your drinking water.

Note: Boiling usually has no impact on chemical or radioactive pollutants, which must be dealt with by other methods.

Portable Water Filters

There are many different portable water filters on the market. A filter is called a "purifier" if it is certified to remove protozoa, bacteria, and viruses. Other certified filters may remove only bacteria or perhaps just cysts. Many home water filters will remove unpleasant tastes and odors, but will not remove microorganisms. *Read the label, but realize that not all similarly rated filters perform the same,* nor do all filter manufacturers perform the same tests in the same manner. You can tell whether a filter's pump is working or whether the filter is clogged, but you can't tell whether the filter itself is working effectively against organisms. Actual lab tests to verify microbiological filter function are expensive, and there is no thorough testing protocol to ensure that all filters are tested in a standardized way by any lab that does the testing. Having personally designed medical intravenous filters, consumer water filters, and commercial filtration systems, I will give you my opinion and recommendations later in this chapter.

Purifying Filters

Almost any backcountry bacteriological filter, including those not given a "purifier" rating, will do a good job of removing protozoa and their cysts, like

Giardia and *Cryptosporidium*. Most "purifying" filters have iodine-impregnated resin beads in the filter media, which release iodine into the water to kill viruses and bacteria. These chemically active resins require sufficiently warm water temperatures and relatively long contact times to kill bacteria and viruses. Some lab tests indicate that most or all iodine-based purifiers may not pass the EPA "purifier" standard without pumping water through the device more than once or at extremely slow flow rates (Vorhis 1997, 13). If viral contamination is a big concern, I personally would not trust the iodine resin in my purifying filter, but would pretreat the water with a chemical treatment before running it through my filter to remove protozoan cysts and the bad taste of the chemicals, or zap it with UV sterilization from a "SteriPEN" after I had filtered it to clarify the water and remove bad tastes and harmful chemicals. There is one certified purifying filter, the First Need Deluxe Purifier, which uses no iodine to remove bacteria and viruses, and is not as prone to the temperature, flow rate, and usage factors that might allow viruses to slip through most other purifiers, but if your water supply is dirty, it will clog this filter in short order.

If you do use a certified "purifying" water filter on dirty water, like a duck pond or urban stream, without secondary chemical treatment, I would be extra careful to run the water through the filters at a *very slow rate* and suggest *running the water through the filter twice*. Katadyn, First Need, Berkey, and Sweetwater make certified "purifying" filters, which cost on the order of $40 to $130, and have fairly low capacities (about 10 to 20 gallons if you are treating reasonably clear, clean water).

Ceramic Versus Carbon Cartridge Filters

If you might be using your backcountry water filter a lot, I would recommend that you purchase a filter with a ceramic filter element, like the Katadyn or MSR units. These units offer far longer life at a much lower cost per filtered gallon than carbon-based or pleated-membrane filter elements. All filter elements have clogging problems that will severely reduce their capacity (useful life), if used with dirty water. Ceramic cartridges will clog faster than the other types of cartridges, but can be serviced fairly easily by scrubbing the outer clogging layer with a scrubbing pad that is supplied with the filter to restore the filter to near its original performance. Some filters have replaceable pre-filters, which help somewhat with clogging, but since the pore size of the pre-filter is usually much larger than the pore size of the main filter, small particles tend to slip through the pre-filter and continue to clog the main filter. Backwashing capabilities can also help extend filter life. A lot of people swear by the backcountry water filters with pleated membranes and carbon block cores, like the Katadyn Hiker Pro or the MSR Sweetwater, which pump water faster and easier than the filters with ceramic-type cartridges (MSR Miniworks and Katadyn Combi Filter) but have the disadvantage that they cannot be field serviced and cleaned when clogged, as with the ceramic-cartridge types of filters.

UV Sterilization—"SteriPEN"

A terrific new invention came out a few years ago called a "SteriPEN." This handy gadget consists of a UV lamp that has a built-in timer to treat 1-quart (1-liter) and 1-pint (½-liter) bottles of water in seconds. It only takes about a minute to kill bacteria, viruses, and protozoa in your drinking water. The catch is that in order to be effective, the water must be clear so the light shines through the water, otherwise the sterilization will not be complete. You can even take it with you into restaurants and use it to zap your glass of drinking water to ensure that you won't get Montezuma's revenge while traveling. All bets are off, however, if you have ice in your drink or are zapping a colored drink like a margarita. The traditional SteriPEN requires batteries, so I suggest you have a backup water treatment along in case the batteries go dead, or your SteriPEN stops working. There is a new model of SteriPEN that has no batteries and uses a hand crank for power.

Mixed Halogens—MSR's MIOX Purifier

Another nifty recent invention is MSR's MIOX purifier. It only weighs four ounces, and is about the size of a felt-tip marker, so it is very compact and easy to use. Developed in conjunction with the U.S. Department of Defense, this compact sterilizer uses rock salt and batteries to generate a small dose of powerful halogens that will sterilize water and deactivate chemical warfare toxins in drinking water. This will work in water regardless of whether it is clear or not. The main drawback is that it does require significant dwell time to ensure that the halogens have had enough time to kill all the microorganisms. The required dwell time is fifteen minutes for bacteria and viruses, thirty minutes for *Giardia*, and four hours for *Cryptosporidium* cysts. The process leaves almost no aftertaste, which is a major plus when compared to traditional iodine or chlorine tablets and drops, which leave a rather unpleasant aftertaste and have similar dwell times. However, having to wait four hours to ensure that *Cryptosporidium* cysts are all dead is a real drawback to this system, which is why a filter or SteriPEN is so appealing.

Water-Treatment Recommendations

There are lots of filters on the market. In this section I provide my opinions on quality filters to help you decide what to buy. See backcountry specialty stores or preparedness/survival suppliers for the best selection of portable water filters.

Note: Most filter manufacturers rate their filter life with an "up to" gallon rating based on use with very clean water. Unless you know that you will only use your backcountry water filter with extremely clean water, figure on a realistic life of roughly one-third the manufacturer's rated life. Sad, but field tests show that this is generally true.

Occasional or Emergency Use

For simplicity, one of the certified purifiers (Katadyn, First Need, MSR, etc.) would be a good choice. If viral contamination is a major concern, I would not rely solely on the iodine resin in most purifying filters, but would either pretreat the water with a chemical treatment, then run it through the purifier to remove protozoa cysts and the bad taste of chemical treatment, or post-treat filtered water with a SteriPEN. Of course, if you are going to do this, you might as well buy a cheaper, longer-lasting filter and treat the water with chemicals or a UV SteriPEN when filtering suspicious water. My personal recommendation is to buy either an MSR or Katadyn filter with a carbon core, and also a SteriPEN. I suggest purchasing a compact Polar Pure iodine crystal kit (it treats up to 2,000 liters of water) as a backup in case your SteriPEN fails. Use the UV SteriPEN to zap clear, sweet-smelling water without bothering to filter it first. If using scummy water, such as city duck ponds or brackish water in the backcountry, first run the scummy water through the filter to clarify the water and remove bad tastes, toxic chemicals, and most (if not all) microorganisms, then zap it with your SteriPEN to make extra sure any stray viruses are killed. Also stock at least one spare filter cartridge, since the cartridges can clog quickly with dirty water. I find that when using filters with ceramic cartridges to treat relatively clear water, the carbon cores in the ceramic-type cartridges tend to stop removing chlorine and other bad tastes long before repeated cartridge cleanings have worn down the ceramic filters to the point where their bacterial filtering capabilities are reduced and they need to be replaced. These types of water filters come with a gauge to tell you when cartridge cleanings have reached the point where replacement is necessary.

The sports-bottle-type bacteriological filters, available from Katadyn or Berkey, are a good, low-cost alternative for storing in the trunk of your car for emergencies, or to carry on day hikes, backcountry runs, and so on. They are also useful as a backup in case the pump on your primary water filter breaks.

Significant Use, Portable

I recommend using a filter with a cleanable ceramic cartridge and a carbon core, such as the Katadyn Combi Filter ($140), MSR MiniWorks ($90), or the MSR WaterWorks II ($145).

For reduction of bacteria, tests indicate that the MSR WaterWorks II and the Katadyn Combi Filter perform the best out of the longer-lasting portable filters. Test users liked the Katadyn Pocket Filter and the MSR MiniWorks best for simplicity and ease of use and service. After testing numerous models, the U.S. Marine Corps selected the MSR MiniWorks for use by its Amphibious Raids and Reconnaissance Division. Katadyn was the third-world traveler's standard for many years, but MSR is giving Katadyn a lot of competition.

The MSR units and the Katadyn Combi Filter have the benefit of activated carbon, which will help remove chemicals, bad tastes, and unpleasant odors until the carbon is used up (the ceramic filter element should continue to provide bacterial and protozoa protection long after the carbon is spent).

Even though these units remove about 99 percent of most viruses, they are not rated as purifiers, so if viruses are a significant concern (for example, if your only source for water is the local duck pond or a river in a highly populated area), you should chemically treat your water before running it through one of these filters or zap it with a SteriPEN after filtering.

Heavy Usage, Not So Portable

If I wanted to provide purified water for several people over a significant period of time, I would buy one of the recommended gravity-fed units. The per-gallon cost of these units is a fraction of the cost per gallon of using a small portable pump purifier, plus you do not have to sit there and pump away for long periods of time to provide a large quantity of purified water.

Gravity-fed units either have a top reservoir that holds the source water while it slowly percolates through the filter media into the bottom reservoir of purified water, or they are siphon-type units designed to siphon water from one container to another. Gravity-fed units require no pumping but cannot produce water nearly as fast as the recommended high-volume, pump-type unit.

Where viruses are a concern, you should chemically treat your water before running it through one of these filters, or zap it with a SteriPEN after filtering.

Recommended gravity-fed units are the various Berkey models, the Katadyn Drip Filter, and the AquaRain model 200 and model 400 filters. The Big Berkey filter, with two "Black Berkey" purification elements ($279) has a rated capacity of 4 gallons per hour, a life of up to 6,000 gallons, and the carbon block filter elements may be cleaned with a Scotch Brite pad to restore the flow rate.

The Katadyn TRK Gravidyn Drip Filter ($250) has a rated capacity of up to 13 gallons per day and a life of about 2,300 gallons before the carbon core is saturated, but will continue to remove bacteria for approximately 13,000 gallons, if necessary. This filter utilizes a set of three silver-impregnated ceramic cartridges with carbon cores.

The AquaRain models use state-of-the-art, award-winning ceramic cartridges from Marathon (a MSR subsidiary) and contain replaceable silver-impregnated activated carbon cartridges for removing chemicals, tastes, and odor. AquaRain model 200 ($199) has a rated capacity of 12 to 15 gallons per day and a life of many thousands of gallons. Their model 400 ($260) has twice as many filter elements and can process 24 to 30 gallons per day. The complete AquaRain unit has not been through EPA purifier certification; however, the Marathon ceramic elements used in the AquaRain unit have been thoroughly tested, indicating an excellent microbiological performance.

Note: Filter life is dependent on water quality, filter surface area, filter thickness, and ceramic hardness. In actual use, the large-capacity Berkey models and the AquaRain model 400 will probably have about double the useful life of the smaller Berkeys, the AquaRain model 200, and the Katadyn unit.

The recommended high-volume, pump-type unit is the pricey Katadyn Expedition Group Filter ($1,200), which will pump more than one gallon per minute (much faster than the gravity-fed units) and has a rated life of 26,000 gallons. Gravity-fed units are considerably less expensive than pump units with equivalent lifetime capacities. This filter has no carbon core, so it won't remove bad tastes, odors, or toxic chemicals. It is very popular with river guides and disaster relief organizations.

Chemical Sterilization

Various forms of chlorine and iodine chemical treatments are commonly used to disinfect drinking water. Chlorination is the most common method of chemically disinfecting water because it is easy to apply, readily available, and inexpensive. Chemical treatments, except for chlorine dioxide (Aquamira, Micropur, and MMS) and the MSR MIOX pen, usually leave an aftertaste that most people find unpleasant. The taste is caused by traces of chlorine or iodine, which are active halogens that can also cause harmful health effects over long periods of time.

Caution: Except for chlorine-dioxide solutions (trade names Aquamira, Micropur, and MMS), and the MSR MIOX mixed halogens, neither chlorine nor iodine disinfection is effective against *Cryptosporidium* cysts.

If treated water has a strong chlorine or iodine taste, you can improve the taste by allowing the water to stand exposed to the air for a few hours, pouring it back and forth several times between containers, adding a pinch of salt, or adding some lemon juice. A pinch of powdered vitamin C (available at health food stores) in a quart of treated water will react with free chlorine or iodine and totally remove the bad taste. Running the water through an activated carbon filter will also remove free chlorine, iodine, and bad tastes.

Caution: Do not remove free chlorine or iodine until the water has set for the proper sterilization time (see table 8-1, below), and do not remove traces of chlorine or iodine from water that is to be stored for long periods of time.

Chlorine Bleach

Liquid chlorine bleaches, such as Purex and Clorox, contain a chlorine compound in solution that will effectively disinfect water. There are some products on the market sold as "bleach" for laundry use that do not contain chlorine and could be harmful, *so be sure to read the label.* The procedure for disinfecting drinking water is usually written on the labels of Purex and Clorox brand chlorine bleaches. When the procedure is not given, use the following percentage of available chlorine as a guide (see table 8-1). Chlorine bleach is not as stable and reliable as the recommended iodine treatments. Chlorine is very pH sensitive, and alkaline waters significantly reduce its antimicrobial effectiveness (Wilkerson 1992, 72).

Caution: Do not use powdered bleach or bleach with conditioning additives, scents, or colorfast additives.

To purify, add four drops of standard liquid chlorine bleach (5 percent concentration) per quart of water, and double that amount for turbid or colored water. The treated water should be mixed thoroughly and allowed to stand for thirty minutes. The water should have a slight chlorine odor. If it doesn't, repeat the dosage and allow it to stand for an additional fifteen minutes. The slight chlorine taste of treated water is additional evidence of safety. Chlorine bleach loses strength over time, so if your bleach is over one year old, the amount used to disinfect should be doubled, and if it is a few years old, it is probably worthless. If you are counting on stored chlorine bleach for your emergency water purification, it is best to rotate your bleach stock once a year.

Chlorine Dioxide

With the discovery that *Cryptosporidium* cysts pose a significant health threat and often survive traditional chlorine water-disinfection treatments, many municipalities have included chlorine dioxide in their water treatment process. Much like ozone water treatments, chlorine dioxide is a powerful oxidizing agent that can kill *Cryptosporidium* cysts and rapidly purify water. It does not leave the active halogen of free chlorine in the water, so it makes for better-tasting water (no aftertaste) than water treated with traditional chlorination.

The Aquamira kit ($14.95) is the first portable water-treatment product to utilize chlorine dioxide. It is a two-part liquid dropper kit, will treat up to 30 gallons per kit, and will purify even frigid water in five to ten minutes. It purifies relatively quickly and leaves no aftertaste.

Katadyn sells their chlorine dioxide tablets under the trade name Micropur MP1 ($14.99) with 30 tablets that treat 1 quart each (7.5 gallons total).

You may also purchase MMS (miracle mineral solutions) commercially, or make it yourself quite cheaply from sodium chlorite (see MMS section in chapter 6 for details). When combined with an activator, MMS releases chlorine dioxide into water solutions for water purification, or when ingested it provides available chlorine dioxide for the body to use in battling various pathogens and toxins.

There are two different procedures for purifying water using MMS. The standard procedure is to mix 2 drops of MMS with the appropriate number of drops of activator solution (2 drops of 50 percent citric acid solution, or 10 drops of either 10 percent citric acid solution, lemon juice, lime juice, or vinegar). Mix the MMS and activator solution and allow to sit for twenty seconds when the 50 percent citric acid activator is used, or three minutes if it is one of the other activators, then add to 1 gallon of water. Mix and wait for fifteen minutes before drinking any of the water.

The alternate procedure for using MMS to purify water is to add 8 drops of MMS per gallon of water, mix, and wait twelve hours before drinking. Personally, I would stick with the standard procedure unless I had no available activator.

Keeping a goodly supply of MMS on hand covers the dual function of providing a reliable low-cost way to quickly purify water as well as providing a powerful tool for battling various diseases when either pharmaceutical medicines are unavailable, or when they are simply not effective at healing some local virus or bacteria that is going around.

Chlorine Tablets

Chlorine tablets containing the necessary dosage for drinking water disinfection can be purchased in a commercially prepared form. Sources for chlorine disinfection tablets are sporting goods stores, army surplus stores, backpacking stores, preparedness/survival suppliers, and so on. Tablets should be used as stated on the instructions. Chlorine tablets can be stored for years. Their small size and precisely measured amount of chlorine in each tablet make them convenient, accurate, and easy to use. For disinfecting large quantities of water, their cost may be prohibitive, but they are a lot lighter and easier to carry than gallons of pure water.

Caution: Traditional chlorine tablets will not kill *Cryptosporidium* cysts.

Redi Chlor tablets, from Continental Technologies, are premeasured tablets of calcium hypochlorite that are handy for disinfecting significant quantities of drinking water. Each tablet treats 5 gallons of water, so a single bottle of 100 tablets treats 500 gallons of water for about $19.95, which is far cheaper than the per-gallon cost of small purifying filters.

Granular Calcium Hypochlorite

Granular calcium hypochlorite is used for chlorinating swimming pools and fairly large quantities of water and for making stock disinfectant solution. It is best stored in a garage or storage building far enough away from other products, since it can cause pitting and corrosion. Granular calcium hypochlorite is packaged for sale in plastic bottles or drums. Sources of calcium hypochlorite are hardware stores, sporting goods stores, pharmacies, chemical suppliers, and swimming pool supply companies.

Caution: Calcium hypochlorite is poisonous and extremely corrosive.

To make a disinfecting solution, dissolve 1 heaping teaspoon of granular calcium hypochlorite (about ¼ ounce) for each 2 gallons of water. This will yield a concentrated chlorine solution of approximately 500 milligrams per liter. To sterilize water, add this chlorine solution in the ratio of 1 part chlorine solution to 100 parts of water to be disinfected (Le Baron 1998, 115). This is roughly equal to adding 1 pint (16 ounces) of concentrated chlorine solution to each 12.5 gallons of water. If this seems unnecessarily complicated, use the Redi Chlor tablets as described under "Chlorine Tablets."

Iodine Disinfection

Iodine is one of the best and most dependable germicides and is widely used as a skin disinfectant for the treatment of superficial wounds. You can use iodine to disinfect your drinking water, and it is commonly impregnated into modern water filter media to kill bacteria and viruses inside water filters. However, iodine is not effective against *Cryptosporidium* cysts. Iodine-treated water has a peculiar odor and taste that some people find unpleasant.

Caution: Pregnant or nursing women, or people with thyroid problems, should not ingest iodine-treated water. The EPA recommends that devices that add iodine to the water should not be used for periods extending beyond two to three weeks at a time.

Tincture of Iodine

Eight drops of 2 percent tincture of iodine (Salvato 1982, 372) can be used to disinfect 1 quart of clear water (8 milligrams per liter dose). Allow water to stand at least thirty minutes before it is used. Studies of the usefulness of elemental iodine show it to be a good disinfectant over a pH range of 3 to 8. It is effective against enteric bacteria, amoebic cysts, *Cerariae*, *Leptospira*, and viruses within thirty minutes.

Iodine Tablets

The use of tetraglycine hydroperiodide tablets is an effective method of disinfecting small quantities of water. Tetraglycine hydroperiodide tablets sell under the brand names of Globaline, Portable-Agua, and Coghland's. Iodine tablets are handy, compact, and light. The tablets are very effective as a water disinfectant if directions are correctly followed. If the water to be treated is cloudy, it should be filtered or treated with double the number of iodine tablets.

You can purchase Portable-Agua with vitamin C–based taste-neutralizer tablets to totally eliminate the iodine aftertaste. Tablets can be purchased from pharmacies, preparedness/survival suppliers, and sporting goods stores. Once opened, iodine tablets have a shelf life of up to one year.

Iodine Crystal Solution

You can purchase a handy, ready-made iodine crystal water-treatment kit from Polar Pure (includes crystals and bottle with thermometer), or you can make your own iodine crystal solution with about 5 grams (⅕ ounce) of iodine crystals and a 2-ounce glass bottle. The Polar Pure kit treats about 500 gallons of water for about $10. Cover the crystals with a small amount of water to preserve them from evaporation (sublimation).

When you are ready to use the iodine solution, fill the 2-ounce bottle with water, put the cap on, and shake the bottle for several minutes. Let the heavy crystals settle, then carefully pour out approximately 3 tablespoons (almost all the solution) into 1 gallon of clear water. *Use only the iodine solution: leave*

Table 8-1 Disinfection techniques and halogen doses (All doses added to 1 quart of water)

Sterilization technique	Quantity for 4 ppm (parts per million)	Quantity for 8 ppm (parts per million)
Iodine tabs (tetraglycine hydroperiodide; Potable-Agua and Globaline products)	½ tab	1 tab
2 percent iodine solution (tincture)	5 drops (0.2 ml)	10 drops (0.4 ml)
10 percent povidone-iodine solution	8 drops (0.35 ml)	16 drops (0.70 ml)
Saturated iodine crystals in water (Polar Pure product)	2½ teaspoons (13 ml)	5 teaspoons (26 ml)
Saturated iodine crystals in alcohol	2 drops (0.1 ml)	4 drops (0.2 ml)
Household bleach (soldium hypochlorite)	(5 percent) 2 drops (0.1 ml)	4 drops (0.2 ml)

Halogen concentration	Sterilization time in minutes at various water temperatures		
	41°F (5°C)	59°F (15°C)	86°F (30°C)
2 ppm	240	180	60
4 ppm	180	60	45
8 ppm	60	30	15

NOTE: Recent data indicate that very cold water requires prolonged contact time with iodine or chlorine to kill *Giardia* cysts (both disinfectants are ineffective against *Cryptosporidium* cysts). These contact times in cold water have been extended from the usual recommendations to account for this and for the uncertainty of residual concentration.

(Source: Adapted from the *Wilderness Medical Society Practice Guidelines for Wilderness Emergency Care*, 1995)

the crystals in the bottle (the crystals are poisonous). Stir the water, and let it stand for approximately thirty minutes. If the water is very cold, let it stand for 1 hour.

You can use the crystals up to about 300 times before they completely dissolve. Be sure to label the bottle "Poison" and keep it out of reach of children. Elemental iodine is poisonous by ingestion (in concentrated form). Elemental iodine crystals are inexpensive and can be obtained at pharmacies and chemical supply companies.

The methods in table 8-1 have been carefully researched, and are time-tested and effective. They are safe when the directions are correctly followed. The raw materials used in purification are inexpensive, but they are *poisonous in concentrated form. Use caution and keep them out of reach of children.*

Treating and Finding Water the Low-Tech Way

With a few simple materials, if you can dig your way to moist soil or find some healthy green bushes, you should be able to provide yourself with drinking water.

Treating Water

Solar Water Disinfection (SODIS)

The solar disinfection of drinking water (SODIS) is promoted by the World Health Organization (WHO), and others throughout the third world, as a viable treatment for disinfecting drinking water and reducing the incidence of waterborne diseases. Health workers stress that boiling, or chemical treatment like chlorination, is much preferred over SODIS, since boiling is 100 percent reliable at killing pathogens, and chemical treatment is close to 100 percent reliable except for hard-to-kill pathogens like *Cryptosporidium*. SODIS is not nearly as reliable as boiling or chlorination, but since boiling requires fuel or other resources that are often in short supply in third-world locations, SODIS is promoted as being far better than drinking untreated water.

The treatment of water with solar radiation was practiced in ancient India more than four thousand years ago, and the modern practice of SODIS using clear water in plastic bottles placed in the sun was developed in Lebanon in the 1980s. The SODIS process uses a combination of UV-A radiation and heat from sunlight to kill pathogens in drinking water. The standard procedure is to fill used, clean, clear PET soda bottles with water and to lay them flat in full sunlight for six hours. Cloudy skies require two days of daylight exposure and the process does not work at all during rainy weather, when rainwater collection is recommended instead.

SODIS requires clear water and works best at water depths of 4 inches or less, so it is not suitable for large containers of water. If the water is murky enough to prevent you from reading newsprint through the filled PET bottle, it won't work for SODIS. Clear plastic bags and glass bottles also work well for SODIS, but window glass does not. Ninety-nine percent of glass bottles let most of the sun's UV radiation pass through the glass, but typical window glass filters out the UV-A radiation, so it won't work for SODIS.

In hotter climates, painting one half of the SODIS bottle black (to act as a solar collector) or placing the bottles on a black or reflective surface will heat the water to higher temperatures, increasing the pasteurization effect. Clear bottles in hot sun can reach temperatures of 131°F (55°C), which kills many pathogenic bacteria over a period of hours. With a black painted surface or a metal container in hot sun, the water temperature can reach 140°F (60°C) or more, where true pasteurization can occur, rapidly deactivating most enteric viruses, bacteria, and parasites (Sobsey 2002, 14). In places like Nepal, where temperatures are cooler but UV-A radiation is higher due to the altitude, it has been found that SODIS treatment is more effective without any paint on the bottles. For an excellent source of both basic information on SODIS and links to numerous technical papers, see www.sodis.ch.

The Bangladesh Sari Filter

In Bangladesh, where annual flooding often contaminates nearly all surface waters and where over half of the tube wells are severely contaminated with arsenic and fluoride, villagers have been trained to make a reasonably effective filter out of a minimum of eight layers of a folded sari. Actual scientific controlled tests have verified the efficacy of these low-tech "sari filters." It turns out that older saris work better than ones made of new cloth, because after several launderings the thread fibers tend to become soft and loose, reducing the pore size compared with pore size on new sari cloth. The folded sari filters are held snugly over the neck of a large water jug as it is dipped in a river or pond until filled. After each use, the sari is first rinsed out in the source water, followed by a rinsing in filtered water, then laid out in the sun for further drying and natural UV sterilization.

Caution: The use of sari filters is not 100 percent safe. In controlled tests, the method reduced cholera infections by 52 percent, and a large number of mothers using sari filtration perceived a significant decline in the incidence of diarrhea within their families. It is better than nothing, but if you have other more sure-fire treatment options, I suggest you use them (Colwell 2003).

Charcoal Filters

You can make your own crude charcoal filters to remove bad tastes, odors, and some pollutants such as organic toxic chemicals and radioactive fallout. The easiest way to make charcoal is to burn some wood and pick the bigger partially burned chunks out of the fire. Place these chunks into a 5-gallon bucket and pour the water to be treated into the bucket. Shake vigorously for a few seconds, then allow to stand for several minutes before filtering this water through a cloth, sand filter, or coffee filter back into a suitable container. If toxic organic chemicals or radioactive fallout are significant concerns, you should filter your water through at least 3 to 5 feet of sand including two 3-inch-thick layers of charcoal. A 50-gallon drum filled with sand and charcoal layers, with a few holes punched in the bottom, could do the job nicely. If you crush the charcoal with some rocks, it will do a better job of filtering.

A more efficient way to make charcoal is with an old-fashioned charcoal kiln, which bakes wood in a closed chamber above a fire. This process makes charcoal without burning the wood sealed into the upper part of the kiln, since that section of the kiln does not allow enough oxygen flow to support combustion. Another traditional method for making charcoal is by first covering a huge pile of wood with a layer of straw or pine needles followed by a thick layer of dirt, leaving a small chimney flue in the top center. Vent holes were scratched into the sides of the dirt and the pine needles or straw were ignited through these vent holes. The chimney and vent holes were partially covered to control the amount of air to ensure that the wood charred into charcoal rather than burned into ash. The charcoal mound was watched carefully for several days, then the chimney and vent holes were completely plugged for several more until the mound cooled down. If the mound keeper was not careful, the pile would build into a roaring fire and burn all the wood to ashes (Wigginton 1979, 97–99).

If the need should ever arise, common household ion-exchange water softeners and carbon or slow sand filters are particularly effective at removing radioactive materials from contaminated water sources.

Solar Still

Under a survival situation in dry climates, you can provide yourself with small quantities of pure water with a homemade solar still, using a clear sheet of plastic and a container to catch dripping water. Dig a hole in the ground in an area with wet or moist soil that is also directly exposed to the sun. If the soil is very wet or damp, you may only have to dig a couple of feet. Place a pail or other catch basin in the center of your pit. If you do not have a container, a piece of plastic or waterproof material covering a depression in the earth will suffice. Cover the pit with the sheet of clear plastic, and seal the edges of the sheeting with more soil or rocks (see fig. 8-1). Weight the center of the sheeting with a stick, stone, or some dirt.

The sun's rays passing through the

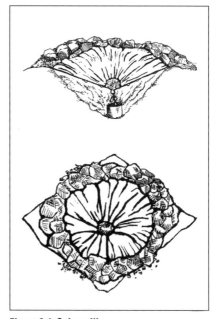

Figure 8-1. Solar still.

plastic sheet will warm the earth, evaporating water from the moist soil. This water vapor rises until it hits the plastic sheeting, which is cooled by the outside air, causing the water vapor to condense and run down the inside of the sheet until it drips off the low point into the container.

Plant Water Pump and Still

A variation on the solar still, this technique uses a living plant as a pump to gather water from under the ground with its roots. You must have a plastic bag or tarp to wrap around a leafy, healthy green plant. Pick a plant that is not too big for your tarp. Dig a small hole on one side of the plant. Wrap your bag or tarp around the plant, lining the shallow hole with the bag or tarp. Tie your bag around the base of the plant and arrange the tarp so that condensing water will trickle down the inside of the tarp and collect in the hole (see fig. 8-2).

Water vapor evaporating off the plant's leaves will condense on the inside of your covering and provide you with a source of water.

Figure 8-2. Plant water pump and still.

Caution: If the plant receives too much sun for too long, it will cook and die under your plastic cover.

Finding Water

Plant Indicators

Look for leafy, green plants that require a lot of water to survive. Cattails, reeds, willows, elderberries, cottonwoods, poplars, and greasewood all require a plentiful supply of water and indicate a high water table. Dig a shallow well at the base of these plants or trees, and you should soon reach wet soil, which will slowly percolate into your pit.

Animal Indicators

Animals and insects are very good indicators for water. Most insects require water and live within flying range of surface water. In particular, watch the directions in which bees fly. Grazing animals, like deer and elk, will travel to water each day. Look for well-worn animal trails, which will usually lead to water. Most birds, except for birds of prey, require significant water several times a day. Look for water in areas where birds congregate, circle, or roost.

Physical Indicators

Dry riverbeds usually offer areas where water breaks the surface or at least comes close to the surface. Dig for water at outside bends in the river or follow the riverbed to areas where bedrock forces the water to the surface. Look for water at the base of cliffs, where green vegetation suggests a water source.

Cactus

Some cacti, such as the barrel cactus (but not the giant Saguaro), contain a watery pulp that can be crushed or sucked to release a jelly-like liquid.

Protecting Your Water Source

Your drinking water source is your lifeblood, so be sure to protect it. Dispose of your sewage in a manner that threatens neither your water supply nor that of your neighbors. Table 8-2 provides some general setback guidelines for protecting your water source.

A pit toilet can be as simple as a plastic bucket or a hole 3 feet deep with a couple of logs to sit across. Or it could be as lavish as a beautifully crafted wooden masterpiece, complete with a proper ventilation system, the privacy

Table 8-2 Water Source Setbacks	
Suggested minimum setbacks for wells	
Pit toilet from dug, bored, or driven well	100 ft
Pit toilet from well with watertight casing, at least 20 ft deep	50 ft
Septic system absorption area from dug, bored, or driven well	150 ft
Septic system absorption area from well with watertight casing, at least 20 ft deep	100 ft
Vault-type outhouse	50 ft
Gravity-draining sewer line or building foundation drain	50 ft
Barn housing animals	50 ft
Manure storage site, automobile wrecking yard, and so on	250 ft
Property line, building, or driveway	10 ft
Sewage lagoon or landfill/dump site	1000 ft
Cemetery	50 ft
Additional setbacks for drinking water springs	
Human habitation/activity downhill from spring	50 ft
Human habitation/activity laterally (sideways) from spring	100 ft
Human habitation/activity uphill from spring	200 ft
(Source: Max Burns, Cottage Water Systems, 1999)	

of four walls, a roof, and a door. The traditional "privy" is about 4 × 4 × 7 feet tall at the front. The seat should be 12 to 16 inches high. A 4- to 5-inch vent pipe should rise from under the seat to about 2 feet above the roof to vent odors. Periodically sprinkling lime or ashes into the pit will help reduce odor, especially in the summer months. Plastic bags lining a plastic bucket make dumping and cleaning a makeshift port-a-potty a task that is only moderately unpleasant.

9

Communication

❝The destruction to communications companies' facilities in the region, and therefore to the services upon which citizens rely, was extraordinary. Hurricane Katrina knocked out more than three million customer phone lines in Alabama, Louisiana, and Mississippi. The wire line communications network sustained enormous damage—dozens of central offices and countless miles of outside plant were damaged or destroyed as a result of the hurricane or the subsequent flooding. Local wireless networks also sustained considerable damage—more than a thousand cell sites were knocked out of service by the hurricane. At the hurricane's height, more than thirty-five Public Service Answering Points (PSAPs) were out of service, and some parishes in Louisiana remained without 911 or enhanced 911 (E911) service for weeks.❞ —Dr. Robert Miller, "Hurricane Katrina: Communications & Infrastructure Impacts," April 2008

Modern communications systems are something we tend to take for granted, until they fail or are no longer available. When a disaster strikes, outside of taking care of any pressing safety or survival issues, what is the first thing most people try to do next? It is usually either to call friends and loved ones to assure them that you are okay, to check in with them to see if they are okay, or to try and tune into some kind of news channel to find more information concerning the disaster. Information might be key to your safety and survival, and it is certainly critical for helping you to regain peace of mind.

Important incoming information might include flood alerts, evacuation orders, boil-water orders, severe weather alerts, chemical spill information, etc. Important outgoing information is usually along the lines of assuring family and loved ones that you are alright, calls to emergency medical services, and calls to report safety issues such as downed power lines or trees. In this day and age, when panic attacks are common each time Blackberry phone service goes down for a few hours, whenever the landlines, cell phones, and Internet all crash at the same time, the general level of anxiety and panic rapidly escalates. Since we live in the information age, when information services go down, there is a tendency for people to project and expect the worst!

When a disaster strikes, people tend to think that they can always rely upon their cell phones, but with the exception of satellite phones, the landlines tend to be more robust and less prone to failure than the cellular systems.

Telephone systems have their own battery backup power supplies, and backup generators, so they are often operable even when there is a widespread power blackout. It is a good idea to have at least one old-fashioned hardwired corded handset (not wireless) that does not plug into an AC outlet, so it will still operate even when the power is out (provided that the landlines are still operating in your area). With many people now relying completely on their cell phones, having dropped their use of landlines, when the cell phones go out in a catastrophe, it can be quite frustrating!

It is a good idea to have multiple levels of redundancy, both for receiving information such as news updates, weather forecasts, and emergency broadcasts, as well as being able to send outgoing communications locally to coordinate with emergency services and friends, and to reach people outside of the disaster area. This chapter covers the basics of communicating in a disaster, including both what to expect as well as the pros and cons of various communications equipment, such as radios, transceivers, shortwave radios, police scanners, CB radios, and telephones. There is no single piece of communications equipment that is guaranteed to provide reliable communication under all potential circumstances, so it is a wise idea to pick up a few of the different options that are discussed in this chapter. Having an out-of-town contact that your family members have all agreed to communicate with in the event of a disaster can be quite important for relaying information, since local communications may be totally tied up, and incoming calls may not get through, but you may well be able to place calls to someone outside of your area.

When Hurricane Katrina struck, local phone systems were not just degraded, they were actually destroyed, and for a very long period of time. Since the fuel and power distribution infrastructures were also critically wounded, whatever services managed to survive initially on battery and generator backup-power supplies, went down when those supplies were depleted, roughly between four and seventy-two hours later. The White House Katrina Report described those results saying, "The complete devastation of the communications infrastructure left responders without a reliable network to use for coordinating emergency response operations."

Radios

At the absolute minimum, you should have a battery-operated portable radio on hand. All of the emergency-preparedness vendors (see sources in appendix 2) stock a variety of radios, many of which have hand-crank spring-powered built-in generators, and/or solar cell power supplies, so they can be operated with or without batteries, and with or without the grid (see fig. 2-1). I keep a Baygen "Freeplay" radio in my 72-hour grab-and-go kit, which has a high-quality built-in hand-crank generator and receives AM, FM, and some shortwave frequencies. The crank winds up an internal spring that powers the generator, so you can crank the radio for a couple of minutes and then it will continue playing for about fifteen more minutes while the spring continues to drive the generator until it needs another rewind. When selecting a solar-powered, or hand-crank generator-powered radio, read the reviews, or ask a trustworthy salesman for his opinion. Many cheap hand-crank radios have terrible reliability and are pretty much guaranteed to fail after a very short period of time, so don't waste your money on a cheap unit.

I suggest you store a lot of batteries, about evenly split between rechargeable ones and standard alkaline batteries. The rechargeable ones tend to have only about half the capacity of the standard alkaline types before they need a recharge. It is a good idea to also store a solar battery recharger so when the grid is down you can recharge your batteries whenever the sun is shining.

Broadband Receivers

To stay informed during an emergency, you really should have a broadband general-coverage receiver that picks up shortwave ("world band") frequencies up to 30 MHz (megahertz). This will enable you to listen to broadcasts from around the world. A good broadband receiver should have an antenna jack to allow for plugging in a larger antenna than the one that comes with your receiver, a headphone jack, an illuminated digital display, and a good signal-strength meter. A synchronous detector with selectable sideband increases adjacent channel rejection while reducing fading and distortion, making the receiver easier to use with better sound quality. Another recommended feature is single side-band (SSB) capabilities, which improves your listening options. The Grundig models pretty much set the standard in the moderate price range, but a lot of people swear by their receivers from Sony, C. Crane, and Radio Shack, so you might want to shop around (see sources in appendix 2).

You may, for example, purchase a compact inexpensive Grundig model G8 Traveler II for as low as around $50, their compact Globe Traveler G3 model (fig. 9-1) with improved reception offered by SSB and synchronous selectable sideband sells for around $150, and their larger desktop Satellite 750 (fig. 9-2) model for around $300. The Grundig Traveler portable receivers are so small they can be easily thrown into your suitcase, but the larger desktop model will provide you with better long-distance reception. People rave about the

Figure 9-1. Grundig Traveler G3 compact portable broadband receiver.
Photo courtesy of Grundig/Eton Corp

Figure 9-2. Grundig Satellite 750 desktop broadband receiver.
Photo courtesy of Grundig/Eton Corp

reception on the Grundig Satellite 750, especially when hooked up to a large outdoor antenna, but you don't hear those kinds of positive comments about the smaller more portable Grundig Traveler models, so if you can afford it, I suggest you buy one of the larger, more expensive desktop models.

The Web site SWLing.com provides a good beginner's guide to short-wave listening, as well as ratings and recommendations for several popular, modestly priced models from a few different manufacturers. For expert advice, or if you have a big budget and wish to spring for a higher end model, see the resource guide in appendix 2 and talk to one of the recommended supplier's salesmen, or contact a local amateur radio operators' club and sit in on one of their meetings so you can ask questions from the guys who spend much of their free time on the airwaves communicating with other folks from all around the world.

Scanners and NOAA Weather Radios

A scanner is a radio receiver (it cannot transmit) that allows you to scan multiple frequencies at one time for two-way radio activity. These devices are commonly known as "police scanners" in that most people use the devices to listen to police radio communications, although fire department monitoring is almost of equal interest, and scanners can also be used to monitor the two-way radios of taxis, mall security, commercial aircraft, ambulances, and so much more. The importance of scanners really comes into play when there is a crisis going on. By listening to a scanner, you can hear the latest updates directly from the emergency personnel involved with the local/regional issues in "real time," meaning you get to hear what is happening at the precise time that it is actually occurring, not having to wait for local news to be filtered through the media to be released at a later time as a news broadcast with sketchy information at best.

NOAA (National Oceanic and Atmospheric Administration) weather radios are special-purpose radios designed to receive detailed local weather alerts, weather forecast information, and emergency alerts. Most newer NOAA radios are designed with the option to sound a loud warning tone and provide important basic visual information on their display each time an emergency alert is issued for your area. For instance, they may alert people to an approaching tornado, a bio-terrorism alert, or an approaching blizzard. You can pick up a basic NOAA radio for very little money, but a better option may be to pick up one of the multipurpose scanners that include NOAA functions plus other popular functions such as police/fire scanning, AM/FM radio, US and Canadian "all-hazards alert," and other scanning bands including military and civilian aircraft. One such all-purpose emergency

Figure 9-3. Uniden Bearcat BC72XLT portable multipurpose radio scanner. Photo courtesy of Uniden

radio product that is reasonably priced and includes all of these functions is the Uniden Bearcat BC72XLT portable handheld radio scanner (fig. 9-3). Most of the newer multipurpose scanners that pick up NOAA radio, have a user-selectable option for emitting an audible alarm signal and displaying descriptive information whenever a local hazard alert is issued, and they also include the ability to scan local two-way radio emergency communications. Such a scanner could be a valuable item to have on hand in the event of a local disaster!

As emergency communications systems evolved, they began to rely on "trunking" systems followed by digital encoding to provide higher signal capacities on a limited number of channels. Similarly, the scanner technologies, selection, and programming to keep up with these communication system changes also become more complex. The original scanners, like cell phones, operated solely on analog signals. As scanner channels became overloaded by too many people trying to communicate at the same time on a limited number of channels, scanner systems developed "trunking" systems, where a computer would automatically select signal channels for routing communications in ways that are similar to telephone trunk lines. The next level of sophistication was introduced with digital coding and multiplexing, similar to the latest digital cell-phone technology, allowing systems to run thousands of simultaneous communications over each individual channel.

Note: With all of these potential complexities, don't count on taking your scanner out of its box during an emergency and immediately tuning in to all the local dispatch communications. Instead I suggest you practice a bit first, and learn the intricacies of your scanner and the local communications networks, so when a true emergency does arise, you will already know exactly how to access the information you are seeking.

A simple, relatively inexpensive analog scanner will work just fine in many locations, but will be totally worthless in others. It all depends upon the local communication protocols and technology used by the emergency communications systems within your area. You might assume that most rural locations would use older analog technology and that the metropolitan areas all have the latest high-tech digital technology, but you would be dead wrong. For example, at the time I am writing this in 2011, they are still using analog technology for fire and police communications in the greater Boston area, so your lower-cost scanners will work just fine in and around Boston. However, in the remote Upper Peninsula area of Michigan, they are using digital technology, so if you purchased a low-cost scanner for use in this area, it would be worthless. How to know what technology is used in your area? Simply go to www.policescanners.net, click on the link for "find a scanner for your area," enter in your zip code information, and this Web site will tell you what type of scanner technology is required for your area. Of course, there are no guarantees that your local public services will not upgrade their systems shortly after you purchase your new scanner!

If you are in an area where the scanners operate on digitally encoded signals, that usually adds a higher level of complexity to getting your scanner programmed for operating efficiently with the local emergency communications networks. And if you like to take your scanner on the road with you, just keeping up with programming changes in each area you pass through would be enough to drive anyone crazy! Uniden has come up with a new scanner product that people are raving about that solves all of these problems and makes scanner use simple again, like the "good old days" of analog signals. It is called the "HomePatrol" scanner. Though pricey (around $500), people love it because it is programmed to be extremely versatile while also being very easy to use. You simply need to input your local zip code information, and the scanner will auto-load the applicable frequencies, trunking systems, alpha tags, and subaudible tones for your area, making it extremely easy to operate, even for those who consider themselves to be somewhat technically challenged. It even has an optional add-on GPS receiver that enables the HomePatrol to automatically detect your geographical location so it can auto-load programming changes on-the-fly while driving from one location to another. There are also high-end portable handheld scanner/transceivers from companies like Yaesu that provide full scanning functions, AM/FM radio, GPS positioning, while allowing you to receive signals on all shortwave frequencies and transmit on a couple of ham bands.

For excellent information on a wide variety of scanner products, check out www.scannermaster.com.

Short-Wave/Ham Radios

In times of disaster, war, and political upheaval, most of the time it is the amateur radio operators, also known as "ham radio operators," that are the first to provide emergency communication services linking the affected areas to the rest of the world. In the recent political upheaval in Egypt, when the people rose up against the government of Hosni Mubarak, one of the first things the government did was to shut down the Internet, the cell phones, and the landlines. However, they did not have the time and resources to go after the amateur radio operators, so those people performed a valuable function of passing information in and out of Egypt while the normal lines of communication had been severed. Even when antennas are down, and the infrastructure totally annihilated, such as occurred in the wake of Hurricane Katrina and the Indian Ocean tsunami, all it takes is a decent shortwave two-way radio, a car battery, and some scavenged wire to provide a makeshift enlarged antenna, and any remote location will have an instant link to the outside world.

Anyone can listen in on shortwave radio conversations from around the world. All you need is a broadband receiver. In order to participate in the broadcast discussion, you need a shortwave transceiver (a transceiver both transmits and receives radio signals) and must also be licensed by the Federal Communications Commission (FCC). Being an amateur radio operator is a unique mix of fun, public service, and convenience. Although hams get involved for many reasons, they all have in common a basic knowledge of radio technology and operating principles, and pass an examination for the FCC license to operate on radio frequencies known as the "amateur bands." These bands are radio frequencies reserved by the FCC for use by hams at intervals from just above the AM broadcast band all the way up into extremely high microwave frequencies.

Now that the knowledge of Morse code is no longer required to pass the FCC exam, it has become quite easy to obtain the basic amateur radio certification for the "technician" level. Children as young as eight years old have passed this certification, and many elderly people enjoy being ham radio operators, daily traveling around the world on the air waves. If ham radio has any interest for you, I strongly suggest you check out the ARRL (Amateur Radio Relay League, also known as the National Association for Amateur Radio) Web site at www.arrl.org. There you will find a wealth of basic information on ham radio as well as information and access to study guides for getting your license. On the ARRL's Web page for membership, you can access a tool for locating local amateur radio operator clubs for networking and to get in touch with experienced operators that might be able to lend you a hand and provide advice for getting started.

Although for most amateur radio operators, their main use of ham radio is for fun and entertainment, it is called the "Amateur Radio Service" because it also has a serious side. The FCC created this "service" to fill the need for a pool of experts who could provide backup during emergencies. In addition, the FCC acknowledged the ability of the hobby to advance the communication and technical skills of radio, and to enhance international goodwill. This philosophy has paid off. Countless lives have been saved where skilled hobbyists act as emergency communicators to render aid, whether it's during an earthquake in Italy or a hurricane in the United States.

Not everyone has the time, money, or inclination to become a ham radio operator, but in times of emergency it could be invaluable to know who your local ham operators are, so you could visit their home to gather critical information when all the other usual channels of communications are down. Not having heard about the ARRL Web site, I first located a couple of nearby ham operators simply by asking some friends if they knew any local amateur radio operators. Had I known about the ARRL Web site, I could have used their online "find a club" tool, entered in my local zip code, and presto—a half dozen ARRL affiliated clubs would have shown up instantly. In my case, I live in a fairly small town, and the local ham operator group did not show up using the ARRL Web tool, but several larger "official" groups in nearby cities did appear. By contacting those groups, one of their members could surely have connected me with a ham operator in my own town.

The Amateur Radio Emergency Service (ARES) consists of licensed amateurs who have voluntarily registered their qualifications and equipment for communications duty in the public service when disaster strikes. Every licensed amateur, regardless of membership in ARRL or any other local or national organization is eligible to apply for membership in ARES. Because ARES is an amateur radio service, only licensed radio amateurs are eligible for membership. These volunteers are trained to step in and provide coordinated emergency communications services in times of disaster and crisis.

The time to develop your network connections with local ham operators is while skies are sunny and things are still working well in your world. If you wait until the next catastrophe, it will be too late. If you wish to become a ham radio operator, it does not take a lot of money and time to get started. For a couple of hundred bucks you can pick up a decent used transceiver, or a basic starter model. In many cases, the guys who are really into this hobby have collected tens of thousands of dollars worth of equipment over decades of active amateur radio operations, but most of them will tell you that they started off quite simply with low-cost gear purchased on a tight budget. Some of these guys talk about attaching an alligator clip to their bed springs to boost their antenna output when they first started out. Since the range and options for ham radio equipment are so extensive, I can't offer you any "best buys" advice on specific starter models, but suggest you network with local experienced "hams," your local Radio Shack salesmen, or contact some of the reputable suppliers listed in appendix 2 for advice on equipment that meets your budget and desires.

CB Radio

The "CB" in CB radio stands for "citizens' band." Though waning in popularity, due to overcrowding of the forty-channel bandwidth for CB combined with the modern explosion in cell phone and Internet use, CB radio still performs a valuable function for truckers and many other people who are on the road for long periods of time, as well as for local communications when the phone lines are down. There is probably no better way to get the latest road and weather conditions in your area, than to turn on a CB radio and listen to the talk between truckers. These guys are on the road all day, and they are constantly chatting with each other to keep tabs on local weather, road conditions, accidents, delays, construction, etc.

CB radio is legally limited to 4 watts of power, but there are after-market power boosters that can illegally boost your transmitter power to many times that figure, which could come in quite handy in an emergency situation. They are normally "line-of-sight" devices, so in mountainous areas such as the one that I live in, different truckers will come in and out of range every few minutes as they pass by on the local freeway. You can pick up a decent CB transceiver by Midland, Cobra, or Uniden for very reasonable prices. Back in the late 1970s or early 1980s, when the FCC started receiving over a million applications each month for licenses, they dropped the licensing requirements, so anyone can buy a CB radio and start using it immediately.

Walkie-Talkies

Small portable handheld two-way radios have come way down in price while offering ever increasing value and function. Many offer privacy options for less interference when calling in crowded areas, plus access to NOAA weather and disaster information services. Most of the newer models operate on multiple channels as combination General Mobile Radio Service (GMRS) and Family Radio Service (FRS) models. The FRS and GMRS bands overlap and share some channels. The FRS models are supposed to have a half watt maximum power limit. GMRS use requires an FCC license, and licensees are permitted to transmit at up to 50 watts on GMRS frequencies (although 1 to 5 watts is more common), as well as have detachable or external antennas. The flooding of the market with combo FRS/GMRS walkie-talkies has resulted in an explosion of people using the GMRS frequencies without an FCC license.

Warning: Read the customer ratings on a model before you make your purchase! All models have range ratings based on perfectly flat totally unobstructed reception. Since there are no universal standards for range ratings, and they are typically overstated, I suggest that you choose a model with a much higher range rating than you might think is necessary.

Antennas

There is an old saying that if you want to receive a weaker signal, or send a stronger one, all you need to do is add more wire, which is partially true. You may wish to purchase a reel type antenna to boost the receive power of your portable radio. Simply attach the antenna and reel out a length of wire that may be woven around your hotel room, campsite, or balcony to improve reception. As a child, I remember buying a roll of 100 feet of antenna wire and stringing it with some cheap insulators between our house and our garage to give me better reception on my homemade radio set.

However, there is much more to antenna technology than just simply adding more wire. Radio enthusiasts may have their own 100-foot-tall radio tower with multiple "tuned" and "steerable" antennas. Some of those special antennas look similar to old fashioned television rooftop antennas. I am by no means an expert on antenna design. For a good primer on antenna theory and design, I suggest you check out www.dxzone.com/cgi-bin/dir/jump2.cgi?ID=7564. I also suggest you protect your home and electronic equipment by installing proper lightning arresters onto your incoming antenna line(s).

10

Self-Defense and Personal Protection

Since there is strength in numbers, the best defense for anybody is a strong community. In a small, tight-knit community you will be able to share resources, skills, tools, and responsibilities, including watching each other's backsides. The well-armed lone wolf survivalist may someday find himself relieved of his weapons and goods by a group of thugs that are tougher, meaner, more plentiful in number, and better organized. After all, even the lone wolf has to sleep sometimes! I am not one of those guys who look forward with gleeful anticipation for the apocalypse to come so I can break out my guns and start shooting with wild abandon. I hope the day never comes when I have to aim a gun at somebody, much less pull the trigger.

However, I do believe in being prepared, and that there is a good chance that many of us, for one reason or another, will experience periods of time where "the rule of law" simply evaporates, at least locally. In that case, it will be ourselves, our friends, and our neighbors that we must count on for protection, safety, and order. My intention in this chapter is to provide useful advice and information, including basic "how-to" instruction sets that may one day save your life, or the life of a friend or loved one.

Even though I grew up hunting and fishing in the Green Mountains of Vermont, I must admit that guns and ammo are not my forte. However, I do have several friends and relatives with decades of practical experience on this subject, and they have been more than willing to bend my ear, take me shooting, and contribute their expertise and opinions to improve this chapter. Similarly, with only a little more than a year of martial-arts training under my belt, I don't claim to be an expert at hand-to-hand combat. I owe a debt of gratitude to my friend Frank Ferris, a highly respected sixth-degree black belt and martial-art/self-defense instructor who graciously shared his time, knowledge, and expertise to help turn the self-defense sections of this chapter into a set of truly valuable practical "how-to" instructions.

This chapter covers the basics of self-defense. The first section discusses firearms, including gun safety, selection, and maintenance. The second section begins with a general talk about self-defense, followed by instructions on basic unarmed martial-arts-style self-defense techniques to deal with specific situations.

Whether or not you choose to equip yourself with one or more firearms is a personal matter. If this is an area where you lack significant experience,

When Allison returned to her apartment one evening, she unlocked the front door and stepped inside, just as she had done a hundred times before. As she walked past her front hall closet, a large muscular man burst from the closet and attacked her. He held an 8" long knife to her throat and threatened to kill her if she resisted. As he ripped her clothes off, Allison punched her attacker with all her might. She hit him repeatedly while receiving two deep cuts from his knife as it slashed across her chest and face, but Allison never gave up fighting. She was able to break free, running out the front door and down the street—naked, bleeding, and screaming, but alive! Allison is absolutely certain that she would have been raped and murdered had she not resisted.

I suggest that you seek professional training, while exercising caution and discernment. I wrote this chapter for the average Joe, or Josephine, and not for the well-armed and trained survivalist. If you are in the latter category, you will probably learn little or nothing from the following pages that you don't already know, but if you are in the former category, read on!

To Arm, or Not to Arm, That Is the Question!

"When I carry a gun, you cannot deal with me by force. You have to use reason and try to persuade me, because I have a way to negate your threat or employment of force. . . . The gun is the only weapon that's as lethal in the hands of an octogenarian as it is in the hands of a weight lifter. It simply wouldn't work as well as a force equalizer if it wasn't both lethal and easily employable.

When I carry a gun, I don't do so because I am looking for a fight, but because I'm looking to be left alone. The gun at my side means that I cannot be forced, only persuaded. I don't carry it because I'm afraid, but because it enables me to be unafraid. It doesn't limit the actions of those who would interact with me through reason, only the actions of those who would do so by force. It removes force from the equation . . . and that's why carrying a gun is a civilized act." —Marko Kloos, "Why the Gun Is Civilization"

I am a firm believer in being prepared for the unexpected. I would much rather learn certain skills, and keep a stock of supplies on hand, but never need them, than find out when it is too late that I wished I had been better prepared. The United States is a heavily armed country. To not have a firearm puts one at a serious disadvantage when confronted with armed hooligans. A firearm is the one thing that puts a small-framed woman or an elderly man on a par with a hulking brute of a man.

Some people say that guns cause more accidental deaths, suicides, shootings of friends or lovers in arguments, and by having weapons turned on their owners by a hoodlum, than they have prevented robberies, rapes, and murders from assailants. People argue both sides of the story, and there is some truth to both sides. Of course, thwarted tragedies do not normally become a statistic, whereas tragic incidents do. You must exercise wisdom and caution in this regard, since there is no "taking back" a bullet once it is fired. Many a child has innocently killed himself, or a friend, while playing with a real gun, and readily available weapons have been the single most common element in domestic arguments that turned lethal. Safety is critical, so I have devoted a section to safety later in this chapter.

If you can't see yourself ever using a weapon, even in a self-defense situation, but you have the financial reserves to invest in some of the resources recommended in this chapter, then perhaps someone you know will be able to put them to good use in times of crisis, providing much needed protection for yourself, your loved ones, and any others you have taken under your wing who may not be so fortunate as to have planned ahead for troubled times.

Firearm Selection

When considering which model(s) and type(s) of guns to purchase there are several basic things to consider:

1. Is the firearm primarily a "working" gun, such as for ranch use, hunting game, and/or outdoor survival? Or is it primarily for use as a "defensive" weapon for personal protection? Though many weapons may work adequately in both of these categories, most weapons are optimized more for one category than the other.

2. Almost any gun in the hands of a trained and practiced expert will be more useful/lethal than the most sophisticated gun in the hands of an "armchair warrior."

3. Guns and their ammunition are sized and optimized for a wide variety of tasks and targets. The same gun that will stop a grizzly bear in its tracks would blow a rabbit to smithereens, may cost on the order of $1 to $5 a shot, packs quite a wallop ("kick") against your shoulder, is quite expensive, and the gun will weigh a lot, but it does the job when smaller-gauge weapons simply won't do. However, a simple .22 caliber rimfire with .22 long-rifle (LR) cartridges and a scope will do a terrific job of taking down small game, deterring marauders, and can take down a deer with well-aimed "head shots." Since you can buy .22 caliber rounds for roughly $.04 each in quantities of 1,000, you could shoot hundreds of rounds during target practice at a cost that won't break the bank.

4. Whenever possible, especially if you may not use your gun for significant periods of time, spend a little extra money for a stainless steel barrel and slide versus traditional carbon steels, which will rust if not properly cared for.

5. Each of my expert shooter friends has a different opinion, and a different set of favorite guns, but the very first "top-of-the-list" gun on more than

Figure 10-1. 10/22 Ruger with scope. Photo courtesy of Cabela's

one of these lists is a 10/22 Ruger rifle with a scope (fig. 10-1). With a 10-round capacity .22 caliber magazine, it offers highly accurate semi-automatic rapid-fire action. Excellent for target practice and small game, it can be effectively used for self-defense when a larger-caliber weapon is not available. They say that at a distance of 50 yards, anyone with a steady hand could put five slugs in five seconds into a nickel-sized bull's-eye using this gun.

6. If you wished to purchase a single firearm that would double for self-defense, hunting small game, and also stop a grizzly bear in its tracks, that would be a 12 gauge shotgun (see fig.10-2). *Caution:* The 12 gauge shotgun has quite a "kick" to it.

   A 20 gauge shotgun has much less kick and is nearly as lethal as a 12 gauge, so lighter-framed men and women may find a themselves much better suited for a 20 gauge shotgun than a 12 gauge. I know a couple who purchased a 12 gauge shotgun and after a single shooting session were so intimidated by the gun's loud blast and kick that they never used it again. However, they are happy with the subsequent purchase of a 20 gauge shotgun. As a "feather-weight" 75-pound preteen male child, I was quite proud of the fact that I could handle shooting a 12 gauge shotgun, but my skeet shooting accuracy improved significantly when I switched to a lighter and less intimidating 20 gauge shotgun. As a self-defense weapon, a 12 gauge shotgun loaded with 00-size buckshot shells will blast a spray of between 9 and 15 each of .33 caliber pellets (number of pellets depends on the length of the shell) that will stop an intruder dead in his tracks. The same shotgun can shoot a rifled "slug" that will pack a huge punch to drop a grizzly or "two-legged large animals," and with shells filled with dozens of smaller-gauge buck shot (#4 through #8) will spray wider patterns of shot to effectively take down fast-moving water fowl and smaller game. Even though using a shotgun to

Figure 10-2. 12 gauge Remington pump-action shotgun. Photo courtesy of Cabela's

fire rounds of buckshot dramatically improves your chances of hitting your target, contrary to popular mythology, a shotgun must be aimed well, especially at close range, where buckshot spread is minimal.

7. After a shotgun and a 10-22 Ruger rifle, you may wish to expand your collection with a .30-06 classic deer hunting rifle and/or one of the military style "defensive" rifles such as the .223 caliber AR-15 (fig. 10-3) and Ruger Mini-14, or the larger caliber .308 (M14/M1A) or .30-06 (M1 Garand). The larger caliber rifles have better accuracy at longer ranges, but are heavier and cost significantly more for each round. For defense within the home, a 12 gauge firing #7½ birdshot loads will stop an intruder without having the rifle's problem of penetrating a wall and possibly harming someone else unintentionally, but for outside use, a rifle has both accuracy and range that is far superior to that of either a shotgun or handgun. Typical hunting rifles are designed for accuracy at over a hundred yards, and hold one to five rounds of ammunition. "Defensive" rifles are generally military-style guns designed to rapidly fire many shots with semiautomatic operation, meaning each time you pull the trigger they fire a shot, and have easily interchanged magazines that may be preloaded and swapped out in a matter of seconds (with practice). The classic military-style AK-47 rifle is world renowned for its effectiveness, high reliability (nearly jam proof), and ease of maintenance, making it an excellent choice for a defensive-style firearm (when equipped with interchangeable magazines, these types of firearms are not legal in some locations). The 7.62×39mm rounds used by the AK-47 offer excellent velocity, penetration, and accuracy, combined with relatively low cost, making it one of the most popular and readily available rifle cartridges around the world. Your rifles should all be properly fitted with slings. Without a sling, the rifle tends to be set down, and will do you no good if it is not within reach when needed.

Figure 10-3. .223 caliber AR-15 "defensive" rifle. Photo courtesy of Bushmaster Firearms

8. As for handguns, since most people purchase a handgun for self-defense, it behooves you to try several different guns to determine what you are comfortable with. A 9mm caliber gun will be smaller and easier to handle for many people, but a .40 S&W or .45 ACP will have much more stopping power. Since handguns require more skill and care than a shotgun or rifle in order to be safely and accurately handled, it is even more important

that you receive qualified instruction and experience shooting different models of handguns before making your selection. When purchasing a semiautomatic handgun for self defense, it is important that you buy a high-quality weapon, since the cheap versions are more prone to jamming, and a jammed gun will be of little use in your defense.

9. The variety of models, gauges, and nuances of firearm selection can be mind boggling to the neophyte. For whatever reason, if you are serious about arming yourself, I suggest you pick up a copy of *Boston's Gun Bible* and Mel Tappan's *Survival Guns*. Unless you are already a firearm enthusiast, these two books will probably tell you more than you ever wanted to know about guns. However, just reading a book is no substitution for experience, so it is also in your best interest to go shooting with friends, and/or seek out professional training where you can try out a variety or firearms to get a feel for what kinds of guns you are most comfortable with.

10. The most common calibers for rifles are .22 LR (long rifle), .223, 7.62×39mm, .308, .30-06. For handguns the most common calibers are 9mm, .40 S&W, and .45 ACP (most police forces have standardized on the .40 S&W). For shotguns the most common calibers are 12 gauge and 20 gauge. In general, you should stick to one of the most common calibers, and limit the number of different caliber guns that you rely upon, so you will not have to stock a huge selection of ammunition, and so you can more easily find ammunition for your guns through trade or barter, should the need arise.

11. Most serious gun enthusiasts and survivalists will purchase "reloading" equipment that enables them to recondition and reload their fired cartridge cases with new primers, powder charges, and bullets. If you shoot thousands of rounds, this will save you money over the long run, and it is also a hedge against some future time when ammunition may be unavailable or the sales severely restricted.

Practice and Training

Just because you may have been a decent shot once upon a time does not mean you have retained that skill. It takes regular practice to maintain or improve your shooting skills. Initially, try to shoot as often as you can, but at least once a week until you feel you have achieved an adequate level of proficiency. After that, make sure that you go shooting at least every month or two to ensure that your skills have not slid into the "near worthless" category, as mine did (serious shooters suggest at least once a week). There is no better way to find out what guns you feel comfortable with, than to go shooting with friends, or receive training from a professional where you are able to try out a variety of models and ammunition. It takes actual use to figure out what type and caliber of gun and ammunition you are comfortable with.

A small cute gun may not stop that attacker when you need it most, or stop that charging bear, but a gun that is too powerful and imposing for its owner will never see much practice, so it probably won't do him or her much good when needed. Salesmen at your local sportsman specialty stores (such as a Cabela's), or enthusiasts at a local gun club, should be able to point you in the right direction for receiving reputable firearms training where you will also be able to try out a variety of firearms. If you can't find a local recommended source, you might try the NRA, Western Rifle Shooting Association (westernrifleshooters.blogspot.com), or Project Appleseed (appleseedinfo .org) for one of their rifle shooting clinics.

Gun Safety

You can never put too much focus on gun safety. Especially if you have children around, either full time or as potential visitors, guns should be securely locked away and the ammunition should be locked in a separate location. Simply storing your ammunition in one place, and your guns in another, is not enough to keep them out of the hands of curious children. I speak that from experience because I was one of those curious children who would sneak shotgun shells from my father's stash so I could cut them apart for salvaging the gunpowder to play with. Like many other male children, I was quite fascinated with fire, guns, and explosives.

According to a review of self-inflicted and unintentional firearm injuries among children and adolescents, written up in the Archives of Pediatrics & Adolescent Medicine, most guns involved in preadult suicides and accidental shootings came from either the child's home or that of a friend or relative, so easy access to guns is a major factor in gun-related tragedies in both adolescence and childhood (Grossman, 1999). I also speak from experience on this one, as I came very close to blowing my brains out with a family shotgun when I was only ten or eleven years old, so don't assume that your innocent young child knows nothing about guns and might not sneak into your stash of guns and ammo one day, tragically changing your life forever! Having narrowly avoided tragedy on that one occasion, none of my family members ever did suffer from a gun-related accident, but many other families have not been so lucky. I strongly urge you to protect your guns and children, visiting or otherwise, by storing guns in a locked location and your ammunition in a separate locked storage area. You may wish to purchase a gun safe that also provides over one hour of protection from fire damage.

Gun Maintenance

Your investment in guns should be cleaned after each use and protected from corrosion, theft, and unintended usage. A gun's barrel is "fouled" with deposits of carbon and other debris as a natural result of shooting it. Buy yourself a gun-cleaning kit with rods, bore cleaner (solvent), gun oil, metal brushes, and plenty of extra disposable gleaning patches. Make sure you have the right size brushes and patches for each of your guns. The bore of the barrel should be brushed with the metal brushes and cleaner to remove built up debris, then swabbed with oil-soaked patches to leave a protective layer of gun oil. For wet climates, James Wesley, Rawles, the well known proprietor of survivalblog.com, recommends using Birchwood Casey Barricade protective oil, and for long-term storage he suggests coating the bore, chamber, and breech face with rust inhibitive grease (RIG).

Caution: Grease must be removed from the bore and firing surfaces before use!

It is a good idea to stock a set of essential spare parts for your guns, such as a firing pin, extractor, various springs, etc. Check with a gunsmith for suggestions for spare parts for your particular model, and store these parts wrapped in an oily cloth to prevent corrosion.

Basic Self-Defense Philosophy

❝Lots of people limit their possibilities by giving up easily. Never tell yourself this is too much for me. It's no use. I can't go on. If you do you're licked, and by your own thinking too. Keep believing and keep on keeping on.❞ —Norman Vincent Peale

To defend oneself and one's loved ones is a basic primal instinct and innate desire that nature built into each and every one of us. True self-defense is about survival. It is a gritty, dirty, no-holds-barred fight for your life. To be victorious, which means saving your life and the lives of those you care about, you must allow yourself to get pissed off! You must channel your anger into the fight against your opponent, not allowing it to cloud your reason, but using it to fuel the fires within that enable you to do what you must do, and never give up. If you can't muster enough anger to allow yourself to do whatever it takes to stop that rapist/murderer/thief/sociopath dead in his tracks, then you will fail, and the consequences may well be disastrous.

The physical self-defense techniques that are outlined in the following pages are very basic tools and principles that may save your life someday. The principles alone will be of some value, but it is their practice, both in your mind as well as against a physical target, such as a padded pole planted in the ground, a punching bag, or a partner wearing protective clothing, that will help program the motions into your muscles and memory that will turn theory into practice when push comes to shove.

People skilled in the martial arts typically practice a series of movements, each set of which is known as a *kata*. Each *kata* is a specific combination of precise offensive and/or defensive movements, such as kicks, blocks, chokes, throws, and punches, designed to deal with one or more opponents in a given scenario. A typical martial artist will practice a few *katas* over and over again, hundreds of times, until each series of movements is mastered, before moving on to a new series of *katas*. In this way, a specific *kata* becomes programmed into the reflex system of the body, so whether in competition, combat, or a self defense situation, the body has a "library" of sets of learned and programmed sequences that may be accessed with lightening speed, bypassing the need to "figure things out." Bruce Lee spoke of learning, memorizing and then forgetting the form, while other martial artists speak of a high concept known as *munen muso,* which can be translated into acting with an undisturbed or seemingly "empty" mind where the natural intuitive self responds unhampered as the situation requires.

Naturally, no amount of self-defense techniques or physical training and conditioning will stop a bullet. Hollywood loves the stereotype of muscle-bound action heroes, like Rambo, whose superhuman strength and uncanny fighting skills carry them safely through a hail of bullets, but real life simply does not work that way. You might say that if you could carry a handgun, why would you ever need to practice and learn the techniques of hand-to-hand combat and self-defense? The answer is that life is messy. You never know when you might be surprised, suddenly finding yourself in a situation where you need to apply one or more of these techniques.

Naturally it is preferable that you receive personal instruction from a true expert, and practice, practice, practice until a number of key techniques for self-defense become so engrained into your being as to become essentially automatic reflex reactions. Since repetition will ingrain these practices into your being, it is in your best interest to ensure that your martial-arts or self-defense instructor is of the highest moral and spiritual integrity as well as having top-notch athletic and instructional skills. There are a lot of bogus macho jerks in the various martial-arts and self-defense disciplines, so choose your instructor wisely.

Unfortunately, the reality is that many of my readers simply will not spend the time and money for professional training. If this is your case, and you have the misfortune to be stuck in some disaster scenario where lawlessness and chaos are the rule of the day, please take the time to at least practice the following techniques within your mind's eye. If you have the opportunity to practice them with a partner, or against an inanimate object, such as a *makiwara*, which is a padded striking post used in training in the martial arts and traditionally made of rice straw bound with a rope, that would be much better.

Remember, there is no single "right answer" or "right technique" for every situation. Ultimately it will be a combination of the inner compass of your intuitional guidance, guts, determination, skill, natural reactions, conditioning, surprise, strategy, and just plain luck that will determine whether or not you will be successful in your attempts to defend yourself in that moment when self-defense suddenly becomes the most important thing in your world. In real-life situations it may well be "all or nothing." There will be no "do-overs" or "time-outs," and there will be no referee standing by to ensure that nobody gets hurt and everybody fights "clean."

Here are a few thoughts and observations:

1. The object of self-defense is to escape with your life, and hopefully your health and well-being intact. If you can avoid the physical conflict altogether, that would be best. Simply "walking tall" with head held high, shoulders back, and an air of self-confidence is often all it takes to persuade a would-be-attacker to pursue an easier target. Predators and bullies usually try to attack what they consider to be easy prey.

2. Sometimes words alone are enough to defuse a situation, and at other times, they may provide a much needed distraction that buys you valuable seconds and a few inches of personal space from which to launch a devastating counterattack that at least temporarily cripples your opponent, damaging or destroying his ability to engage in further combat or pursuit. Sometimes eye contact can back someone off. An alert look could create enough doubt in a bully's mind that he chooses to go for another target. Again, trust your intuition, use your "feelers," and don't make it easy for an assailant by feeling and acting vulnerable or inattentive.

3. Sometimes, such as the case of my friend Allison's story, simply breaking loose and sprinting out the door to a public area is all that is required to reach safety.

4. At other times, if you have weaker people in your party (such as other family members), or there is no nearby "safe" location, then simply breaking free is of no value. If your opponent is bigger, stronger, and faster than you are, what good would it do you to just break free and run? He will simply catch up with you and be more careful the next time. In this case, you must use all of the skill, knowledge, strength, determination, will power, and strategy that you can muster to launch an explosive and crippling offensive that renders your opponent physically incapable of striking again, incapable of pursuit, or in the least to have inflicted enough pain and suffering that your opponent decides to find easier prey elsewhere.

5. Survival in a true self-defense scenario involves decisive aggressive action! The goal is to avoid injury and death. If unsuccessful at avoiding conflict, in order to minimize your chances of injury and maximize your chance of success, your attacker must be neutralized quickly and decisively. A counterattack must be initiated as soon as possible, with explosive action,

preferably simultaneous to your defense, shifting the aggressor immediately to the defensive. Most criminals are looking for a victim, not a battle, and will be surprised when an opponent inflicts immediate injury and extreme pain, often dropping their attack to make a hasty retreat.

6. Assess the situation. If someone has a gun and is pointing it at you, what do they want? If they simply wanted to shoot you, they would have done so already. Are they trying to force you into a car, or a private location, where they may do with you as they wish? Are there potential makeshift weapons around, such as a table lamp, paperweight, vase, cane, stick, etc., that you might use to your advantage? Are you on home turf where if the lights went out, you would be at an advantage knowing your way around in the dark? What is your opponent's body language telling you? Body language, both yours and your opponent's, speak volumes when we know what we are looking for. During the assessment phase, which could be just a few seconds in duration, gathering a little information can make a big difference. How is your assailant standing? Is he concealing something? Is he tired? What is he wearing? What is the terrain? Are there exits or objects that you could pick up to use as a makeshift weapon? Are other people nearby? Simply the act of calmly and consciously assessing your opponent may generate enough concern and doubt on his part that he chooses to leave you alone.

7. Many women have a fear of violent attack and/or sexual assault. This fear happens to be well grounded in fact, given the statistic that one in six women will be the victim of at least one attempted or completed rape over the course of their lifetime (for Native Americans the rate is a staggering one in three) (RAINN 2011). Rape-aggression defense (RAD, see www.rad-systems.com for more information) is a practical empowering program for women interested in a quick and definitive self-defense program.

8. Trust your instincts! Nature has built into each and every one of us an inner radar and compass to both warn us of impending danger, and to instinctively guide us toward optimal action. Millions of years of natural selection means that those human beings lacking in these traits simply died out and left the gene pool. Trust me, you were born with what it takes, but you need to allow your genetic heritage to shine through. Your "bad feeling" about that seemingly harmless nice-looking man in the elevator, or about parking next to that windowless van (always a warning signal) in the parking garage, might be a warning about something you need to pay attention to.

9. Stay aware of your surroundings. Pay attention to easy hiding spots, such as thick hedges, windowless vans, alleys, bridges, etc.

10. When threatened, you may be at a stalemate until your aggressor is close enough to touch. Odds are that your attacker is untrained, so any training on your part will be to your advantage. Once your opponent reaches for you, he has opened the door for you to go on the attack. Remember, if he is grabbing you with his hands, that usually leaves at least both your feet

free, and possibly your hands too, so use these available appendages to go on the immediate offensive.

11. Take a class and practice. There are many fine self-defense programs, and many excellent teachers. Talk to people and find a class/teacher with a good reputation. For example, the "Krav Maga" system of self-defense and practical fighting skills was developed by the Israelis as a hand-to-hand combat training program for soldiers, law enforcement personnel, and civilians, both male and female It is simple enough for users to reach a reasonable level of proficiency in a short period of time, and is quite effective, enabling a smaller person with some training to quickly and easily knock down and disable an opponent who is much larger and more intimidating in stature. If you have not done so already, I highly recommend you invest some time and energy into your "real-life insurance policy" by taking a class in one of the many professionally taught self-defense systems that does not require years of practice to become reasonably proficient. A more in-depth martial-art system that offers balance to the equation is the DanZan Ryu Jujitsu of Professor Henry S. Okazaki, its founder. This comprehensive martial art offers something for everyone, including hand-to-hand combat, multiple weapons usage, bodywork, and folk medicine. It is never too late and you are never too old to start learning a system such as this one.

12. Attack vulnerable areas. When your life is at stake and failure is not an option, your primary hope for a positive outcome is to explosively and decisively attack your opponent's most vulnerable areas without hesitation. The "eyes, throat, and groin" (a self-defense mantra in itself) of a 300-pound human gorilla are just as vulnerable to attack as those body parts are on the rest of us. The head offers several vulnerable areas as well as the top of the foot, shins, knees, and available joints such as fingers, wrists, and elbows. Hitting the areas where major bodily organs are located will severely disrupt the assailant's system. These include the liver, kidneys, heart, and solar plexus, to name a few. The body is full of pressure points and soft tissue that will avail you the time or the inches you need to make your escape, or follow through with a more deadly attack. These include the pocket behind the ear lobes (specific techniques to follow), the trachea, and other areas that surround the neck. The goal is to make your attacker unable or unwilling to continue the attack.

Self-defense, like emergency preparations in general, is much like car insurance. You pray to God you will never need to use it, but if that day should ever come when you do need it, you thank God you took the time to learn a few powerful and effective techniques of self-defense.

The Value of Speed and Surprise

If you are older, or a nonthreatening looking male or female, your looks could be used to your advantage. Deception is excellent self-defense. By all means, avoid a confrontation if you can, but if you are unsuccessful in these efforts, use body language and voice to momentarily disarm and distract your opponent. Once your opponent reaches toward your body, touches you, or attempts to strike a blow, you have a brief moment of opportunity where you may take control of the situation. If your attacker has no clue that you have the knowledge and skills to defend yourself with crippling blows to vulnerable parts of his body, he is much less likely to be cautious and protective, so do not go into some cheesy self-defense stance you learned in the martial-arts class you took decades ago.

Keep your hands above your waist in a nonthreatening stance such as the "thinking posture," or perhaps scratch your chin or nervously play with your hair. Turn your body to the side, standing at an angle to your attacker that minimizes your exposure of vital areas, and be ready to block your opponent's advance while launching a crippling counterattack. You must use the element of surprise to your best advantage. You might be able to buy inches of room to increase your options, and seconds to initiate your counterattack. When your opponent is at close range, an alarming look to the side, a feint, or a gesture toward an imaginary friend could provide that instant of distraction that you need to strike your opponent's eyes, throat, or groin or other highly vulnerable areas. Distractions are everywhere—throw things if you can, and use your voice (*kiai* or spirit yell). This will muster up your will, off-balance your opponent, and alert others to the situation.

Vulnerable Parts of the Body

There are numerous "pressure points" and sensitive body areas that are vulnerable to attack, but we are going to focus on those areas of the body that will be most accessible, and easiest to strike while providing excellent results without the necessity for significant precision, training, or strength. Which areas you strike, and how you strike your blows, will be dependent upon instinct, training, and what is most convenient and accessible at the moment. There is a world of information available on this fascinating subject, and I encourage you to expand your knowledge and training in this area. The experts involved in helping to produce this chapter recommend balancing your martial-art and self-defense skills with altruism and healing skills, since life and death are two aspects of the same coin.

Vulnerable areas to strike:

1. **Eyes.** Gouging the eyes with the thumbs, an extended finger, or a swinging blow from the butt of your elbow will rapidly impair your opponent (see fig. 10-4). As always, be aware that a wounded animal is often more dangerous than an unwounded one, so be effective or prepare to deal with the consequences. In *The Art of War*, Sun Tzu suggests you do

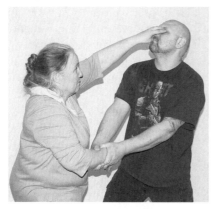

Figure 10-4. Finger strike to the eyes.

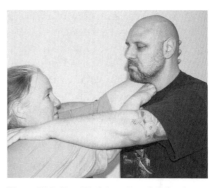

Figure 10-5. Knuckle jab to the windpipe (note her left hand behind his head, pulling it toward her fist)

Figure 10-6. Elbow strike to the throat (debilitating strike whether you hit the throat or the jaw or the temple).

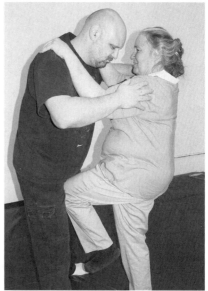

Figure 10-7. Knee strike to the groin.

not "burn your enemy's kitchen" or leave him no retreat, or wound him unnecessarily. This will cause him to fight with a reckless abandon for which you may be unprepared. Don't make matters worse for yourself. Be decisive in your attack, causing as much damage as you can! You do not want to fight the same opponent twice.

2. **Throat.** A firm blow to the throat with your elbow, fist, or knee will drop your attacker instantly (figs. 10-5 and 10-6). It is not hard to collapse the windpipe, so by all means "go for the throat" of your opponent while doing your best to protect your own.

3. **The groin.** In general, assuming your attacker is male, a blow to the groin will drop your attacker in short order. The male groin is sensitive enough

that a swinging blow of a wide-open palm or fist will probably do the trick, though a hard knee jab (fig. 10-7), elbow swing, or foot kick will almost always provide a knock down that will keep your assailant down for a long time. *Caution:* Sometimes it will take several seconds after a groin strike hits a male assailant before it produces the desired incapacitating effect. On occasion a drugged-out assailant, or one with an abnormal physical response (or a protective cup, or thick padded clothing), will not succumb to a full-contact groin strike, so do not ease up on your counterattack until your opponent is clearly incapacitated!

4. **Knees.** When a person is standing with his full weight on a straight, or nearly straightened leg, his knee may be severely damaged by a crippling kick, aimed at either the side or the front, that is well within the physical capabilities of most people. When your assailant is behind you, use what is commonly known as a "bicycle kick" (fig. 10-8). Bend and raise your knee to "cock" it before launching explosively backwards to dislocate and tear your opponent's knee joint, striking the knee from either the front or the side.

You do not have to be an athlete to do this, but you must be determined and not hold back. As with all strikes, always hit or kick through your target. It is not the surface that you are attacking, but what is beyond. Follow through. The side of the knee will buckle quite easily. Not only will the knee be damaged by these techniques but the assailant will be taken to the ground. This will give you the option of escape or further aggressive action. If you are facing toward your attacker, a classic karate "side kick" will deal a crippling blow to either the kneecap or the side of the knee. It will take a heavier blow to buckle the knee from the front, than from the side, but you will have to settle for whatever direction you have access to. For either the side kick or the bicycle kick, launch as much of your body's force and momentum through the heel of your extended leg with as much explosive power as you can muster. The knee, like many other joints (elbow, etc.) is susceptible to hyperextension, and permanent damage will be incurred. Unlike your toes, which break fairly easily, the heel of your foot can both take and deliver a severe pounding without damage to the heel.

Figure 10-8. "Bicycle kick" to the side of the knee.

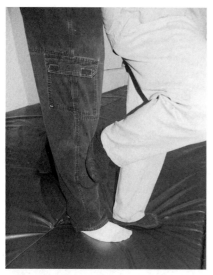

Figure 10-9. Explosively rake your foot down the opponent's shin to help it stay on target (this is called "tracking"), crushing your opponent's foot.

Many times we are wearing shoes, boots or even high heels—all wonderful weapons at our immediate disposal!

5. **Instep/shin.** An attack to the instep or shin of your assailant could break the leg or ankle. Regardless, it will be intensely painful, and quite effectively incapacitate your assailant. If your arms are pinned tightly by your assailant, and you are in a standing position, his instep may be the most accessible and vulnerable body part to counterattack that gets him to release his grip. Raise your well bent knee, effectively cocking your leg, before extending it explosively while allowing the side of your foot to scrape down your opponent's shin to ensure that the heel of your foot lands on target with a crippling blow to the top of his foot (fig. 10-9).

6. **Chin.** An upward blow to the chin, either straight up with a vigorous palm thrust (fig. 10-10) or head butt, or somewhat from the side with an elbow swing or hammer fist, will usually deliver a knockout blow. In the least, it should "ring your opponent's bell" and "rattle his cage" enough to cause a drop of his guard that will create an opening with the opportunity to attack other sensitive areas, such as the eyes, throat, or groin.

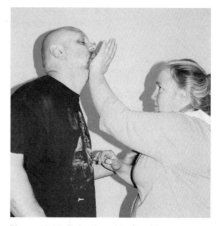

Figure 10-10. Palm thrust to the chin.

7. **Jaw.** A side blow to the jaw from an elbow swing, or a hammer fist (make a fist and swing it as hard as you can, striking on the flexed side of your hand that is opposite the thumb) will often break the jaw and/or knock out your opponent (fig. 10-11). This spot is called the "knock-out button" where the maxilla meets the mandible. As always, be aware of your own fist alignment, which you can learn from a trained martial artist, since you do not want to injure your own hand.

Figure 10-11. Hammer fist to the jaw (swing from the side as hard as you can).

8. **The ears.** The area in the hollow directly behind the ear lobes is an extremely sensitive pressure point. If you are tightly held, you may not have room for delivering a swinging blow, but if you can reach the area behind your opponent's ear lobes (fig. 10-12), with one or both of your hands, driving your thumbs into that hollow and up toward the top of his head, will deliver excruciating pain to your assailant and he will most likely pull back, opening himself up to attack on other vulnerable areas, such as the groin, throat, eyes, or knees.

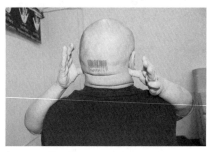

Figure 10-12. Thumb attack to pressure points behind the ears.

Figure 10-13. Swinging strike of cupped hand to "box" the opponent's ear.

9. The ears are quite sensitive in more ways than one. Cup your hand(s) and swing hard to strike either one or both ears. This "boxing" of the ears will be excruciatingly painful, most likely bursting your attacker's eardrum (fig. 10-13).

10. **Neck/carotid artery.** This is not just a trick in the movies. A swift firm blow to the side of the neck with an elbow swing,

Figure 10-14. Karate or judo chop to the side of the neck (carotid complex).

karate chop, or a hammer fist will spasm the carotid complex supplying blood and oxygen to the brain and will severely compromise your opponent (fig. 10-14).

11. **Solar plexus.** The solar plexus is the area in the center of your gut between your belly button and your rib cage. A blow to the solar plexus, with a fist, knee, a kick, or the elbow (fig. 10-15), could "knock the wind out" of your opponent or worse, buying you precious time to make your escape or deliver more crippling blows to further incapacitate your opponent. A firm blow to the solar plexus region can also break the ribs and sternum.

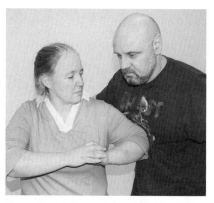

Figure 10-15. Elbow strike to the solar plexus (swing from the side as hard as you can).

12. **Nose.** Though not necessarily a knockout blow, a palm thrust, elbow swing, head butt, or firm fist to the nose (fig. 10-16) will easily break it, generating much pain and profuse bleeding. This strike will affect vision by watering the eyes as well. Blood has its own psychological effect on your opponent, especially if it is his and not yours. This will usually cause your opponent to let down his guard, at least momentarily, allowing you to mount an attack on his more critically vulnerable areas.

Figure 10-16. Palm thrust to the nose.

13. **Shins.** The bony front edge of the shin is sensitive (the peroneal nerve can be struck about two-thirds of the way down the shin), but not very vulnerable to damage. However, an angled blow to the muscle immediately adjoining the front bony part of the shin, delivered by a knee,

Figure 10-17. Bicycle kick to the side of the shin.

elbow, or kick (fig. 10-17), will cause intense pain, may well get him to drop his grip or attack, and at least temporarily impair the ability of your assailant to run.

Strategies for Defending Against Common Scenarios

This is a short list for a number of common scenarios. Again, since it will take a considerable amount of practice under the tutelage of a skilled instructor to transform a neophyte from a clumsy armchair warrior into a confident well-oiled fighting machine, I urge you to pick up some of the recommended references (see appendix 1) *and* seek professional self-defense training. Self-defense training is recommended for folks of all ages, body types, and genders, but especially for those lacking in confidence in this area, such as the elderly, most women, and men who may be somewhat overweight or slight in build and stature.

1. **Grabbing your hand(s).** An assailant might grab your hand (these techniques also work when two hands grab on one, or when both hands are grabbed) for several reasons, such as intimidation, to prevent you from reaching for a gun or physical object, to drag you into a car, or for immobilization. When you know what you are doing, it is quite easy to break free of the grasp of a much stronger and bigger assailant. Common methods of breaking free from an assailant's grip on your hands or wrists are (1) leverage (fig. 10-18), (2) circular rotating movements (fig. 10-19), and (3) "stripping" movements (fig. 10-20). For the leverage method, rotate your wrist slightly so the narrow direction of your wrist is aimed to pull through your opponent's finger tips and thumb. Bend at the elbow and snap your arm toward yourself to break it out of your opponent's grasp. If your other hand is free, you may wish to assist the first hand by grasping the fingers of your trapped hand and pulling them toward your body as you bend at the elbow to break free from your assailant's grasp.

Figure 10-18. *A,* start of "leverage" method of breaking free from opponent's grasp (note defensive raised position of other hand). *B,* finish of "leverage" method of breaking free from opponent's grasp (bend arm sharply at the elbow while pulling hand toward self to easily lever your hand out of opponent's grip).

Figure 10-19. For the circular method, rapidly and vigorously rotate your hand in a small circle either to the outside or the inside to quickly pry your wrist from your opponent's grasp.

Figure 10-20. *A*, start of "stripping" method of breaking free from opponent's grasp (note "cocked" position of right arm). *B*, middle of "stripping" method of breaking free from opponent's grasp (drive free hand vigorously toward wrist of opponent). *C*, end of "stripping" method of breaking free from opponent's grasp (strike opponent's wrist with all your might).

For the "stripping" method, raise your free hand by cocking the elbow, then rotate your body and hips as you straighten your elbow, striking your opponent's wrist with your free hand using a "palm strike" as you pull back on the restrained hand. The pulling force and motion of the restrained hand combined with the opposing stripping action of the free hand will knock your opponent's grasp from your wrist.

Remember: At this point in time your feet and legs are probably free, so if you are significantly threatened, you should immediately counter attack using a knee or foot against your opponent's groin, instep, solar plexus, etc.

2. **Bear hug from behind.** When grabbed from behind with a "bear hug," and your arms are pinned, raise your leg to a "cocked" position before striking vigorously behind you with a "bicycle kick" (fig. 10-21). You can also use the "instep stomp."

   You may also be able to accomplish the same thing by flinging your head back in a "head butt" aimed toward your opponent's jaw or nose, provided his head is stationed in a vulnerable position. It is not necessary to be stronger than your opponent. All you need to be is stronger than his thumb. An alternate method is to grab his thumb with several fingers and pull hard (fig. 10-22). When his thumb breaks, or dislocates at the joint, he will let go!

Figure 10-21. "Bicycle kick" to the knee to get opponent to release a "bear hug."

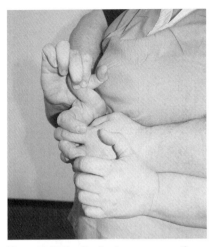

Figure 10-22. Peeling back your opponent's thumb to get him to release a "bear hug."

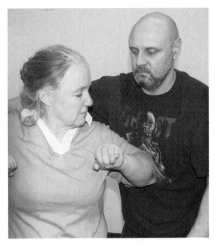

Figure 10-23. Elbow strike counter attack to the solar plexus.

Don't forget to launch your counterattack the moment that your opponent has released his grip using elbows and well-placed strikes (fig. 10-23).

3. **Choking.** If your attacker is trying to slip his arm around your neck to apply a choke hold, one defensive technique is to grab the arm with both hands and yank downward before he has had a chance to interlock both of his arms and apply the choke (fig. 10-24). Speed is essential, always remembering your feet are free to distract and attack from below.

Another technique for thwarting choke holds is to drive an arm or hand up alongside your neck to get a limb inside the choking hold, wire, rope, etc., before it is too late (fig. 10-25). For good reason, the classic piano wire or rope chokes have been favored by Mafia hit men and made

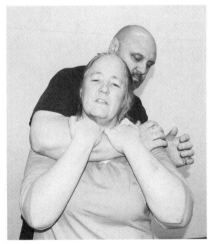

Figure 10-24. Thwarting a choke hold by yanking attacker's arm downward.

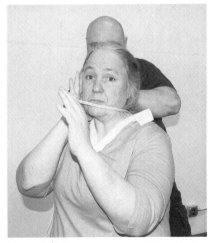

Figure 10-25. Thwarting a strangle by inserting a limb underneath the attacker's rope or wire.

famous in movies like *The Godfather*. They are noiseless, fast, and very deadly.

Various choke holds are common in the martial arts and have been quite controversial in law enforcement over the years. But these techniques are most valuable and effective when applied correctly. These holds apply leveraged pressure against the carotid arteries and jugular veins in the neck, cutting off blood flow to the brain and can result in loss of consciousness in a few seconds.

Caution: In the case of a carotid artery choke ("sleeper hold"), or a wire/rope strangle, you will have only a few seconds before loss of consciousness to thwart the strangle attempt with an inserted limb or a counter attack, such as an instep strike, bicycle kick to the knee, or groin strike.

4. **Knife.** Knife and gun defense are a study all their own. The number-one rule in defending yourself from a knife attack is expect to be cut. A knife fighter will carve you up and close the distance on you before you can blink. Many prisoners practice with shivs (makeshift sharpened objects) all day and they are very, very good. There are systems of study available that can get you into some sort of even ground, but it takes training. We will assume that the knife wielder is not experienced. Use distractions and consider escape if you are without an equalizer of your own. That means you are facing an edged weapon with empty hands, and have no weapon of your own. Remember that the weapon is the person holding the knife and not the knife itself. Distance is your friend, so keep it. Keep your hands close to your chest and body as they will be easy targets if outstretched. It is common for a defender to let the attacker make the first move. The Duke of Wellington said to one of his officers, and I paraphrase, "How am I to know what to do if we do not know what Bonaparte does?" This is good thinking. Be patient. Let opportunity show itself. Sometimes it is better to let the assailant extend and make the first move. It is vitally important to realize the deadliness of this kind of situation. You may have only one opportunity for your survival. This is what the student of war calls "death ground," and with a knife or a gun this strategy is all too real. Scream, throw things, kick sand—whatever you need to do to defend your life, for it is all at stake. Think of your

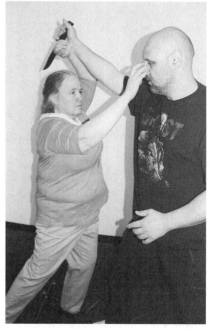

Figure 10-26. Blocking a stabbing knife strike combined with counter attack to the eyes.

family and your right and desire to live. You will prevail if your fighting spirit is more worthy. "Defanging the snake" is a term we use for taking out the weapon-bearing limb. There are ways to simultaneously hit the back and front of a hand to release a grip but you must be very good and very fast. There are methods of trapping and then stripping the knife that work. There are methods of controlling or breaking the wrist or arm that are also effective (figs. 10-26 and 10-27).

Figure 10-27. Blocking a knife thrust combined with counterattack knee to the solar plexus.

5. **Gun.** The gun has a similar story to the knife. We already mentioned that if a gun is pointing at you and has not gone off then the person holding the weapon has something else in mind. Think about this intently. Whether it's a wallet or the keys to a safe—give it to him. If he wants to take your children, then it is time to implement a strategy and not be a victim. Many good men and women have gone down fighting for others. We are all on this earth a short time. Live right. Die right. The following are things to remember about a gun. Bullets shoot in a straight line, so when you try to deflect an arm holding a gun, step to the side out of the line of fire. Cover is good to find. As with a knife it is possible to disarm a gun, but the gun needs to be within your reach. The wrist can be manipulated, the arm can be broken (fig. 10-28). All the vital points we have mentioned and

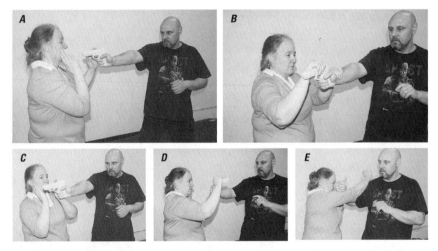

Figure 10-28. Blocking a gun aimed at the head. *A*, step 1: hands raised in ready position. *B*, step 2: turn sideways as you push gun away. *C*, step 3: grab wrist and gun, while pulling wrist as you strip the gun away. *D*, step 4: pulling wrist while stripping the gun wrenches it from assailant's hand, potentially damaging the trigger finger. *E*, step 5: gun is now out of assailant's hand and under your control.

captured throughout this very brief exposé on self-defense can be attacked and the effect will be there. Self-defense works—if you work it.

Common Sense, the Law, and Self-Defense

❝As a martial-arts teacher and student, as a father and a good citizen, I have had to face myself and my students with the reality of these situations and ask the hard questions. I recommend you all do the same. I have studied with the military, law-enforcement officers, and hundreds of martial-arts enthusiasts. Self-defense is all about taking life or limb in the interest of self-preservation. We must think this through beforehand and make the decision now to be ready and willing to strike out against lethal unwarranted aggression and not wait to think about these things until we are suddenly confronted with a potentially deadly situation. This will prepare us for the future and better guide the outcome. I believe that with a righteous heart combined with strong technique we cannot lose.❞—Frank Ferris, sixth-degree black belt, Sensei, High Sierra Jujitsu, instructor of DanZan Ryu Jujitsu and a major contributor to this chapter

Everyone has the right to defend him- or herself, and that right is protected by the law. However, the law is open to many different interpretations, and simply because you are acting within your legal rights, and they are protected by the law, does not mean you may not be brought to court for your actions. These days, it seems that anyone can bring a lawsuit against anyone else for nearly anything, so you may be dragged into court for what seems like totally reasonable actions on your part, though judges will usually throw obviously frivolous cases out of court before they get very far along. I am not a lawyer, and cannot offer you advice on legal matters, but I can give you my opinions concerning the popular consensus on these matters.

In general, it is perfectly legal to defend yourself, but it is not legal to take retribution on another person. For example, if you use self-defense to defend yourself from attack, and throw your attacker to the ground, breaking his arm, that should be within your legal right, but once your attacker has been subdued, and is lying unconscious on the ground, if you kick him repeatedly and viciously causing great bodily harm, you may well be in a heap of legal trouble. The standard advice given for these situations is to always say you were "afraid for your life" and that is why you acted in such a way. That may, or may not, be the case. The judge, jury, and police are usually directed to use the "reasonable person" test to determine the "reasonableness" of your actions. You are typically legally allowed to use whatever force a "reasonable person" might use in your situation, which is open to interpretation.

Let's say you are a 5'6" 120-pound woman fighting off a 6' tall 200-pound male rapist. In this case, if you succeeded in knocking down your opponent, and picked up a nearby lamp stand and bashed his head repeatedly to ensure that he could not arise and continue his attack, chances are that all would agree you were acting as a "reasonable person" using reasonable force given the situation. However, if you are a 180-pound man, and a 125-pound unarmed purse snatcher grabs your wife's purse, and as he is running away you draw a pistol and put three bullets in his back, you will probably have a hard time getting away with using the reasonable person defense and may well be charged with manslaughter.

Let's face it, if you are truly in a life-and-death situation, you should probably do whatever you must to ensure the safety and well-being of yourself and your loved ones, and worry about the legal ramifications later.

PART THREE

Specific Disasters and Crises: Preparations and Strategies

[11]

Fire!

Fire Statistics

The following statistics from the National Fire Protection Association (NFPA) are for fires in the United States in 2009 (Karter 2010):

- There were 3,010 civilian deaths from fire, 2,565 of which occurred in the home.
- There were 260 civilian deaths from motor vehicle fires.
- Only 105 civilian fire deaths occurred in nonresidential structures.
- U.S. fire departments responded to an estimated 1,348,500 fires resulting in an estimated $12,531,000,000 in property losses and 17,050 civilian injuries.

In general, fires cause more loss of life and property in America than all natural disasters combined! Statistically speaking, the easiest and most cost-effective way to reduce the chances that you, your home, or your family might suffer great loss in a future fire event, is to improve the fire safety of your home, and the fire awareness of your loved ones. This chapter covers fire safety in the home, what to do when a fire strikes, and how to improve the fire resistance of your home and property.

Fire Safety Within the Home

Smoke Detectors

Probably the single most important fire-safe thing you can do for your home and family is to make sure that it is properly equipped with smoke detectors, and that they are in good working order. Smoke detectors should be installed in every bedroom, the kitchen, hallways, and at least one on every floor of your home. Where possible, smoke detectors should be hardwired into your home's electrical system, and should also have their own battery power to provide protection when the AC power in your home goes out. It is a good idea to install combination CO (carbon monoxide) and smoke detection units.

For new construction, codes require that all smoke detectors are of the new type that are hardwired to communicate with each other. That way, if one smoke detector goes off, they all go off. Since there may be only a matter of

In October 1993, when a vicious wildfire broke out in Laguna Beach, a southern California beach town, firefighter John Henderson was called down from his home in the Sierras of northern California to fight this blaze. The combination of extremely dangerous fire conditions, brought on by three consecutive drought years coupled with 60 to 70 mph hot and dry Santa Ana winds, quickly whipped the fire into an unstoppable conflagration, burning hundreds of homes to the ground! When John rounded a corner on the Pacific Coast Highway, just north of Laguna Beach, he saw a sight that he will never forget. He and his partner watched the firestorm rush down the dry hills toward the ocean. The heat of the firestorm was so intense that, even after blowing across four lanes of pavement, it was hot enough to ignite a mile-long stretch of wooden telephone poles on the ocean side of the road. From a distance, he said they looked like a string of matchsticks stuck in the sand, igniting one after the other until there were perhaps a hundred telephone poles burning at once.

a few minutes of time to escape a fire once it has grown to the point where it trips a smoke detector, the new interconnected systems improve the chances that everyone in the home will escape safely. For retrofit situations, you can purchase smoke detectors that use a wireless interconnect to communicate with each other. In the case of either wireless or hardwired intercommunicating smoke detectors, the detectors may be of different types (ionization or photoelectric types, combination CO and smoke detecting, etc.) as long as all detectors are made by the same manufacturer and designed to communicate with each other. When retrofitting rooms for smoke detectors, in most cases the units will operate solely from batteries.

You may find it hard to believe, but children will often sleep through the screech of a smoke detector alarm. Statistical tests show that more children will respond to their parent's voices than to the screech of a smoke detector. Make sure you train your children to both recognize and respond to a smoke detector alarm, but also remember to add your own voice to that alarm when confronted by a real-life situation!

Be sure to change your smoke detector batteries, and test their function, at least once a year. An easy way to remember this is to get in the habit of changing smoke detector batteries, and testing their function, on the same time each year, such as when you set the clocks back at the end of Daylight Saving Time every fall. Locate the manual "test" button on the outside of your smoke detector. It may be simply a small raised area in the housing with a slot around it and the word "test" printed on that part of the housing. Push this flexible button and listen for an ear-piercing audible alarm.

Caution: If the light on your smoke detector blinks slowly, or it beeps at you intermittently, that probably means that its batteries are running low and need changing.

Fire Extinguishers

A portable fire extinguisher can save lives and property by putting out a small fire or containing it until the fire department arrives; but portable extinguishers have limitations. Because a fire can grow and spread quite rapidly, the number-one priority for residents is to get out safely. Fire extinguishers have a rating label that tells you what types of fires they are designed to work on, as well as their relative fire-fighting capacity. A class "A" fire extinguisher is designed to work on standard fires such as wood, paper, textiles, etc. A class "B" fire extinguisher is designed to work on flammable liquids such as grease, gasoline, and oil fires. A class "C" fire extinguisher is designed to work on electrical fires. For home usage, it is recommended that you select a multi-class fire extinguisher, such as an ABC-type extinguisher capable of fighting a normal fire as well as grease and electrical fires (NFPA 2001).

The numbers on the fire extinguisher label also indicate relative size of the fire extinguisher. On a multi-class-rated fire extinguisher, the number immediately preceding the "A" is the equivalent number of water units (a unit is 1.25 gallons) of fire-fighting capacity that are contained inside the fire extinguisher. The number before the "B" is the number of square feet of grease fire that the extinguisher is sized to fight. For example, a fire extinguisher with a 3-A:40-B:C UL rating has a rated firefighting capacity equivalent to 3 × 1.25 = 3.75 gallons of water for standard fires, 40 square feet of grease fire fighting capacity, and is also rated to handle electrical fires.

Safety Tips

- Use a portable fire extinguisher when the fire is confined to a small area, such as a wastebasket, and is not growing; everyone has exited the building; the fire department has been called or is being called; and the room is not filled with smoke.

- To operate a fire extinguisher, remember the word *PASS*:

  Pull the pin. Hold the extinguisher with the nozzle pointing away from you, and release the locking mechanism.

  Aim low. Point the extinguisher at the base of the fire.

  Squeeze the lever slowly and evenly.

  Sweep the nozzle from side-to-side. See figure 11-1.

- For the home, select a multipurpose extinguisher (that can be used on all types of home fires) that is large enough to put out a small fire, but not so heavy as to be difficult to handle.

- Choose a fire extinguisher that carries the label of an independent testing laboratory, such as UL or CSA.

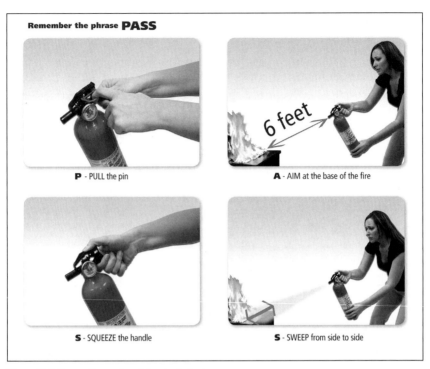

Remember the phrase PASS

P - PULL the pin

A - AIM at the base of the fire

S - SQUEEZE the handle

S - SWEEP from side to side

Figure 11-1. Proper fire-extinguisher technique.

- Read the instructions that come with the fire extinguisher and become familiar with its parts and operation before a fire breaks out. Local fire departments or fire equipment distributors often offer hands-on fire extinguisher trainings.

- Install fire extinguishers close to an exit, and keep your back to a clear exit when you use the device so you can make an easy escape if the fire cannot be controlled. If the room fills with smoke, leave immediately.

- Know when to go. Fire extinguishers are one element of a fire response plan, but the primary element is safe escape. Every household should have a home fire-escape plan and working smoke alarms.

Painters Masks and Gas Masks

Caution: Smoke inhalation can rapidly incapacitate and kill!

A painter's-style respirator mask with charcoal canisters (see fig. 17-10), or a gas mask (see fig. 17-9), could provide much needed protection from smoke inhalation to give you that extra minute or two to rescue a pet or child from a burning building, provided you know exactly where they are located so you don't waste precious time looking for them. A wet towel held over the mouth and nose, drenched clothing, or a prepackaged gel-soaked blanket or hood can also provide partial short-term protection from extreme heat.

Escape Ladders

Consider purchasing a dedicated coiled escape ladder for second-story and higher bedrooms that do not have window access to a roof that is close enough to the ground to hang and jump. The escape ladder should be mounted in a permanent box directly underneath an openable window (ensure that the window operates properly and has not been painted shut), and not buried in the bottom of some closet.

Home Fire-Safe Checklist/Defensible Space

- Clear dead brush from property and trim tall weeds short.
- Clean rain gutters and roof valleys of all dead leaves and pine needles.
- Place smoke detectors in all bedrooms, hallways, kitchens and at least one on every floor of your home.
- Put fire extinguishers in kitchen, garage, and workshop areas.
- Inspect and chimney sweep chimneys and woodstove pipes annually to prevent creosote buildup. Creosote is a black greasy gooey layer that is combustible, and is a common byproduct of incomplete wood combustion. Chimney fires destroy many homes each year.
- Store flammables (gasoline, kerosene, oily rags, paint thinner, etc.) in approved flame-resistant containers and away from living areas. Garage areas should have one-hour fire-wall code-approved construction (typically ⅝-inch sheetrock wall covering, or better).
- Clear ground of pine needles, dead leaves, etc. Rake them once in the spring and let them fall in the fall. Remove dead vegetation and debris.
- Thin out thick stands of shrubs and trees to create a separation.
- Remove "ladder fuels" like lower tree branches and shrubs underneath trees to keep wildfire from climbing and spreading. Prune all dead limbs from trees.
- Plant "green zones" of moist, fire-resistant plants that will act as a barrier, and not fuel for fires.
- Swimming pools, ornamental ponds, etc., provide extra water reserves for fighting fires, and may be tapped by either fire trucks' onboard pumping systems or lighter-duty homeowner firefighting pump systems (see fig. 11-2).

Figure 11-2. Portable firefighting high-volume self-contained water pump for rural homes. Source: High Desert Fire Equipment, Sparks, NV

- Consider installing fireproof window shutters that will help prevent the heat of an approaching firestorm from shattering your windows or transmitting enough radiant heat to ignite items inside the home.

- Your house number should be clearly visible from the street for identification by emergency vehicles.

- In remote rural areas, it may be a smart idea to purchase a high-volume gasoline-powered home fire-fighting pump (see fig. 11-2). Gel systems have the capability to get the most out of limited water supplies, and the sticky gel is a fire resistant gooey coating that provides much longer lasting protection than a simple water spray, when applied to walls, decking, and roofing.

Extreme Fire Alert, or Approaching Fire

Here is what to do if your home and loved ones are in the path of a fire:

- Stay tuned to local radio stations, but keep your eyes and ears open, not counting on authorities for proper warning. *Stay safe! It is best to err on the side of caution!*

- Keep pets and children close at hand and ready for rapid evacuation.

- Place 72-hour emergency kits in car(s) along with important documents and computer backup files. Park cars facing toward the driveway exit for a speedy evacuation.

- When concerned about an approaching fire, a lawn sprinkler left running on your roof improves the chances for saving your home.

- Hose down bushes and hedges next to your home, and trim back if you feel it may be helpful or necessary.

- Close all windows and doors. Block foundation and roof vents to slow penetration of superheated firestorm gases inside the building envelope.

- Close fireplace or chimney dampers to minimize the "chimney effect" from drawing air up your chimney. Whatever volume of air draws up your chimney, will be replaced by superheated air from the outside firestorm.

- Remove drapes from windows and move furniture into center of rooms away from windows.

- Turn off natural gas lines at the meter (you may need to contact your gas company to have a qualified workman safely turn your gas back on) and propane lines at the tank. Place a lawn sprinkler on your propane tank.

- Remove gas grills and portable propane tanks far from the home, as well as combustibles such as portable gasoline cans.

When a Fire Strikes Your Home

Crawl Under the Smoke

Remember that hot air rises, so if you step into a hallway filled with choking, blinding smoke, drop to your knees to see if that will get you into a bearable level of smoke so you can speed-crawl your way to safety.

Putting Out a Clothing Fire with a Blanket, or by Rolling on the Ground

Normal types of fires need oxygen in order to burn. When hair or clothing catches on fire, quickly smother the fire with a towel, blanket, or jacket tightly wrapped around the burning area on the victim. Alternately, get the victim to roll on the ground to smother the flames, or grab and hug the victim while using your own body to smother the flames.

Bust Through Sheetrock Walls

In an emergency situation, realize that most homes are built with interior walls covered in sheetrock. If necessary to avoid a fire-and-smoke-filled hallway, or to gain access to a room to rescue a family member, realize that this sheetrock can be easily kicked through to allow a person to slip between the studs from one room to another without using a door or window.

Fire Safety and the Structure of Your Home

If current scientific predictions of global warming prove anywhere near correct, then the horrific 2007 fires outside of San Diego, and the 1993 Laguna Beach fires, are simply a preview of future wildfires that will endanger hundreds of thousands of homes in the coming years. Whether you are a homeowner wishing to improve the fire resistance of your current dwelling, or are planning to build a new home, there are a number of actions you can take to improve the chances that your home will survive a local wildfire. These guidelines are typically applied to homes located in areas where long periods of dry weather are common, such as many of the southwestern states. However, due to climate change, people in many areas where the threat of wildfires was previously a non-issue may soon find it a valid and growing concern.

Lessons from the 1993 Laguna Fire

- Many if not most homes burned from the inside out when firestorm heat radiated through closed windows and slipped inside through foundation and roof vents to ignite interior curtains, rugs, etc. Double-pane windows and heavily insulated walls will slow the rate of heat penetration into interior spaces.

- The only buildings to survive the Laguna Fire had insulated walls, double-pane windows, and blocked or minimized venting. A well-insulated, well-sealed building envelope, and high thermal mass, will slow interior heating and ignition.

- Minimize venting, and screen all vent openings to prevent flaming embers from entering vents. Removable fire-wall vent blocks should be placed in front of foundation and roof vents during periods of extreme fire danger to keep hot air from easily penetrating the building envelope.

- One of the few Laguna homes in the path of the firestorm to survive had a 40-foot-wide strip of the green succulent "ice plant" (creating an excellent "defensible space") and a concrete tiled roof (an exceptionally fire resistant roof). The firestorm blew right over the top of the ice plant and the house, dropped burning embers on the concrete tile roof, roasted a 10-foot-wide swath of ice plant, but failed to ignite the building's structure.

- Stucco, cement, or earthen walls are preferred. If wood siding is desired, it should be applied over a ⅝-inch sheetrock fire wall for improved fire resistance. Cement-based weather board can look like wood but give you cement board's superior fire resistance. Even with a stucco or cement weather-board sheath, an underlying wood-framed wall might ignite if the firestorm gets hot enough.

- All projections (roof eaves, etc.) should be protected on the underside with cement stucco or cement board (like Certainteed or Hardie Board) that looks like wood. A less-preferred alternative is to paint natural wood with fire-resistant coating to improve its resistance to ignition by burning embers. Hot air rises and can easily ignite roof overhangs in a firestorm.

- Coat wood decks with multiple layers of a fire-resistant urethane deck covering (Pacific Polymers or similar) or treat wood decking with fire-resistant coatings (Fire Stop or similar). *Note:* Chemical treatments, such as Fire Stop, will inhibit ignition by burning embers, but will not prevent ignition due to a superhot firestorm. A stucco coat (¾ inch or thicker) on the underside of wooden decks was credited with saving two homes in the Laguna Beach fire. There is a new fly-ash composite decking board from LifeTime Lumber that has a "Class A" fireproof rating, and is LEED certified for its recycled content, that can be used to build high-quality fireproof decks. Trex and many of the other similar competing composite decking manufacturers have come out with "Class B" fire-resistant wood/plastic composite decking to meet California's new wildland fire codes.

- Use only "Class A" fire-rated roofing systems, which are rated to prevent both the roofing material itself, and roofing underlayment (plywood) from catching fire when covered with burning embers. Most asphalt and fiberglass shingles are Class A rated, but metal roofing usually requires the use

My buddy Jim Bolton, an experienced Reno fireman, tells me that when they enter a neighborhood, they take mental notes about which homes have maintained a defensible space and which have not. They don't waste their time focusing on homes without a defensible space, but spend their time defending homes where they stand a decent chance of success, while keeping a watchful eye on nearby flames. These are brave guys, risking their necks where most of us would not go, but they have wives and kids, so when a vicious fire storm gets dangerously close, they simply have to leave the neighborhood and let nature take its course.

of Versashield underlayment (or equal) to achieve this rating. "Living" roofs (planted sod) have excellent fire resistance as well as thermal mass and insulation. With Class A roofing, the eaves and overhangs are the most vulnerable areas of the roof owing to the fire down below.

(Adapted and expanded from John Underwood, "Fire Resistant Details: Studying the Houses That Survived the 1993 Laguna Beach Fire Storm Yields Lessons in Building to Withstand the Heat," Fine Home Building.com)

There are a number of building systems that are inherently fire resistant. Basically, if it is earth or concrete based, it is very fire resistant. Also, if you fill the wall with foam or straw, to eliminate dead air spaces and the chimney effect, and sheath the wall with stucco, earthen plasters, or cement board, even if it is wood-framed it will have good fire resistance. Do your best to make your roof, eaves, and decks fire resistant too, since your home will only be as fire resistant as its weakest link. Obviously, traditional stone, brick, and concrete-block construction are also quite fire resistant, provided their roofs are not a weak link in the system.

With burning embers settling on rooftops, in many cases it is the roof that forms the weak link in the fire-resistance chain. Traditional wooden shake and shingle are notorious for catching on fire from burning embers. For fire-resistant roofing, consider the following options:

- Use only "Class A" fire-rated roofing.
- Class A roofing must withstand burning embers on roof without igniting plywood sheeting.
- Most modern composition (asphalt) shingles are "Class A" fire-rated.
- Metal roofs transmit heat easily to the underlying plywood, so they tend to be not as fire resistant as you might imagine, unless they are underlaid with an insulating flame-resistant lining. They are usually only Class A fire resistant with the addition of Versashield underlayment (or similar).
- I recommend two layers of Versashield FR underlayment (or similar) FR barrier for extra fire barrier between metal roofing and its underlying plywood sheeting.

When to Make a Stand, and When to Pack and Go

Remember the story of Andrew and Mary Hall at the beginning of chapter 2? They had the wisdom to pack-and-go when their home was threatened by a nearby bush fire during supercritical fire conditions in Australia, but chose to make a stand at the home of friends who had a much more defensible space, and who were also well equipped with a large reservoir of water and extensive personal firefighting equipment. On what has become known as "Black Saturday," others in their town were not so lucky in the bush fires that took the lives of 173 people, wiping out whole towns, with entire families found incinerated in their cars while trying to escape the inferno.

It bears repeating that *when it comes to wildfires, it is better to err on the side of caution than to risk all in a moment of valor!*

12

Earthquake!

❝On November 18, 1755, the earth beneath the waters off Cape Ann heaved. Within seconds, the seismic wave generated there traveled to the twisting lanes and wharves of pre-Revolutionary Boston. According to historical accounts, chimneys toppled from roofs, steeples parted from churches, and gables crumbled from building fronts and shattered on the lanes below. The weather vane atop Faneuil Hall snapped. Vibrations were felt from Halifax, Nova Scotia, to Chesapeake Bay. Estimated at a magnitude of 6.2, the Cape Ann earthquake is one of New England's strongest in recorded history.

But it's not the aberration you might think. In an average year, 30 to 40 earthquakes strike New England. . . . In 1929, a magnitude 7.2 quake centered off the southern coast of Newfoundland generated a tsunami that killed at least two dozen people; the quake was felt as far away as New York City.

A study by Boston College seismologist John Ebel, published earlier this year, zeroes in on the epicenter of the 1755 Cape Ann earthquake. Ebel, who has spent the last 25 years studying local quakes, also proposes a new idea: that all New England earthquakes—including the 1755 one and a 1638 magnitude 7 quake probably centered in New Hampshire—might be the aftershocks of an even larger historical quake. He says another large one may be looming. Our earthquake threat is made more pressing by what distinguishes Boston among other American cities: its elegant brick-and-mortar architecture, which in many cases sits on lose, unstable soil. . . . Yet earthquakes do happen here. Why then isn't Boston ready for the next one?❞ —Jeremy Miller, "Boston's Earthquake Problem," *The Boston Globe*, May 28, 2006

Given the series of devastating earthquakes over the past few years, ranging from the mega quakes in Japan, Chile, and the Indian Ocean tsunami, to the smaller but still deadly quakes in Kobe and Haiti, people are concerned that we are entering a period of heightened global seismic activity, and that means they should be prepared for potential earthquakes even if they live in an area that has been relatively free of quakes in recent history.

Most Americans think earthquakes are only a problem in California and possibly Alaska, but that isn't necessarily the case. Realize that earthquake predictions are based on statistical averages. Living in an area that is not known for earthquakes does not mean you won't ever experience a major earthquake. What it does mean is that you have a smaller chance of experiencing one. It is a little-known fact that the largest earthquakes on record in the United States did not happen in California but along the Mississippi

River in New Madrid, Missouri, in late 1811 and early 1812. The quakes were so powerful that they shook down chimneys 360 miles away in Cincinnati and changed the course of the Mississippi River for more than 100 miles.

Earthquake prediction is based on the study of past earthquake patterns. It generates statistics about the probability of an earthquake within a certain magnitude range occurring in a specified region over a specified period of time. A typical prediction for the San Francisco Bay Area might read something like, "The San Francisco Bay Area is overdue for a significant earthquake. We believe that this area has a 70 percent chance of having an earthquake in the 7.5 to 9.5 range sometime in the next thirty years." Except in rare instances when undeniable geological signs indicate that a major quake is imminent, modern scientific methods cannot give accurate earthquake warnings. And we think weather forecasters have a hard time being accurate!

This chapter discusses earthquake preparations, specific techniques and strategies to improve your chances of surviving a serious earthquake, how to improve the earthquake resistance of your home, and what to do in the aftermath of an earthquake.

What to Expect When an Earthquake Strikes

In the aftermath of a major earthquake, the public utilities usually fail, and fires tend to break out due to broken gas mains and lack of water. Most government workers are either injured themselves, or at home caring for family members. If the earthquake is a significant one, with widespread damage and casualties, in all likelihood you will be on your own for several days or more. In this case, medical attention for the wounded and rescue efforts for those trapped under debris will be the first priority, with water second, followed by shelter and food.

The magnitude of an earthquake is usually measured on the Richter scale, or the newer "moment magnitude scale," which are both roughly equivalent logarithmic scales—meaning that each point of magnitude is a factor ten times as strong as the point below. For example, a magnitude 7.0 earthquake is ten times as strong as one of magnitude 6.0, 100 times as strong as one of magnitude 5.0, and 1,000 times as strong as one of magnitude 4.0. However, the magnitude of the quake tells only part of the story. The extent of the damage will depend on a number of factors in addition to the quake's magnitude, including the geophysics of the local soil and rock, the age and quality of the local buildings and bridges, and the local seismic building codes (or lack thereof).

The epicenter of the 1989 Loma Prieta quake was about 10 miles outside of Santa Cruz, California, and 60 miles from San Francisco. The worst damage was focused in the downtown area of Santa Cruz, which was built on gravelly wet soils next to the San Lorenzo river, 60 miles away in the Marina District in San Francisco, which is built on loose, poorly compacted fill from the 1906 San Francisco quake, and in Oakland where the Cypress Freeway was also built on gravelly soils. At each of these locations, the magnifying effect of gravelly soils combined with liquefaction and older construction methods/ materials to result in catastrophic structural failures and fatalities.

Construction codes, age and type of materials of construction, and soil conditions each have a lot to do with how well a community will fare during an earthquake. Generally speaking, a 5.0 quake will shake things up a bit, throwing items of shelves and possibly breaking fragile appliances like televisions and computers, but will not cause a lot of structural damage unless it strikes old masonry buildings or a third-world location with poor building practices. When a 5.3 magnitude quake shook us out of bed in 1998, it didn't cause any appreciable damage, but if a quake of that same magnitude had struck downtown Boston, between liquefaction and the old brownstone buildings that Boston is known for, it would probably have caused extensive damage and killed a lot of people.

Earthquakes in the magnitude range close to 7.0, such as the 6.7 Northridge quake, the 7.0 Port-au-Prince, Haiti, quake, and the 6.8 Kobe, Japan, quake, will be quite frightening and will cause significant destruction ranging from the flattening of Port-au-Prince, that killed an estimated 316,000 and left a million people homeless, to the Northridge quake in Southern California that resulted in 33 deaths, injured an estimated 8,700 people, and caused $20 billion in damages. It is hard to imagine what it would feel like to experience a mega-quake, like the magnitude 9.5 1960 great Chilean earthquake, which was 316 times as strong as the Haiti quake, or the 2004 Indian Ocean tsunami earthquake, which had a magnitude of 9.1 to 9.3!

How to Improve the Earthquake Resistance of Your Home

- Tie down your water heater with steel strapping bolted securely to wall studs. Seismic water heater straps are available at most hardware or building supply stores. Water heaters are quite heavy and will often topple over during an earthquake, breaking gas and water lines and causing much damage to your home.

- Do not hang any heavy paintings, or other heavy items, on the wall above your bed.

- If your building is of older construction, inspect the foundation to see if the building frame is bolted into the foundation. If not, a qualified trades-man should perform a seismic retrofit to bolt your home-framing sill plates onto the foundation. If your home was built before the 1950s, and you are concerned about its seismic safety, you will probably need to hire a civil engineer and licensed contractor to make the seismic upgrades.

- If your building is of older, non-reinforced masonry construction, it will have extremely poor seismic resistance and should be structurally retrofitted and upgraded. In order to properly complete this work, it will require enlist-ing the help of a qualified structural engineer and contractor.

- Attach heavy bookcases and other tall furniture to wall studs with metal strapping, or specially designed seismic straps. Use Velcro or plastic straps to secure computers in place. Earthquake putty or clay can be used to help secure pots and other ornamental items to shelves.

- Use child locks on your kitchen cabinets to prevent your dishes from flying out of the cabinets during an earthquake.

Earthquake Prep Checklist

- Store a sturdy pair of shoes and leather work gloves under each bed. Broken glass often covers the floor during quakes.

- If you live in a climate subject to freezing temperatures, store extra anti-freeze (preferably the nontoxic RV type) for winterizing your toilet bowls and sink traps.

- Keep a backup propane, kerosene, or wood heater (and fuel) for emergency space heating, and a portable camping stove for cooking food and boiling water.

- Store a roll of plastic sheeting, 50 feet minimum (available at hardware or contractor's supply stores).

- Keep well-stocked, 72-hour emergency kits in the car (or other outside loca-tion), including spare clothing. See chapter 2 for details.

- Keep spare car keys stored on your car (or other outside location). If your clothes, wallet, and keys disappear in a collapsed house on a cold winter's day, you will be grateful for a spare key!

- Keep a permanent shutoff wrench attached to your gas shutoff (available at surplus, hardware, and survival stores).

- If you are an urban dweller and have no car, or store your car under a large building, you might consider arranging with friends or relatives to store some supplies in their garage, garden shed, and so on.

- Store off-site backup copies of computer files, family photos, and important papers (marriage license, social security card, bank accounts, stock certifi-cates, immunization records, etc).

The "Three-Second Rule"

In a medium-sized quake (5 to 6 magnitude), you could probably dash outside, but in a large quake of roughly 7.0 or greater, you can figure on approximately three seconds before objects will come flying (including daggers of broken glass), buildings might start collapsing, or in the least you will be knocked off your feet and thrown around. It is during this time that the current expert advice is to "drop, cover, and hold on." "Drop" gets you off your feet where you are less likely to be knocked over and injured. "Cover" means getting under the cover of a table, desk, etc., where you have some semblance of cover and protection from flying objects (glass, dishes, boards, etc.) and falling debris, or if you can't get to a protective cover of some sorts, cover your head and neck area with your hands and forearms. "Cover" can also mean hugging an interior wall that will provide structural support that may help support the ceiling and protect your position. "Hold on" means literally just that. Grab on to a wall or solidly anchored object. In a severe earthquake you risk injury from being thrown about, and if you are able to hang on to a relatively stable object this will reduce your risk of injury.

The "Triangle of Life" versus "Drop, Cover, and Hold On"

An e-mail article by Doug Copp under the title of the "Triangle of Life" has been widely circulated on the Internet. Some of the recommendations in this article have been repeated by the media as fact, but have been broadly questioned and refuted by other disaster experts. The gist of the article is that rather than ducking *under* the cover of an item like a table, the safest place is to drop and roll to a location *beside* a heavy structural item such as a couch, refrigerator, piano, bed, etc. The philosophy is that when a building "pancakes" (collapses), as is much more common in third-world locations than in Europe and North America, a heavy item that has significant structural strength will be more likely to hold up against collapsing building structures, and that the resulting triangular space alongside the bulky strong item will provide a relatively safe haven where a person might survive; whereas if you crawled underneath a table or desk, it would tend to collapse and squash you like a pancake.

Studies of injuries and deaths caused by earthquakes over the last several decades, as noted above, show that you are much more likely to be injured by falling or flying objects (TVs, lamps, glass, bookcases, etc.) than to die in a collapsed building. "Drop, cover, and hold on" (as described above) will better protect you from these injuries. In traditional buildings, the space under a sturdy table or desk is likely to remain even if the building collapses. Pictures from around the world show tables and desks standing with rubble all around them, and even holding up floors that have collapsed. Experienced rescuers agree that successfully predicting other safe locations in advance is nearly impossible, as where these voids will end up depends on the direction of the shaking along with many other factors.

The exception to the "drop, cover, and hold on" rule is if you are in a country/building lacking engineered construction, and if you are on the ground floor of a non-reinforced earth-based or mud-brick (adobe) building with a heavy ceiling. In that case, you should try to move quickly outside to an open space, and if that is not possible as a last resort attempt to find a "triangle of life."

There are no hard-and-fast rules that work all the time in all situations. The hope is that being aware of these concepts will be of some assistance when making split-second decisions in a time of crisis.

Immediate Actions to Take and Coping Strategies

Caution: If you smell gas, or the quake was severe, immediately turn off the outside electrical and gas utility supply to your house (gas utility personnel may need to turn it back on).

- Drop, cover, and hold on as described above.

- *If a gas leak is suspected, do not light an open flame or turn on an electric switch.* All common electric switches arc when turned on or off, and may ignite explosive gases. If you suspect a gas leak and need to turn on a flashlight, turn it on or off outside, in the open air. Glow sticks are a safe light source that will not ignite flammable gases.

- Check for injuries and damage.

- Your car, when parked outside, can provide safe, secure shelter during periods of aftershocks when you may feel insecure sleeping in an indoor location.

- After a major earthquake, public water systems are usually incapacitated or contaminated. See water-purification suggestions in chapter 8 and the 72-hour grab-and-go survival kit section in chapter 2.

- Disease can be a huge problem after a major earthquake. People tend to be stressed out, underfed, underclothed, dehydrated, injured, and often wet or cold. Sanitary conditions are generally poor at best. See chapter 6 for suggestions on staying healthy in a crisis or pandemic.

13

Hurricanes and Floods

When a hurricane is approaching, and/or floodwaters are rising, it is the wrong time to wish you had planned ahead. I strongly suggest that you use this chapter, along with the first 8 chapters (the "core" of this book) to help you plan ahead to cope with hurricanes and floods. When deciding whether to pack and go (evacuate), or to stay and make a stand, if your life is at stake, or the lives of your loved ones, it is wiser to err on the side of caution. The vast majority of nearly 2,000 deaths attributed to Hurricane Katrina could have been avoided had those people evacuated ahead of time. Remember, whenever there is a hurricane warning, there will be a run on items like matches, flashlights, candles, plywood, milk, bread, first-aid kits, and generators. The procrastinators get the dregs of what is left on the shelves after they have been picked over, which in some cases is nothing of any use in an emergency!

This chapter covers hurricane and flood survival tips, how to improve the resistance of your home to hurricanes, checklists of items to have on hand and action items to take care of beforehand, and tips for dealing with the aftermath, including toxic mold (in the case of flooding).

Hurricane and Flood Survival Tips

Here is a list of essential items and tips for surviving a flood or a hurricane:

1. **Axe and life preservers.** Stash an axe and life preservers in the upper story, or attic, of your home. Remember, most of the drowning victims of Hurricane Katrina were people who stayed in their homes and found themselves trapped by rising waters with no place to go. Many drowned in their attics, unable to break through the roof to the outside. A few bucks spent on these items ahead of time could save your life! Having a small boat on hand, such as an inflatable raft or canoe, is a good idea, but it shouldn't take the place of a life preserver, which will keep you afloat, and your head above water, even if knocked unconscious.

2. **Water is critical.** Water is absolutely essential for human survival; it plays a part in all of the body's biochemical reactions. You may not believe it, but most of us could survive for several weeks without food, yet a single day without water in extreme heat can kill a person. Water requirements vary depending on activity level and temperature. The absolute minimum for survival, with little or no activity and cool conditions, is about 1 quart of drinking water per day, and 2 quarts of water per day will usually

Several years ago, my friends David and Nancy flew to the island of Kauai for their vacation. On the first day of their vacation, they went for a walk on the beach. As they gazed out to sea, they watched a dark and sinister looking cloud build and boil on the horizon. When the waterline receded about 20 feet out to sea, they knew that something serious was about to hit. They rushed back to their rented cottage, a mile down the beach and a few houses back from the shore. By the time they reached their cottage, the winds had increased to over 80 miles per hour as Hurricane Iniki approached the Island. Since David was an employee of the public utility district in a mountain community, he knew the importance of preserving a supply of potable water. Immediately, he filled all the sinks and bathtubs in the house with water and instructed the other occupants not to flush toilets or wash with the stored water.

As the day progressed, winds increased to an almost unbelievable 175 miles per hour. The terrified occupants crouched in corners, away from windows, and watched fearfully as large chunks of the neighboring houses blew by. Their house was constantly pelted with flying debris and the roar of the wind was deafening. Hours later, when the storm cleared, there was an eerie silence. Downed trees cluttered the roads, making automotive travel impossible. The stores quickly ran out of food and water. The water that David had stored in the bathtubs and sinks provided drinking water for several households. It took more than three weeks to restore electricity and water to most of the island.

sustain moderate activity at an acceptable level of comfort under moderate conditions (you will feel somewhat dehydrated). More than 1 quart of water every hour can be required to perform heavy physical labor under extremely hot conditions. Typically allow for at least 1 gallon per person per day, and in desert climates, or hot humid climates, a realistic figure is to allow for 3 gallons per day per person.

3. **Fill your bathtub and tape off your toilets.** After a major hurricane or flood hits, the public water system may be polluted, or entirely shut down, for weeks. Immediately fill your bathtubs, sinks, and other available containers with water. This will provide your household with a short-term supply of clean, potable water. There is a supply of clean, potable water in the toilet tanks, hot-water heater, and piping in your house. When you notice that the tap water has stopped flowing, conserve the water in your toilet tanks (the tanks, not the bowl, contain potable water) and immediately notify all other occupants to not flush the toilets. *Caution:* Do not drink the toilet tank water if you use an automatic toilet cleaner with blue toilet water.

4. **Drain your water heater and pipes.** Water heaters are supplied with a vent located near the top of the tank and a drain near the bottom of the tank. Open the top vent (pull on the little lever on the spigot) and drain the tank into containers as needed. If there is dirt and sediment in the water coming out of the tank, *do not discard this water.* Simply allow the sediment to settle and drink the water off the top. *Make sure you turn off the electricity or gas to your water heater before draining or it will be ruined!* Crack an upper faucet and open a lower hose bib or faucet to drain a gallon or two of water out of your home's piping.

5. **Water filters and treatment chemicals.** I know from experience that after having gone without water for more than a day in extreme heat, most anyone would willingly drink from the scummiest, most disgusting source of water, if that was the only available option! If you must evacuate your home, carrying a personal water supply on your back would be extremely difficult (at a gallon per person per day, a family of four would go through 100 pounds of water in three days). Floodwaters are usually extremely contaminated with farm waste, human sewage, and industrial chemicals, so I highly recommend you purchase a bacteriological backcountry-type water filter that has a carbon core to also remove toxic chemicals, bad tastes, and odors. You can chemically treat surface water with household tincture of iodine (5 drops per quart) and pure chlorine bleach (4 drops per quart) and by allowing water to stand for thirty minutes. See chapter 8 for full water-treatment details and my personal water-filter recommendations (I design these things for a living, so I know what I am talking about). Boiling for just one minute will kill all waterborne organisms, but will do nothing to remove toxic chemicals, bad tastes, and odors.

6. **72-hour grab-and-go survival kit.** Every family should have at least one grab-and-go kit that can be thrown in the car on a moment's notice, or carried on your back, if the need should arise. Grab-and-go kits should provide the basic emergency food, water, shelter, and first-aid supplies that you, and your family, will need to survive the critical first three days after a disaster. See chapter 2 for a full list of all the supplies I recommend to include in a well stocked grab-and-go kit.

7. **Store your grab-and-go kits in "dry packs."** If you live in hurricane country, or an area prone to flooding, I strongly recommend you purchase a "dry pack" for each of your grab-and-go kits. Dry packs are a special combination backpack and waterproof bag used by river guides. They have removable padded shoulder straps, are made of extremely tough waterproof material, and are 100 percent sealed against water intrusion, so in addition to keeping your stuff dry in a deluge, they can also double as floatation devices to help keep you afloat in floodwaters. A dry pack stocked and ready to go for every member of your family is cheap insurance if you live in an area prone to hurricanes and/or floods!

Figure 13-1. A "dry pack" provides waterproof storage. Photo courtesy of Eastern Mountain Sports (EMS)

8. **Colloidal silver generator.** After a hurricane or flood, homemade colloidal silver will purify drinking water and will help fight infection and viruses when high-tech pharmaceuticals may be unavailable or ineffective. All hospitals use silver-based ointments to fight infection in severe burn victims, where traditional antibiotics are simply not enough to fight the infection over large areas of burned skin. See chapter 6 for more details.

9. **Disaster plan.** Formulate a disaster plan, including out-of-town contacts (relatives, family, friends, etc.) and a central meeting place where your family should gather if separated and local communications are cut. When a widespread disaster strikes, you will usually be able to reach friends or family outside of the disaster area long before local communications can be reestablished. See chapter 2 for full details on preparing your family disaster plan. If you live near a coastal area, make an evacuation plan with a known destination at least 50 miles inland.

10. **Waterproof LED headlamp.** I highly recommend that you purchase a waterproof backcountry type headlamp with LED bulbs. Headlamps leave your hands free to carry things, or work on things. LED bulbs use a fraction of the power, are far more shock resistant, and last far longer than traditional lightbulbs, so your batteries (don't forget to stock spares) last many times longer. If you had to, you could even swim across a raging river in total darkness with your dry bag, a life preserver, and a headlamp.

How to Improve the Hurricane Resistance of Your Home

Here is a list of things you can do to improve the chances that your home will survive a hurricane in decent shape. These items are best attended to well ahead of time, since the materials to accomplish many of these tasks are usually in short supply shortly after a hurricane warning is issued, and these tasks require careful attention and focus to be properly executed.

- Protect your windows, if possible. The best protection is offered by roll-down hurricane shutters that are quite popular in the Caribbean, but any storm shutters are better than nothing.

- Plywood works too, use ½ inch or thicker exterior grade plywood, such as "CDX." Mark each plywood storm window covering with an understandable code so you can use them again the next time a hurricane approaches. A coating of paint will ensure that your plywood shutters survive their time in storage to protect you another day. For a speedy installation, use a cordless drill to drive deck screws. To ensure that high winds don't suck the plywood right off the screw heads, place wide washers (fender type) under the heads of each deck screw.

- Ensure that your roof is in good shape, with no loose or missing tiles or shingles. Install special hurricane clips on the edges of metal roofing to reduce the likelihood of your roof peeling off in high winds. I suggest you enlist a qualified roofing contractor for hurricane-readiness roofing inspections and upgrades.

- Caulk all seams on your home's exterior sheeting, and around windows. Winds over 100 mph can drive a lot of water through a tiny crack!

- If your home is more than a few years old, check for proper structural hurricane clips and ties between the roof rafters and the wall framing. You will probably need a licensed contractor or home inspector for this job, and a contractor to do the upgrades. For buildings subject to moist salty air, especially ocean-front homes, inspect your existing hurricane clips and Simpson Strong Ties for corrosion, and replace or upgrade as necessary. Old hurricane clips that are mostly rusted through will do little to hold down the roof of your home in ferocious hurricane winds!

- Inspect the home's foundation for resistance to erosion from floodwaters, and take erosion control measures if you suspect that the foundation might be endangered by floodwaters. Remember, if your foundation fails, your whole house goes down!

- Keep trees and palm fronds well trimmed, and your property free of clutter and loose debris. Remember, a branch, board, or other loose debris can become a lethal weapon when driven by 100-plus mph winds!

- Review your insurance papers and read the fine print. Floods are not covered by most homeowner's policies unless you have a specific clause or policy for flood insurance. Many Hurricane Katrina victims found out the hard way that their insurance policies were inadequate!

When a Hurricane Is Closing In . . .

When it looks like a hurricane is headed for your area, here is a checklist of items that should be attended to:

- ❏ Make sure your car is filled with gasoline and your grab-and-go kits are packed.
- ❏ Make sure that rain gutters are clean and windows covered.
- ❏ Fill all available tubs, basins, and containers with potable drinking water.
- ❏ Turn refrigerators and freezers to lowest settings in anticipation of power failure. If power fails, eat refrigerated and frozen foods first before moving on to canned and dry foods.
- ❏ Stay tuned to radio and TV. Also a NOAA weather radio if you have one.
- ❏ Unless planning to weather the storm in your home, evacuate early before roads are jammed. Stay flexible, not rigid! Storms do not always behave according to what the weatherman predicts, so you may need to change plans on a moment's notice.
- ❏ Store lawn furniture and loose yard items in a secure location, before they

become lethal projectiles! Some people throw lawn furniture into their swimming pools to be retrieved after the storm passes.

❏ Let friends and family know your evacuation plans and out-of-town contacts.

❏ If you have a swimming pool, chlorine-shock your pool to protect against contamination from debris and flood waters.

❏ For insurance purposes, take "before" pictures of your home and key possessions.

The Aftermath

After a severe hurricane or flood has struck your area, chances are good that the utilities will be down for quite a while, perhaps for several weeks. Here are some other things you might expect and look out for, as well as action items to perform in the aftermath of a hurricane:

• Until the authorities tell you the tap water is safe, expect that it will have been contaminated from floodwaters, so all tap water should be filtered, chemically treated, or boiled before drinking.

• Snakes and other wild animals will seek shelter from the storm on higher ground and may be prevalent or agitated, so be aware! Normally docile animals may behave in unexpected ways.

• Watch for downed power lines. A chain saw is a useful tool to bring along when attempting to drive a car after a major storm with high winds.

• Check on your neighbors.

• Check for gas leaks and damaged electrical lines. If you smell gas, or suspect a leak, turn the gas off at your meter or fuel tank and call your gas company. *Caution:* Do not light a match, turn on a light switch, or even a flashlight in the presence of gas, or an explosion may occur!

• Take "after" pictures of damage for insurance purposes.

• Open windows and doors for drying out your home to reduce the likelihood of mold damage.

• You can "wash" furniture and textiles in the sun to kill mold spores using the sun's ultraviolet rays. *Caution:* This technique will not save severely mold-damaged items.

Toxic Mold: Flooding's Evil Twin

Mold and flooding go hand in hand. Even though it has been more than five years since Hurricane Katrina struck, there are rows upon rows of abandoned New Orleans homes that are filled with toxic black mold, rendering them unfit for human habitation. In the aftermath of any flood, the presence of significant visible mold inside a home makes it clear that drastic measures are mandated, such as the use of a professional mold-remediation team with respirators and Tyvek protective clothing (including Tyvek booties and hoods). In other cases, mold can be a hidden demon, thriving inside walls and crawl spaces, devastating occupants' lives without leaving obvious clues as to the cause of their misfortune. This book is not about mold remediation. However, since floods and toxic mold problems tend to go together, I will provide you with some basic information to help you understand when your problem is serious enough that you should seek professional medical help, or the help of a qualified mold-remediation service.

One of the problems with toxic mold is that it could be harming your health even though you may not see or smell any mold, and that its effects can creep up on you quite insidiously, just a little bit at a time, until one day you come to the realization that you feel sick all the time and can no longer lead a normal life. The symptoms of toxic mold poisoning are quite varied, and most medical doctors will not recognize these symptoms as being caused by toxic molds.

Not all molds are equal! Some molds have relatively low toxicity, meaning that you may see and smell obvious signs of a mold infestation, yet if it is a low-toxicity mold, it might not cause any noticeable negative health effects. Whereas a super-toxic mold, like the deadly *Stachybotrys* black mold, could be hidden inside your home's walls, or behind the floor boards, not smell at all "moldy," yet be the cause of a catastrophic loss of health. In my experience, a "musty" smell means mold, and a "moldy" smell means lots of mold. Whether or not your problem is serious depends upon many variables, such as the type of mold, mold mycotoxin concentrations in household air, personal sensitivity and/or allergies to molds and mold mycotoxins, rate of home ventilation air changes, moisture issues in the home, and so on.

Health Effects of Mold and Other Fungi

“Mayo Clinic researchers say they have found the cause of most chronic sinus infections—an immune system response to fungus. They say this discovery opens the door to the first effective treatment for this problem, the most common chronic disease in the United States.” —*Science Daily*, "Mayo Clinic Study Implicates Fungus as Cause of Chronic Sinusitis," Sept. 10, 1999

Many molds, not just black mold, give off a highly toxic substance that can severely affect your health, particularly in the case of children, seniors, and anyone with allergies or a compromised immune system. In severe cases, black molds have been known to kill healthy soldiers and horses that were sleeping on straw bedding infected with *Stachybotrys*. Here is a partial list of symptoms:

- The most common effects are respiratory ailments, including shortness of breath, wheezing, chronic sinusitis, and exacerbated asthma. Side effects of sinus issues include acid reflux and postnasal drip.

- Signs of mold-toxin overload often include poor low-contrast visual distinction (which makes night driving difficult), panic attacks, feelings of claustrophobia, headaches, tremors, seizures, confusion, and the inability to concentrate.

- Migraines and shimmering vision are common effects that my wife and I have each experienced when we spent too much time in a mold-contaminated room.

- Burning or itchy eyes, dizziness, and/or nausea.

- Rashes and/or spontaneous bruises on the skin. Itching, welts, or hives.

- Behavior changes, such as restlessness, hypersensitivity, and irritableness.

- Low-grade fever (can feel like a flu that seems to never go away).

- Compromised immune system (a normally healthy person suddenly starts "catching everything").

- Chronic fatigue and/or hair loss.

- Fungi and molds can cause related lung diseases and cancers.

- In severe cases, toxic mold poisoning can lead to lung and brain hemorrhaging, permanent brain damage, and death.

  (Adapted from Michael Pugliese, *The Home Owner's Guide to Mold*, and Gary Rosen and James Schaller, *Your Guide to Mold Toxins*)

Caution: When it comes to toxic-mold contamination, your health, home, and all of your possessions are at stake. Delays could cost you everything you own and even your life.

Dealing with Mold

Any kind of flooding should be dealt with immediately, because mold will start to grow on wet or moist surfaces in twenty-four to forty-eight hours, especially in warm climates. Since mold loves to eat/grow on the paper that covers regular sheetrock, unless it has been specifically treated with chemicals designed to prevent mold growth, water-damaged sheetrock must be removed and replaced. A small amount of mold growing on the front side of sheetrock in a bathroom or laundry area, or by a water heater or sink, could be a sign of a much more serious problem hidden behind the sheetrock. If you have any concerns, I suggest that you pull off a small section of sheetrock so you can use a mirror to look inside the wall at the sheetrock's back side.

If your carpets and furniture are wet from flooding, if you find signs of mold, or feel sick and suspect that mold may be the cause, I suggest that you immediately pick up one or two books on this subject and start educating yourself further on this important topic. Time is of the essence. If your situation looks at all serious, you should immediately call a certified mold specialist. When I was living in Hawaii, if I knew then what I know now about mold, I could have saved me and my family more than $100,000 in losses, long-term health issues, much heartache, and suffering. When dealing with all but very small amounts of toxic black molds, such as *Stachybotrys*, you should wear a respirator and protective clothing. When in doubt, it is best to err on the side of caution and bring in a certified mold-remediation professional.

Mold Tips

In my experience, a person who has been severely sickened by toxic-mold exposure tends to develop a sensitivity to molds and must be much more careful about their environment than the average person. We have found a number of things that seem to improve the environment for the mold-sensitive person over the short term, but we have not found any "quick fix" type of mold-remediation actions that works to permanently eliminate mold. Here are several tips that we learned from personal experience and from the late Vincent Marinkovich, MD, a renowned mold specialist:

- You should eliminate (if possible) and/or encapsulate all active mold inside your home, including inside wall cavities and basements. Encapsulation should be with materials specifically designed to encapsulate mold long term, as mold will often grow through a coat of common paint in just a few months.

- Once mold has a hold on your house, all personal items will be contaminated with mold spores and could recontaminate your home after mold remediation has been completed and you move back into your home.

- If you are suffering from mold-related health issues, move out of the home, if at all possible, and leave the mold remediation to someone else. All of your personal possessions and furniture from the problem home will be contaminated with molds, spores, and mycotoxins. Some things can be cleaned and decontaminated, but it is sometimes safest and cheapest to simply purge everything and start over. Hard-surfaced furniture may be washed with a strong chlorine bleach solution (wear gloves and a painter's respirator). I have also found that a product called Moldzyme that is quite effective for decontaminating hard surfaces, as well as for washing textiles.

I add a capful of the concentrate to each load of laundry. I have found that some items of clothing that gave me a burning reaction did not give me a reaction after washing with a capful of Moldzyme. I buy it a quart at a time in concentrated form.

- All mold experts stress that moisture control is critical to controlling mold growth. If you don't eliminate the source of the moisture, through patching leaks, proper drainage, proper ventilation, and the use of dehumidifiers when necessary, then the mold will come back. Mold will not usually grow in an environment that has less than 47 percent relative humidity.

- If you have been in a severely compromised physical condition, it is safest to replace your personal possessions, mattresses, sofas, and so on. You can buy supertight-weave mold-and-allergen-barrier zippered pillow and mattress covers for all your pillows, mattresses, and box springs. These covers will protect new items from contamination, and protect you from older items that are moderately contaminated. Good sources for these items are: http://www.natlallergy.com/ and http://www.allergybuyersclub.com/.

- It is important to evaluate the effectiveness of mold remediation with before-and-after mold-count measurements in the major rooms in your house, including all rooms where any mold work was done. There's no point in moving back in if the house still has high mold counts.

- There are different schools of thought on killing and cleaning mold. Some say that liquid chlorine bleach (always use a respirator and eye/skin protection when cleaning with strong bleach solutions and other toxic chemicals) and fastidious cleaning, including a thorough rinsing, is the best way to kill and clean mold without leaving a toxic residue behind that could further contribute to the health problems of an already sick person. On the other hand, Michael Pugliese says he has been called in to perform several mold remediations after his predecessors had relied on bleach and the mold came back. Pugliese says that bleach is not an adequate mold decontaminant, and will not kill certain highly dangerous black molds. Instead, you should use EPA-registered treatment from companies such as BBJ Environmental Solutions and Envirocare Corp. to ensure that surfaces are treated with low-toxic solutions to prevent the regrowth of mold at a later date.

- You will never get all the mold out of upholstered furniture and wall-to-wall carpeting, and they should be junked. We got rid of all of our home's wall-to-wall carpeting, and replaced it with hardwood flooring and tile. We have a number of rubber-backed throw rugs that we wash once every other week with a capful of Moldzyme in each load of laundry.

- When you super-ozone a room or entire house, it will temporarily remove mold spores and toxins from the air, but I have never seen it fix the problem long term. If you can smell ozone, it is harmful to your lungs. If the ozone is not strong enough to harm your lungs, it will not harm the mold. Use an ozone generator, such as ones from Air-Zone, with a built-in timer to allow the ozone to shut off and dissipate for several hours before reentering the room.

- Some people find that misting their home regularly with Moldzyme and/ or Heartland Microbes (in Sanger, Texas) keeps their mold reactions down to a manageable level.

- Refrigerator cooling coils, personal computers with air-cooled cabinets, and other electronic devices with dark, air-cooled chambers will harbor mold spores inside their dusty recesses that you will never be able to entirely eliminate. If you move out of a home with a severe toxic mold problem, and bring any of these items with you to your new home, you stand a good chance of infecting your new home with the same toxic molds. However, if the new home does not have a moisture problem, and the old one did, those mold spores may not take hold in the new home.

- HEPA-type air filters, such as the ones made by Honeywell and Austin Air, placed in all rooms and running twenty-four hours a day will drastically reduce your airborne mold counts and mold reactions. Using good-quality pleated filters (not the cheap, see-through type) on a central heating and/or air-conditioning system and running the fan continuously will circulate the air in your house efficiently and clean it at the same time. *Note:* You should religiously service the pre-filters in HEPA-type air filters and your HVAC system filters on a regular basis.

- Dr. Marinkovich would often start people off on the relatively benign anti-fungal prescription of Nystatin. He custom-formulated a nose spray based on the heavy-duty prescription antifungal known as Nisoral. He sometimes prescribed Diflucan, but your liver must be monitored when taking oral doses of heavy antifungal drugs such as Nisoral and Diflucan.

- Dr. Marinkovich also recommends a strict anti-yeast diet (there are many books on the subject, such as Dr. Crooks' *The Yeast Connection*). Since molds and yeasts are related, anti-yeast diets tend to also help the body heal mold-related health issues.

- Some people have reported excellent results using MMS (see chapter 6) to help them recover from mold-related health issues.

- There may be another way to detoxify your body from mold neurotoxins. By a stroke of luck, during a Maryland Lakes disaster when fish were dying and many people were getting sick, Dr. Ritchie Shoemaker stumbled upon an effective pharmaceutical for eliminating many biotoxins from the body. When dozens of people who were sickened by the biotoxins in the local lakes filled Shoemaker's Maryland office, he gave cholestyramine (trade name Questran) to an older woman to treat her diarrhea. Not only did her diarrhea disappear, but also most of her neurotoxin symptoms simply evaporated. Since then, Dr. Shoemaker has treated thousands of patients with cholestyramine and has found it to be very good at binding and eliminating neurotoxins (Rosen and Schaller 2006, 73). My wife was suffering from debilitating daily mold-related migraines. The use of a single daily dose of cholestyramine has made a night-and-day difference, reducing her migraines from a daily occurrence to rare occasions!

[14]

Tornadoes

Darden describes a family of five who lived on a farm outside of Higdon, Alabama, a small community in the northern part of the state. They had no storm shelter, but they did live in a home that he says was well built.

On Saturday, Darden and a partner visited the family. 'The mother and three daughters were there at the time,' he recalls. Looking at the wall-free ground floor—all that remained of the home—'I introduced myself and said: "Thank God y'all were not home."' Her response? 'Oh, we were here.' With no storm shelter and nothing but a slab foundation left, 'I really thought she was joking,' he continues. 'I asked: "'Where were you at?"'

She led the two men to a spot on the storm-swept slab, where nothing but a small patch of hardwood flooring and a scrap of carpeting remained—parts of each pulled up by the tornado. The rest of the flooring vanished into the vortex and hasn't been found. The patch is all that was left of the interior hallway in which the family huddled. 'They were not touched,' he says, in a voice tinged with amazement. 'They were not sucked up. They didn't have a scratch on them.' —Pete Spotts, "Lessons from the Wreckage: How Alabama Could Help Tornado Preparedness," *Christian Science Monitor*, May 4, 2011

Who could not be shocked and saddened by the images of massive devastation left in the wake of the record-breaking string of tornadoes that struck the central, southern, and eastern parts of the United States in the spring of 2011? With winds clocked at speeds of over 300 mph (500 km/hr), combined with their unpredictable and erratic nature, tornadoes can be both awe inspiring and terrifying at the same time. Though nothing can guarantee absolute safety in the path of a tornado, outside of a shelter with reinforced concrete and steel walls, understanding something about the nature of tornadoes, safety tips for surviving a tornado strike, and which common folklore is to be trusted or ignored, will improve your chances for making the right decision when confronted by a tornado. The above-mentioned story illustrates the value of seeking shelter on the bottommost floor of a building and at the innermost area with no windows, such as a hallway, bathroom, or closet.

This chapter starts out with a list of tornado facts and common myths, so you might understand more about tornadoes, is followed by a section on tornado prediction and warnings, and ends with a list of tornado safety tips and recommended strategies. For an excellent up-to-date online source of information on tornado safety, statistics, history, forecasting, and scientific research, I highly recommend "The Online Tornado FAQ: Frequently Asked Questions about Tornadoes" by Roger Edwards at the Storm Prediction Center, which may be accessed at www.spc.noaa.gov/faq/tornado/.

Tornado Facts and Myths

- It is commonly believed that tornadoes happen mostly in the spring, but the peak of tornado season varies with location, and tornadoes can occur any month of the year. For example, the peak of tornado season in the northern plains and upper Midwest is June or July but it is from May to early June in the southern plains, and even earlier in the spring for the Gulf Coast.

- There is a myth that tornadoes can only spawn and strike in relatively flat areas, but they have actually occurred in high areas of the Rocky Mountains, Sierra Nevada, and Appalachian Mountains. Though more frequent in the flatter areas of the plains states and the southeast, tornadoes have been spotted in such varied locations as Vermont, upstate New York, Nevada, and one hiker spotted and photographed a tornado at 12,000 feet in the Sequoia National Park of California (Edwards 2011).

- A common myth is that trailer parks attract tornadoes. They certainly do not attract tornadoes, but due to their light weight and lack of heavy-duty anchoring to strong structural foundations, trailers are extremely vulnerable to damage from tornadoes.

- Another common myth is that you should open your windows to allow the pressure to equalize should a tornado strike your home. Do not waste your time opening windows. If a tornado strikes, it will blow out the windows, and the last place you should be is near a window, where there is the greatest danger from flying debris and glass.

- There is a common myth that owing to the direction of rotation of tornadoes in the Northern Hemisphere the southwest corner of a building is the safest place to be. This myth is totally false. Corners are areas of buildings that are most prone to damage. The safest areas are in the center of the building in a windowless room or closet, and on the lowest level (in the basement if there is one).

- There is a common myth that highway overpasses provide protection from tornadoes. In fact, the underside of a highway overpass often acts as a wind tunnel, channeling high winds and debris, and there are a number of reported deaths of people who parked under an overpass while seeking shelter from approaching tornadoes.

Tornado Prediction and Warnings

A *tornado watch* is issued by the National Weather Service (NWS) when they have determined that local conditions are ripe for generating tornadoes. Once a tornado watch has been issued, it is advisable to stay tuned to your local radio and television stations for further updates. If you live in tornado country, the use of a NOAA weather radio is highly recommended, especially those models that have a battery backup and can emit an audible warning whenever a severe weather alert is issued. This is the time to turn on the audible alarm switch on your NOAA radio to alert you if the watch is upgraded to a warning. Once a tornado watch has been issued, stay alert using your eyes, ears, and other senses to watch for signs of an approaching tornado, and make sure you have access to a safe shelter. Watch for unusual behavior on the part of pets and animals that might be an indication of an approaching tornado.

Once a tornado has been spotted visually, or on weather radar, a *tornado warning* is issued. Once a warning has been issued, you should take immediate precautions and seek shelter. If you live in a mobile home or other poorly protected building, you should seek shelter elsewhere, if possible. Bring your radio with you to listen for status updates and an "all-clear" signal when the warning is over.

Note: Sirens and severe weather alerts may provide advance tornado warnings, but tornadoes can occur in any season and without warning!

Tornado Survival Tips and Strategies

- If you are at home, seek shelter in the bottommost floor, and innermost area, such as an inner hallway, bathroom, or closet. Stay away from windows, outer walls, and building corners. Do not waste time opening windows.

- If you have a "safe room" (a specially constructed room protected by reinforced concrete and/or steel), a basement, root cellar, or storm cellar, those are the safest places to be. In the basement, the safest place is under a sturdy table or mattress, and in a position that is not directly below heavy items on the floor above, such as a refrigerator or piano.

- Protect yourself as best as possible. Wear a bicycle or hockey helmet, if you have one. Crouching in a bathtub or shower stall can provide improved protection, as can lying under a sturdy table or overturned couch.

- If you are in a car, do not try to outrun a tornado as it can travel at speeds in excess of 70 mph. However, it is worth taking a moment to watch the tornado closely, comparing its motion to a fixed object on the ground, so as to gauge its direction of travel. If you see it moving to one side or the other, and can travel in the opposite direction, then do so. If it does not appear to move to the left or right, it is headed straight for you. In that case, you must make a decision. If you have the option of traveling to the right or left, then do so, but if you are stuck in traffic, or the tornado is very close, you must abandon your vehicle and seek shelter, since tornadoes can easily pick up cars and even tractor trailers, sometimes throwing them hundreds of yards. If possible, pull your car to the side of the road and do not park in lanes of traffic, since with the heavy rains that often accompany tornadoes, a driver traveling at high speeds might not see your car parked in the middle of the road.

• If you are stuck in your car with an impending tornado strike, crouch down as low as you can, with your seatbelt buckled, staying away from the windows, and shielding your head with your arms and hands.

• If you are in the open, perhaps having abandoned your car, seek shelter in a building or culvert, or lie down flat in a ditch or depression and cover your head with your hands. Not a pleasant thought, but people have survived tornadoes by doing this! Stay away from cars and trees, since they will become heavy flying objects with the power to kill and maim.

• Do not park under an overpass, since these tend to act as wind tunnels funneling debris and magnifying winds.

• Avoid shopping malls, theatres, gymnasiums, and other buildings with large open interior spaces where the roof might easily collapse. If inside of such a building, with no time to seek shelter elsewhere, seek shelter under a doorjamb or next to an interior wall that may provide some structural support and protection in the event of a building collapse.

15

Winter Storms: How to Handle the Cold Without Power

The challenging winter survival situations that people are most likely to face during their lifetime, will probably fall under the first two of the following three primary categories of winter survival situations:

1. A major power failure has occurred, and you are stuck in your home without any electrical power for several days (or more) during extremely cold winter weather.

2. You are traveling in your car during a winter storm, and get stuck in the snow, or you are driving in traffic that has come to a halt during a severe winter storm and people are abandoning their cars.

3. You are without substantial shelter and must sleep outside during severe winter weather, due either to being lost (perhaps you skied out of bounds at a ski resort?) or perhaps there was a major disaster, such as an earthquake, and you had to abandon your home and do not have an available shelter to go to.

This chapter covers how to prepare your home and automobile for harsh winter conditions, what to do when the power goes out for an extended period of subfreezing weather, and how to survive in extreme cold and harsh winter weather, both indoors and outside.

Severe Winter Weather in the Home Without Power

As millions of people found out during the record-breaking ice storm of January 1998, when the power goes out, without a backup source of heat (unless you happen to live in a well-insulated solar home), the temperature inside most homes gradually cools until it approaches the temperature of the outside environment. If the power outage is caused by a winter storm, and the average outside temperature is well below freezing, within a day or two (sometimes in just a few hours) all the pipes and fresh food in your house will start to freeze.

Key Items to Have on Hand in Your Home

Whether you live in a harsh northern climate, or a more southern climate that only sees subfreezing weather on occasion, it is a good idea to keep the following items on hand:

In the winter of 2008, during an unusually warm spell of crystal-clear sunny weather, my wife, Josie, and I decided to exchange the deep snows surrounding our home in the High Sierra Mountains for a few days of beach weather. We packed up our trailer and drove to an ocean-side campground near Santa Cruz, California, where we enjoyed almost unbelievable 80-degree beach weather in the middle of January. A few days later the weather turned, and what had been a record-breaking January heat wave transformed into a record-breaking cold snap with ocean-side nighttime temperatures dipping into the 20s, causing local pipes, crops, and palm trees to freeze.

With the change in weather, Josie started feeling like she was coming down with the flu, and said "we have to go home." Knowing that it would be at least 30 degrees colder at our house, I reluctantly agreed, packed up our travel trailer, and headed back to our home in the snows of Tahoe. The moment we set foot inside our front door, we knew something was wrong. Our home was stone cold. When we left for our trip, we had set the furnace thermostat at around 60°F, but with outside temperatures well below zero, the interior of our house was so cold that all of our indoor plants were frozen solid. I immediately ran to the kitchen faucet and found it to be frozen too. Checking the bathrooms next,

when I took the lid off the toilet tanks, I found that each tank contained a surreal three-dimensional forest of 10-inch-long ice daggers suspended in slushy water. Had we returned a few hours later, all of our toilets would have been frozen solid and shattered by the expanding ice!

Immediately I built a fire in our wood-stove and crawled under the house to check our furnace. It appears that Murphy's Law had struck when we were out of town. The igniter on our furnace just happened to fail during the coldest snap in several years, when no one was there to realize that anything had gone wrong. I got a heater going in the insulated crawl space under our house, and a few hours later the pipes thawed out. Miraculously no pipes had burst and our kitchen faucet was the only plumbing fixture to split from the expansion of ice when it froze solid. We had narrowly avoided a major catastrophe. Had we come home the next day, as I had suggested, we would have returned to find every plumbing fixture (including the valves inside the clothes and dishwasher), plus most of the pipes inside our walls, split and ruined (probably at least $20,000 in damage). And if the pipes had thawed before we returned home, the split pipes would have flooded the entire structure, ruining the sheetrock and flooring, and quite possibly turning our home into a toxic mold pit.

- Enough comforters and warm clothing so that you and your family could sleep and function inside your home 24/7 if it was as cold inside your house as it gets outside during a winter's cold snap. Electric blankets and most furnaces won't work without electricity. This is a very real worst-case scenario that happens all too often during extended wintertime blackouts.

- Backup sources of heat for both cooking and space heating. A woodstove is my favorite, as it can be used for both, and is quite safe and comfortable. During extended power failures, a large wood pile will usually last much longer than stored propane, kerosene, or gasoline, and if you live in a forested area, in a pinch you could forage for dead wood to burn in your stove. See chapter 4 for more information on these items, and for safety precautions concerning carbon monoxide poisoning.

- Typical "ski clothing" or backcountry clothing for extreme weather such as mittens, insulated boots, woolen or insulated pants, and a heavy coat or down jacket. Even if you are not an outdoorsman, having that kind of clothing on hand is cheap insurance for dealing with an extended power failure during extreme winter weather. When the rest of your body is properly clothed, a warm hat is critical for maintaining body heat. In general, the head loses heat at the same rate as the rest of the uncovered parts of the body, and it only accounts for about 7 percent of the surface area of the body, but when the rest of your body is covered with heavily insulated clothing, that 7 percent of uncovered head area will account for the majority of heat loss.

- A backup electrical power generator. Even just a small quiet portable 2 kW generator can make a huge difference on your level of comfort and convenience during a blackout. Though not big enough to generate sufficient power to directly heat your home or power an electric hot-water heater, it can provide enough power to run the fans on a furnace, keep your refrigerator operating, and turn on a few lights, a radio, and a computer. See chapter 4 for more information on these items.

A "Winterizing" Checklist for the Home

Some of you may live in cold climates and have a standard winterizing procedure that you go through every fall before the freezing weather sets in, and thus have no need for the following checklist. For others who experience brutally cold weather only on rare occasions, this checklist could be quite helpful for preparing your home ahead of time when alerted by the weather forecast that a freeze warning is in the offing.

- Remove garden hoses from hose bibs, otherwise attached hoses may hold water inside the outlet of your hose bibs, resulting in split fixtures during a hard freeze.

- If you do not have "freeze proof" style hose bibs, wrap each hose bib in foam or fiberglass insulation covered by duct tape or plastic. *Note:* "Freeze proof" hose bibs mounted on the exterior of a home have an extended lengthy valve stem that projects several inches inside the home's wall, so the pressurized "wet side" of the valve is actually located inside the home in a freeze-protected area, and the part of the valve that is exposed to freezing exterior temperatures drains free of water after each use. Freeze-protected hose bibs extending vertically from buried outdoors pipes, such as in a garden area, have a long stem that goes into the ground to where the actual valve is mounted on the piping buried below the frost level in the earth (typically between 12 inches and 6 feet below the surface, depending upon the recommended frost-free bury depth for your area). In order to work properly, both types of freeze-protected hose bibs must drain the water from potentially freezing zones of the hose bib after each use.

• If you have a home with a crawl space underneath the first floor, and you live in a climate that experiences freezing temperatures at least some of the time, you probably have an enclosed foundation with screened foundation vents located at standard intervals along the perimeter of your crawl space walls beneath the level of the first floor. These vents are important to allow for air circulation under your home to prevent excessive moisture buildup and subsequent mold or rot problems. In our location, these foundation vents are typically blocked from the inside with a piece of foam or fiberglass insulation, or some other type of covering to block air flow during the freezing months to help hold heat inside the crawl space to prevent pipes from freezing. In the spring these vent blocks are removed to allow for ventilation and air circulation during the warmer months.

• It is a good idea to actuate your home's main water shut-off valve twice a year, such as when you do your fall and spring winterizing routine. Some of these valves have a tendency to lock up over the years if they are never actuated, meaning that if you suddenly find yourself in a situation where you need to shut off your water and drain your plumbing during a hard freeze, and you find your main shut-off valve is locked up from years of neglect, you will be out of luck and your pipes may freeze and burst. Plumbing codes and standards of construction vary depending upon location and age of construction. If you can't find your home's main water shut-off valve, you may need to call out a plumber to locate it for you.

Draining and Freeze-Protecting Your Plumbing

When the power goes out for just a few hours, you won't normally need to be concerned with the possibility that your plumbing will freeze. When the power goes out for a day or more, and the outside temperatures are well below freezing, it is absolutely critical that your plumbing be protected. Depending on a variety of factors, including how well your home is insulated, and how cold it is outside, it may be days after the power goes out before your plumbing starts to freeze, or it may be just a few hours.

Water expands when it freezes. When the water in your plumbing is frozen hard, it will usually split copper piping and ceramic fixtures such as toilet bowls and tanks, and stands a decent chance of damaging the rest of the piping and plumbing fixtures in your home, including the solenoid valves inside your dish and clothes washers.

Note: Protecting your plumbing from a hard freeze is of vital importance! Once your piping and/or plumbing fixtures have split from a hard freeze, in addition to having to replace all damaged pipes and fixtures (some of which may be buried inside of walls), if left unattended, once the plumbing thaws out you will have a flood on your hands that could totally trash your home.

The most vulnerable plumbing in your home will be plumbing that is next to, or running through, exterior walls, such as the pipes under many kitchen sinks that are located under an outside window. The exterior walls of your home will cool down first, and in extreme cold snaps, even with the heat on inside your home, some people have recurring freezing issues with plumbing that runs through exterior walls (this is common in my area when temperatures fall well below 0°F).

If you have some source of heat in the house, the simplest and easiest mode of defense is to open the cabinet doors under sinks along exterior walls to allow warmer interior air to circulate under the sink. You can also crack all of your faucets to keep a trickle of water flowing through your pipes and fixtures, though this will not protect your toilets or other appliances such as your dish and clothes washers.

Caution: During extremely cold weather, if your drain pipes flow through unheated freezing areas, such as a garage's external walls, and you are trying to keep your plumbing from freezing by cracking a faucet, you risk clogging your drain pipe with ice. A trickle of cold water flowing through a drain pipe in an area that is well below freezing will slowly close off this pipe due to successive layers of ice building up along the inside of the pipe's walls. An occasional flush with hot water from a shower or bath, or an extended flush with a high volume of cold water, will clear the ice from the inner walls of your drain pipes.

If the power is out, and you have a source of backup heat, such as a woodstove or kerosene space heater (which must be ventilated to avoid carbon monoxide poisoning), you should check to see whether or not the areas of your home that are far removed from the source of heat are subject to freezing temperatures. If so, then you may need to keep a faucet cracked and flowing in those faucets furthest from the source of heat.

Valuable tip: Where I live in the High Sierras, below-zero nighttime winter temperatures are common, and −40°F (−40°C) temperatures are not that unusual. In our climate, most homes are equipped with a "stop and drain" type of main water shut-off valve. These valves are designed to drain the water out of the homes' plumbing lines whenever this valve is turned to the "off" position, which simplifies the process of draining and winterizing your plumbing. However, many older homes, or homes in other parts of the country, will not have this type of automatically draining valve. If the ability to freeze-protect your plumbing is a valid concern, and your home does not have a "stop and drain" type of water shut-off valve, then you should contact a plumber to see about having one installed.

Draining Your Plumbing:

When the outside temperatures are well below freezing, and you have no access to an adequate source of heat, the only safe course of action is to drain the pipes and plumbing fixtures in your home. If you must vacate your home in extremely cold weather, being able to drain your plumbing is the only safe way to ensure that subfreezing temperatures will not ruin your plumbing, and possibly flood your home when it thaws out. The plumbing in your home may be quite different from what is described here, so you should familiarize yourself with your own home's plumbing. You may need to contact a local plumber to help you understand how best to drain your pipes in the event of an extended power blackout during a period of extremely cold weather. A plumber may be required for installing modifications to your home's plumbing so it may be easily drained when necessary to protect your home from freeze damage.

The following general guidelines should give you a decent start (see fig. 15-1):

1. Locate your home's main water shut-off valve and turn the water off.

2. Crack all the faucets in your home, both hot and cold. For single-handle control valves, where the hot and cold mixture are controlled with a single handle rather than a separate hot and cold faucet, move the control to a central position where both the hot and cold would be on at the same time (a "warm" setting). Cracking each faucet allows air to bleed into the system through the faucets to replace the water draining out of the lowest valve(s).

3. Crack all external hose bib faucets.

4. Turn off the gas or electricity supply to your hot-water heater.

5. Drain your hot-water heater by attaching a hose to the hose bib faucet near the base of your hot-water heater. Make sure that hot-water faucets in the home are open while draining the hot-water tank!

6. Unhook your clothes-washer hoses and drain the water out of them into a bucket. You may need to open the back of your washer and pull the hoses off the water pump and the solenoid valves to allow those parts to drain. Simply running your washer for a few minutes will not pump the water out of its internal components.

7. Flush your toilets to get almost all the water out of the toilet tanks. Using a sponge or rag, remove most of the water from the toilet bowl itself.

8. Pour about a cup of nontoxic RV-type antifreeze (pink antifreeze available in gallon jugs at most hardware stores) into all of the sink drains and toilet bowls (after they have been flushed) to freeze-protect the traps of your sinks and toilets. You should not use green automotive antifreeze for this

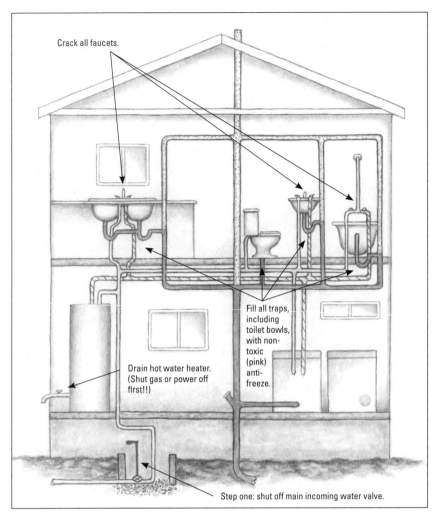

Crack all faucets.

Fill all traps, including toilet bowls, with non-toxic (pink) anti-freeze.

Drain hot water heater. (Shut gas or power off first!!)

Step one: shut off main incoming water valve.

Figure 15-1. Draining your plumbing system.

task, since it is toxic. Alternately, you can use a rag or sponge to remove all the water from your toilet-bowl traps, and unhook sink traps from below to drain the water out of them. *Caution:* Once the water is removed from your sink and toilet traps, there is nothing left inside the traps to block smelly sewer gas from entering your home through the sink and toilet drain lines!

Draining a Hot-Water Heating System:

If you have a hot-water heating system, and you are vacating your home or have no power and/or heat to prevent it from freezing, then you must also drain your hot-water heating system.

1. Shut off the main water supply to the heating system.

2. Turn off the gas or electricity supply to the hot-water heater/boiler for your heating system.

3. Unplug or turn off any recirculating pumps in the system, so they don't run dry and burn out.

4. Open radiator and expansion-tank drain valves. Position pans under each drain valve to catch spillage.

5. Drain the hot-water heater/boiler for your heating system, and its piping, by opening a valve at the system's lowest point, which is usually on the bottom of the boiler. Typically you will run a hose from the drain valve to a floor drain, or to the outside. *Caution:* Use a rubber hose, or red-colored high-temperature hose, since the hot water may ruin a cheap plastic hose.

How to Thaw Frozen Plumbing

Inspect piping for sections that are frosty or bulging. You may be able to feel a frozen section with your bare hand. Check plumbing in, or adjacent to, exterior walls first, and also look for plumbing at low spots under the house where cold air would tend to pool and cause pipes to freeze. If you are able to locate the frozen section of piping, it is possible to thaw that part out using a hair dryer, or by wrapping the pipe in a towel and pouring extremely hot water onto the towel. The use of a propane torch for thawing frozen pipes is not recommended owing to potential for causing more damage, so if you do use a torch, keep it moving and don't allow any portion of piping to overheat.

I have thawed out frozen pipes under my house by manually lighting my furnace and disconnecting a duct so that the hot air from my furnace poured directly into my crawl space, and not into the main part of the house. As you start to thaw your piping, continuously inspect different parts of your home to ensure that a split pipe or fixture is not causing a flood once the water starts flowing again. I recently met one couple who had a split pipe under their house that went undiscovered for weeks, causing a huge mold and rot problem that resulted in the loss of both their home and their health.

Staying Warm in a Home Without Power

If you have no heat, or a very limited source of heat, you will be more comfortable if you close off a small room and everyone stays in that one room. Covering your living area's windows with thick curtains or blankets, especially at night, can make a huge difference in heat lost to the outside. The human body puts out an average of about 100 watts of power when at rest, which is a significant amount of heat, and roughly 500 watts of power when working hard. It takes about seven candles to put out as much heat as a single human body at rest, so you should conserve and use that body heat! If it is freezing cold inside your home, pitching a small tent inside a room, or making a "fort," like little kids tend to do, out of blankets and furniture, will make good use of available body heat to keep a small volume of space warmer and more comfortable.

Stuck in Your Car During Severe Winter Weather

Every winter, thousands of people are stranded while driving in the snow. On more than one occasion, I have been overly confident in my abilities to drive in hazardous icy and snowy conditions, forgetting that I may know how to drive in the snow, but that does not mean the other guy does. When driving in winter weather, it is best to heed the old Yankee saying, "Hope for the best, but plan for the worst!"

Prep for Winter Driving

- Make sure that your car's antifreeze and windshield washer fluid can handle the predicted lowest temperatures. It is both frightening and dangerous when you find yourself blinded by a slushy spray that coats your windshield, only to discover that your washer fluid is frozen and worthless. You can pick up an inexpensive plastic meter with different colored balls inside it for measuring to what temperature your car's antifreeze is good for freeze protection.

- Carry chains and make sure they really fit your tires and that you know how to install them. It is a good idea to practice putting your chains on in broad daylight on dry pavement. It is much harder to figure these things out in the middle of a blinding snow storm at night when you are cold and wet and lying on your belly in a foot of new snow. The night before I wrote this, I was helping a motorist around the corner who was stuck on a hill with wet snow that had packed to ice. He had a pair of brand-new cable chains, but had no clue how to install them. That particular style of cable chain was pretty near impossible to properly tighten when installed in the snow, rather than on pavement, so after spending a half hour trying to get the cable chains properly installed, we ended up towing him with a rope and a four-wheel-drive pickup. Some states outlaw tire chains, but in a dicey situation on treacherous roads I figure it is better to be safe and use the chains than to worry about breaking a rule. If you have a set of traditional tire chains, you should also carry spare chain repair links and at least one set of chain tensioners (not for use with cable chains).

- Bring along a flashlight. It will be very useful for flagging down cars, warning people of an accident, and an absolute must for installing tire chains in the dark. I personally prefer a waterproof backcountry-style headlamp over a standard flashlight, because it leaves my hands free and shines wherever I point my head. Have you ever tried installing tire chains by yourself while holding your flashlight in your teeth?

- Carry extra food, water, and clothing, including a warm hat, mittens or gloves, and a warm jacket that preferably has a waterproof but breathable outer shell, such as one made from Gore-Tex. Make sure you have boots that are adequate for trudging through miles of snow. Tennis shoes just don't cut it in the snow, and frozen toes are no fun!

- Carry a snow scraper for clearing your windshield, a broom for brushing snow off your car, a compact shovel for digging your vehicle out of a snow bank, and sand or a piece of burlap for traction in case your wheels become stuck.

- Check the weather forecast and updated road conditions.

- Stash a spare key on your car. Motorists sometimes get locked out of their vehicle while installing tire chains. I like to bring along a waterproof poncho, tarp, or rain jacket and rain pants for lying in the slush while installing tire chains.

Stay in Your Car or Abandon It?

People ask me this question, and I tell them there is no single right answer, though there is an optimal answer for each situation. Assuming you are stuck either in traffic that has come to a stop, or along the side of a road, here are a few thoughts and guidelines:

- Is your car in a dangerous position where there is a significant chance you may be run into by another car? If so, abandon your car and relocate yourself to some nearby place where you aren't in danger!

- How much gasoline do you have in your tank? Do you have enough spare clothing to stay warm inside your car without running the engine? If not, and you may be stuck for a long time, ration your gasoline by turning your car on for a few minutes at a time to warm the heater, then turn it off again. In my part of the country, major freeways over mountain passes can stay closed for days, and I have been stopped in traffic for eight hours while waiting for accidents to be cleared. At times like these, it is common for motorists to run out of gas while idling to keep their car heaters going.

- What is your footwear like? Are you equipped to walk for miles in the snow, and spend the night outside if necessary?

- If your clothing is not really adequate for spending long hours outside in the snow, is there enough passing traffic to hitch a ride to a nearby town, or is all traffic stopped and the road shut down? If your chances of hitching a ride are slim, and your car is parked in a safe spot, you are probably better off staying inside your vehicle.

- In a desperate situation, lacking suitable boots for snow-country travel, you could use a knife to slice up your car seat cushions to make strips of thick insulation that could be wrapped around your feet and lower legs to provide the insulation needed to protect your feet from freezing while trudging for miles through the snow. Wires from your car could be twisted until they break to provide cordage for tying the insulation around your feet and legs. If you lacked a knife, a piece of plastic or metal trim could be pried off your car, or perhaps broken from an item like your glove box, to provide a sharp edge for slicing your seat cushions into usable pieces of insulated fabric. Also, the mirrors of your car could be broken to provide a sharp piece of glass, though it would not do any good to break the windows, since they are made from tempered safety glass and would shatter into tiny unusable pieces.

Clothing Notes

When circumstances dictate that you must spend many hours outside in extreme weather, your clothing can make the difference between life and death. The Inuit Eskimos of the Canadian North can spend days outside in bitterly cold weather protected solely by their deerskin clothing, as can modern-day mountaineers in their high-tech protective gear.

Here are some observations and suggestions pertaining to clothing for surviving outdoors in extreme weather:

- **Dressing in layers**: In general, dressing in layers is preferable to dressing in a super thick coat. Layers allow you to adjust your clothing for comfort depending upon your level of activity. The last thing you want to do is to soak your clothing with sweat during periods of heightened activity, then sit there shivering and shaking with cold, wet, sweat-soaked clothing when you are inactive for a while.

- **Underlayer**: Both natural and synthetic fibers tend to be either "hydrophobic," meaning water does not stick to them, or "hydrophilic," meaning water loving. Cotton, for example, is hydrophilic, which makes it great for keeping cool in the heat, since it soaks up a lot of moisture and that helps maintain a high level of evaporative cooling in the heat. However, cotton is a terrible material for cold-weather protection, since it soaks up moisture and is a very poor insulator when wet. For cold weather protection, your underlayer should be a "wicking" hydrophobic material, such as wool, polypropylene, or polyester thermal underwear. These materials retain most of their insulating value when wet, and rapidly wick moisture away from your skin, keeping you more comfortable and warmer, especially when exercising and working up a sweat. Cheap woolen long underwear can be scratchy and itchy, but quality woolen thermal underwear, made from premium materials, like baby-soft Merino wool, is a pleasure to wear. Polypropylene thermal underwear wicks moisture extremely well, but smells horrible after a few days in without washing, and the smell can be difficult to get out of the fabric without special soap, so I personally lean toward woolen or polyester thermal underwear.

- **Insulating layers:** I like to dress in a woolen or fiber-pile (usually polyester) sweater layer followed by a fiber-pile insulating jacket that will stay warm even if it gets wet. Thinsulate insulating material makes for warm insulated jackets and pants that are not bulky and retain much of their insulating value when wet. In my winter trips to the backcountry, I also carry an extremely warm, thickly insulated, and fully baffled down parka. I usually only pull this jacket out when I am setting up camp, as it is too warm to wear when I am active, but it sure is nice when I am sitting around, or if I have to hunker down and sleep in the snow. My down parka and sleeping bags are lightweight and extremely warm, but totally worthless when wet.

- **Outer shell:** It takes a tremendous amount of heat to evaporate water (it takes approximately 540 times as much heat to evaporate one gram of water as to raise the temperature of one gram of water by 1°C), and most insulating layers lose some of their insulating value when wet, so keeping yourself dry is extremely important! Protective clothing for extreme weather should either have an integral shell of "breathable" windproof and waterproof material, such as Gore-Tex (or equivalent), or you can also dress with a separate pair of Gore-Tex pants and a Gore-Tex jacket to go over your insulating layers. If your outer shell layer is waterproof, but not breathable, you will drench your clothing from the inside-out with your sweat. In cold temperatures, your body will always try to maintain a high moisture level on your skin's surface, so it will be pumping moisture through your sweat glands to maintain this high humidity level around your skin, and this moisture will condense inside your clothing's insulating layers, if it can't escape through the shell.

- **Boots and socks:** Of critical importance is a comfortable pair of warm, insulated boots that will keep your feet dry in the snow. For a reasonable price, Sorel-type boots, with a removable wool felt liner, rubber waterproof lower section, and uppers of breathable leather or nylon, provide a viable cost-effective solution for most people. Mountaineering boots work great, but are quite expensive. Ugg brand boots (or Ugg boot look-alikes), with their lamb's wool inside layer, and suede leather outer surface, are warm and comfortable, look great, but absorb moisture too easily to work well for even moderately long-distance travel through the snow. Tennis shoes and street shoes in the snow are a sure bet for trouble and frozen feet. I usually prefer to use a thin, wicking, liner sock covered by a thick woolen or synthetic outer ski sock. On multiday winter trips to the backcountry, I like to place a thin plastic bag directly on the skin of my foot, or between my liner sock and the ski sock, to act as a "vapor barrier," which prevents foot perspiration from wetting my socks and leading to cold feet. When I first tried this technique, I was amazed at the major difference it made for keeping my feet warm and dry.

- **Hat or hood:** A warm hat is critical. I like to wear a thick, tightly knit, woolen hat that I supplement with the hood on my parka to keep my head dry when it is snowing, or to add to the insulating value of my hat when it is extremely cold. As a ten year old child, I was skiing at Mt St. Anne outside of Quebec City on a clear frigid day, where the temperature was −40°F (−40°C). When I got off the ski lift, I was so cold that I skied non-stop to the bottom of the mountain. What a mistake! Even though I was wearing a thick woolen ski hat, the arctic air had penetrated through the knit fabric of my hat and froze my ears solid. When I got inside the base lodge, I touched my ears, and they felt like frozen leather. When I bent one ear, it stayed bent at 90 degrees until I bent it back into a normal position. Once my ears thawed out, I started screaming from the pain! For the rest of our family vacation to Quebec, my ears were a painful swollen oozing mess, wrapped in gauze and antiseptic ointment.

• **Mittens and gloves:** In general, mittens are much warmer than gloves, because each finger is in direct contact with the finger next to it, so they stay warmer. In the backcountry, I tend to bring both gloves and warm mittens. The gloves are helpful for setting up camp, when I need more manual dexterity than mittens provide, and for skiing when I am active and staying plenty warm. The mittens are critical when it is very cold and I am not so active. For most purposes, downhill ski gloves and mittens will work fine, but in the backcountry, and for ice climbing, I prefer a thick, densely knit woolen "Dachstein" mitten (available at mountaineering and backcountry stores) that is nearly waterproof and stays warm when wet. These mittens are usually worn with a nylon outer shell that has a leather or rubberized palm for an improved grip.

Tips for Surviving Outside in Extreme Weather and Subfreezing Temperatures

Every year people get lost in the backcountry near where I live in the High Sierras, and end up spending one or more unplanned nights outside in the snow and extreme cold. Some of those folks live to tell the tale, and some of them don't. Hopefully you will never need to spend unexpectedly long hours outside in extreme weather, but in case you do, here are a few tips:

• **Stay dry.** If at all possible, keep your clothing dry, including hat, gloves, and boots. It takes a huge amount of energy to dry clothing using just body heat, and wet clothes will not insulate nearly as well as dry clothing. If you must lie down to sleep, break fresh green pine boughs off evergreen trees to make a somewhat insulated "bough bed" that will help you stay drier and warmer than lying directly on the snow.

• **Check for numb hands and feet.** The extremities of your body will tend to cool and freeze first, so keep a watchful eye on your hands and feet. At the first signs of numbness, you should stop what you are doing and get the blood circulating again, or you will risk frostbite and potentially perma-nent damage due to freezing your flesh. For the feet, brace your arms against something, stand on one leg, and vigorously swing the other leg back and forth, like a ringing bell in a bell tower. The centrifugal force of the swinging motion will usually restore blood circulation and warm your toes, unless they are already truly frozen and not just cold. If they burn and hurt, that is OK, and the painful condition should only last a few minutes, unless the feet had actually suffered frostbite. The easiest technique for restoring feeling and circulation to the hands is similar to the previous technique for the feet. Swing your arms in wide rapid circles to help drive blood into the fingertips. Alternately, take your gloves or mittens off and stick your bare hands under your jacket and into your armpits until your hands are warm.

- **Check each other for signs of hypothermia and frostbite.** A few years back a father and son skied out of bounds into the Granite Chief Wilderness and survived several nights outside until they were rescued. The father kept the son moving most of each night to keep his feet and hands from freezing, and to help prevent him from succumbing to hypothermia. This winter, a female snowboarder descended out of bounds into the Granite Chief Wilderness. She perished from exposure while trying to hike her way out of the wilderness, not realizing that in the direction she chose, it is about a fifty-mile snow-covered backcountry trek to reach the nearest all-season road. If you have no companion to help you check for frostbite and/or hypothermia, you must be vigilant and do this for yourself. Frostbite on the skin shows up as a bright white patch of skin, usually surrounded by pinkish colored flesh. It is caused by freezing of the flesh, and actual frost crystals start forming on the skin's surface. See below for more details on both frostbite and hypothermia.

- **When in doubt, backtrack.** Surprisingly few folks who get lost in the wilderness try to backtrack. Downhill skiers and snowboarders who travel out of bounds inherently dislike the idea of hiking back up the mountain the same way they came down, but this course of action would have saved many a life. However, when snows are incredibly deep, like they can be in the high mountains, backtracking may not be a viable option.

- **Seek shelter:** Tree wells and snow caves can provide shelter from storms and extreme cold. Snow is an excellent insulator, but try to keep yourself from getting wet both while building your snow shelter and when staying inside the shelter. See illustrations and text on snow shelters near the end of chapter 7.

- **Build a fire.** Your chances of starting a fire in extreme weather, using primitive methods, like a fire drill, or flint and steel, are pretty slim, but if you happen to have matches or a cigarette lighter on hand, by all means build a fire! Look for standing dead wood, or branches sheltered underneath fallen logs that may be drier than the rest of the available wood. For kindling, look for branches on trees that have a bunch of dead brown pine needles. The dead pine needles on these branches will usually burn even if they are fairly wet. Make sure you knock the snow off any overhead branches before you start your fire, so they won't dump snow on your fire as it heats up. You can build a fire directly on top of the snow. Just lay down a bunch of braches to keep your drier wood separated from direct contact with the snow. See chapter 7 for more details on building a fire from scratch.

Warning Signs and Treatment for Hypothermia

Hypothermia, and its evil twin, hyperthermia, are both very dangerous, life-threatening conditions. The human body is designed to function in a relatively narrow core body-temperature range that is within a few degrees of 98.6°F (37°C). When the body's core temperature rises a few degrees above this, hyperthermia (overheating) occurs, and when it drops a few degrees lower, this condition is described as hypothermia (overcooling). When left uncorrected, either case can rapidly lead to impaired mental and physical performance followed by death. When people die in the wilderness due to either overheating (hyperthermia) or overcooling (hypothermia), their cause of death is usually referred to as "exposure."

Recognizing the signs and symptoms of hypothermia is extremely important. Most people who died of exposure probably had ample time to recognize the situation, and may have been able to do something about it had they realized what was going on. The following are warning signs of hypothermia:

- Shivering
- Decreased awareness and inability to think clearly
- Numbness, especially in the extremities
- Pale skin color and skin cold to the touch
- Poor dexterity

As hypothermia advances, and the body core temperature approaches the "death zone," the following symptoms may occur:

- Apathy
- Feelings of blissful warmth
- Sleepiness and the desire to lie down and take a nap
- The victim may start to feel hot and start shedding clothes
- Difficulty or inability to walk
- Slurred speech followed by inability to speak, or speech not making any sense whatsoever
- Ashen cold skin, looking like a corpse that can still move a little
- May or may not have waves of uncontrollable shivering

Treatment for hypothermia:

- It is absolutely critical that core temperature be raised as soon as possible.

- Monitor pulse and breathing. Give victim artificial respiration, or CPR, if necessary.

- Get the victim out of wet or frozen clothes and immerse in a warm bath (not hot, optimum is from 102°F–105°F (39°C–40.5°C), if available. Change victim into dry warm clothes. Alternatively, wrap victim in pre-warmed blankets.

- Drink plenty of hot liquids, such as tea, coffee, or simply just hot water.

- If prior options are not available, have a warm person crawl into a single sleeping bag alongside the hypothermic victim for body heat transfer from the warm body to the hypothermic body. *Note:* Simply placing a hypothermic victim inside a sleeping bag by themselves is usually not good enough, since their body will at that point be pretty much shut down and not generating enough body heat on its own to rapidly restore correct body temperature.

- Seek medical attention—hypothermia is life threatening, so time is of the essence!

Frostbite

Frostbite can seriously damage the body, and left untreated can result in gangrene, infection, and death. Great efforts should be taken to avoid frostbite. The seductive danger of frostbite is that once a part of the body is frozen, it doesn't hurt any more, whereas warming a numbed part of the body up, either prior to reaching the frostbite stage, or after it has already frozen, can be intensely painful.

Here is some information and tips pertaining to frostbite:

- Frostbite occurs when the flesh stars freezing and frost crystals start forming on the skin.

On a solo trans-Sierra backcountry ski trip, while I was setting up my camp for the night, I made the mistake of not bothering to stop what I was doing in order to swing my feet and regain the circulation in my toes. My route had taken me to lower elevations in the warmth of the midday, and the snow had been quite wet, soaking through my old leather ski mountaineering boots. It was a clear night as I was pitching my tent, and the temperature had dropped to well below zero. Figuring I would soon be inside my sleeping bag, boiling a hot pot of tea on my camp stove, I did not pay attention to my numb toes. Turns out I froze the last half inch of my big toe. It blistered up, became quite sore, and turned black. I eventually lost my toenail and a large chunk of blackened flesh peeled off the tip of my big toe, but I did not need any surgery or have to deal with infection problems or gangrene, so I consider myself lucky, having learned a valuable lesson that could have been a lot worse.

- Frostnip is the first stage of frostbite where just the surface is frozen. It can be quite painful, but there is no permanent damage, though the surface layers of skin may peel off a few days later, and the affected areas may be more sensitive to cold for many subsequent years.

- Second-stage frostbite is similar in treatment and scope to a second-degree burn. It causes blistering and oozing wounds that tend to look more serious that they really are, usually healing within a few weeks' time.

- Serious frostbite is where deep tissues are frozen, usually resulting in permanent damage to nerves and other tissues. Frozen areas often turn black, and gangrene infection of frostbitten tissues may occur, which can result in amputation or death.

- The best treatment for frostbite is prevention. When the body cools, in order to preserve core temperature and keep the brain functioning reasonably well, the body will reduce blood flow to the extremities, so hands and feet tend to start freezing first. Pay attention to feelings of numbness in hands and feet. As recommended above, swing the hands and feet in wide rapid arcs to help drive blood into the extremities to restore circulation and feeling to numb fingers and toes. If you have a partner, visually check ears, nose, and cheeks for the telltale white blotchy signs of frostbite. If you do not have a partner, check these areas with your fingers to feel for numbness and the sense that areas of exposed flesh may be freezing.

- If your fingers, feet, or toes are badly frozen, you have a decision to make. Once frozen, they will perform like lumps of clay, but they will not hurt. If they were not badly frozen, thawing is best and will minimize the damage, provided you can keep affected areas from refreezing. The worst thing you can do is thaw them out only to have them refreeze. Foot travel on thawed feet that had been seriously frozen will be excruciating, and the damage to your flesh will be worsened with each freeze-thaw cycle. If you have a long ways to travel on foot to reach safety, best to leave those extremities frozen, since once thawed, the feet and/or fingers will swell and blister, making foot travel pretty much impossible as well as excruciatingly painful. Pray you never have to make a choice like this one.

- When thawing out frozen flesh, or near-frozen fingers and toes, studies show the best results are from warming and thawing quickly in running or circulated warm water (not hot. As mentioned above, the optimum is 102°F–105°F (39°C–40.5°C), though there will be less pain if the frozen flesh is thawed slowly in cold water before switching to warm water. At first, the cold water will actually feel hot to your numb flesh. Once feeling returns to your flesh, you can switch to warm water. If you choose to skip the cold water soak and go straight to dipping your frozen flesh into warm or hot water, I know from personal experience that the pain will be excruciating! If the person is already hypothermic, best to immediately use warm water to help elevate the core temperature as soon as possible.

- Handle the frostbitten area gently, and do not massage it! Severe swelling and blistering are common. Keep affected areas elevated to reduce swelling, and protect them from contact with bed clothes via the use of sterile gauze.

To Eat Snow, or Not to Eat Snow, That Is the Question!

A common question that people ask is if it is okay to eat snow when you are thirsty, and with no potable water to drink. The answer is, "It depends . . ." It takes a considerable amount of heat to melt ice (in technical terms, this is referred to as "the heat of fusion"). Though not nearly as much energy is required to melt a gram of ice, as it takes to evaporate a gram of water (i.e., drying wet clothing with body heat), it requires about 80 times as much energy to melt a gram of ice as it does to raise the temperature of a gram of water by just 1°C! So, the question to ask yourself is, "Does my body need to conserve heat more than it needs to satisfy its thirst?"

If you are already cold and shivering, to eat snow to satisfy your thirst is going to hasten the risk of hypothermia, a potentially life-threatening condition. If you are in a situation where conserving body heat is going to be a potentially serious issue, try to minimize eating snow, as this will dissipate significant amounts of much needed body heat. However, if you are physically active, and perhaps even building up a sweat, then go right ahead and eat some snow. When I used to take frequent backcountry ski mountaineering trips, I would often tuck a water bottle in between my sweater and my shirt. Whenever I drank from my water bottle, I would top it off with snow, before tucking it back inside my clothing. My body heat would usually fully melt this slushy mixture by the time I took my next water break. I found this technique to be much more convenient than stopping to melt snow for drinking water using my backcountry stove.

16

Electromagnetic Pulses and Solar Storms

❝It is not possible to precisely predict the time to restore even minimal electrical service due to an EMP eventuality given the number of unknowns and the vast size and complexity of the system with its consequent fragility and resiliency. Expert judgment and rational extrapolation of models and predictive tools suggest that restoration to even a diminished but workable state of electrical service could well take many weeks, with some probability of it taking months and perhaps more than a year at some or many locations; at that point, society as we know it couldn't exist within large regions of the Nation. The larger the affected area and the stronger the field strength from the attack (corollary to extent of damage or disruption), the longer will be the time to recover. Restoration to current standards of electric power cost and reliability would almost certainly take years with severe impact on the economy and all that it entails.

. . . There is a point in time at which the shortage or exhaustion of critical items like emergency power supply, batteries, standby fuel supplies, replacement parts, and manpower resources which can be coordinated and dispatched, together with the degradation of all other infrastructures and their systemic impact, all lead toward a collapse of restoration capability. Society will transition into a situation where restoration needs increase with time as resources degrade and disappear. This is the most serious of all consequences and thus the ability to restore is paramount.❞ —John S. Foster, Jr., et al., "Report of the Commission to Assess the Threat to the United States from Electromagnetic Pulse (EMP) Attack," April 2008

Electromagnetic pulses (EMPs) and solar super storms are two different, but related, categories of events that are often described as high-impact, low-frequency (HILF) events. Events categorized as HILF don't happen very often, but if and when they do, they have the potential to severely affect the lives of many millions of people. At the lower end of the impact range, an HILF event might cause serious disruption and infrastructure damage to regions covering several hundred square miles, similar in scope to the destruction and disruption caused by Hurricane Katrina, the Haitian earthquake, or the Indian Ocean tsunami. At the higher end of the range of potential impact, the social and economic fabric of entire countries might collapse, and at its worst, an HILF event could result in such widespread damage to the fabric of our technological society that it would result in the end of the modern world as we know it.

What is generally referred to as an EMP is a deliberate detonation of a nuclear device at a high altitude, roughly defined as somewhere between 24 and 240 miles, or 40 and 400 kilometers, above the surface of the earth. Nuclear detonations of this type have the potential to negatively affect electronics, and electrical power grids, along their line of sight, covering huge distances on the order of an area 1,500 miles (2500 kilometers) in diameter, which would correspond to a circular area stretching roughly from Quebec City in Canada down to Dallas, Texas.

Similar in many respects to EMP are "solar super storms," which also have the ability to severely affect electronics and electrical power grids. Though it may appear to the naked eye that our sun is the one thing in our world that we can depend upon to be there day after day, things are not always as they appear. It turns out that our sun is not nearly as consistent as it appears to the eye, having an ever-changing surface that is in a constant state of flux. There are periods when the sun's surface is quite active, with fluctuating sunspots and intermittent "coronal mass ejections" (CMEs) in which massive amounts of high-energy charged particles are launched from the surface of the sun and hurtle through space at tremendous velocities. The more active of these periods are referred to as "solar maximums." It is when a CME is launched toward our planet, and massive high-velocity charged particles from the sun impinge upon the earth's ionosphere, that we experience a geomagnetic storm, the largest of which are referred to as "solar super storms." The relatively quiet periods of diminished solar activity are referred to as "solar minimums."

In relatively recent history, our planet has been subject to both solar super storms and high-altitude nuclear tests. In all recorded cases, our civilization has survived these types of events. However, our modern society is increasingly dependent upon microelectronics, the use of an ever-increasingly complex and widespread electrical power grid, electronic telecommunications, and electronic data storage devices, all of which are highly sensitive to electromagnetic disturbances such as those resulting from significant EMP events. Scientists, engineers, and strategic government planners have recognized the serious nature of these threats to our society, and have spent a great deal of time analyzing their extents, including studying past events as well as developing simulated EMP apparatus to test the effects of EMP and geomagnetic storms on modern electronic components and systems.

Studies include the effects of aboveground nuclear tests performed before the Partial Nuclear Test Ban Treaty went into effect in October 1963, as well as the effects of geomagnetic storms that have occurred within relatively recent history. There is a huge body of data pertaining to the electromagnetic effects of at least twenty-one different aboveground nuclear detonations, ranging in size from 10 kilotons to 10 megatons (for comparison, the effective size of the nuclear bombs dropped on Hiroshima and Nagasaki were estimated at 13 kilotons and 21 kilotons, respectively), and burst heights from 90 to 500 kilometers. As for geomagnetic storms, from the 1850s to today, there are records of roughly one hundred significant solar storms.

The more significant of these events include the 1989 geomagnetic solar storm that induced huge electric currents that fried a major power transformer in the HydroQuebec system, causing a cascading grid failure that knocked out power to 6 million customers for nine hours; a May 1921 solar super storm that produced ground currents roughly ten times as strong as the Quebec incident; and the 1859 great-granddaddy solar storm of recorded history known as "the Carrington Event." It is important that we understand something about these potential events and their effects on critical components in the big machine that keeps our technological world running smoothly, so that we might prepare ahead of time to cope with their consequences. This chapter outlines what might happen during such an event, how to plan and prepare ahead of time to cope and survive if such an event should ever occur, and how best to respond once such an event has actually taken place.

The Super Solar Storm of May 1921

Hundreds of newspapers, in both the Northern and Southern Hemispheres, reported on the unusually brilliant and far-reaching aurora displays on the night of May 14–15, 1921. This great geomagnetic storm affected the Northern Hemisphere as far south as Mexico and Puerto Rico, and the Southern Hemisphere as far north as Samoa. In San Juan, Puerto Rico, the aurora was described as, "The Sky in the north was brightly alight and filled with a golden haze. Five great bars of extra brightness, extending from the horizon to the zenith, starting from a common axis, with diverging arcs about equal, extended through the golden haze and gave a wonderful effect." In other parts of the world, closer to either of the earth's poles, the aurora was described as "pulsating," "crimson," "a strange green phosphorescence like wreaths, clouds, and odd shapes," and in a host of other ways (Silverman 2001).

Except for the tropical latitudes, telegraph communications around the world were disrupted during this solar storm, fuses were blown, the relatively crude electronic equipment of the day behaved quite erratically, and the Central New England railroad station in Brewster, New York, was burned to the ground by a fire that started in the station's telegraph due to currents induced by the geomagnetic storm (Silverman 2001). It has been estimated that if an event like that one occurred today, in the United States alone it would put over 350 main-grid transformers at risk of serious damage, potentially knocking out power to over 130 million Americans.

The Carrington Event

The great geomagnetic solar storm of 1859 was actually a combination of two closely spaced, massive solar-induced worldwide geomagnetic events, the first one beginning on August 28 and the second one on September 2. From August 28 to September 4, much of the world was dazzled by an "otherworldly" array of brilliant nighttime light shows. Hikers in the Rocky Mountains were awakened in the middle of the night thinking it was morning. A "perfect dome of alternate red and green streamers" was observed over New England, and citizens in Havana, Cuba, described the sky as appearing "stained with blood and in a state of general conflagration." More pertinent to the concerns of this book, telegraph systems around the world experienced major outages and disruptions. In some cases telegraph poles and stations caught on fire, and in others telegraph operators disconnected their batteries and sent telegraph messages using only the electromagnetically induced currents produced by the solar storm's aurora.

On September 1, 1859, the British amateur astronomer, Richard Carrington, observed "two patches of intensely bright and white light" ejecting from a large complex of sunspots located near the center of the side of the sun facing the earth. Carrington noted that this outburst was followed by a severe magnetic storm that hit the earth the following day. It was not until the 1970s that scientists realized it was the coronal mass ejections (CMEs), and not eruptive flares, that are the cause of non-recurrent solar-induced geomagnetic storms. It turns out that when masses of large solar particles reach the earth as a result of CMEs, they leave a "fingerprint" in the form of nitrates that are created in the upper atmosphere and settle out over the following weeks. These nitrates are stored in arctic ice layers, providing scientists with a record and comparison of the magnitude and chronology of prior solar super storms, such as the Carrington Event.

Ice-core-sample analysis indicates that the Carrington Event was the most powerful geomagnetic event in at least the prior 500 years, and best estimates are that the Carrington Event was stronger than the solar super storm of May 1921 by 50 percent or more.

Disruptions Caused by Aboveground Nuclear Tests

On the night of July 8, 1962, the United States detonated a 1.4-megaton thermonuclear device at an altitude of 240 miles (400 kilometers) above Johnston Island in the mid-Pacific in what was called the Starfish Prime test. It was monitored by hundreds of scientific instruments at widespread installations across the Pacific and outer space. Owing to a physicist's miscalculations, the EMP was far larger in size than expected, with the result that many of the measurement systems went completely off the scales for which they had been calibrated. In spite of the fact that the automobiles, electric power grid, telecommunication devices, and other electronic devices of that day were far less susceptible to an EMP than today's microelectronics, there were numerous reports of streetlight failures and automobile starting-system problems on the island of Oahu, and telephone service failures on the island of Kauai, roughly 780 miles (1400 kilometers) away from the detonation site.

On the morning of October 22, 1962, the Soviets detonated a 300-kiloton thermonuclear device over central Kazakhstan at an altitude of 174 miles (290 kilometers). Though the intention of the test was to study the EMP effects, the Soviets were quite surprised by the magnitude of those effects. A major aboveground telephone line was knocked out by induced currents estimated at 1,500 to 3,400 amps, and a 600-mile-long (1000 kilometer) underground power line was also knocked out. The EMP started a number of electrical fires, including one at the city of Karagandy's electrical power plant. Radios were damaged at a range of 360 miles (600 kilometers) from detonation, and a radar was disabled at a range of 600 miles (1000 kilometers). Additionally, a number of the military's diesel generators were damaged. Note that all of these items were less susceptible to EMP damage than today's electronics containing integrated circuits and microelectronic controls, except for those electronics specifically designed to be hardened against EMP damage.

Subsequent analysis of the thermonuclear devices used in both the American Starfish test, and the Russian Kazakhstan test, show that these devices were quite inefficient at generating high levels of EMP, as compared to much smaller and simpler nuclear fission bombs, such as the more primitive 500-kiloton device known as the Mark 18, first tested by the Americans in 1952. There are a number of countries in today's world, including Pakistan and Israel, that have more sophisticated nuclear devices at their command, and with the breakup of the Soviet Union combined with wealthy individuals from places like Saudi Arabia contributing to the support of terrorist organizations, such devices may well have already fallen into the hands of terrorists, or will eventually do so.

There is a lot of hype about EMPs and solar super storms; some of it true and some of it blown out of proportion. Before I talk about how to prepare to weather the storms caused by a terrorist act involving a nuclear-generated EMP, or an "act of God" caused by a solar super storm, I will spend a little time summarizing some of the most important findings on these subjects based upon information from two highly credible government-sponsored reports—*Severe Space Weather Events: Understanding Societal and Economic Impacts Workshop Report* and *Report of the Commission to Assess the Threat to the United States from Electromagnetic Pulse (EMP) Attack.*

What to Expect from an EMP

❝The electromagnetic pulse from a high-altitude nuclear explosion is one of a small number of threats that can hold our society at risk of catastrophic consequences. The increasingly pervasive use of electronics of all forms represents the greatest source of vulnerability to attack by EMP. Electronics are used to control, communicate, compute, store, manage, and implement nearly every aspect of United States' (U.S.) civilian systems. When a nuclear explosion occurs at high altitude, the EMP signal it produces will cover the wide geographical region within the line of sight of detonation. This broadband, high-amplitude EMP, when coupled into sensitive electronics, has the capability to produce widespread and long lasting disruption and damage to the critical infrastructures that underpin the fabric of U.S. society.

. . . A single EMP attack may seriously degrade or shut down a large part of the electric power grid in the geographic area of EMP exposure effectively instantaneously. There is also the possibility of functional collapse of grids beyond the exposed area, as electrical effects propagate from one region to another. . . . Some critical electrical power infrastructure components are no longer manufactured in the United States, and their acquisition ordinarily requires up to a year of lead time in routine circumstances. Damage to or loss of these components could leave significant parts of the electrical infrastructure out of service for periods measuring in months to a year or more. . . .

Electrical power is necessary to support other critical infrastructures, including supply and distribution of water, food, fuel, communications, transport, financial transactions, emergency services, government services, and all other infrastructures supporting the national economy and welfare. Should significant parts of the electrical power infrastructure be lost for any substantial period of time, the Commission believes that the consequences are likely to be catastrophic, and many people may ultimately die for lack of the basic elements to sustain life in dense urban and suburban communities.❞ —John S. Foster, Jr., et al., "Report of the Commission to Assess the Threat to the United States from Electromagnetic Pulse (EMP) Attack," April 2008

When a nuclear device is detonated aboveground, it generates three different categories of electromagnetic effects, and these are referred to as E1, E2, and E3 effects. The E1 is the direct, freely propagating electromagnetic-field effect that happens immediately, on the order of less than one nanosecond to a few nanoseconds. The E1 effects are particularly damaging to modern integrated circuits in electronic controls, such as supervisory control and data acquisition (SCADA) systems, digital-control systems (DCS), and programmable logic controllers (PLC), which form critical elements in every aspect of our modern world's infrastructure. The E1 effects induce high-voltage currents in any kind of significant wiring runs that connect various sensing elements in data acquisition and control systems.

For example, the systems that remotely control our gas and oil pipelines, oil and chemical refining processes, water and sewage distribution and treatment systems, power generation and distribution systems, and food storage and distribution systems, all contain sensitive digital-processing circuits and remote-sensing devices that are connected by wiring harnesses and are inherently susceptible to failure caused by induced currents and voltage spikes from E1 effects. The E1 effects occur at such incredibly fast rates, that there is generally no time for electronic protective circuits to switch into action and protect these sensitive and critical devices from damage.

Warning: The cooling and control systems that keep nuclear reactors functioning properly, and prevent their cores from melting down (like what happened during the recent catastrophic multiple failures in Japan's Fukushima Daiichi nuclear reactors), are entirely dependent upon complex combinations of SCADAs, PLCs and DCSs—those types of electronic equipment that are most sensitive to crippling damage from EMPs and solar super storms. In the event of an EMP from a terrorist's suborbital nuclear detonation, or a solar super storm, it is quite likely that a large number of nuclear power plants will simultaneously experience cooling failures and catastrophic reactor core melt downs. After the Japan earthquake and tsunami spawned multiple reactor-cooling-system failures in the Fukushima reactors, widespread concerns about radiation contamination caused a run on supplies of potassium iodide, dosimeters, Geiger counters, gas masks, and related items, effectively wiping out the world's short-term stock of radiation-related emergency supplies. One-third of the U.S population lives within fifty miles (83 km) of a nuclear reactor. If you happen to be one of these people, I strongly suggest you read chapter 17, "The Unthinkable: Surviving a Nuclear Disaster," and make your pertinent disaster plans and purchases in a timely manner.

The intermediate-time EMP effects are categorized as E2 effects. These are similar in electrical frequency to lighting strikes, but their occurrence will be much like many thousands or millions of lightning strikes occurring simultaneously over thousands of square miles. In many cases, the protective circuits designed to protect devices and power-distribution systems from lightning damage may well be adequate, but in those cases where the rapid E1 effects have damaged the device's lightning-protection elements, the E2 effects falling immediately on the heels of the E1 effects will cause the destruction of those devices.

The late-time EMP effects are categorized as E3 effects, and may last for a minute or more. E3 pulses are quite similar to the geomagnetic-induced currents from solar storms. E3 effects are known to induce huge currents and voltages on long runs of electrical wires and conductors. Geomagnetic storms, such as the one that fried the major HydroQuebec grid transformer, are known to cause major damage to electrical-system components at much lower levels than might reasonably be experienced during an E3 EMP event.

Based upon E3-type effects observed during previous geomagnetic storms, in combination with EMP simulation testing on electrical components and systems, and data gathered from Soviet and American aboveground nuclear testing prior to the partial test ban treaty in 1962, the following are some anticipated effects from a nuclear-device-generated EMP:

- Extended grid collapse due to failed major-grid power transformers as well as critical SCADA and PLC systems. Owing to cascading effects, the grid failure is likely to extend far beyond the region directly affected by the EMP. For example, on August 10, 1996, during a triple-digit heat wave, sagging power lines in Oregon shorted against insufficiently trimmed tree limbs, causing a cascading blackout that cut power to 7 western states, parts of Baja, Mexico, and parts of two Canadian provinces. The grid had been operating near peak capacity because of massive loads from air-conditioning units operating during the heat wave, and the shorted lines threw it over the edge into short-term collapse, affecting millions of customers.

- Cellular telephone systems are particularly susceptible to EMP and will likely fail immediately owing to direct E1 and E3 effects.

- Landline telecommunication systems that were not damaged by the initial E1 and E3 effects, will likely fail within four to seventy-two hours as battery backup supplies run down, and generator backup power for central telephone substations run out of fuel reserves. In many locations, landlines with corded handsets that do not need 110-VAC connections will still work from between a few hours to three days, after which all local telephone services, including 911 emergency services, will cease to operate within the affected area, which is exactly what happened across a wide area devastated by Hurricane Katrina.

- There will be a brief period, lasting a few hours to a few days, where backup generators that were not damaged by the E1 and E3 effects will still be functional and provide some semblance of services, until they run out of fuel and cease to operate.

- Most smaller electrical devices that were not plugged in, or turned on, at the time of the EMP will still be operable, provided they were not connected to long runs of cable such as Ethernet network lines or the local grid.

- If the EMP happened during normal waking hours, roughly 10 to 15 percent of cars and trucks that were on the road at the time of the EMP will stop operating immediately, causing major traffic tie-ups. Cars not operating at the time of the EMP will be mostly functional, though many will have annoying issues. Realize that today's cars all have complex microelectronic controls that are highly susceptible to EMPs, and the last time a car was exposed to a real nuclear EMP was in 1962 when they had electromechanical systems that were far more resistant to EMP than today's cars, so it is quite possible that the simulated EMP testing programs have underestimated effects on automobiles. In general, since automobiles have spark plugs that emit significant short-range electromagnetic pulses, they are designed to be fairly hardened against this sort of thing and will be more resistant to EMPs than most other modern electronic devices that were not specifically designed to be hardened against EMPs. *Note*: I recently met a retired naval officer who had spent nearly thirty years in the U.S. military's nuclear program. He assured me that if a nuclear device designed for optimal EMP effect was detonated at the proper elevation above the United States, its effect on modern motor vehicles would be far worse than the effect predicted by the official report, which was based on an "average" (not optimized for EMP) nuclear device, effectively crippling nearly all vehicles that contain microelectronics and an electronic fuel-injection system across an area totaling thousands of square miles.

- Most streetlights and traffic signals will be damaged by the E1 and E3 effects, contributing to major traffic problems in metropolitan and suburban areas.

- The magnetic data on personal computers, banks, and business systems will probably survive, but microelectronic control circuits in most of the devices that read and write that data (computer hard drives, tape drives, etc.), if operating at the time of the EMP, will be damaged or destroyed.

- The one-to-three-day supply of food in supermarkets will be rapidly depleted owing to the destruction of the electronic SCDA- and PLC-based systems that control today's highly automated "just-in-time" delivery systems. Loss of the grid means that food-storage refrigerator systems will stop functioning when backup generator fuel runs out in one to three days' time.

- The electronic SCADA "eyes, ears, and voice" systems that would normally diagnose, dispatch, and coordinate repairs to the grid and telecommunication systems will be crippled, making it nearly impossible to coordinate repairs to these systems, as well as the complex effort to manually restart sections of the downed power grid.

- The volume of trained manpower capable of manually diagnosing and repairing the complex power grid and telecommunications systems is simply not there, making such a monumental task nearly impossible. There is neither the volume of trained manpower nor the spare parts that will be required to accomplish this task.

- Most older-style electromechanical devices, such as relays and mechanical switches, will be unaffected by the EMP.

- Older pre-fuel-injection vehicles will be less likely to be affected.

- Battery-powered shortwave "ham radio" communications will probably be down for a few hours due to electromagnetic interference. Unless protected by a "Faraday cage" most radios inside the EMP area will probably be damaged by the E1 effects, however, some of these systems will probably survive, returning to service after a few hours, until they run out of a source of backup power.

What to Expect from a Solar Super Storm

The Metatech Corporation was commissioned by FEMA and the Electromagnetic Pulse Commission to study the potential impacts of severe geomagnetic storms on the U.S. electric power grid. Using a scenario with a geomagnetic storm of the same size as the 1921 solar super storm, roughly 50 percent less severe than the Carrington Event, their study estimated that more than 300 of the large, custom, major power transformers in the U.S. would be exposed to levels of induced currents putting them at probable risk for either total failure or severe enough damage so as to require replacement.

There are roughly 2,000 of these large custom-built power transformers, rated at or above 345 kV, that service the entire U.S. electric power grid. These large custom-built power transformers are no longer manufactured in the United States. Under normal circumstances, meaning the world is functioning reasonably well and everything is moving smoothly, the delivery time for one of these transformers used to run one to two years. However, owing to the rapidly expanding economies in China and India, the recent high demand for these transformers has bumped delivery for a single large custom transformer to where it is now running almost three years!

Worldwide production capacity for these custom transformers is currently less than 100 per year. A worldwide super solar storm, of a magnitude similar to the 1921 event, or the Carrington Event, would wipe out many hundreds of these transformers, including roughly a third of the large power transformers in the United States, and a higher percentage in countries at latitudes located closer to the north or south pole (there are fewer solar-storm-induced effects as you get closer to the equator). Widespread destruction of these power transformers would completely overwhelm the world's manufacturing capacity for such devices, and that is if all the manufacturing facilities for such things were in areas that still had a power grid that was intact, which is highly unlikely. Such an event would have a devastating effect worldwide from which it would take many years, if ever, for the world to recover. It would be much like rebuilding Europe after World War II, only the chances are that we would not have a technological superpower that was still intact to provide the technology and manufacturing base to drive the recovery effort.

The geomagnetic effects of a solar super storm similar in size to the 1929 super storm will cause less damage to sensitive electronics than an EMP event, so long as they are not connected to long runs of wiring that are susceptible to induced currents from E3-type effects. However, the geographical extent of a solar super storm will almost certainly cover a much broader area of the planet than that caused by an EMP. Thus the long-lasting effect on the grid, and society in general, could mean the end of the world as we know it, if the geomagnetic storm was of a size and duration similar to the 1929 super storm or the Carrington Event.

Planning Ahead for EMP or a Solar Super Storm

Planning ahead to survive and thrive after an EMP event or solar super storm, requires longer-term strategies, more supplies, and a varied, self-reliant skill set that far exceeds those required for surviving most other crises or catastrophes. If you happen to live in a rural area that grows more food than it uses, your chances are much better than if you live in a city or in an area that is not conducive to growing your own food. In that case, if you are able to produce your own food, or trade and barter goods, skilled services, or manual labor for food and essential items, then you stand a decent chance of coming through this ordeal in good shape.

If you wish to plan ahead to survive a major EMP event or super solar storm, this book provides a good start, but you should expand your survival skill set, as well as your stock of long-term supplies. In that case, I suggest you start by picking up a copy of *The Encyclopedia of Country Living*, by Carla Emery, *How to Survive the End of the World as We Know It* by James Wesley, Rawles (editor of www.survivalblog.com), *When Technology Fails* by Matthew Stein, at least one or two books on wild edible plants native to your area that include clear color photographs of plants at various times of the year, as well as a number of other books and resources listed in appendix 1 and 2. You should also consider stockpiling guns and ammunition (see chapter 10) for self-defense and hunting purposes. Even if you do not have any desire (or training) to ever use a rifle or handgun, in the least you may use them for trade and barter, as well as lend them to others in your survival network (or extended family), who may be better trained and qualified to use them for communal protection and for hunting game.

Protection of Electronic Devices from EMP and Solar Storms

A detailed discussion of the technological strategies for protecting electronic devices from EMP and solar super storms is beyond the scope of this book, but I will give you a few general guidelines. Detailed technical instructions are offered in the Department of the Army Technical Manual TM 5-690, *"Grounding and Bonding in Command, Control, Communications, Computer, Intelligence, Surveillance, and Reconnaissance (C4ISR) Facilities,"* which may be downloaded for free on the Internet (see bibliography for details).

- Severe solar storms are likely to be devastating to the grid, and subsequently life and society in general, but not harmful to your personal electronics, computers, automobiles, etc., provided you have adequate surge protection on your lines.

- EMP-simulation tests indicated that most electronic devices that are self-contained and not operating at the time, wired to an antenna, or connected to significant lengths of wires will be unharmed by EMPs or solar storms. Complex digital microelectronics, such as personal computers, are quite sensitive to EMPs.

- Significant lengths of wires, such as network cables, grid connections, telephone lines, and possibly even local wires that connect your renewable-energy-system components to each other, may experience induced currents of high voltage and high amperage that are potentially damaging to solid-state circuits and microelectronics.

- Wires entering the building should be lightning protected with suitable ground-path circuits.

- You can protect sensitive electronics (anything with integrated circuits, logic boards, and microelectronics) with homemade "Faraday cages." A Faraday cage is simply a continuous metal enclosure that surrounds a device. Do not pierce your Faraday cage with any power cords or antennas, or those items will bring induced currents into your device, potentially ruining it. Your Faraday cage must be insulated from electrical contact with the device it is meant to protect. Any fully enclosed metal box will act as a Faraday cage, or you can make a simple Faraday cage by first insulating your device with a couple of layers of plastic garbage bags, or layers of rolled plastic film, then covering it with a continuous layer of aluminum foil. Tape overlapping sections of foil to itself to form a continuous metal shielding layer.

- "Nested" Faraday cages work even better. To make a nested Faraday cage, start with a single-layer aluminum-foil Faraday cage and add one or two more layers of foil with an insulating layer of plastic between each layer of foil.

- Aluminum window screen material is also good for making Faraday cages.

- A simple small ready-made "Faraday cage" for protecting sensitive electrical components is any old microwave oven (cut the power cord off to prevent it from acting as an antenna). Alternately, a common galvanized garbage can with a tight-fitting lid would do an excellent job as a low-cost Faraday cage.

- Grounding Faraday cages for optimal EMP protection is quite tricky. In the Soviet EMP nuclear tests, large currents were induced in buried power lines, causing extensive damage. Unless you are an EMP expert, it is probably best to leave your Faraday cages ungrounded, and resort to nested Faraday cages for sensitive equipment like computers and solid-state shortwave radios.

- Store plenty of batteries, and a battery-operated shortwave radio. After an EMP or solar storm event, it is quite likely that your shortwave radio may be the only source of outside information about what has actually occurred. A battery-powered shortwave radio stored inside a nested Faraday cage is probably your best form of insurance to stay connected and informed after an EMP event. (See chapter 9 for more information on radios.)

- Most magnetic media will probably survive an EMP event, but the key word is "probably." Optical media, such as CDs and DVDs will certainly survive. Even if all your computer equipment is fried, data stored on optical media will survive, and one can hope that at some point in time new computer equipment will arrive from outside the affected area, allowing you to once again access your stored data.

- For more specific information on tools and techniques for personal protection from an EMP, see the online article, "Getting Prepared for an Electromagnetic Pulse Attack or Severe Solar Storm" by Jerry Emanuelson, available at www.futurescience.com/emp/emp-protection.html.

Coping Strategies

If you are one of the ones with the time and money to prepare a sustainable survival retreat, complete with a renewable energy system, garden, greenhouse, and fully stocked with spare parts (including key electrical components like inverters) and survival supplies, as soon as you realize your area has been struck by an EMP or debilitating solar storm, you should head for the hills and retreat to your refuge from the coming storm, provided you can get there before it is occupied by others. If you are lucky enough to live in such a place full-time, then congratulations are in order. However, if you are like the other 99.9 percent of the population, here are some strategies that you may find helpful:

- If you believe that your area may have been subject to a significant EMP or solar super storm, and you live in a metropolitan or suburban area, try to get out of town as soon as possible. If the event turns out to be minor, that is terrific—you get to go back to your home and community. Better to be overly cautious than sorry!

- In case you need to ditch your car somewhere down the line, be sure to pack your camping gear, backpacks, and sturdy hiking boots. Don't forget the moleskin and cloth first-aid tape for taping your hot spots before they blister! *Note:* Duct tape will suffice if you have nothing else.

- If traffic is totally tied up, do not waste precious gasoline idling your car in endless traffic jams. Pull over somewhere and try to get some sleep if possible. The middle of the night, when most people are sleeping, may be your best chance for "getting out of Dodge" using your automobile.

- If you have a ham radio, a multi-channel scanner, or have developed a survival network the includes a local ham radio operator (see chapter 9), try to get up-to-date information about what is really happening before you decide on exactly where to go and what to do. If it was an EMP event, then your best bet is to head for an area outside of the EMP range, if at all possible.

- Remember that when struck by a solar super storm, or an EMP, if it was a severe event, the situation will degrade quickly and significantly with each new day, as backup supplies of fuel for generators begin to dry up, leaving telecommunication, food distribution, water, sewage, and refrigeration systems incapacitated, and fuel systems running out of fuel.

- Make sure you bring along your grab-and-go kits, key self-reliant instruction manuals, illustrated edible plant guide(s), medical supplies, personal self-defense and hunting supplies, and whatever food provisions you have room for inside your vehicle (or push cart if no gasoline-powered vehicle is available).

- Realize that the U.S. population is a heavily armed population. Since every Tom, Dick, and Harry will be out hunting for game, the game will be quite scarce in almost no time at all, so your best bet for maintaining food stocks (unless, of course, you have your own survival retreat with a large garden/greenhouse) is if you have good foraging skills and a well-illustrated guide to wild edible plants in your area, or a large surplus stock of valuable survival goods to use for trade and barter.

I can assure you that a civilization-disrupting solar super storm is guaranteed to happen. Since there have been at least two such events in the past 160 years, it is sure to happen again. Nobody knows when it will happen, but it is just a matter of time. Whether or not a crippling EMP event will ever occur is dependent upon human free will. Most people who analyze these things believe the odds are somewhere in the range of 50–70 percent that a terrorist organization, or rogue state, will launch such an attack on the United States, and its effects will be devastating to a large population covering a huge area. At the minimum, this will be on a par with the scope of the area crippled by Hurricane Katrina, and at the other end of the spectrum fomenting the collapse of our entire country.

For more information on EMPs and solar storms, you may download the government reports mentioned earlier (see the bibliography for specific report information), and there are numerous articles and Web sites that are devoted to these subjects. One such Web site, which is posted by an electrical engineer and includes numerous valuable links, is www.futurescience.com/emp.html.

17

The Unthinkable: Surviving a Nuclear Disaster

❝Five years ago I visited the still highly contaminated areas of Ukraine and the Belarus border where much of the radioactive plume from Chernobyl descended on 26 April 1986. I challenge chief scientist John Beddington and environmentalists like George Monbiot or any of the pundits now downplaying the risks of radiation to talk to the doctors, the scientists, the mothers, children and villagers who have been left with the consequences of a major nuclear accident.

It was grim. We went from hospital to hospital and from one contaminated village to another. We found deformed and genetically mutated babies in the wards; pitifully sick children in the homes; adolescents with stunted growth and dwarf torsos; fetuses without thighs or fingers and villagers who told us every member of their family was sick.

This was 20 years after the accident, but we heard of many unusual clusters of people with rare bone cancers. One doctor, in tears, told us that one in three pregnancies in some places was malformed and that she was overwhelmed by people with immune and endocrine system disorders. Others said they still saw cesium and strontium in the breast milk of mothers living far from the areas thought to be most affected, and significant radiation still in the food chain. Villages testified that 'the Chernobyl necklace'—thyroid cancer—was so common as to be unremarkable; many showed signs of accelerated ageing....

At the end of 2006, Yablokov [member of the Russian academy of sciences, and adviser to President Gorbachev at the time of Chernobyl] and two colleagues, factoring in the worldwide drop in births and increase in cancers seen after the accident, estimated in a study published in the annals of the New York Academy of Sciences that 985,000 people had so far died and the environment had been devastated. Their findings were met with almost complete silence by the World Health Organization and the industry....

Fukushima is not Chernobyl, but it is potentially worse. It is a multiple reactor catastrophe happening within 150 miles of a metropolis of 30 million people. If it happened at Sellafield, there would be panic in every major city in Britain. We still don't know the final outcome, but to hear experts claiming that nuclear radiation is not that serious, or that this accident proves the need for nuclear power, is nothing short of disgraceful.**❞**
—John Vidal, "Nuclear's Green Cheerleaders Forget Chernobyl at Our Peril," *Guardian. co.uk*, April 1, 2011

When the Russian nuclear reactor at Chernobyl blew the roof off its containment building and burned out of control for several weeks, it spread many tons of radioactive contamination over large parts of Russia and many other European countries. By a factor of 100:1, the radioactive materials injected into the environment from this single nuclear reactor accident exceeded the combined amounts of radioactive contamination released by the Nagasaki and Hiroshima bombs! (Greenpeace 2006, 8). Immediately following the Chernobyl accident, 237 people suffered from acute radiation sickness, and only 31 of them died within the first three months, which on the surface does not seem that bad. However, a small industrial city was abandoned (Pripyat), 336,000 people had to be relocated, and the entire Northern Hemisphere was contaminated with increased levels of radiation, including serious contamination in thirteen different European countries, the worst of it falling on Russia, the Ukraine, and Belarus. The most recent epidemiological evidence, published under the auspices of the Russian Academy of Science, suggests that in the Ukraine, Russia, and Belarus alone, the Chernobyl accident resulted in an additional estimated 212,000 deaths between 1990 and 2004, and nearly 1 million people worldwide. It has also been estimated that the Chernobyl radiation contamination caused roughly 3 million people to suffer significant health problems such as cancers, tumor, suppressed immune system response, birth defects, and chronic fatigue (Greenpeace 2006 and Vidal 2011).

After a partial reactor-core meltdown caused the evacuation of all personnel from the U.S. nuclear reactor on Three Mile Island, it was three days before American officials were certain that this reactor was not going to burst its containment vessel and contaminate a huge geographical area in much the same way as the Russian reactor in Chernobyl later did. It has been said that if a World War II–style war were to break out in Europe today, and not a single nuclear weapon was detonated, the destruction of Europe's nuclear power plants by conventional bombs would render all of Europe uninhabitable for tens of thousands of years! I am not trying to scare anyone, but I do wish to provide my readers with a commonsense understanding of the various types of nuclear threats, and offer concise practical information that could help them make rational life-saving decisions should they ever find themselves in the unfortunate situation of being nearby, or downwind from, a nuclear disaster.

Roughly one-third of all Americans live within fifty miles of a nuclear power plant. Since an EMP or super solar storm has significant potential to start a chain of events in practically any nuclear power plant in the world that could be quite similar to what happened at the Fukushima reactor complex, this chapter provides important information about preparing for, and dealing with, such an event that might one day affect millions of people. This chapter starts by introducing the three main categories of nuclear threats, followed by strategies for coping with each of these three types of nuclear disasters. It also details specific tools, tips, and techniques both for preparing to survive a nuclear event, as well as coping with the aftermath.

Radiation Basics and Types of Nuclear Threats

❝And what about our reactors? In the United States we have twenty-three reactors of the same General Electric design as Fukushima No. 1. We also have atomic plants built on fault lines. For example, the Diablo Canyon Nuclear Power Plant's units 1 and 2 not far from Santa Barbara, and outside San Clemente there's the San Onofre Nuclear Generating Station, which has three reactors, two of which are still running. Environmentalists protested and bitterly opposed the opening of these plants along the California coast in a region of regular and often violent seismic activity. But as in Japan, their concerns were brushed aside with assurances that all contingencies had been taken into account.

The American fleet of 103 atomic reactors is old and rickety. But more dangerous than the old and brittle equipment, according to Bradford, may be overconfidence among regulators and managers. 'The phrase "it can't happen here" is an invitation to disaster,' said Bradford. Mix technological arrogance with the profit motive, and you get slipshod management, corner-cutting and repeated lying.❞ —Christian Parenti, "Nuclear Hubris: Could Japan's Nuclear Disaster Happen Here?" *The Nation*, **March 14, 2011**

There are three different types of nuclear threats: (1) the detonation of a nuclear bomb, which may be a "fission"-type of nuclear device, such as the bombs that were dropped on Nagaski and Hiroshima, or a "fusion"-type of device that yields a much larger explosion that will flatten an area may times the size of what would be destroyed by a fission-type explosion; (2) a nuclear reactor "meltdown," internal gas explosion, or some other event that breaches the reactor's safety mechanisms and the structural housing that surrounds the reactor core, leaking radioactive contamination into the environment; or (3) a "dirty bomb," which is a non-nuclear type of explosive device that has been encased in highly radioactive materials that are dispersed into the environment when the explosive is detonated.

There are also three main types of radiation that may be given off by radioactive materials and nuclear detonations. The first type of radiation is direct electromagnetic radiation, similar to the sun's rays, only of a higher intensity, mostly in the form of intense heat and/or high-energy "gamma radiation" radiating directly from a nuclear detonation's fireball, and from radioactive material dispersed by a nuclear detonation. Gamma rays are a form of electromagnetic radiation that have enough energy to penetrate through flesh and building walls, quite similar to X-rays, only more powerful, more penetrating, and more destructive to living tissues. Gamma rays are the most immediately damaging form of radiation, and are what the thick dense walls of fallout shelters are specifically designed to block.

The second and third types of radiation are alpha and beta particles. Radioactive debris, such as nuclear-blast "fallout," emits gamma rays, alpha particles, and beta particles. Beta particles are simply free-flying high-energy electrons, which can penetrate light clothing or about ⅛ inch of flesh, causing surface "beta burns" when radioactive fallout is left on the skin for more than a few minutes. Alpha particles don't have much penetrating power, being stopped by skin and clothing, so they don't pose much of a threat unless they are emitted by radioactive particles that have been ingested and become lodged in organs of the body, where over time they may contribute to cancerous growths and tumors.

"Fallout" is composed of small radioactive particles resulting from a nuclear detonation, or the release of airborne radioactive debris from a damaged nuclear reactor, or the explosion of a dirty bomb. In the case of a ground or low-altitude burst, thousands of tons of these particles are carried far into the atmosphere by the classic mushroom cloud of a nuclear blast. The heavier of these particles tend to settle out of the air fairly quickly, and may look like grains of rice, salt, ash, or fall as "black rain." Tiny microscopic particles of fallout may stay airborne for weeks, traveling many thousands of miles while floating on air currents. The most highly radioactive components in the fallout from a nuclear detonation decay quite quickly, so the more time that elapses from the moment of detonation, the less radioactive the fallout becomes, regardless of whether it is in the air, on the ground, or in the water. The longer fallout particles remain in the air before settling to the ground, the less radioactive they will be when they hit the ground. (See fig. 17-1.)

Fallout-contaminated clothing should be shaken off regularly and before entering your shelter. Washing in contaminated water is better than nothing, but it is preferable to wash in a source of clean, uncontaminated water if available. Radiation sickness is characterized by vomiting, loss of hair, skin burns, spontaneous bruising/hemorrhaging, plus other symptoms typical of shock, and is usually a result of the cumulative exposure to radiation. Radiation damage to the body is cumulative, meaning that it is a combination of the radiation dose rate multiplied by the elapsed time of exposure to radioactive sources (fallout, ingested materials, etc.). There is no way of knowing exactly how much radiation one has been exposed to unless one

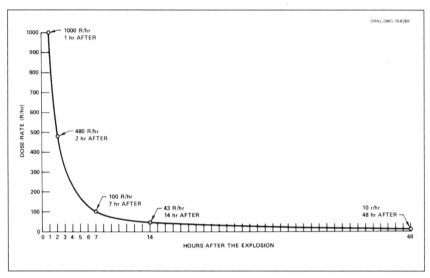

Figure 17-1. Decay of the dose rate of radiation from fallout, taken from the time of detonation, not from the time of deposit on the ground or in water. Source: Cresson H. Kearny, *Nuclear War Survival Skills*

is wearing a high-tech "dosimeter," (see sources in appendix 2) which indicates cumulative exposure to radioactivity, or unless one has made a low-tech homemade "Kearny Fallout Meter" (KFM), which I will talk about more a little later in this chapter.

The new standard for measuring radiation is the millisievert, or sievert (1 sievert is equal to 1,000 millisieverts). Previously, radiation levels and exposure were typically measured in Roentgens (R), rads (radiation absorbed dose) and rems (roentgen equivalent man). Roentgens were the original measure of radiation, named after the German physicist who discovered X-rays and invented the first X-ray machine. Roentgens were primarily used to measure the strength of X-rays and gamma rays. Since different types of radiation do not have the same effect on the human body, the "rem" was developed to more accurately describe a radiation-dosage level as it pertains to its effect on the human body, and the sievert is a similar "dose-equivalent" measurement of radiation. One mSv is equal to 0.1 rem. A rem is essentially a roentgen multiplied by a factor that takes into account the specific type of radiation's effect on a human body, and for our purposes assume that Rs, rems, and rads are essentially interchangeable.

The lethal dose of radiation varies considerably from person to person, but it is generally accepted that about 50 percent of the people exposed to a dose of roughly 4,500 mSv (450 rems) will eventually die from radiation poisoning. By comparison, the average background radiation rate for a person living in America (varies by location) is approximately 3 mSv per year, the standard

Table 17-1. Short-Term Health Effects of Radiation	
Exposure (mSv)	**Health Effect**
0–250	• May be changes in blood chemistry, but no long-term effects
250–1,000	• May cause nausea and vomiting for 1–2 days • May cause hair loss in 2–3 weeks • Disabling sickness not common
1,000–,000	• Nausea and fatigue • Vomiting if dose is 1,250 mSv or more • May cause hair loss in 2–3 weeks • Longer term reduction in some types of blood cells • Most people will recover without medical treatment
2,000–3,000	• Nausea and vomiting on first day of exposure • Hair loss in 2–3 weeks • Up to a two week latent period followed by appetite loss, general malaise, sore throat, pallor, diarrhea, and moderate emaciation • Most people will recover unless they succumb to ancillary infection
3,000–6,000	• Nausea, vomiting, and diarrhea in first few hours • Up to a one week latent period followed by appetite loss, fever, and general malaise in the second week • Followed by bleeding, inflammation of mouth and throat, diarrhea, and emaciation • Some deaths in 2–6 weeks, followed by eventual deaths of 50% at exposure of 4,500 mSv (worse as exposure increases)
6,000–10,000	• Nausea, vomiting, and diarrhea in the first few hours • Rapid emaciation and death in the second week
Over 10,000	• Destruction of intestinal lining. Damage to the central nervous system. Death between hours and two weeks.
(Source: Adapted from JP Laboratories "Effect of Radiation" and U.S. EPA "Radiation Protection: Health Effects")	

limit of exposure to radioactivity for nuclear workers in the United States is 20 mSv per year, and the criteria imposed for relocation after Chernobyl was a lifetime exposure of 350 mSv. It is now common in some parts of Iran, India, and Eastern Europe for background radiation levels to exceed 50 mSv per year.

In the event of a nuclear catastrophe, if you are able to determine the nature of this disaster, to some extent this will dictate what strategies and course of action should be followed. If the disaster is related to a nuclear power plant that has breached its containment vessel, as long as the reactor continues to release significant radioactivity into the environment, the accumulated radioactivity downwind will continue to rise with time, and your best bet is to get out of the downwind vicinity as soon as possible, while doing your best to prevent breathing contaminated air or ingesting contaminated food and water.

Radioactive iodine tends to concentrate in the thyroid gland, often resulting in tumors in the years following the ingestion of food or water that was contaminated by radioactive fallout. A simple way to avoid this problem is to ingest clean iodized salt, so the body takes in uncontaminated iodine rather than drawing its iodine from contaminated food, though it is claimed that there is really not enough bioavailable iodine in iodized salt to properly accomplish this task and so a more effective prophylactic treatment is to eat sea vegetables that contain high amounts of natural iodine, or take potassium iodide (KI) tablets. If you have planned ahead for the possibility of a nuclear event, and have a supply of potassium iodide tablets, then you should begin taking them as soon as you are aware that a nuclear disaster has occurred in your vicinity.

After the collapse of the Soviet Union in the early 1990s, there was a drastic reduction in the probability that our world might end in a conflagration of thermonuclear detonations, and many breathed a giant sigh of relief. Unfortunately the collapse of the Soviet Union also left thousands of nuclear devices and massive amounts of radioactive materials under the jurisdiction of a variety of relatively unstable governments. These dangerous materials have at times been guarded by people who were being paid very little, if anything, so one might assume that there has been ample opportunity for well-funded terrorist groups to bribe the appropriate officials and purchase some of these materials. In addition to the potential for a terrorist group or unstable government to detonate a nuclear weapon or a "dirty bomb," due to the presence of nuclear reactors in many parts of the world, there is always the potential for an earthquake (as happened at the Fukushima reactors in Japan), industrial accident, act of war, or terrorist action to breach the containment vessel of a nuclear reactor, resulting in widespread radioactive contamination.

In the event of a nuclear-device detonation, the initial extremely dangerous levels of radiation will decay and diminish fairly quickly, so your best shot at avoiding serious radiation sickness or death is to hole up in an area that is heavily shielded from radiation emanating from deposits of radioactive fallout until the worst of the high levels of radiation have subsided, then remove yourself to an area that is upwind from the contaminated zone. There were huge numbers of people who survived the bombings of Nagasaki and Hiroshima, and they had no idea whatsoever of what was going on.

In the case of a "dirty bomb" detonation, in all likelihood there will not be high levels of radioactivity, such as from the detonation of a nuclear device or the breach of a reactor containment vessel, so the short-term danger will not be very high. However, the longer you remain in the contaminated zone, the greater your chance of ingesting radioactive contamination that may contribute to long-term negative health effects including cancers, tumors, chronic fatigue, depressed immune-system response, and untimely death. After a terrorist attack or nuclear power plant accident, unless you are very close to the site of the actual detonation, if you are armed with proper information and make good decisions, you stand a decent chance of coming out of your ordeal in relatively good shape.

Radiation and Protection Basics

In the event of an actual nuclear detonation, short-term high-level radiation will be a huge threat. This comes in two forms. The first is the radiation burst coming from the actual detonation, and the second is in the form of highly radioactive "fallout." You will have no control over the initial radiation burst, since that will travel at the speed of light, reaching victims before they hear anything or even have a chance to blink or shield their eyes. If possible, avoid looking at a blast's fireball. This will help prevent blindness caused by exposing your eyes to the thermal radiation emitted by a nuclear fireball. A nuclear detonation tends to create its own weather pattern, causing shifting winds and usually resulting in a rainstorm even if the detonation was on a clear day. It is absolutely imperative that you find shelter from direct contact with fallout and black rain, as they contain highly radioactive materials. Fallout poses threats from contamination through breathing and ingesting radioactive particles, as well as from exposure to direct radiation that is emitted from the fallout when it settles to the earth and on top of objects such as rooftops and cars.

The radioactive components of fallout that give off the most deadly radiation (gamma rays) decay very quickly. Fallout will lose about 90 percent of its gamma radiation after the first seven hours and will decay about 90 percent more over the next forty-eight hours (leaving only 1 percent of the original level of radioactivity), making it relatively safe for you to leave your place of shelter and seek a location outside of the contaminated zone. If you have the good fortune to have access to a true fallout shelter with adequate food, water, its own independent power source, and a HEPA-type air-filtration system, your safest course of action is to stay put for two weeks, at which point the gamma radiation will have subsided to roughly one-thousandth of what it was originally (Deyo 2006, 389).

Dense materials, such as earth, stone, concrete, and water, will provide the best shielding from gamma radiation emitted by freshly fallen radioactive fallout. For every 3.6 inches (9 cm) of packed earth, gamma radiation

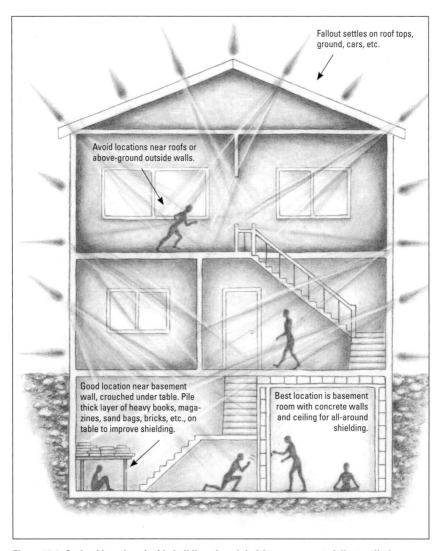

Fallout settles on roof tops, ground, cars, etc.

Avoid locations near roofs or above-ground outside walls.

Good location near basement wall, crouched under table. Pile thick layer of heavy books, magazines, sand bags, bricks, etc., on table to improve shielding.

Best location is basement room with concrete walls and ceiling for all-around shielding.

Figure 17-2: Optimal locations inside buildings for minimizing exposure to fallout radiation.

is cut by a factor of two. According to FEMA, the minimal recommended makeshift fallout shelter shielding is provided by the following equivalents: 5 to 6 inches (13 to 15 cm) of bricks; 7 inches (18 cm) of earth; 8 inches (20 cm) of hollow concrete blocks; 10 inches (25 cm) of water; 14 inches (35 cm) of books or magazines; or 18 inches (45 cm) of wood (Deyo 2006, 401). The more shielding the better.

For quick shelter inside existing buildings, a basement location is usually best, provided that air circulation is minimized to prevent the circulation of fallout into your shelter from outside. In general, the basement locations that will receive the fewest gamma rays will be sitting crouched against an earth-

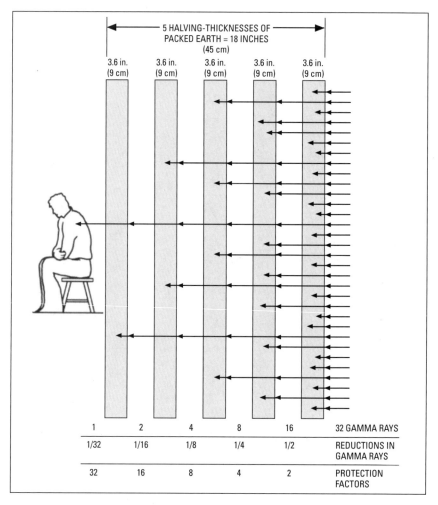

Figure 17-3: Shielding effect of packed earth. Each 3.6 inches of thickness of packed earth cuts radiation penetration by 50 percent. Source: Kearny, *Nuclear War Survival Skills*

protected wall to minimize the "angle of incidence" exposure to gamma rays entering through the more marginal radiation shielding provided by walls and ceilings that don't have an outer layer of packed earth (Kearny 1999). See figure 17-2 for the best locations for minimizing your exposure to radiation from fallout, when sheltering inside an existing building.

A true fallout shelter with HEPA-type air filtration, a protected supply of water, an independent power source, and a month's supply of food would be best, but if you already have all of that put together, then you are way ahead of the game and don't need to be reading this section of this book. In general, the center of the bottom story in a large multistory building would be a good location, unless the HVAC system is still active (unlikely) and circulating radioactive contaminated air throughout the building. Avoid ground floors along outside walls, floors located directly beneath roofs, and any other locations adjacent to where fallout may settle onto flat or gently sloping surfaces. The farther you are away from a highly radioactive gamma-ray source (such as freshly settled radioactive fallout), and the greater the thickness of dense shielding materials that separate you from that source, the better. A cave would be an excellent place in which to weather a nuclear storm. Simply stay as far away from the mouth of the cave as possible. Subway stations, underground areas in airports, and underground parking garages would also be good choices (steel and concrete in the walls and ceiling of a structure provide excellent shielding).

The idea is to get as much mass as you can between you and any location where fallout might settle. Remember, the distance through air does not matter. It is the distance that gamma rays travel through dense items such as dirt, stacked books, packed earth, water, steel, and concrete that matters most when it comes to blocking damaging radiation emanating from fallout (see fig. 17-3).

By pushing a sturdy table against a basement wall, and stacking a bunch of books and magazines on top of the table, you would significantly reduce the gamma ray exposure to anyone sitting underneath the table. Remember, the first couple of days, and especially the first seven hours, are the most critical times to try and get the maximum shielding from gamma ray radiation while the fallout is at its maximally lethal radiation intensity. After forty-eight hours, the fallout will have reduced to roughly 1 percent of its original radiation level. The more shielding you can take advantage of, and the longer the period of time, the better.

Protecting Yourself from Radioactive Contamination

The primary ways for radioactive contamination to lodge inside your body is to breathe it in through your lungs, ingest contaminated food or water, or absorb it through your skin. If you have access to a common painter's respirator with carbon-filter canisters (way better than nothing), an army surplus gas mask (better), or a hazmat gas mask (better), or a self-contained breathing apparatus (best), these will eliminate most or all of the radioactive particles from the air you breath. Their continuous use is highly recommended during the critical first forty-eight hours after a nuclear disaster, or if you need to travel through a contaminated zone during your evacuation. Running water through a water filter with a carbon-block cartridge will similarly filter out most radioactive components from drinking water, since they will generally be stuck to larger particles that are removed by the filter. Beware of drink-

Figure 17-4. High-quality HEPA filter by Austin Air. Photo courtesy of Austin Air

ing from contaminated open waters. After the World War II bombing of Hiroshima, thousands of people sought refuge in the local rivers and ponds, unwittingly ingesting large amounts of radioactive material from the contaminated water.

If you can't find shelter in a suitable basement room, I suggest you find a windowless room in the center of a building that has sheetrock or plaster on the walls (sheetrock is a dense material that is also quite effective at blocking air flow). Try to seal off the door, and any windows, with duct tape and plastic sheeting to minimize air penetration. If you happen to have access to a tank of compressed air, such as a scuba diver's air tank, you may open the tank's valve every so often to allow a supply of fresh air to bleed into the room, providing "positive pressure," which ensures that air primarily flows toward the outside from the room in which you are sheltering, thus preventing contaminated air from flowing into the shelter. If you must go outside, I suggest you shake your clothes often, change clothes at the door to your shelter, and leave your contaminated clothing in an entry area so as to minimize contamination of your shelter area. If you have a source for electric power, the use of a HEPA-type portable air filter will continuously sweep radioactive particles out of the air inside your shelter. The filter itself will become progressively more radioactive as it filters particles out of the air, so keep your distance from it.

If a breached nuclear reactor containment vessel is contaminating the area in which you are located, as was the case with both the Chernobyl and Fukushima nuclear reactor disasters, your best bet is to get out of the contaminated zone as soon as possible, since the radioactive fallout from the breeched reactor will continue to accumulate over time, and radiation poisoning has a cumulative effect. The longer you are in the contaminated area, the more radiation you will receive and the more radioactive material you will ingest or absorb into your body. You should do your best to avoid drinking contaminated water, breathing contaminated air, or ingesting contaminated food.

Radioactive heavy metals will be concentrated by the food chain, so the most dangerous kinds of foods with the highest levels of radioactive heavy metals will be dairy products and meat from animals that were grazing on feed that was contaminated by radioactive fallout from the nuclear disaster. In the case of Chernobyl, if the authorities had quarantined all of the meat, dairy products, and produce within the 58,000 square miles of heavily contaminated land, then they could have avoided the vast majority of hundreds of thousands of cases of deaths, massive birth defects, and chronic health problems attributed to ingesting radioactive materials from the Chernobyl fallout.

In the case of a terrorist's "dirty bomb," the primary danger is from ingesting radioactive contamination that could make you sick in the short term and cause cancer in the long run. There will be only small amounts of the highly radioactive gamma-type of radiation, which is a huge initial concern after a nuclear bomb detonation, but not in a "dirty bomb" detonation, so once the local winds have had a chance to clear out the radioactive smoke and dust particles from the detonation, your best bet is to get out of the downwind contaminated area as soon as possible. Filtering the air you breathe and the water you drink will improve your chances of avoiding ingestion of radioactive particles.

Building a Makeshift Short-Term Radiation Shelter

The easiest and most expedient makeshift fallout shelter is an improved basement-type shelter, where an earth-covered exterior basement corner wall forms the two main walls that are the starting point for your shelter. Using sturdy furniture, or quickly scavenged items like doors taken off their hinges and removed from upper household stories, the object is to build a small room-within-a-room, where you stack sand bags, books, wood, etc.—whatever dense materials you can find, on top of the roof and next to the two temporary side walls to improve their gamma-ray-shielding properties.

In his classic book, *Nuclear War Survival Skills*, Cresson Kearny suggests building a makeshift shelter by digging a 3-foot-wide by 4-foot-deep (1 m × 1.25 m) trench, covering it with 7-foot-long (2m) logs and heaping earth on top of these logs. A backyard ditch shelter can be built in a few hours by two people with picks and shovels, provided the ground is not frozen, too wet, or too rocky. The object is to try to provide at least 4½ feet (1.4 meters) of head height in the ditch, covered by at least 30 inches (.75 meters) of packed dirt covering. If the dirt covering is arched (see fig. 17-5), then the arch will take a lot of the load of the cross members holding up the roof of the shelter, and also provide better blast resistance. The shelter roof should be supported

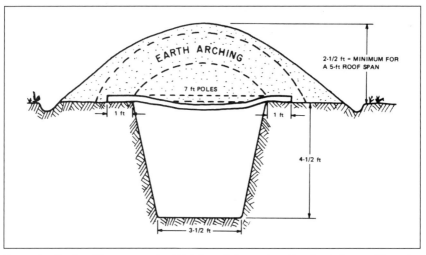

Figure 17-5. Earth arching over a makeshift fallout shelter roof enables the shelter to withstand higher blast pressures. Source: Kearny, *Nuclear War Survival Skills*

by 7-foot-long (2 m) wooden poles laid crosswise, or alternatively by doors scavenged from the home. If the trench is lined with plastic sheeting, it will be much less damp and much more comfortable inside the shelter. If available, plastic sheeting should be buried within the roof during construction to waterproof that too. Such a shelter would provide a protection factor (PF) of 300, meaning it would reduce the inhabitant's fallout exposure to gamma radiation by a factor of 300:1 as compared to a person out in the open with no protection at all!

Cresson Kearny's *Nuclear War Survival Skills* offers a multitude of basic plans for home fallout shelters, both the makeshift and permanent types, including plans for aboveground, as well as buried versions. Kearny also includes plans for homemade ventilation schemes and ventilation air pumps as well as a homemade fallout meter (the "Kearny Fallout Meter" also referred to as a KFM) that provides a low-cost reasonably accurate radiation-dose-rate meter, when combined with a watch to keep track of elapsed time. You may purchase the latest edition of Kearny's book from the Oregon Institute of Science and Medicine in Cave Junction, Oregon, or download each chapter for free at www.oism.org/nwss/index.htm.

Building a Makeshift "Safe Room"

In the event of a "dirty bomb" or a chemical spill/terrorist attack, your best bet for safety is to stay inside a relatively airtight "safe room" in the middle of your home (see fig. 17-6) for several hours until the toxic chemicals,

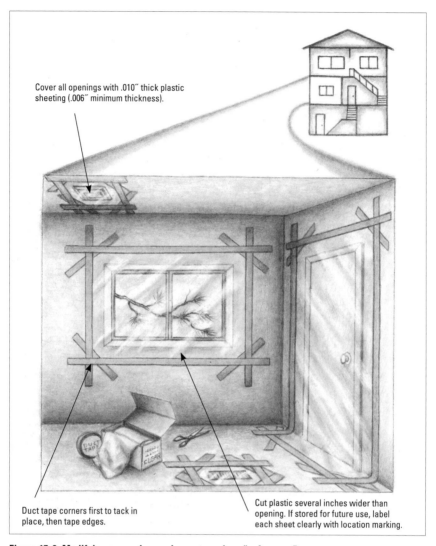

Cover all openings with .010″ thick plastic sheeting (.006″ minimum thickness).

Duct tape corners first to tack in place, then tape edges.

Cut plastic several inches wider than opening. If stored for future use, label each sheet clearly with location marking.

Figure 17-6: Modifying a room in your house to make a "safe room."

or radioactive cloud of particles, has had time to disperse. Unlike protection from fallout, the preferred location for a "safe room" of this type is located on an upper-story floor due to the fact that most toxic chemical gases are heavier than air and will tend to settle more toward the ground floors. Building your safe room ahead of time, with its own HEPA filtered positive pressure air supply, provides your family with a tested, highly reliable personal protected space. If I lived in an area near a chemical plant, or a metropolitan area that I suspected might be a terrorist target, this is the way I would go.

In that case, I would use 10-mil (.010"/.25 mm thick) polypropylene plastic sheeting and duct tape to cover all the windows, electrical outlets, and openings in the room to ensure it was airtight. I would also stock this room with a quality HEPA filter (see fig. 17-4) and a regulated tank of air to provide positively pressured filtered air inside your safe room. Cracking the valve on your air tank provides a small continuous air flow that creates a "positive pressure" in your safe room with the excess air leaving the room through the few cracks that were not 100% sealed by the duct tape and plastic, preventing any nonfiltered outside air from entering your safe-room space. A large-capacity deep-cycle marine-type battery, and a low-cost inverter, would provide a few hours of backup power for your HEPA filter in the event that the grid power goes out during a crisis. Make sure you store a port-a-potty in your safe room to allow people to relieve themselves, and perhaps one of those easily erected beach sunshade tents to provide privacy to people while relieving themselves. Don't forget water, snacks, and provisions for pets to also relieve themselves. Readymade filter systems for safe rooms are available from www.americansaferoom.com.

Even if you do not live in an area with a significant risk of chemical exposure or terrorist attack, it is still a wise choice to keep the duct tape and plastic sheeting on hand just in case. In the case of a local event necessitating the use of your safe room, a hastily sealed space will provide improved protection for several hours. However, if you did a very good job of sealing your room, you must consider oxygen depletion in a sealed room occupied by people. For a 100-square-foot 10 ft. × 10 ft. × 8 ft. (3 m × 3 m × 2.5 m) perfectly sealed room, occupied by four people, the maximum occupancy time, without a source of oxygen or outside filtered air, would be 2.5 hours tops (Deyo, 2006, 383). If you are staying inside a sealed temporary safe room that lacks an oxygen supply or source of filtered outside air, I suggest you set a timer every half hour to check for signs of oxygen depletion, including rapid shallow breathing, dizziness, headaches, foggy thinking, or weakness. Falling asleep in a tightly sealed room occupied by several people might mean that none of you ever wake up!

Special Supplies to Have on Hand to Cope with a Nuclear Incident

Potassium Iodide (KI)

Studies of people who have been exposed to radioactive fallout have shown a high rate of thyroid cancers and tumors, and that children and pregnant women are especially susceptible. The body uses iodine to make hormones in

Table 17-2. FDA Potassium Iodide Dosage Guidelines	
Adults and children over 150 lbs.	130mg
Children aged 3 to 18 (under 150 lbs.)	65mg
Young children (1 year to 3 years)	32mg
Young children (1 month to 1 year)	32mg
Infants (birth through 1 month)	16mg
(Source: FDA guidelines, effective as of 2005, courtesy of Anbex, Inc., manufacturer of IOSA KI tablets)	

the thyroid gland. Radioactive iodine is generated in nuclear explosions, and when unsuspecting people drink contaminated water, or eat contaminated food, radioactive iodine tends to be absorbed into the thyroid gland, leading to long-term generation of thyroid cancers and tumors. Potassium iodide (KI) treatments effectively saturate the thyroid with clean non-radioactive iodine so the body will not absorb radioactive iodine into the thyroid. A prescription is not necessary to obtain KI tablets, and they are available at many pharmacies and online locations. KI tablets are quite stable. They have an official shelf life of seven years, but in truth should last indefinitely.

Caution: Potassium iodide will not prevent or treat radiation-sickness symptoms. Its sole use is as a prophylactic to help prevent the long-term development of thyroid tumors due to the absorption of radioactive iodine, and must be administered during the period of exposure to radioactive materials, and preferably starting before exposure (it will do no good if administered later).

Prussian Blue

Since the 1960s, Prussian blue, originally made from Prussian blue dye, is a medicine that has been used to treat people contaminated with radioactive cesium or thallium. Prussian blue binds to these materials in the body, effectively acting as a chelating agent, helping the body to dump these materials into the intestine for elimination at about four times the rate that would naturally occur. Therefore, the use of Prussian blue decreases the amount of time the body will be subject to potentially damaging levels of these harmful materials. Unlike KI tablets, Prussian blue is a prescription-only medication designed to treat a specific type of contamination after it has occurred. The CDC has included Prussian blue in the Strategic National Stockpile, a special collection of drugs and medical supplies the CDC keeps on hand for times of national emergency. Prussian blue could be particularly helpful for treating people contaminated by a "dirty bomb" detonation.

Herbal and Alternative Remedies and Supplements

Vitamins C and E will help the body detoxify and repair soft tissues. People have reported that they have used hair-analysis tests to verify that MMS (see chapter 6) will help the body to eliminate heavy metals, so MMS could be a valuable self-help treatment to purge radioactive heavy metals from the body. Chlorella, an algae that is most effective when processed to its "cracked wall" form, and the herb cilantro are natural products that have been scientifically proven to chelate heavy metals, helping the body to eliminate them. In my opinion, an extremely valuable supplement for helping the body to detoxify and dump radioactive heavy metals is Modifilan (see www.modifilan.com). It is a seaweed extract made from a brown kelp that has been used to help Russian industrial workers clean heavy metals, and other toxins, out of their bodies. Developed in the late 1960s, Modifilan first came into widespread usage after the Chernobyl nuclear catastrophe. In addition to helping the body detoxify and dump heavy metals, Modifilan is also an excellent source of bio-available iodine, selenium, manganese and other essential minerals.

Dosimeter

In the event of a nuclear disaster, traditionally it has been quite difficult, or expensive, to determine how big of a radiation dose one has received. For the most part a "wait and see" attitude was employed in which, based

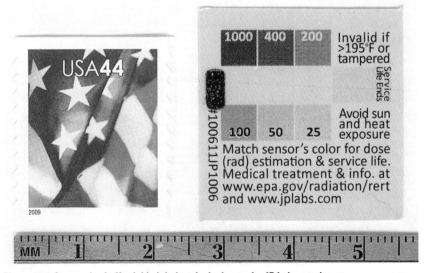

Figure 17-7. Stamp-sized affordable label-style dosimeter by JP Laboratories. Photo courtesy of JP Laboratories

upon your symptoms and distance from the nuclear event, one might estimate roughly how much radiation was received. However, after the Chernobyl accident it became clear that large numbers of people might need an inexpensive dosimeter that would provide a visual indication of the level of radiation exposure. One such device is a low cost (roughly $2 each) label from JP Laboratories that has a built-in color-coded meter. Much like those labels that read temperature by changing color, this label reads cumulative radiation dose by changing color (see www.jplabs.com).

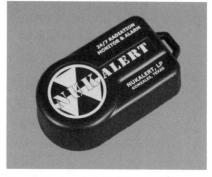

Figure 17-8. Key chain NukAlert audible radiation alarm and level meter. Photo courtesy of NukAlert

Another nifty product you may want to add to your radiation protection arsenal is called a NukAlert pocket key-chain device that detects elevated radiation levels and sounds an audible alarm that is calibrated in such as way as to provide an audible signal that varies corresponding with different levels of radiation exposure. This device is more expensive, running on the order of $150 each (see www.nukalert.com).

Gas Masks and Protective Clothing

If I lived anywhere near a chemical plant that stockpiled highly toxic chemicals, I would certainly plan on purchasing a supply of gas masks (with spare

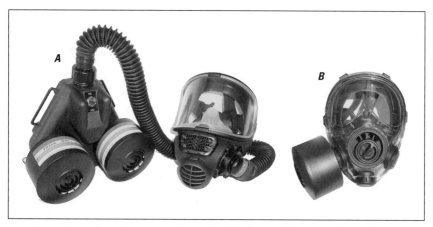

Figure 17-9. Gas mask with NATO spec 40 mm thread to fit standard NBC canisters. *A*, gas mask with battery-operated positive-pressure pump. *B*, standard gas mask. Photo courtesy of Approved Gas Masks

Figure 17-10: NIOSH approved P95 respirator ("poor man's gas mask").
Photo courtesy of Approved Gas Mask

canisters, see fig. 17-9), and possibly hazmat-style protective clothing for myself and family. I could say the same about living near a nuclear power plant, or a nuclear-fuel processing facility. Depending upon your budget, your location (do you live near a likely terrorist target?), your level of paranoia, and the state of the world, you may, or may not, feel it is necessary to do the same in case of a nuclear disaster.

I do have a few army surplus gas masks on hand—one for everyone in my family, and I certainly hope that I never need to use them. The respiratory protective gear that I use on a regular basis, and rely upon considerably, are NIOSH approved P95 respirators with replaceable carbon canisters that filter out over 95 percent of particulates as well as most toxic volatile organic compounds (see fig. 17-10). These types of respirators are reasonably inexpensive (on the order of $30) and are available at most hardware stores. They are often referred to as "painters masks," and I sometimes call them a "poor man's gas mask."

I use my P95 respirators whenever I am using spray paint, working with solvents, or dealing with heavy dust and/or toxic mold. Since we live in wildfire country, they also provide protection from smoke inhalation whenever the smoke settles in thickly from nearby forest fires. This style respirator has a soft rubber flange that conforms and seals against the face much better than the cheaper cloth or paper type of particulate face masks. P95-style respirators would do a decent job of protecting against breathing in radioactive contaminants in a nuclear disaster, provided the strap is adjusted tightly and the mask conforms well to the face. Of course, they will not provide the same level of protection afforded by a true gas mask, or hazmat mask, that covers the entire face, including the eyes, or a self-contained breathing apparatus (SCBA). There is a relatively new improvement to the traditional gas mask, which is a battery-operated, air-pumping filter pack that pumps purified air into the gas mask via a flexible hose. By providing a "positive pressure" inside the gas mask, this design practically guarantees that hazardous gases will not seep into the mask via a poor facial seal caused by facial hair, imperfect fit, loose strapping, etc. (see fig. 17-9).

True "air-purifying respirators (APR), also known as gas masks, can be purchased through safety supply houses, emergency-preparedness stores, or from specialty gas mask and protective clothing suppliers that you can find on the Internet. There are dozens of models and variations ranging from very basic to complete Military Spec "NBC" (Nuclear-Biological-Chemical) full-body suits with gas masks (see fig. 17-11). On the low end, protective clothing could be as simple as a set of inexpensive throwaway Tyvek painter's coveralls, which

Figure 17-11. Full-body complete Mil-Spec NBC protective gear.
Photo courtesy of Approved Gas Masks

won't really offer significant protection against chemical, nuclear, or biological hazards, but can be thrown out once contaminated. On the higher end are Mil-Spec suits designed to protect from nerve gas, biological, and nuclear hazards. For a huge selection of reasonably priced protective clothing sets, gas masks, and SCBA gear, check out www.approvedgasmasks.com. They even have full-body protective bags to cover your pets and babies!

Removing Radioactive Fallout from Drinking Water Using a Low-Tech "Dirt Filter"

According to Cresson Kearny, and testing at the Oak Ridge National Laboratory, simple earth filters will remove about 98 percent of the radioactive fallout contamination from water, and will do a better job of removing radioactive iodine than ion-exchange water softeners, boiling water distillation, or carbon filtration. I personally believe that a good high-quality pressed-carbon block filter would do an excellent job of removing radioactive fallout particulates, but perhaps this type of filter did not exist at the time that Kearny performed his tests back in the 1960s and 1970s. At any rate,

Kearny describes how to build an effective homemade dirt filter for removing fallout from drinking water as follows:

1. Perforate the bottom of a 5-gallon (20-liter) bucket, waterproof trash can, or similar container using a nail or drill.

2. Place a layer of clean pebbles or gravel about 1½ inches (4 cm) deep in the bottom of your container.

3. Cover the pebbles with a layer of porous cloth, such as burlap or a piece of a towel. Cut the cloth into a circular shape roughly 3 inches (8 cm) larger in diameter than the inside of the container.

4. Take soil containing some clay (nearly any soil will do) from at least 4 inches below the surface of the ground (nearly all fallout particles remain at or near to the surface, unless they fell on sand or gravel).

5. Pulverize the soil then gently press it in layers over the cloth that covers the pebbles, so that the cloth is held snugly against the sides of the can. Do not use pure clay, since it is not porous enough, or pure sand, since it is too porous. The soil in your bucket filter should be 6 to 7 inches (15 to 18 cm) thick.

6. Completely cover the top of the soil with another layer of porous cloth, such as towel material. This will keep the soil from eroding away when the water is poured into the filter, and the cloth will pre-filter some of the coarser particles. A dozen small stones placed on top of the perimeter of the cloth will help hold it in position.

7. Support the filter can on a rack of rods or sticks placed on top of a container to catch the filtered water.

The contaminated water should be poured into the filter can, preferably after letting it settle for a few hours to settle the largest particles to the bottom. As the filter flow rate starts to slow down, you may boost its rate by removing the top cloth, rinsing it in water, and replacing the top ½ inch (1 cm) of soil with new soil before putting the top cloth back into position. Eventually you will need to rebuild the filter with all new soil. Treat your water as usual (chlorine bleach drops, boiling, carbon filter, etc.) to ensure that it has no harmful organisms residing in it (Kearny 2006, 73).

If the threat of a nuclear disaster is keeping you up at night, I suggest you pick up a copy of Cresson Kearny's classic *Nuclear War Survival Skills*, which is considered to be the definitive guide to this subject. *Dare to Prepare* by Holly Drennan Deyo is another fine book that offers a summary of much of the information from Kearny's book plus a wealth of related material and updated information. These books both provide detailed information pertaining to radiation, fallout, shelter design, and preparations for surviving a nuclear disaster.

Be a Survivor!

❝Nothing in this world can take the place of persistence. Talent will not; nothing is more common than unsuccessful people with talent. Genius will not; unrewarded genius is almost a proverb. Education will not; the world is full of educated derelicts. Persistence and determination alone are omnipotent. The slogan "press on" has solved and always will solve the problems of the human race.❞ —Calvin Coolidge

Being a survivor takes guts, determination, perseverance, and action, but don't forget to smell the roses, enjoy the sunsets, and still have fun whenever you can. Remember to lighten up about your survival preparations. Play some music, laugh, be joyful, and make a game out of it whenever possible, especially if you have children whom you wish to instill with a certain amount of "buy in" to your survival training and preparations. This chapter delivers my final words of wisdom and encouragement, urging you to move forward along your path of preparedness and being a survivor.

The ability to laugh helps people manage under the worst conditions. As mentioned earlier, my father-in-law, Joseph Jussen, was both a Dutch resistance fighter during World War II and a Dutch marine during the Indonesian revolution. Having survived capture, torture, and numerous sticky situations where many of his comrades were killed, throughout his life he maintained a tremendous sense of humor and loved nothing more than to make people laugh. His favorite saying was, "Make you happy!" When you are kind, thoughtful, loving, and cheerful, not only will you be loved in return, but your comrades will bend over backwards for you, covering your backside, knowing that you would do the same for them.

Remember, there is more strength and security in numbers than there is in being the well-armed and well-stocked lone wolf. No single person can know it all, stay awake 24/7, have eyes in the back of his head, or be skilled at everything (medicine, survival, self-defense, healing, engineering, mechanics, gardening, hunting, trapping, cooking, sewing, etc.). With community, friends, and neighbors, you have a much larger pool of talent and resources than a single person or family can provide.

If you have the good fortune and foresight to be well stocked with both supplies and skills, and happen to experience a time of crisis and need, perhaps your knowledge and supplies will be a savior to many others. I firmly believe in the old saying that, "whatever goes around comes around." Much as some will say that their stash of stuff is for themselves and their family only, the truth is that disasters usually bring out much more of the best in people than the worst in people, and the spirit of sharing and selfless service is often what touches people's hearts the most, leaving effects that travel far beyond the limited scope of the experience, like waves in a pond rippling off into the distance from the splash of a small pebble. It would be a sorry world indeed, and many would question the value of living, if all we had to look forward to was a bleak *Mad Max* world where personal survival depended solely upon your ability to forage for grubs and worms while killing the other guy before he killed you first.

Follow Your Inner Compass

❝When I dare to be powerful, to use my strength in the service of my vision, then it becomes less and less important whether I am afraid.❞ —Audre Lorde

Through millions of years of natural selection, Mother Nature has bred into each and every one of us the most awesome survival tool—an inner compass capable of guiding us while making decisions that could literally mean the difference between life and death. I urge you to start developing and nurturing this personal built-in guidance system. You can do this by asking your internal guidance system to help you make decisions in your daily life, right now, today, while skies are blue and things in your world are still working reasonably well.

My mother in-law, Jackie Jussen, told me the following story. Orphaned at the age of five, Jackie was raised by her grandmother on a remote coffee plantation on the island of Java, Indonesia. Living far from any sizable community, her grandmother relied on natural herbal medicines. When a neighbor's son was deathly ill with malaria, Jackie's grandmother used her herbs to nurse him back to health. The neighbor was a Japanese immigrant and presented her with the gift of a kimono, which bore the seal of a powerful Japanese family.

Years later, during the World War II Japanese occupation of Java, civilians were forbidden to listen to the radio. All radios were registered with the state and fitted with official seals to indicate whether the radio had been used. Jackie's grandmother broke the seal on her radio so she could hear foreign news. When officials discovered the broken seal, she was ordered to appear in court. To maintain order and obedience, Japanese wartime justice was typically cruel and swift. Infractions, such as breaking the seal on the radio, usually resulted in a public beheading in the square immediately after sentencing. As her grandmother prepared to leave for the court hearing, an inner voice told her to wear the kimono. When the magistrate saw the seal of a royal family on her kimono, he asked her how she had come to own this kimono. Upon hearing her story, he reprimanded her, but spared her life.

If you are spiritual or religious, by all means pray and ask for help and guidance in your life from God, Jesus, Buddha, Allah, the Holy Spirit, or whatever other higher power you feel connected to. If you are not religious, you can still harness this inner compass simply through your intention and the desire to ask and receive guidance from within. One way to know if it is your mind/ego that is speaking, or if it is truly the voice of inner guidance, is the quality of the voice. If it is changing and wavering, you can be assured that it is your mind talking. If this inner voice is steady and steadfast, and has a calm unwavering quality, it is almost certainly your inner compass speaking. Most of the time this voice is rather quiet, but occasionally when there is extreme danger lurking nearby, it might feel as if you have an inner guide that is literally screaming at you. So, even though the "quiet" characteristic is often a good indicator, it is certainly not always the case!

Many survivors of life-threatening ordeals relate that at some point in their experience it seemed as if they suddenly tapped into an inner strength and a higher power that had not been there before—in all likelihood making the difference between life and death. Since we can't interview the ones that did not make it back alive, to see what their experience was, let us learn from those that did.

Be Brave and Steadfast!

❝I learned that courage was not the absence of fear, but the triumph over it. The brave man is not he who does not feel afraid, but he who conquers that fear.❞ —Nelson Mandela

It is easy to let your disaster prep plans slide when everything in your world seems to be going just fine. Just remember that you have picked up this book for a reason, and don't let your friends or family talk you out of it. So what if you spend a few days and some money planning ahead, and preparing to cope with potential future disasters that may never come? If they don't ever arrive, then you can thank your lucky stars, count your blessings, and be grateful that you never had to dig into your "disaster insurance policy." After all, who among us would regret never getting to use your car insurance policy because you managed to avoid ever being in an accident?

And if that day should ever come when you are stuck in a true disaster or crisis, think of how grateful you will be that your had the foresight, perseverance, and discipline to learn valuable new skills, make emergency plans, and stock up on provisions and tools to help you and your family cope with a variety of situations.

Don't worry, don't be scared, just be prepared! With preparedness comes self-confidence. It is much easier to be brave in the face of danger when you have the self-confidence that comes from learning and practicing skills, making preparations, and planning ahead to cope with a variety of likely scenarios. The bravery of a fool is easily shattered at the first encounter with difficulties, but the bravery of those who have practiced inner calm and awareness—who are in touch with their own inner compass and know they have done their best to plan ahead for friend, family, and self, is solid as a rock and not easily shaken.

Prep for Tomorrow, but Live for Today

I have always believed, and I still believe, that whatever good or bad fortune may come our way we can always give it meaning and transform it into something of value. —Hermann Hesse

Once you have made your plans, bought your provisions and gear, and stocked up on whatever amount of food you feel is needed to cover yourself and family for the foreseeable future, take a breather and pat yourself on the back, but don't forget to live! Remember, classic survivors tend to be joyful people with a positive, cheerful outlook tempered by a dose of practical realism. Don't let fear and paranoia consume your daily life to the point where you can't put your future concerns out of mind long enough to enjoy the simple pleasures in life. Remember, if the alarm bell of fear is ringing 24/7, you will be so accustomed to the noise that you won't be able to hear when your inner compass is desperately trying to gain your attention because a clear and present danger is just around the corner!

This is serious stuff, but don't take it too seriously. Make a plan, set some goals, and create a timeline that includes several milestones. Each time you reach a new milestone, reward yourself with a break and a breather. All work and no play will be hard on your friends and family, plus it will make your job of enlisting the "buy in" of others that much more difficult. No one likes a "stick in the mud." Your disaster prep, plans, and training are much more likely to succeed if you are part of a group with common goals and values, than if you are a survival team composed of me, myself, and I. The present moment is all you can ever truly have, so don't forget to take time to live and experience those precious moments between now and the time spent on future plans and preparations.

In closing, I urge everyone to do your best to change the world, *and* do your best to be ready for the changes in the world!

Appendices

1. Recommended Reading

Note: This is not an exhaustive list, but will give you a good start. Even though a few of the books overlap significantly in content, each author has their own areas of expertise and focus, providing information lacking in similar books.

Self-Reliant Living and Preparedness

If you are concerned with becoming more self-reliant in an increasingly unstable world, and perhaps being prepared to deal with longer-term societal breakdowns, then the following references could be quite helpful:

The Encyclopedia of Country Living: The Original Manual for Living Off the Land & Doing it Yourself by Carla Emery

When Technology Fails: A Manual for Self-Reliance, Sustainability, and Surviving the Long Emergency by Matthew Stein

Storey's Basic Country Skills: A Practical Guide to Self-Reliance by John and Martha Storey

How to Survive the End of the World as We Know It: Tactics, Techniques, and Technologies for Uncertain Times by James Wesley, Rawles (Editor of www.SurvivalBlog.com)

Country Wisdom and Know-How: Everything You Need to Know to Live Off the Land by the editors of Storey Publishing's Country Wisdom Boards

Dare to Prepare by Holly Drennan Deyo

When All Hell Breaks Loose: Stuff You Need to Survive when Disaster Strikes by Cody Lundin

Just in Case: How to be Self-Sufficient when the Unexpected Happens by Kathy Harrison

The Transition Handbook: From Oil Dependency to Local Resilience by Rob Hopkins

Back to Basics: A Complete Guide to Traditional Skills edited by Abigail R. Gehring

Survival +: Structuring Prosperity for Yourself and the Nation by Charles Hugh Smith

The Modern Homestead Manual: What It Really Takes to Succeed Beyond the Sidewalks and Power Lines by Skip Thomsen and Cat Freshwater

The Foxfire Books edited by Eliot Wigginton (the first six books in this series are quite valuable, but especially the first two)

Cooking with Stored Food

The Amazing Wheat Book by Learta A. Moulton
Cooking with Food Storage Made Easy by Debbie G. Harman
Just in Case: How to Be Self-Sufficient when the Unexpected Happens by Kathy Harrison
Cookin' with Home Storage by Peggy Layton and Vicki Tate
I Can't Believe It's Food Storage: A Simple Step-By-Step Plan for Using Food Storage to Create Delicious Meals by Crystal Godfrey
The Morning Hill Solar Cookery Book by Jennifer Stein Barker
Cooking with Sunshine: The Complete Guide to Solar Cuisine with 150 Easy Sun-Cooked Recipes by Lorraine Anderson and Rick Palkovic

Edible Plants and Wild Medicinal Herbs

Nature's Garden: A Guide to Identifying, Harvesting, and Preparing Edible Wild Plants by Samuel Thayer
The Forager's Harvest: A Guide to Identifying, Harvesting, and Preparing Edible Wild Plants by Samuel Thayer
Edible Wild Plants: A North American Field Guide, by Thomas S. Elias and Peter A. Dykeman
Identifying and Harvesting Edible and Medicinal Plants in Wild (And Not So Wild) Places, by Steve Brill, with Evelyn Dean
Edible and Medicinal Plants of the West, by Gregory L. Tilford
A Field Guide to Medicinal Plants: Eastern and Central North America (Peterson Field Guide Series), by Steven Foster and James A. Duke

Firearms and Self-Defense

Boston's Gun Bible by Boston T. Party
Survival Guns by Mel Tappan
The Little Black Book of Violence: What Every Young Man Needs to Know about Fighting by Lawrence A. Kane and Kris Wilder
Krav Maga For Beginners: A Step-by-Step Guide to the World's Easiest-to-Learn, Most-Effective Fitness and Fighting Program by Darren Levine, John Whitman, and Ryan Hoover
Complete Krav Maga: The Ultimate Guide to Over 230 Self-Defense and Combative Techniques by Darren Levine and John Whitman

Krav Maga: How to Defend Yourself Against Armed Assault by Imi Sde-Or and Eyal Yanilov

First Aid, Medicine, and Self Healing

Where There Is No Doctor: A Village Health Care Handbook by David Werner, Carol Thuman, and Jane Maxwell

Medicine for the Outdoors: The Essential Guide to First Aid and Medical Emergencies, 5th Edition by Paul S. Auerbach, MD

Medicine for Mountaineering & Other Wilderness Activities, edited by James A. Wilkerson, M.D, Ernest E. Moor, MD, and Ken Zafren, MD

Ditch Medicine: Advanced Field Procedures for Emergencies by Hugh L. Coffee

Wilderness Medicine: 5th Edition by Paul S. Auerbach, MD

Where There Is No Dentist by Murray Dickson

The Pill Book: The Illustrated Guide to the Most Prescribed Drugs in the United States edited by Harold M. Silverman, PharmD.

Prescription for Nutritional Healing: A Practical A–Z Reference to Drug-Free Remedies Using Vitamins, Minerals, Herbs and Food Supplements by James F. Balch, MD, and Phyllis A. Balch, CNC

The Encyclopedia of Natural Medicine, Revised 2nd Ed., by Michael T. Murray, ND, and Joseph E. Pizzorno, ND

Encyclopedia of Herbal Medicine: The Definitive Reference to 550 Herbs and Remedies for Common Ailments by Andrew Chevallier, FNIMH

The Herbal Medicine Maker's Handbook: A Home Manual by James Green

Herbal Antibiotics: Natural Alternatives for Treating Drug-Resistant Bacteria by Stephen Harrod Buhner

Holistic Herbal: A Safe and Practical Guide to Making and Using Herbal Remedies, by David Hoffman

Everybody's Guide to Homeopathic Medicines: Safe and Effective Remedies for You and Your Family by Stephen Cummings, MD, and Dana Ullman, MPH

Healing with Homeopathy: The Doctor's Guide by Wayne B. Jonas, MD, and Jennifer Jacobs, MD, MPH

The Cure for All Diseases, by Hulda Regehr Clark, PhD, ND

Growing Food

How to Grow More Vegetables: (and Fruits, Nuts, Berries, Grains, and Other Crops) Than You Ever Thought Possible on Less Land Than You Can Imagine by John Jeavons

All New Square Foot Gardening: Grow More in Less Space! by Mel Bartholomew

Four-Season Harvest: Organic Vegetables from Your Home Garden All Year Long by Eliot Coleman

The Winter Harvest Handbook: Year-Round Vegetable Production Using Deep-Organic Techniques and Unheated Greenhouses by Eliot Coleman

The Vegetable Gardner's Bible: Discover Ed's High-Yield W-O-R-D System for All North American Gardening Regions by Edward C. Smith

Gaia's Garden: A Guide to Home-Scale Permaculture by Toby Hemenway

Gardening When It Counts: Growing Food in Hard Times by Steve Solomon

The Encyclopedia of Country Living: The Original Manual for Living Off the Land and Doing It Yourself by Carla Emery

The Organic Gardener's Handbook of Natural Pest and Disease Control: A Complete Guide To Maintaining a Healthy Garden and Yard the Earth-Friendly Way edited by Fern Marshall Bradley, Barbara W. Ellis, and Deborah L. Martin

Seed to Seed: Seed Saving and Growing Techniques for Vegetable Gardeners by Susan Ashworth

The Humanure Handbook: A Guide to Composting Human Manure by Joseph C. Jenkins

Edible Forest Gardens: Ecological Design and Practice for Temperate Climate Permaculture, Volume Two: Design & Practice by Dave Jacke, with Eric Toensmeier

Periodicals

The following magazines have excellent articles on various facets of self-reliant living, plus numerous advertisements for useful products. You might want to check out their Web sites to see what they have to offer:

Back Home Magazine. Call (800) 992-2546 or see their Web site at www.backhomemagazine.com

Backwoods Home. Call (800) 835-2418 or see their Web site at www.backwoodshome.com

Countryside & Small Stock Journal. Call (800) 551-5691 or see their Web site at www.countrysidemag.com

Home Power Magazine. Call (800) 707-6585 or see their Web site at www.homepower.com

The Mother Earth News. Call (800) 234-3368 or see their Web site at www.motherearthnews.com

Survivalist Magazine. Call (866) 437-6570 or see their Web site at www.survivalist.com

Preserving and Storing Food

Ball Complete Book of Home Preserving: 400 Delicious and Creative Recipes for Today edited by Judi Kingri and Lauren Devine

Preserving Food Without Freezing or Canning: Traditional Techniques Using Salt, Oil, Sugar, Alcohol, Vinegar, Drying, Cold Storage, and Lactic Fermentation by the Gardeners & Farmers of Terre Vivante

Root Cellaring: Natural Cold Storage of Fruits and Vegetables by Mike & Nancy Bubel

Stocking Up: The Third Edition of America's Classic Preserving Guide by Carol Hupping

Wild Fermentation: The Flavor, Nutrition, and Craft of Live-Culture Foods by Sandor Elix Katz

A Guide to Canning, Freezing, Curing and Smoking of Meat, Fish and Game by Wilbur F. Eastman

Raising Livestock

Backyard Livestock: Raising Good, Natural Food for Your Family by Steven Thomas and George P. Looby, DVM

The Complete Guide to Small Scale Farming: Everything You Need to Know about Raising Beef Cattle, Rabbits, Ducks, and Other Small Animals by Melissa Nelson

Storey's Guide to Raising Chickens: Care, Feeding, Facilities by Gail Damerow

Salad Bar Beef by Joel Salatin

You Can Farm: The Entrepreneur's Guide to Start and Succeed in a Farming Enterprise by Joe Salatin

Storey's Guide to Raising Sheep: Breeding, Care, Facilities by Paula Simmons and Carol Ekarius

Storey's Guide to Raising Dairy Goats: Breeds, Care, Dairying by Jerry Belanger

Basic Butchering of Livestock and Game by John J. Mettler Jr. DVM

The Complete Herbal Handbook for Farm and Stable by Juliette De Bairacli-Levy

Veterinary Guide for Animal Owners by C.E. Spaulding, DVM

The Merck Veterinary Manual edited by Cynthia M. Kahn and Scott Line

Renewable Energy

The Renewable Energy Handbook: A Guide to Rural Energy Independence, Off-Grid and Sustainable Living by William H. Kemp

Photovoltaics: Design and Installation Manual by Solar Energy International

Solar Hot Water Systems: Lessons Learned, 1977 to Today by Tom Lane

Solar Water Heating: A Comprehensive Guide to Solar Water and Space Heating Systems by Bob Ramlow and Benjamin Nusz

Wind Power: Renewable Energy for Home, Farm and Business by Paul Gipe

Alcohol Can Be a Gas: Fueling an Ethanol Revolution for the 21st Century by David Blume

Biodiesel, Basics and Beyond: A Comprehensive Guide to Production and Use for the Home and Farm by William H. Kemp

Microhydro: Clean Power from Water by Scott Davis

Survival, Backcountry Travel, and Primitive-Living Skills

The SAS Survival Handbook: How to Survive in the Wild, in Any Climate, on Land or at Sea by John "Lofty" Wiseman

Primitive Wilderness Living & Survival Skills: Naked into the Wilderness by John and Geri McPherson

98.6 Degrees: The Art of Keeping Your Ass Alive by Cody Lundin

Wilderness Survival by Gregory J. Davenport

The National Outdoor Leadership School's Wilderness Guide: The Classic Handbook, Revised and Updated, by Mark Harvey

Mountaineering: Freedom of the Hills by The Mountaineers, edited by Ronald C. Eng

The Gift of Fear: And Other Survival Signals That Protect Us from Violence by Gavin de Becker

Nuclear War Survival Skills by Cresson H. Kearny

Mammal Tracks and Signs: A Guide to North American Species by Mark Elbroch

2. Recommended Resources

Note: This is not an exhaustive list, but will give you a good start. The sources listed here are reputable, but please realize that dealers do change over time and their listing here is not an official endorsement on my part.

General Survival and Preparedness Suppliers

B&A Products, 700 East Shawntel Smith Blvd., PO Box 1376, Muldrow, OK 74948; phone: (918) 427-3600; Web site: www.baproducts.com.

Best Prices Storable Foods, P.O. Box 3182, Quinlan, Texas 75474; phone: (903) 356-6443; fax: (903) 356-6233; Web site: www.internet-grocer.net.

Captain Dave's Survival Center, PO Box 72298, Durham, NC 27722; phone: (877) 413-2837; Web site: www.captaindaves.com.

C.F. Resources, PO Box 405, Kit Carson, CO 80825; phone: (719) 962-3288; Web site: www.cfamilyresources.com.

Emergency Essentials, 653 North 1500 West, Orem, UT 94057; phone: (800) 999-1863; Web site: www.BePrepared.com.

Epicenter Supplies, 384 Wallis St. #2, Eugene, OR 97402; phone (541) 684-0717; Web site www.theepicenter.com.

Freeze Dry Guy, P.O. Box 1476, Grass Valley, CA 95945; phone: (866) 404-3663; Web site: www.freezedryguy.com.

Major Surplus & Survival, 435 W. Alondra Blvd., Gardena, CA 90248; phone: (800) 441-8855; Web site: www.majorsurplusnsurvival.com.

Nitro-Pak Preparedness Center, 151 North Main St., Heber City, UT 84032; phone: (800) 866-4876; Web site: www.nitro-pak.com.

Powervision Emergency Food Storage Solutions, 128 W. Windsong, Pleasant Grove, UT 84062; Web site: www.permapak.net.

Preparedness Now, PO Box 148, Humansville, MO 65674; phone: (417) 754-1222; Web site: www.preparednessnow.com.

Ready Made Resources, 239 Cagle Road, Tellico Plains, TN 37385; phone: 800-627-3809; fax: 423-253-2113; Web site: www.readymade resources.com.

Safety Central, 311 East Perkins St., Ukiah, CA 95482; phone: (707) 472-0288; Web site: www.safetycentral.com. A preparedness superstore.

USA Emergency Supply, PO Box 4884, Chapel Hill, NC 27515; Web site: www.usaemergencysupply.com.

Walton Feed, Inc., 135 North 10th Street, Montpelier, ID 83254; phone (800) 847-0465; fax: (208) 847-0467; Web site: www. waltonfeed.com.

Goods for Simple Living

Lehman's. A major supplier of goods for simple living. Lehman's, PO Box 41, Kidron, OH 44636; phone: (877) 438-5346; Web site: www .lehmans.com.

Cumberland General Store. For a catalog, phone (800) 334-4640, or send $5 to: Cumberland General Store, PO Box 4468, Alpharetta, GA 30023. Web site: www.cumberlandgeneral.com.

Growing Food

Bountiful Gardens, 18001 Shafer Ranch Road, Willits, CA 95490; phone: (707) 459-6410; fax: (707) 459-1925; Web site: www.bountiful gardens.org.www.bountifulgardens.org

Fedco, PO Box 520, Waterville, ME 04903; phone: (207) 873-7333; fax: (207) 872-8317; Web site: www.fedcoseeds.com.

Gardener's Supply Company, 128 Intervale Road, Burlington, VT 05401-2850; phone: (888) 833-1412; fax: (800) 551-6712; Web site: www.gardeners.com.

Peaceful Valley Farm & Garden Supply, PO Box 2209, Grass Valley, CA 95945; phone: (888) 784-1722; fax: (530) 272-4794; Web site: www.groworganic.com.

Nichols Garden Nursery, 1190 North Pacific Highway, Albany, OR 97321-4580; phone: (800) 422-3985; fax: (800) 231-5306; Web site: www.nicholsgardennursery.com.

Park Seed Company, 1 Parkton Ave., Greenwood, SC 29647; phone: (800) 213-0076; fax: (888) 709-7333; Web site: www.parkseed.com, www.organicseed.com.

Richters Herbs, 357 Highway 47, Goodwood, Ontario, L0C 1A0, Canada; phone: (905) 640-6677; fax: (905) 640-6641; Web site: www.richters.com.

Redwood City Seed Company, PO Box 361, Redwood City, CA 94064; phone: (650) 325-7333; fax: (650) 325-4056; Web site: www.ecoseeds.com.

Seed Savers Exchange, 3094 North Winn Road, Decorah, IA 52101; phone: (563) 382-5990; fax: (563) 382-5872; Web site: www.seedsavers.org.

Guns, Ammunition, Etc.

Caution: Gun laws vary from state to state. Use caution when crossing state lines to purchase firearms, especially at gun shows, as arrests have occurred owing to violation of state laws concerning the purchase and transportation of firearms across state lines.

AIM Surplus, 3801 Lefferson Rd., Middletown, OH 45044; phone (888) 748-5252; fax (513) 424-9970; Web site www.aimsurplus.com.

Ammoman.com, 151 Cooper Road, West Berlin, NJ 08091; phone: (856) 767-8835; fax: (856)-767-3877; Web site: www.ammoman.com.

Bushmaster Firearms International, LLC, PO Box 556, Madison, NC 27025; phone: (800) 883-6229; fax: (336) 548-8736; Web site: www.bushmaster.com.

Cabela's, phone: (800) 237-4444; Web site: www.cabelas.com.

Cheaper Than Dirt, PO Box 162087, Fort Worth, TX 76161; phone: (800) 559-0943; Web site: www.cheaperthandirt.com.

Dan's Sporting Goods, #84, Route 380, Apollo, PA 15613; phone: (724) 727-2648; fax: (724) 727-2649; Web site: www.dansammo.com.

J&G Sales, 440 Miller Valley Road, Prescott, AZ, 86301; phone: (928) 445-9650; fax: (928) 445-9658; Web site: www.jgsales.com.

MidwayUSA, 5875 West Van Horn Tavern Rd., Columbia, MO 65203; phone: (800) 243-3220; fax: (800) 992-8312; Web site: www.midway usa.com.

Natchez Shooters Supply, PO Box 182212, Chattanooga, TN 37422; phone: (800) 251-7839; fax: (423) 892-4482; Web site: www.natchezss .com.

Miscellaneous Supplies

Approved Gas Masks (AGM) Box 9509, San Diego, CA 92169: phone: (877) 246-1010; fax: (301) 931-6655; Web site: www.approvedgasmasks. com. AGM offers a wide selection of in-stock gas masks, protective clothing, hazmat supplies, NBC kits, etc.

Basco, 2595 Palmer Ave., University Park, IL 60466; phone: (800) 776-3786; Web site: www.bascousa.com. Basco is a bulk supplier of food and water storage containers and seals.

KI4U, Inc., 212 Oil Patch Lane, Gonzales, Texas, 78629; phone: (830) 672-8734; Web site: www. ki4u.com. KI4U is an excellent source for potassium iodide, dosimeters, Geiger counters, plus other products and practical information relating to nuclear events and radioactive contamination.

New England Cheesemaking Supply Company, P.O. Box 85, Ashfield MA 01330; phone: (413) 628-3808; fax: (413) 628-4061; Web site: www .cheesemaking.com.

Life Sprouts, PO Box 150, Hyrum, UT 84319; phone: (800) 241-1516.

Shelter Logic, 150 Callendar Road, Watertown, CT 06795; phone: (800) 932-9344; fax: (203) 931-4754; Web site: www.shelterlogic.com. Shelter Logic (used to be called Cover-It) manufactures a multitude of different sizes and shapes of instant greenhouses, barns, sheds, garages, hangars, etc. Their structures range from small backyard varieties to huge structures for commercial growers and airports.

Nutrition & Healing

Frontier Natural Products Coop, PO Box 299, 3021 78th St., Norway, IA 52318; phone: (800) 669-3275; fax: (800) 717-4372; Web site: www .frontiercoop.com.

Herbs Pro.com, Universal Herbs Inc., 33453 Western Ave., Union City, CA 94587; phone: (510) 324-2900; fax (510) 324-5300; Web site: www .herbspro.com.

Herbalcom, 803 E. Lincoln Way, Ames, IA 50010; phone (888) 649-3931; fax (877) 818-4115; Web site: www.herbalcom.com.

Vitacost.com, 4780 North Lamb Rd., North Las Vegas, NV 89115; phone: (800) 793-2601; Web site: www.vitacost.com. This is a great source for a wide variety of highly discounted vitamins and supplements.

Dr. Clark Research Association, 8135 Engineer Rd., San Diego, CA 92111; phone: (800) 220-3741; Fax: (866) 662-0086; Web site: www .drclark.com.

Outdoor Clothing and Backcountry Gear

Check your yellow pages under "backpacking" for local suppliers of quality backcountry gear, or shop at the large suppliers listed below.

Cabela's, phone: (800) 237-4444; Web site: www.cabelas.com.

Campmor, Inc., PO Box 700, Saddle River, NJ 07458; phone: (888) 226-7667; Web site: www.campmor.com.

EMS (Eastern Mountain Sports), EMS Direct, 327 Jaffrey Road, Peterborough, NH 03458; phone: (888) 463-6367; Web site: www.ems .com.

REI (Recreational Equipment Inc.), 1700 45th Street, East, Sumner, WA 98352; phone: (800) 426-4840; Web site: www.rei.com.

Radio Equipment, Supplies, and Information

AES (Amateur Electronic Supply), 5710 W Good Hope Rd., Milwaukee, WI 53223; phone: 800-558-0411; Web site: www.aesham.com.

ARRL, the national association for Amateur Radio, 225 Main Street, Newington, CT, 06111-1494; phone: (860) 594-0200; fax: (860) 594-0259; Web site: www.arrl.org.

C. Crane Company, Inc., 1001 Main Street, Fortuna, CA 95540; phone (800) 522-8863; fax: (707) 725-9060; Web site: www.ccrane.com.

Ham Radio Outlet, 390 Diablo Rd., Suite 210, Danville, CA 94526; phone 877-892-1745; fax: 510-534-0729; Web site: www.hamradio.com.

Radio Shack, phone: (800) 843-7422; Web site: www.radioshack.com

Scanner Master Police Scanners Corporation, 260 Hopping Brook Road, Holliston, MA 01746; phone: (800) 722-6637; fax: (508) 429-0800; Web site: www.scannermaster.com.

Survival and Primitive-Living Skills

Aboriginal Living Skills School, PO Box 3064, Prescott, AZ 86302; phone: (928) 713-1651; Web site: www.codylundin.com. Cody Lundin's primitive-living skills school and Web site.

Alderleaf Wilderness College, 18715 299th Ave SE, Monroe, WA 98272; phone: (360) 793-8709; Web site: www.wildernesscollege.com.

Complete Survivalist, PO Box 9, Boynton Beach, FL 33425; phone: (866) 437-6570; fax (714) 455-2091; Web site: www. survivalist.com.

Earth Knack Stone Age Living Skills, PO Box 508, Crestone, CO 81131; phone: (719) 256-4909; Web site: www.earthknack.com. Robin Blankenship's primitive-living skills school.

Equipped to Survive, Web site: www.equipped.com.

Hollowtop Outdoor Primitive School, PO Box 697, Pony, MT 59747; phone: (406) 685-3222; Web site: www.hollowtop.com. Thomas J. Elpel's primitive-living skills school.

Hoods Woods, phone: (208) 665-5537; Web site: www.survival.com.

Prairie Wolf, PO Box 96, Randolph, KS 66554; phone: (785) 293-5310; Web site: www.prairiewolf.net. John and Geri McPherson's primitive-living skills Web site.

Society of Primitive Technology, PO Box 905, Rexburg, ID 83440; phone or fax: (208) 359-2400; Web site: www.primitive.org.

SurvivalBlog.com, Web site: www.survivalblog.com. James Wesley, Rawles, best-selling author and renowned survival expert edits this huge online forum and survival blog.

Survival-Gear.com, 2204 N. Horace Walters Rd, Raeford, NC 28376; phone: (910) 878-5722; Web site: www.survival-gear.com.

Glossary

4WD: Four-wheel drive (as in vehicle).

AC: Alternating current (type of electrical power).

AM: Amplitude modulation (type of radio wave and radio receiver).

APR: Air-purifying respirator.

AR-15: Civilian semiautomatic rifle variation of the U.S. Army M16 rifle.

Carbine: Similar to a rifle, but with a shorter barrel for easier maneuverability in close quarters (commonly used as a combat weapon).

CB: Citizens' band radio for two-way communications. Broadcasting on the VHF (very high frequency) citizens' band radio does not require a license. Very popular with truckers, and handy in emergencies.

CCW: Carrying a concealed weapon (usually in reference to a permit to carry such a weapon).

CDC: Centers for Disease Control (U.S. federal government agency).

CLP: Cleaner, lubricant, protectant. A mil-spec lubricant useful for cleaning, lubricating, and corrosion-protecting guns and other metal hardware, sold under the trade name Break-Free CLP.

CME: Coronal mass ejection. Massive amounts of high-energy particles launched from the surface of the sun to hurtle through space at high velocities. Typically associated with geomagnetic storms.

CPR: Cardiopulmonary resuscitation. A technique for manually maintaining breathing and blood circulation in the event of cardiac failure.

DC: Direct current (type of electrical power).

DCS: Digital control system (highly susceptible to EMP damage).

Dirty Bomb: A non-nuclear explosive device encased in highly radioactive material, specifically designed to spread radioactive contamination upon detonation.

EMP: Electromagnetic pulse.

EMT: Emergency medical technician.

EPA: Environmental Protection Agency (U.S. federal government agency).

ER: Emergency room.

FDA: Food and Drug Administration (U.S. federal government agency).

FEMA: Federal Emergency Management Agency (U.S. federal government agency).

FIFO: First in, first out.

FM: Frequency modulation (type of radio wave and radio receiver).

GPS: Global positioning system.

Grid: The nationwide electrical power distribution system.

GSE: Grapefruit seed extract, a broad-band antibacterial and antifungal extract available at most health food stores.

HDPE: High-density polyethylene, a common plastic used in milk and juice bottles, water containers, and most 5-gallon plastic buckets. Often manufactured as "food grade," but not always.

HEPA: High-efficiency particulate air (filter).

HILF: High-impact low-frequency (events). Events that don't happen very often, but if they do, their consequences are catastrophic.

Inverter: An electronic device that converts DC electric to AC (typical output is 110 VAC and /or 220 VAC).

IR: Infrared.

km: Kilometer, or one thousand meters. Equal to a distance of 0.6 miles.

KW or kW: Kilowatt, a metric unit of power equivalent to one thousand watts.

kV: Kilovolt, one thousand volts.

LDPE: Low-density polyethylene, a common plastic used to make plastic trash, sandwich, and grocery bags. Often manufactured as "food grade," but not always.

LDS: Latter-Day Saints, also known as Mormons.

LED: Light-emitting diode.

LR: Long rifle, commonly referring to a longer cartridge size with higher velocity and range than standard-size cartridge ammunition.

M4gery: Civilian semiautomatic version of U.S. military-issue 5.56mm NATO carbine. Typically with a 16" barrel to meet the U.S. minimum rifle-barrel length requirement, versus the 14.5" military-issue barrel, and a collapsing stock (pronounced "em forgery").

Mag: Magazine for a pistol or rifle to hold multiple rounds of ammunition.

MIL-SPEC or Mil-Spec or mil-spec: Military specification, as pertains to products made to exacting standards and specifications of military organizations.

MMS: Miracle mineral solution. A two-part solution that people claim helps the body to heal a wide variety of diseases and physical issues. Originally called miracle mineral supplement.

MRE: Meals ready to eat. Preserved military ration meals, typically packaged in extra-thick sealed plastic bags, ready to be eaten anywhere anytime.

mSv: millisievert, a dose-equivalent measurement of radiation.

NATO: North Atlantic Treaty Organization.

NBC: Nuclear-biological-chemical (as in devices to protect against contamination from any one of these types of contaminants).

NiMH: Nickel-metal hydride, a type of rechargeable battery.

NIOSH: National Institute for Occupational Safety and Health (U.S. federal government agency).

NOAA: National Oceanic and Atmospheric Administration (U.S. federal government agency).

NWS: National Weather Service.

Off-grid: Not connected to the power grid. Typically referring to homes in remote locations that are powered by solar power, wind turbines, gasoline or diesel generators, etc.

OSHA: Occupational Safety and Health Administration (U.S. federal government agency).

PLC: Programmable logic controller (highly susceptible to EMP damage).

PV: Photovoltaic. PV modules are solar panels that convert the sun's energy directly into DC electrical power.

PVC: Polyvinyl chloride, a common plastic used to make water and sewer pipe (among many other things).

RF: Radio frequency, or rimfire, depending upon context.

SCADA: Supervisory control and data acquisition (highly susceptible to EMP damage).

Scanner: A special radio that is designed to scan a wide variety of channels, typically in the police, fire, weather, and/or emergency bands, looking for active signals. Each model of scanner is usually designed to scan only a specific set of radio channels and bands.

SCBA: Self-contained breathing apparatus.

SPC: Storm Prediction Center, a branch of the NOAA.

S&W: Smith & Wesson, an American gun manufacturer.

TEOTWAWKI: The end of the world as we know it (acronym coined by Mike Medintz).

Transceiver: A radio that both transmits and receives.

UHF: Ultra high frequency.

USDA: United States Department of Agriculture (U.S. federal government agency).

USGS: United States Geologic Survey (U.S. federal government agency).

UV: Ultraviolet light, also known as a "black light."

VAC: Volts, alternating current.

VDC: Volts, direct current.

VHF: Very high frequency.

WHO: World Health Organization.

YOYO: You're on your own. When things fall apart, at least for a while, and the government is not providing essential services such as police and fire protection, and when the utilities are down, such as electrical power, gas, and water.

Bibliography

Abernethy, Iain. "Kicking: Below the Belt?" Available at http://www.shotokankata.com/ Articles/kicking_below_the_belt.htm. Accessed March 2011.

Allsopp, Michelle, Richard Page, Paul Johnston, and David Santillo. *Oceans in Peril: Protecting Marine Biodiversity.* Washington, DC: Worldwatch Institute, 2007.

Anbex, Inc. "New Dosage Guidelines [for potassium iodide]." Available at http://www.anbex .com/guidelines.php. Accessed March 2011.

Balch, James F., MD, and Phyllis A. Balch, CNC *Prescription for Nutritional Healing: A Practical A–Z Reference to Drug-Free Remedies Using Vitamins, Minerals, Herbs and Food Supplements.* New York: Avery Publishing Group, 1997.

Barker, Jennifer Stein. *The Morning Hill Solar Cookery Book.* Canyon City, OR: Morning Hill Associates, 1999.

BBC News. "Virtually Untreatable TB Found." September 6, 2006. Available at http://news .bbc.co.uk/2/hi/health/5317624.stm. Accessed November 2007.

————. "Fall in Tiny Animals a 'Disaster'." July 10, 2008. Available at http://news.bbc .co.uk/2/hi/uk_news/scotland/highlands_and_islands/7499834.stm. Accessed February 2010.

Bearak, Barry, and Celia W. Dugger. "Power Failures Outrage South Africa." *New York Times,* January 31, 2008.

Beck, Robert C., DSc. *A First Aid Kit of the Future: The Beck Protocol.* Kelowna, British Columbia, Canada: Sharing Health From the Heart, Inc., 2002.

Becker, Gavin de. *The Gift of Fear: And Other Survival Signals That Protect Us from Violence.* New York: Dell Publishing, 1999.

Belson, Ken. "Certainties of Modern Life Upended in Japan." *New York Times,* March 15, 2011. Available at http://www.nytimes.com/2011/03/16/world/asia/16japan.html. Accessed March, 2011.

Beshiri, Roland. "How Farmers Weathered Ice Storm '98," *Statistics Canada.* Available at http://web.archive.org/web/20060308012756/http://www.statcan.ca/english/kits/agric /ice.htm. Accessed February 2011.

Bosely, Sarah. "Are You Ready for a World Without Antibiotics?" *Guardian,* August 12, 2010.

Brill, Steve, and Evelyn Dean. *Identifying and Harvesting Edible and Medicinal Plants in Wild (and Not So Wild) Places.* New York: Hearst Books, 1994.

Brown, Lester R. *Plan B 4.0: Mobilizing to Save Civilization.* New York: W. W. Norton and Company, 2009.

Bubel, Mike, and Nancy Bubel. *Root Cellaring: Natural Cold Storage of Fruits and Vegetables.* Pownal, VT: Storey Publishing, 1991.

Buhner, Stephen Harrod. *Herbal Antibiotics: Natural Alternatives for Treating Drug-Resistant Bacteria.* Pownal, VT: Storey Books, 1999.

Burns, Max. *Cottage Water Systems: An Out-of-The-City Guide to Pumps, Plumbing, Water Purification, and Privies.* Toronto, Ontario: Cottage Life Books, 1999.

Catton, William R., Jr. *Overshoot: The Ecological Basis of Revolutionary Change.* Champaign, IL: University of Illinois Press, 1982.

Centers for Disease Control and Prevention. "Emergency Preparedness and Response: Fact

Sheet, Prussian Blue." Available at http://www.bt.cdc.gov/radiation/prussianblue.asp. Accessed March 2011.

Clark, Hulda Regehr, PhD, ND *The Cure for All Advanced Cancers.* Chula Vista, CA: New Century Press, 1999.

————. *The Cure for All Diseases.* Chula Vista, CA: New Century Press, 1995.

————. *The Cure and Prevention of All Cancers.* Chula Vista, CA: New Century Press, 2007.

CNN News. "America's Food Supply Vulnerable?; Saudi Arabian Oil and Terror," aired December 6, 2004. Transcript available at http://transcripts.cnn.com/ TRANSCRIPTS/0412/06/pzn.01.html. Accessed November 2007.

————. "Italy Recovering from Big Blackout," September 28, 2003. Available at http:// www.cnn.com/2003/WORLD/europe/09/28/italy.blackout/index.html. Accessed October 2007.

————. "Major Power Outage Hits New York, Other Large Cities," August 14, 2003. Available at http://www.cnn.com/2003/US/08/14/power.outage/. Accessed March 2008.

————. "Sagging Power Lines, Hot Weather Blamed for Blackout," August 11, 1996. Available at http://www.cnn.com/US/9608/11/power.outage. Accessed June 2000.

Coleman, Eliot. *Four-Season Harvest: Organic Vegetables from Your Home Garden All Year Long.* White River Junction, VT: Chelsea Green Publishing, 1992.

Colwell, Rita R., et al. "Reduction of Cholera in Bangladeshi Villages by Simple Filtration." *Proceedings of the National Academy of Sciences of the United States of America,* January 14, 2003. Available at http://www.pubmedcentral.nih.gov/articlerender.fcgi?artid=298724. Accessed December 2007.

Committee on the Societal and Economic Impacts of Severe Space Weather Events. "Severe Space Weather Events—Understanding Societal and Economic Impacts Workshop Report." The National Academies Press, Washington DC, 2008. Available at http://www .nap.edu/catalog.php?record_id=12507. Accessed September 2010.

Cummings, Stephen, MD, and Dana Ullman, MPH (contributor). *Everybody's Guide to Homeopathic Medicines: Safe and Effective Remedies for You and Your Family.* New York: J. P. Tarcher, 2004.

Danks, Lisa Marie. *Building Your Ark: Your Personal Survival Guide to the Year 2000 Crisis.* West Fork, AR: DAL Enterprises, 1998.

Department of the Army. Technical Manual TM 5-690, "Grounding and Bonding in Command, Control, Communications, Computer, Intelligence, Surveillance, and Reconnaissance (C4ISR) Facilities." Department of the Army, 2002. Available at www .wbdg.org/ccb/ARMYCOE/COETM/tm_5_690.pdf. Accessed December 2010.

Deyo, Holly Drennan. *Dare to Prepare!* Pueblo West, CO: Deyo Enterprises, LLC, 2006.

Diamond, Jared. *Collapse: How Societies Choose to Fail or Succeed.* New York: Viking Penguin, 2005.

Dickson, Murray. *Where There Is No Dentist.* Berkeley, CA: The Hesperian Foundation, 1999.

Duke, James A., PhD *The Green Pharmacy: New Discoveries in Herbal Remedies for Common Diseases and Conditions from the World's Foremost Authority on Healing Herbs.* Emmaus, PA: Rodale Press, 1999.

————. "Half the Story Is Worse Than No Story at All: Dr. Duke Responds to the *Washington Post.*" Unpublished letter sent to author, April 18, 2000.

─────. "Nature's Medicine: The Green Pharmacy." *Mother Earth News,* December/January 2000.

Earthquake Country Alliance. "Protecting Yourself During an Earthquake... Drop, Cover, and Hold on!" Available at http://www.earthquakecountry.info/dropcoverholdon/. Accessed February 2011.

Edwards, Roger. "The Online Tornado FAQ: Frequently Asked Questions about Tornadoes." *Storm Prediction Center,* May 2011. Available at www.spc.noaa.gov/faq/tornado/. Accessed May 2011.

Eisler, Peter. "Powerful New Pollutants Imperil Drinking Water Supply." *USA Today,* October 21, 1998.

Elias, Thomas S., and Peter A. Dykeman. *Edible Wild Plants: A North American Field Guide.* New York: Sterling Publishing Company, 1990.

Emanuelson, Jerry. "Getting Prepared for an Electromagnetic Pulse Attack or Severe Solar Storm." *Future Science,* LLC. Available at www.futurescience.com/emp/emp-protection .html. Accessed March 2011.

─────. "Nuclear Electromagnetic Pulse." *Future Science, LLC.* Available at http://www .futurescience.com/emp.html. Accessed March 2011.

Emery, Carla. *The Encyclopedia of Country Living: An Old-Fashioned Recipe Book.* Seattle, WA: Sasquatch Books, 1998.

─────. *The Encyclopedia of Country Living: The Original Manual for Living Off the Land & Doing it Yourself,* 10th edition. Seattle, WA: Sasquatch Books, 2008.

Farber, Dr. M. Paul. *The Micro Silver Bullet.* Houston, TX: Professional Physicians Publishing & Health Services Inc., 1998.

Foster, Dr. John S., Jr., Earl Gjelde, Dr. William R. Graham (Chairman), Dr. Robert J. Hermann, Henry (Hank) M. Kluepfel, Gen. Richard L. Lawson, USAF (Ret.), Dr. Gordon K. Soper, Dr. Lowell L. Wood, Jr., Dr. Joan B. Woodard. "Report of the Commission to Assess the Threat to the United States from Electromagnetic Pulse (EMP) Attack: Critical National Infrastructures." April 2008. Available at http://www .empcommission.org/. Accessed September 2010.

Fox News. "Man Claims Skin Treatment Turned Face Permanent Blue." December 20, 2007. Available at http://www.foxnews.com/story/0,2933,317564,00.html. Accessed January 2008.

Friedman, Kenneth, PhD *The New Silver Solution.* Alpine, UT: American Biotech Labs, 2006.

Global Footprint Network. *Living Planet Report, 2010: Biodiversity, Biocapacity and Development.* Jointly published by the Global Footprint Network, WWF, and the Zoological Society of London, 2010.

Goddard Institute for Space Studies. "Global Land-Ocean Temperature Index in .01 C." Available at http://data.giss.nasa.gov/gistemp/tabledata/GLB.Ts+dSST.txt. Accessed October 2007.

Godfrey, Howard. *Emergency Preparedness the Right Way.* Bowman, CA: BookSurge Publishing, 2009.

Golden Genesis Company. *Solar Electric Design Guide,* 1999.

Gonzales, Laurence. *Deep Survival: Who Lives, Who Dies, and Why.* New York: W. W. Norton and Company, 2004.

Goodall, Dr. Jane. "Remembering the Marshall Islands." Jane Goodall Institute, 2006. Available at http://www.pacificpeoplespartnership.org/marshallislands.html. Accessed March 2011.

Gray, Kevin. "Factbox: Dodging the 'Death Tube'-Tornado Survival Tips." Reuters, April 29, 2011. Available at http://www.reuters.com/article/2011/04/30/us-usa-weather-safety-factbox-idUSTRE73S7BU20110430. Accessed May 2011.

Greenpeace. "The Chernobyl Catastrophe Consequences on Human Health." Greenpeace, Amsterdam, The Netherlands, 2006. Available at http://www.greenpeace.org/international/en/publications/reports/chernobylhealthreport/. Accessed March, 2011.

Grossman, David C. MD, MPH; Donald T. Reay, MD; Stephanie A. Baker, MD. "Self-Inflicted and Unintentional Firearm Injuries among Children and Adolescents." *Archives of Pediatrics & Adolescent Medicine*, August 1999. Available at http://archpedi.ama-assn.org/cgi/content/short/153/8/875. Accessed March 2011.

Handal, Kathleen A., MD, and the American Red Cross. *The American Red Cross First Aid and Safety Handbook.* New York: Little, Brown and Company, 1992.

Hansen, James, Makiko Sato, Pushker Kharecha, David Beerling, Robert Berner, Valerie Masson-Delmotte, Mark Hansen, James, Reto Ruedy, Makiko Sato, and Ken Lo. "If It's That Warm, How Come It's So Damned Cold?" January 15, 2010. Available at http://www.realclimate.org/index.php/archives/2010/01/2009-temperatures-by-jim-hansen/. Accessed July 2010.

Harrington, H.D. *Edible Native Plants of the Rocky Mountains.* Albuquerque, NM: University of New Mexico Press, 1998.

Hellweg, Paul. *Flintknapping—The Art of Making Stone Tools.* Canoga Park, CA: Canyon Publishing Company, 1984.

Howden, Daniel. "Deforestation: The Hidden Cause of Global Warming." *Independent,* May 14, 2007. Available at http://environment.independent.co.uk/climate_change/article2539349.ece. Accessed May 2007.

Hoyos, Carola, and Javier Blas. "World Will Struggle to Meet Oil Demand." *The Financial Times,* October 28, 2008. Available at http://www.odac-info.org/node/4976. Accessed October 2008.

Humble, Jim. *The Miracle Mineral Solution of the 21st Century,* 4th Edition. Self-published E-book, Part I, Part II, and the "Author's Message." Available at http://miraclemineral.org and http://jimhumble.biz/. Accessed February 2011.

Hutton, Primrose, and Jerry Ongerth, PhD. "Performance Evaluation of Ten Commercially Available Portable Water Filters." Department of Water Engineering, University of New South Wales, Australia, February 1997.

Jonas, Wayne B., MD and Jennifer Jacobs, MD, MPH *Healing with Homeopathy: The Doctor's Guide.* New York: Warner Books, 1998.

Joseph, Lawrence E. "The Sun Also Surprises." *New York Times,* August 15, 2010. Available at http://www.nytimes.com/2010/08/16/opinion/16joseph.html. Accessed August 2010.

JP Laboratories. "Effect of Radiation." Available at http://www.jplabs.com/html/effect_of_radiation.HTM. Accessed March 2011.

Karter, Michael J. Jr. *Fire Loss in the United States During 2009.* Quincy, MA: National Fire Protection Association, 2010.

Kearny, Cresson H. *Nuclear War Survival Skills: Updated and Expanded 1987 Edition.* Cave Junction, OR: Oregon Institute of Science and Medicine, 1999.

Kelland, Kate. "Scientists Find Superbugs in Delhi Drinking Water." Reuters, April 7, 2011. Available at http://www.reuters.com/article/2011/04/07/uk-bacteria-superbugs-india-idUSLNE73600F20110407. Accessed May 2011.

Kennedy, Jack. "Could a Solar Storm Send Us Back to the Stone Age?" *Spaceports,* August 9, 2010. Available at http://www.csmonitor.com/Science/Cool-Astronomy/2010/0809 /Could-a-solar-storm-send-us-back-to-the-Stone-Age. Accessed September 2010.

King, M., PhD, and C. Bailey, MS. "Carbon Monoxide Related Deaths, United States, 1999–2004." *National Center for Environmental Health,* CDC, December 21, 2007. Available at http://www.cdc.gov/mmwr/preview/mmwrhtml/mm5650a1.htm. Accessed February 2011.

Klein, Gerda Weissmann. *One Survivor Remembers,* Los Angeles, CA: HBO & Teaching Tolerance, 1996. (Academy Award–winning film based on the book *All But My Life* by Gerda Weissmann Klein, 1957).

Kloos, Marko. "Why the Gun Is Civilization." Available at http://munchkinwrangler. wordpress.com/2007/03/23/why-the-gun-is-civilization/. Accessed March 2011.

Knudson, Tom. " 'Death by GPS' in the Desert." *Sacramento Bee,* January 30, 2011.

Laherrère, Jean. "Forecast of Oil and Gas Supply to 2050" *Petrotech 2003: Hydrocarbons Resources,* 2003. Available at http://www.oilcrisis.com/laherrere/Petrotech090103.pdf. Accessed May 2008.

Layton, Peggy. *Emergency Food Storage Survival Handbook: Everything You Need to Know to Keep Your Family Safe in a Crisis.* New York: Three Rivers Press, 2002.

Lean, Geoffrey. "Global Warming Is Three Times Faster Than Worst Prediction." *Independent,* June 4, 2007. Available at http://environment.independent.co.uk/climate_ change/article2609305.ece. Accessed June 2007.

Le Baron, Wayne. *Preparation for Nuclear Disaster.* Commack, NY: Nova Science Publishers, 1998.

Lindemann, Peter A. "Colloidal Silver: A Closer Look." Available at http://www.elixa.com /silver/lindmn.htm. Accessed August 2006.

Long, Laurie Ecklund. *My Life in a Box: A Life Organizer* (third edition). Fresno, CA: AGL Publishing, 2009.

Lucas, Rex A. *Men in Crisis: A Study of a Mine Disaster.* New York: Basic Books, 1969.

Lundin, Cody. *When All Hell Breaks Loose: Stuff You Need to Survive When Disaster Strikes.* Layton, UT: Gibbs Smith, Publisher, 2007.

———. *98.6 Degrees: The Art of Keeping Your Ass Alive.* Layton, UT: Gibbs Smith, Publisher, 2003.

Macalister, Terry. "US Military Warns Oil Output May Dip Causing Massive Shortages by 2015." *Guardian,* April 11, 2010. Available at http://www.guardian.co.uk/business/2010 /apr/11/peak-oil-production-supply. Accessed April 2010.

Maclean's. "Kobe Earthquake," January 30, 1995. Available at http:// thecanadianencyclopedia.com/index.cfm?PgNm=TCEParams=M1ARTM0010379. Downloaded 9/22/2007.

McCaughey, Betsy. "To Catch a Deadly Germ." *New York Times,* November 14, 2006.

McPherson, John, and Geri McPherson. *Primitive Wilderness Living and Survival Skills: Naked Into the Wilderness.* Randolph, KS: Prairie Wolf, 1993.

———. *Primitive Wilderness Skills, Applied and Advanced.* Randolph, KS: Prairie Wolf, 1999.

Metcalf, Mark. *Colloidal Silver: Making and Using Your Own.* Forest Grove, OR: Silver Solutions, 1998.

Miller, Dr. Robert. "Hurricane Katrina: Communications & Infrastructure Impacts." From a compilation of the Proceedings of the First Annual Homeland Defense and Homeland

Security Conference. U.S. Army War College. Available at www.carlisle.army.mil/... /Hurricane%20Katrina%20Communications%20&%20Infrastructure%20Impacts.pdf. Accessed March 2011.

Miller, Jeremy. "Boston's Earthquake Problem." *Boston Globe,* May 28, 2006. Available at http://www.boston.com/news/globe/magazine/articles/2006/05/28/bostons_earthquake_ problem/. Accessed July 2007.

Mueller, John. "Is There Still a Terrorist Threat?: The Myth of the Omnipresent Enemy." *Foreign Affairs,* The Council on Foreign Relations, September/October 2006. Available at http://www .foreignaffairs.org/20060901facomment85501/john-mueller/is-there-still-a-terrorist-threat -the-myth-of-the-omnipresent-enemy.html?mode=print. Accessed March 2008.

Muller, Robert. *Most of All, They Taught Me Happiness.* Garden City, NY: Doubleday Company, 1978.

Mullin, Ray C. *House Wiring with the National Electrical Code: Based on the 1999 National Electrical Code.* Albany, NY: Delmar Publishers, 1999.

Mumford, Stephen D. *Infallibility and the Population Issue.* From an address to Population Strategy Meeting IV, Barbara Jordan Conference Center Kaiser Family Foundation Washington, DC, October 4, 2010. Available at http://www.populationmedia. org/2010/10/27/infallibility-and-the-population-problem/. Accessed October 2010.

Murray, Michael T., and Joseph E. Pizzorno, N.D. *The Encyclopedia of Natural Medicine,* 2nd edition. Rocklin, CA: Prima Publishing, 1997.

Naiman, Ingrid. "Artemisia annua." Available at http://www.cancersalves.com/botanical_ approaches/individual_herbs/artemisia.html. Accessed January 2008.

National Fire Protection Agency (NFPA). "Fire Extinguishers." November 2001. Available at http://www.nfpa.org/itemDetail.asp?categoryID=277&itemID=18264&URL=Safe ty%20Information/For%20consumers/Fire%20&%20safety%20equipment/Fire%20 extinguishers. Accessed February 2011.

New York Times. "Experts Mostly Back Way U.S. Reacted in TB Case." July 5, 2007. Available at http://www.nytimes.com/ 2007/07/05/us/05tb.html?_r=1oref=slogin. Accessed July 2007.

————."Study Sees 'Global Collapse' of Fish Species." November 3, 2006. Available at http://www.nytimes.com/ 2006/11/03/science/03fish.html. Accessed November 2008.

————. "TB Patient Is Isolated after Taking Two Flights." May 30, 2007. Available at http://www.nytimes.com/2007/05/30/us/30tb.html?ex=1338177600en=24ae4499127b61 9cei=5088partner=rssnytemc=rss. Accessed May 2007.

————. "Until All the Fish Are Gone." January 21, 2008. Available at http://www .nytimes.com/2008/01/21/opinion/21mon1.html?scp=1sq=st=nyt. Accessed January 2008.

NOAA (National Oceanic and Atmospheric Administration). "NOAA: 2010 Tied For Warmest Year on Record." NOAA, 2011. Available at http://www.noaanews.noaa.gov /stories2011/20110112_globalstats.html. Accessed May 2011.

Null, Gary, PhD, Carolyn Dean, MD, ND, Martin Feldman, MD, Deborah Raiso, MD, and Dorothy Smith, PhD. *Death by Medicine, Part I and Part II.* Available at http://www .healthe-livingnews.com/articles/death_by_medicine_part_1.html and http://www.healthe -livingnews.com/articles/death_by_medicine_part_2.html. Downloaded February 2011.

Parenti, Christian. "Nuclear Hubris: Could Japan's Disaster Happen Here?" *The Nation,* March 14, 2011. Available at http://www.thenation.com/article/159213/nuclear-hubris -could-japans-disaster-happen-here. Accessed March 2011.

Party, Boston T. *Boston's Gun Bible.* Gillette, WY: Javelin Press, 2002.

Perko, Sandra J., PhD, CCN. *The Homeopathic Treatment of Influenza: Surviving Influenza Epidemics and Pandemics Past, Present, and Future with Homeopathy—Special Bird Flu Edition.* San Antonio, TX: Benchmark Homeopathic Publications, 2005.

Pfeiffer, Dale Allen. *Eating Fossil Fuels: Oil, Food, and the Coming Crisis in Agriculture.* Gabriola Island, British Columbia, Canada: New Society Publishers, 2006.

Platt, Anne McGinn. "Water-Borne Killers." *World Watch,* March/April 1996.

Plumer, Brad. "Is There Enough Food Out There for Nine Billion People?" *The New Republic,* February 3, 2010. Available at http://www.tnr.com/blog/the-vine/there-enough -food-out-there-nine-billion-people. Accessed November 2010.

Population Information Network (POPIN) of the United Nations Population Division. "World Population Growth From Year 0 to Stabilization," June 7, 1994. Available at gopher://gopher.undp.org:70/00/ungophers/popin/wdtrends/histor. Accessed April 2000.

Pugliese, Michael, CMR, CMT. *The Homeowner's Guide to Mold.* Kingston, MA: RS Means Company, Reed Construction Data, 2006.

Radabaugh, Joe. "Making and Using a Solar Cooker." *Backwoods Home Magazine,* Issue 30, Nov/Dec 1994. Available at http://www.backwoodshome.com/articles/radabaugh30.html. Downloaded February 2011.

Radiation Emergency Assistance Training Center. "Guidance for Radiation Accident Management." Available at http://orise.orau.gov/reacts/guide/injury.htm#biological. Accessed March 2011.

RAINN (Rape, Abuse, & Incest National Network). "Who are the Victims? Breakdown by Gender and Age." Available at http://www.rainn.org/get-information/statistics/sexual -assault-victims. Accessed March 2011.

Rawles, James Wesley. *How to Survive the End of the World as We Know It: Tactics, Techniques, and Technologies for Uncertain Times.* New York: Plume/Putnam Penguin Group, 2009.

Read, Piers Paul. *Alive: The Story of the Andes Survivors.* New York: Avon Books, 1992.

Renders, Eileen, N.D. *Food Additives, Nutrients, and Supplements A-To-Z: A Shopper's Guide.* Santa Fe, NM: Clear Light Publishers, 1999.

Robertson, Dougal. *Survive the Savage Sea.* New York: Bantam Books, 1973.

Rosen, Gary, PhD, and James Schaller, MD. *When Traditional Medicine Fails: Your Guide to Mold Toxins.* Tampa, FL: Hope Academic Press, 2006.

Runyon, Linda. *A Survival Acre.* Phoenix, AZ: APOA Books, 1995.

Sachs, Allan, DC, CCN. *The Authoritative Guide to Grapefruit Seed Extract: A Breakthrough in Alternative Treatment for Colds, Infections, Candida, Allergies, Herpes, and Many Other Ailments.* Mendocino, CA: LifeRhythm, 1997.

Sack, Kevin. "Deadly Bacteria Found to Be More Common." *New York Times,* October 17, 2007.

Salvato, Joseph A. *Environmental Engineering and Sanitation.* New York: John Wiley and Sons, 1982.

Sands, David R. "Global Food Riots Turn Deadly." *Washington Times,* April 10, 2008.

Santini, Jean-Louis. "Scientists Warn Research Slowdown Poses Global Threat." *AFP,* September 13, 2010. Available at http://www.google.com/hostednews/afp/article /ALeqM5jpSCk6SJcrl-MfAnLpYV2CQFO8UA. Accessed October 2010.

Sardone, Susan Breslow. "Sea Sick: The Norwalk Virus Strikes." *Your Guide to Honeymoons/ Romantic Travel.* Available at http://www. honeymoons.about.com/od/cruising/a/Seasick. htm. Accessed December 2007.

Schultz, Stefan. "Military Study Warns of a Potentially Drastic Oil Crisis." *Spiegel,* September 1, 2010. Available at http://www.spiegel.de/international/germany/0,1518,715138,00 .html. Accessed September 2010.

Science Daily. "Mayo Clinic Study Implicates Fungus as Cause of Chronic Sinusitis," September 10, 1999. Available at http://www.sciencedaily.com/releases/1999/09 /990910080344.htm. Accessed January 2008.

Seager, Ashley. "Steep Decline in Oil Production Brings Risk of War and Unrest, Says New Study." *Guardian Unlimited,* October 22, 2007. Available at http://www.guardian.co.uk /oil/story/0%2C%2C2196435%2C00.html. Accessed October 2007.

SEMP (Suburban Emergency Management Project). "The Catastrophic 1953 North Sea Flood of the Netherlands." January 11, 2006. Available at http://www.semp.us /publications/biot_reader.php?BiotID=317. Downloaded March 2008.

Sharing Health From the Heart. *A First Aid Kit of the Future: The Beck Protocol.* Thousand Oaks, CA: Sharing From the Heart/The Reality Zone, 2007.

Shearer, Harry. "New Orleanians Learn They Have to Help Themselves Rebuild after the Worst Disaster to Shatter Their World." *San Francisco Chronicle,* August 26, 2007.

Siebert, Al, PhD. *The Survivor Personality: Why Some People Are Stronger, Smarter, and More Skillful at Handling Life's Difficulties . . . and How You Can Be Too.* New York: The Berkeley Publishing Group, 1996.

Sillin, John O. "The Blackout of 2003: Why We Fell into the Heart of Darkness." *Public Utilities Reports, Inc.,* September 15, 2003. Available at http://www.pur.com/pubs/4251. cfm. Accessed October 2007.

Silverfacts.com. "Silver Safety," updated August 20, 2007. Available at http://www.silverfacts .com/safety.html. Downloaded January 2008.

Silverman, S. M., and E. W. Cliver. "Low-latitude auroras: the magnetic storm of 14-15 May 1921." *Journal of Atmospheric and Solar-Terrestrial Physics* 63, 2001.

Sobsey, Mark D. "Managing Water in the Home: Accelerated Health Gains from Improved Water Supply." World Health Organization, 2002. Available at http://whqlibdoc.who.int /hq/2002/WHO_SDE_WSH_02.07.pdf. Downloaded February 2008.

Spigarelli, Jack A. *Crisis Preparedness Handbook: A Comprehensive Guide to Home Storage and Physical Survival.* Alpine, UT: Cross-Current Publishing, 2002.

Spotts, Pete. "Lessons from the Wreckage: How Alabama Could Help Tornado Preparedness." *Christian Science Monitor,* May 4, 2011. Available at http://www.csmonitor .com/USA/2011/0504/Lessons-from-the-wreckage-How-Alabama-could-help-tornado -preparedness. Accessed May 2011.

Stein, Matthew. *When Technology Fails: A Manual for Self-Reliance, Sustainability, and Surviving the Long Emergency.* White River Junction, VT: Chelsea Green Publishing Company, 2008.

Stern, Nicholas. *The Economics of Climate Change: The Stern Review.* Cambridge, UK: Cambridge University Press, 2007.

Stevens, James Talmage. *Making the Best of Basics: Family Preparedness Handbook.* Seattle, WA: Gold Leaf Press, 1997.

Still, Dean. "Larry Winiarski's Rocket Stove Principles." April 2002. Available at http://www .bioenergylists.org/stovesdoc/Still/Rocket%20Stove/Principles.html. Downloaded February 2011.

Tappan, Mel. *Survival Guns.* Boulder, CO: Paladin Press, 2009.

Tebbetts, Charles. *Self-Hypnosis and Other Mind-Expanding Techniques.* Glendale, CA: Westwood Publishing Company, 1997.

Tierney, Kathleen J., and Goltz, James D. *Emergency Response: Lessons Learned from the Kobe Earthquake.* Disaster Research Center, 1997.

Torassa, Ulysses. "Berkeley Clinic Finds Hardy Bugs in Infections: Antibiotic Resistance Also Seen in Midwest." *San Francisco Chronicle,* October 14, 2001.

Touber, Tijn, and Kim Ridley. "Could Homeopathy Prevent a Pandemic?" *Ode Magazine,* January 2006.

Tzu, Sun. *The Art of War.* Lindenhurst, NY: Tribeca Books, 2011.

Underwood, John. "Fire Resistant Details: Studying the Houses That Survived the 1993 Laguna Beach Fire Storm Yields Lessons in Building to Withstand the Heat." FineHomebuilding.com. Available at http://www.taunton.com/finehomebuilding/how-to /articles/fire-resistant-details.aspx. Accessed August 2007.

University of Michigan Health System. "Gun Safety for Kids and Youth." Available at http:// www.med.umich.edu/yourchild/topics/guns.htm. Accessed March 2011.

U.S. Census Bureau. "U.S. and World Population Clocks – POPClocks" Available at http:// www.census.gov/main/www/popclock.html. Accessed December 7, 2007.

U.S. Department of Agriculture, National Institute of Food and Agriculture. "About Us: Introduction" Available at http://www.csrees.usda.gov/qlinks/extension.html. Accessed May 2011.

U.S. Environmental Protection Agency. "Health Effects: Radiation Protection." Available at http://www.epa.gov/radiation/understand/health_effects.html. Accessed March, 2011.

U.S. Joint Forces Command. "The Joint Operating Environment (JOE) 2010." Available at http://www.fas.org/man/eprint/joe2010.pdf. Accessed November 8, 2010.

Vidal, John. "Nuclear's Green Cheerleaders Forget Chernobyl at Our Expense: Pundits Who Downplay the Risks of Radiation are Ignoring the Casualties of the Past. Fukushima's Meltdown May Be Worse." *Guardian,* April 1, 2011. Available at http://www.guardian.co.uk /commentisfree/2011/apr/01/fukushima-chernobyl-risks-radiation/print. Accessed May 2011.

————. "Global Food Crisis Looms as Climate Change and Fuel Shortages Bite." *Guardian,* November 2, 2007. Available at http://www.guardian.co.uk/environment/2007 /nov/03/food.climatechange. Accessed December 2007.

Vorhis, Dan. "Portable Water Filters: A Designer's Perspective," Seattle, Washington, 1997. Available at http://www.marathonceramics.com/designrev.html. Accessed December 2, 1999.

Wackernagel, Mathis, et al. "Tracking the Ecological Overshoot of the Human Economy." *Proceedings of the National Academy of Sciences* (PNAS), vol. 99, no. 14, 2002. Available at http://www.pnas.org/cgi/reprint/142033699v1. Accessed March 2008.

Wackernagel, Mathis, and William Rees. *Our Ecological Footprint: Reducing Human Impact on the Earth.* Gabriola Island, British Columbia, Canada: New Society Publishers, 1996.

Wall Street Journal. "Climate Changes: MIT Study Says Temperatures Could Rise Twice as Much." May 19, 2009. Available at http://blogs.wsj.com/ environmentalcapital/2009/05/19/climate-changes-mit-study-says-temperatures-could -rise-twice-as-much/. Accessed May 2009.

Weiss, Eric A. MD. *A Comprehensive Guide to Wilderness and Travel Medicine.* Oakland, CA: Adventure Travel Kits, 1997.

Whittaker, John C. *Flintknapping: Making and Understanding Stone Tools.* Austin, TX: University of Texas Press, 1994.

Wigginton, Eliot, ed. *Foxfire 5: Iron Making, Blacksmithing, Flintlock Rifles, Bear Hunting.* New York: Anchor Books, Doubleday, 1979.

Wikipedia. "Northeast Blackout of 2003." Available at http://en.wikipedia.org/wiki/2003_North_America_blackout. Accessed July 2007.

Wilderness Medicine Newsletter. "Heat Loss Through the Head and Hypothermia." Available at http://wildernessmedicinenewsletter.wordpress.com/2007/02/14/heat-loss-through-the-head-and-hypothermia/. Accessed February 2011.

Wilkerson, James A. MD, ed. *Medicine for Mountaineering & Other Wilderness Activities.* Seattle, WA: The Mountaineers, 1992.

Wiseman, John. *The SAS Survival Handbook: How to Survive in the Wild, in Any Climate, on Land or at Sea.* London: Harper Collins Publishers, 1996.

Worthington, Amy. "The Radiation Poisoning of America." *Idaho Observer,* October 7, 2007. Available at http://www.worldhealth.net/p/the-radiation-poisoning-of-america.html. Accessed January 2008.

Index

abdominal wounds, 94
Aboriginal Living Skills School, 355
abrasions, 92
acorns, 165
AEDs (automatic external defibrillators), 89–90
AES (Amateur Electronic Supply), 354
AIM Surplus, 352
Alderleaf Wilderness College, 355
Alive, 142
aloe vera gel, 120
amaranth, 168–169
American Biotech Labs (ABL), 135–136
Ammoman.com, 352
animal bites, 103
antennas, 227
antibiotic-resistant bacteria, 6–7, 115, 118–119, 132
antibiotics, 25–26
Approved Gas Masks (AGM), 353
argyria, 132, 136
arnica, 120
ARRL, 354
ASAP gel ointment, 116, 135–136
astragalus, 120
Australia Black Saturday fire, 20–21, 264
The Authoritative Guide to Grapefruit Seed Extract (Sachs), 122
automatic external defibrillators (AED), 89–90

Backer, Howard, xi
backpacking, 32, 51
bacteria and viruses, 117–119, 196–198. *See also* antibiotic-resistant bacteria
Balch, James F., 119
Baldwin, Margo, xi
bandages and dressings, 96
Bangladesh sari filters, 212
B&A Products, 350
Basco, 353
Bateman, Jeb, xii
Beck, Bob, 133, 137
Becker, Robert, 137
Beck Protocol, 116, 137–138
Best Prices Storable Foods, 350
Bettman, Barry, xii

bites and stings, 103–105
black mustard, 165
Black Saturday fire, 20–21
Blankenship, Robin, 192
blankets, 25
bleeding, 90–92
blood electrification, 137
Bolton, Jim, xii
bone tools, 191
boots/shoes, 52–53
Bountiful Gardens, 351
bow hunting, 172–174
broadband receivers, 219–221
bulrush, 166
burdock, 166
Bushmaster Firearms International, LLC, 352

Cabela's, 352, 354
calendula, 120
camping equipment, 48–53
Campmor, Inc., 354
candles, 26, 75
Captain Dave's Survival Center, 351
cardiopulmonary resuscitation. *See* CPR
Carrington event, 8–9, 307, 313–314
cash, 27
cattails, 166
Cavanagh, Brad, 144
CB radios, 226
C. Crane Company, Inc., 354
C.F. Resources, 351
charcoal filters, 212–213
Cheaper Than Dirt, 352
checklists
    basic supplies, 36–37
    earthquake preparation, 268
    electromagnetic pulse attacks, 317
    home fire-safe/defensible space, 259–260
    hurricanes and floods, 271–274
    life-in-a-box, 30–31
    short-term preparedness, 23
    tornadoes, 284–285
    winter storms, 286–289
chemical contaminants, 198–199
chemical sterilization, 205–211
Chernobyl nuclear meltdown, 319–320

chest wounds, 94
chicory, 167
childbirth, 111–114
children, communication with, 54–55
choking, 95
Cipro antibiotics, 116
Clark, Hulda Regehr, xii
climate change, 14–15
clothing, 27, 49, 296–298
cold storage, 44–46
colloidal silver, 25–26, 116, 120, 132–135, 137, 274
communications
    antennas, 227
    broadband receivers, 219–221
    CB radio, 226
    with children, 54–55
    radios, 218–219
    scanners and NOAA weather radios, 221–223
    short-wave/ham radios, 223–225
    walkie-talkies, 226–227
Complete Survivalist, 355
Conrad, Bill, xi
cookware, 52
cordage, 186–189
coronal mass ejections (CMEs), 305–307
CPR (cardiopulmonary resuscitation), 85–87
Cumberland General Store, 351
cuts, 92–93

dandelions, 167–168
Dan's Sporting Goods, 352
Dare to Prepare (Deyo), 340
Deep Survival (Gonzales), 149
deforestation, 16
dehydration, 153, 161
desertification, 16
Deyo, Holly Drennan, 340
dimethyl sulfoxide. *See* DMSO
disaster plans, 32, 274
dislocations and fractures, 97–101
DMSO, 120–121
dock plants, 167
documents, 30–31
dosimeters, 336–337
Dr. Clark Research Association, 354
dry-ice fumigation, 41
dry packs, 273
Duffy, Jim, xii

Earth Knack Stone Age Living Skills, 355
earthquakes
    aftermath of, 266–267
    Cape Ann (1755), 265
    Haiti, 3
    Japan (2011), vii, 10–11
    Kobe, Japan, 3–4, 20
    major metro area scenario, 10–12
    New Madrid, 265–266
    preparations for, 267–269
    response to, 269–270
Eastern Mountain Sports (EMS), 354
Ebel, John, 265
echinacea, 121
edible plants, 33
Edwards, David, x
elderberry extract, 116, 121
elderly, 54
electrical outages. *See also* electromagnetic pulse (EMP) attacks; generators
    New York City (2006), 4–5
    solar storms and, 7–9, 305–307, 313–318
electromagnetic pulse (EMP) attacks
    effects of, 309–313
    nuclear tests and, 308–309
    overview, 304–306
    planning for, 314–318
    scenarios, 7–9
Elpel, Thomas J., 192
Emanuelson, Jerry, xii
Emergency Essentials, 351
emergency preparedness. *See* preparedness
Emery, Carla, xi, 314
EMP. *See* electromagnetic pulse (EMP) attacks
The Encyclopedia of Country Living (Emery), 314
Epicenter Supplies, 351
Epsom salts, 121
Equipped to Survive, 355
escape ladders, 259
Esdaile, James, 138
eye first aid, 106

fallout, 322–323. *See also* nuclear disasters
fasting, 160–161
Fedco, 352
Ferris, Frank, xi, 228
fiddleheads, 168
fire. *See also* fire building

Australia's Black Saturday, 20–21, 264
Laguna fire (1993), 261–263
safety, 255–263
statistics, 255
firearms, 229–235
fire building, 32, 153–160
fire extinguishers, 257–258
first aid. *See also* medicine and health
    ABCs of, 82–85
    bandages and dressings, 96
    bites and stings, 103–105
    bleeding, 90–92
    childbirth, 111–114
    choking, 95
    consent and liability, 82
    CPR, 85–87
    eyes, 106
    fractures and dislocations, 97–101
    heart attack, 87–90
    heat-related trauma, 102–103
    initial evaluation, 81
    kits, 28–29, 146–147
    moving the injured, 106–110
    shock, 96–97
    sprains and strains, 101–102
    wounds, 92–94
fishing, 179–181
flashlights, 26
flint and steel, 155–156
flint knapping, 190–191
Flintknapping: Making and Understanding Stone Tools (Whittaker), 190
Flintknapping: The Art of Making Stone Tools (Hellweg), 190
floods, 271–274, 276–281. *See also* hurricanes
flu virus, 117–118. *See also* influenza pandemics
food preparedness. *See also* hunting and gathering
    basic supplies, 36–37
    calculating needs, 37–39
    long-term planning, 34–36
    long-term storage, 41–46
    short-term, 26
    sprouts, 35, 46–48
    storage tips, 39–40
food supply/famine, 16–17, 34
footwear, 52–53
fractures and dislocations, 97–101
Frances, Karen, xi

Freeze Dry Guy, 351
Frontier Natural Products Coop, 353
frostbite, 301–303
Fukushima nuclear meltdown, 321

game. *See* hunting and gathering
garbage bags, 27
Gardener's Supply Company, 352
garlic, 121
gas masks, 258, 337–339
generators
    appliance power consumption, 69
    installing and using, 67–74
    overview, 65–67
    safety, 75
global warming. *See* climate change
goldenseal, 121
Gonzales, Laurence, 144, 149
Good Samaritan laws, 82
goosefoot, 168
grab-and-go survival kits, 24–28, 31, 144–147
grapefruit seed extract, 116, 122
grasses, 163
greenhouse gases. *See* climate change
guns, 229–235

Hall, Andrew/Mary, xii, 264
Ham Radio Outlet, 354
ham radios, 223–225, 313
headlamps, 26, 274
head wounds, 94
healing remedies. *See* medicine and health
health issues. *See* medicine and health
heart attacks, 87–90
heating, 56–63. *See also* fire building
heat-related trauma, 102–103
Heimlich maneuver, 84, 95
Hellweg, Paul, 190
Henderson, John, 256
Herbalcom, 354
herbal remedies, 124–125
Herbs Pro.com, 353
high-impact, low-frequency (HILF) events, 304
historical perspectives, xiv
Hollowtop Outdoor Primitive School, 355
homeopathy, 116, 122
honey, 122
Hoods Woods, 355
How to Survive the End of the World as We Know It (Rawles), 314

Humble, Jim, xii, 131
hunting and gathering
    bow hunting, 172–174
    fasting, 160–161
    fishing, 179–181
    insects, grubs and worms, 181–182
    mice and rats, 42, 177
    plants, 162–172
    skinning and cleaning, 177–179
    traps and snares, 174–177
hurricanes
    aftermath, 276
    home protection, 274–275
    Iniki, 4, 272
    Katrina, ix, 217–218, 276
    New York City scenario, 9–10
    preparation for, 275–276
    survival tips, 271–274
    toxic mold and, 276–281
hypnosis, 138–139
hypothermia, 300–301
hyssop, 122

ice storms, 20. *See also* winter storms
identity papers, 30–31
incisions, 92–93
infection, 92–94
influenza pandemics, 5–7. *See also* flu virus
Iniki hurricane, 4, 272
insects, grubs and worms, 181–182
intuition, 31–32, 144, 149–151, 342–343
ionic silver, 132

Japan
    2011 earthquake, vii, 10–11
    2011 tsunami, ix
    Fukushima nuclear meltdown, 321
    Kobe earthquake, 3–4, 20
J&G Sales, 353
Jussen, Jackie, 342
Jussen, Joseph, 148, 341

Kalcker, Andreas, xii
Katrina hurricane, ix, 217–218, 276
Kaupert, Andreas, xii
Kearny, Cresson, 331–332, 339, 340
KI4U, Inc., 353
Kiley, Debbie, 144
knives, 26–27, 189–191
Kobe earthquake, 3–4, 20
Koepcke, Julianne, 149

labor and childbirth, 111–114
Labrie, Cannon, xi
lamb's quarter, 168
lanterns, 75–76
Lehman's, 351
liability, 82
life-in-a-box checklist, 30–31
Life Sprouts, 353
lighting, 75–76, 274
Long Island Express hurricane, 9–10
Long, Laurie Ecklund, xii
Lord, Gary, xi
Lucas, Rex, 142
Lundin, Cody, 177, 192
Lyme disease, 104–105

magnetic pulsing, 137
Major Surplus & Survival, 351
map and compass, 26–27
Marinkovich, Vincent, xii, 279, 281
matches, 25
Mckee, Merri, xi
McPherson, John/Geri, xii, 190, 192
medicine and health. *See also* first aid
    ASAP gel ointment, 116, 135–136
    Beck Protocol, 116, 137–138
    colloidal and ionic silver, 25–26, 116,
        120, 132–135, 137
    compact medical kit, 146–147
    hypnosis, 138–139
    miracle mineral solution (MMS), 116,
        122–123, 126–131, 336
    remedies, 116, 119–126
    viruses and bacteria, 117–119
Men in Crisis: A Study of a Mine Disaster
    (Lucas), 142
Metatech Corporation, 313
mice and rats, 42, 177
MidwayUSA, 353
MIOX purifiers, 202
miracle mineral solution (MMS), 116,
    122–123, 126–131, 336
*The Miracle Mineral Solution of the 21st
    Century* (Humble), 131
Moeller, Keith, 136
mold, 276–281
money, 27
MRSA (Methicillin-resistant Staphylococcus
    aureus), 132, 136
mustard plants, 165

nano-particle silver solution, 116, 135–136
Natchez Shooters Supply, 353
neem oil, 123
New England Cheesemaking Supply
  Company, 353
New York City, 4–5, 9–10
Nichols Garden Nursery, 352
Nielsen, Richard, xii
Nitro-Pak Preparedness Center, 351
NOAA weather radios, 221–223
nuclear disasters. *See also* electromagnetic
  pulse (EMP) attacks
    Chernobyl, 319–320
    Fukushima, 321
    makeshift shelters, 331–334
    protection from radiation, 325–331
    radiation and types of threats, 321–326
    supplies to have, 334–340
    Three Mile Island, 320
nuclear tests, 304–306, 308–309. *See also*
  electromagnetic pulse (EMP) attacks
Nuclear War Survival Skills (Kearny),
  331–332, 340

ocean health, 15–16
oil production, 12–14
Okazaki, Henry S., 239
O'Leary, Jeremy, xi
oregano oil, 123
ovens, 63–64. *See also* heating; stoves
overpopulation, 17–18
ozonated water, 138

pandemics, 5–7
parasites, 123, 198
Pardeu, Jolie, xi
Park Seed Company, 352
Peaceful Valley Farm & Garden Supply, 352
peak oil, 12–14
Pedersen, Gordon, 136
personal records, 27
pets, 55
pharmaceutical substitutes, 124–125
pigweed, 168–169
pine nuts/needles, 169
plantain, 169
plants
    edibility test, 162–163
    foraging, 164
    grasses, 163
    poisonous, 172

roots and tubers, 164
seaweed, 164
seeds and grains, 163–164
tree bark, 163
wild edible plants guide, 164–171
plant water pump and still, 214
plumbing, 76–77, 288–293
police scanners, 221–223
population growth, 17–18
potassium iodide, 334
power, 64–65. *See also* generators
Powervision Emergency Food Storage
  Solutions, 351
Prairie Wolf, 355
preparedness
    72-hour grab-and-go survival kits,
      24–28, 31, 273
    compact survival kit, 144–147
    first-aid kits, 28–29
    life-in-a-box checklist, 30–31
    overview, 21–22
    short-term checklist, 23
    survival skills, 31–33
Preparedness Now, 351
Prescription for Nutritional Healing (Balch),
  119
pressure points, 90–91
*Primitive Wilderness Living and Survival
  Skills* (McPherson), 190
privies, 215–216
protection. *See* self-defense
protozoa, 197
Prussion blue, 335
puncture wounds, 93
purslane, 169

radiation. *See also* nuclear disasters
    contaminants, 198–199
    makeshift shelters, 331–334
    overview, 321–326
    protection from, 325–331
radios, 24, 218–219
Radio Shack, 134, 354
ramps (leeks), 169–170
rats and mice, 42, 177
Rawles, James, Wesley, xi, 314
Ready Made Resources, 351
Red Cross First Aid and Safety Handbook, 81
Redwood City Seed Company, 352
REI (Recreational Equipment, Inc.), 354
respirator masks, 258, 337–339

Richards, Dennis, xii
Richters Herbs, 352
Robertson, Dougal, 142
rocket stoves, 60–63
rodents, 42
root cellars, 44–46
roots and tubers, 164
rope, 27, 186–189
rose hips, 170
Rosen, Gary, xii

Sachs, Alan, 122
Safety Central, 351
Sambucol, 121
Scanner Master Police Scanners
  Corporation, 354
scanners, 221–223
Schmidt, Mike, xi
Schwartz, Kristen, xi
scurvy, 161
seaweed, 164
seeds and grains, 163–164
Seed Savers Exchange, 352
self-defense
    defending against common scenarios,
      246–251
    firearms, 229–235
    legal considerations, 251–252
    philosophy of, 235–239
    speed and surprise, 239–240
    vulnerable parts of the body, 240–246
72-hour grab-and-go survival kits, 24–28,
  31, 273
sewage, 215–216
sewing kits, 27
sheep sorrel, 170
shelf-life, 42–44
shelter construction, 33, 182–185, 331–334
Shelter Logic, 353
shock, 96–97
Shoemaker, Ritchie, 281
shoes/boots, 52–53
short-term preparedness checklist, 23
short-wave/ham radios, 223–225
Siegal, Bernie, 149
Sims, F.W., 138
skinning and cleaning game, 177–179
sleeping bags/mats, 50–51
smoke detectors, 255–256
snakebites, 103–104
snares and traps, 174–177

snowshoes, 185
Society of Primitive Technology, 355
solar ovens, 63–64
solar stills, 213–214
solar storms, 7–9, 305–307, 313–318
solar water disinfection (SODIS), 211–212
Sota Instruments, 134, 138
Spanish flu pandemic, 5–6
spider bites, 104
spilanthes-usnea extract, 116
splicing, 189
sprains and strains, 101–102
sprouts, 35, 46–48
Stein, Elisha, xi
Stein, Joshua, xi
Stein, Josie, ix
Stein, Matthew, viii, 314
SteriPENs, 202
stings and bites, 103–105
St. John's wort, 123
Stone, Patricia, xi
stoves, 27–28, 51–52, 55–56, 60–63. See
    also solar ovens; woodstoves
Stroud, Les, 192
surgical masks and gloves, 116
SurvivalBlog.com, 355
Survival-Gear.com, 355
survival skills. See also hunting and
  gathering; water purification
    basic strategies, 142–144
    cordage, 186–189
    fire starting, 32, 153–160
    intuition, 31–32, 144, 149–151
    personality traits, 147–149, 341–344
    shelter construction, 33, 182–185,
      331–334
    snowshoes, 185
    survival kits, 24–28, 31, 144–147
    tools, 189–191
    top ten skills, 31–33
Survive the Savage Sea (Robertson), 142
swine flu. See influenza pandemics

tea tree oil, 125–126
tents, 48–49
Three Mile Island, 320
tick bites, 104–105
toenail fungus, 125
toiletries, 26
tools, 26–27, 189–191
tornadoes, 282–285

tourniquets, 91–92
traps and snares, 174–177
Traumeel cream, 126
tree bark, 163
tsunamis, ix

USA Emergency Supply, 351
usnea, 126
utensils, 27

vacuum packaging, 42
Van Bruggen, Ralph, xii
viruses and bacteria, 117–119, 196–198. *See also* antibiotic-resistant bacteria
Vitacost.com, 354
vitamin C, 126, 130, 336
vitamin E, 126, 336
Vorhis, Dan, xii

walkie-talkies, 226–227
Walton Feed, Inc., 351
Warner, Susan, xi
water. *See also* water purification
    conservation of, 153
    contaminants, 195–199
    dehydration, 153, 161
    emergency measures, 151–152, 194–195
    location indicators, 214–215
    ozonated, 138
    requirements for, 151–152, 193, 271–272
    sewage and, 215–216
    stocking up, 193–194
watercress, 170–171
water purification. *See also* water
    72-hour grab-and-go survival kit, 24–25

chemical sterilization, 205–211
    filters, 200–202, 212–213
    heat sterilization, 200
    hurricane or flood and, 273
    MIOX purifiers, 202
    planning ahead, xiii
    plant water pump and still, 214
    radioactive contamination and, 339–340
    recommendations, 203–205
    solar stills, 213–214
    solar water disinfection (SODIS), 211–212
    SteriPENs, 202
    as a survival skill, 32–33
When Technology Fails (Stein), xvi, 314
whistles, 26–27
Whittaker, John C., 190
wildfires. *See* fire
wild leeks, 169–170
wild onions, 171
winter storms
    clothing, 296–298
    eating snow, 303
    frostbite, 301–303
    hypothermia, 300–301
    ice storms, 20
    inventory for, 286–288
    outdoor survival, 298–300
    staying warm, 293–294
    stuck in car, 294–296
    thawing frozen plumbing, 293
    winterizing homes, 288–293
woodstoves, 58–60
wounds, 92–94

YOYO time, ix

About the Author

Mat Stein is an environmentalist, best-selling author, MIT-trained engineer, and green builder. As an inspiring speaker and visionary thinker, he is dedicated to helping people wake up and unite to shift our collective course from collapse to global renaissance. As an expert at self-reliance, emergency preparation, and survival, Mat's writings and work help people prepare to weather the storms we are facing due to continuing climate change and ecological decline, coupled with a fossil-fuel-based economy that has recently passed the peak in world oil production and is struggling to cope with impending near-term shortfalls.

Mat is the author of the best-selling book *When Technology Fails: A Manual for Self-Reliance, Sustainability, and Surviving the Long Emergency* (Chelsea Green 2008), a comprehensive manual on sustainable living skills, survival, and disaster preparations. He has appeared on over a hundred radio and television programs and is a repeat guest on dozens of shows, including *Fox News, MSNBC, Lionel, Coast-to-Coast AM*, and the *Thom Hartmann Show.* He also has written a number of articles on the subject of sustainable living and is a guest columnist for the *Huffington Post*.

As the owner of Stein Design & Construction, Mat has built hurricane-resistant, energy-efficient, and environmentally friendly homes. The mechanical engineering side of his firm specializes in product design and development. Among other things, Mat has designed consumer water-filtration devices, solar PV roofing panels, medical bacterial filters, emergency chemical-drench systems, computer disk drives, and portable fiberglass buildings.

Mat has been an active outdoorsman since he was a small child, an extreme skier and climber (over a hundred Yosemite Valley ascents, including several El Capitan and Half Dome big walls), and volunteers as a guide and cross-country ski instructor for the blind with the Sierra Regional Ski for Light program. He and his wife, Josie, live in the High Sierra Mountains near Lake Tahoe, California.

About the Foreword Author

James Wesley, Rawles is the editor of www.SurvivalBlog.com. He is a former U.S. Army intelligence officer and the author of *How to Survive the End of the World as We Know It: Tactics, Techniques, and Technologies for Uncertain Times; Patriots: A Novel of Survival in the Coming Collapse;* and *Survivors: A Novel of the Coming Collapse.*